Creating Web Pages

Web Pages

FOR

DUMMIES®

5TH EDITION

Creating Web Pages

FOR

DUMMIES®

5TH EDITION

by Bud Smith and Arthur Bebak

Foreword by Kevin Werbach

IDG BOOKS WORLDWIDE

IDG Books Worldwide, Inc.
An International Data Group Company

Foster City, CA ◆ Chicago, IL ◆ Indianapolis, IN ◆ New York, NY

Creating Web Pages For Dummies®, 5th Edition

Published by
IDG Books Worldwide, Inc.
An International Data Group Company
919 E. Hillsdale Blvd.
Suite 400
Foster City, CA 94404
www.idgbooks.com (IDG Books Worldwide Web site)
www.dummies.com (Dummies Press Web site)

Library of Congress Control Number: 00-101846

ISBN: 0-7645-0733-8

Printed in the United States of America

10 9 8 7 6 5 4

5B/RT/QX/QQ/IN

Distributed in the United States by IDG Books Worldwide, Inc.

Distributed by CDG Books Canada Inc. for Canada; by Transworld Publishers Limited in the United Kingdom; by IDG Norge Books for Norway; by IDG Sweden Books for Sweden; by IDG Books Australia Publishing Corporation Pty. Ltd. for Australia and New Zealand; by TransQuest Publishers Pte Ltd. for Singapore, Malaysia, Thailand, Indonesia, and Hong Kong; by Gotop Information Inc. for Taiwan; by ICG Muse, Inc. for Japan; by Intersoft for South Africa; by Eyrolles for France; by International Thomson Publishing for Germany, Austria and Switzerland; by Distribuidora Cuspide for Argentina; by LR International for Brazil; by Galileo Libros for Chile; by Ediciones ZETA S.C.R. Ltda. for Peru; by WS Computer Publishing Corporation, Inc., for the Philippines; by Contemporanea de Ediciones for Venezuela; by Express Computer Distributors for the Caribbean and West Indies; by Micronesia Media Distributor, Inc. for Micronesia; by Chips Computadoras S.A. de C.V. for Mexico; by Editorial Norma de Panama S.A. for Panama; by American Bookshops for Finland.

For general information on IDG Books Worldwide's books in the U.S., please call our Consumer Customer Service department at 800-762-2974. For reseller information, including discounts and premium sales, please call our Reseller Customer Service department at 800-434-3422.

For information on where to purchase IDG Books Worldwide's books outside the U.S., please contact our International Sales department at 317-596-5530 or fax 317-572-4002.

For consumer information on foreign language translations, please contact our Customer Service department at 1-800-434-3422, fax 317-572-4002, or e-mail rights@idgbooks.com.

For information on licensing foreign or domestic rights, please phone +1-650-653-7098.

For sales inquiries and special prices for bulk quantities, please contact our Order Services department at 800-434-3422 or write to the address above.

For information on using IDG Books Worldwide's books in the classroom or for ordering examination copies, please contact our Educational Sales department at 800-434-2086 or fax 317-572-4005.

For press review copies, author interviews, or other publicity information, please contact our Public Relations department at 650-653-7000 or fax 650-653-7500.

For authorization to photocopy items for corporate, personal, or educational use, please contact Copyright Clearance Center, 222 Rosewood Drive, Danvers, MA 01923, or fax 978-750-4470.

is a registered trademark under exclusive license to IDG Books Worldwide, Inc. from International Data Group, Inc.

About the Authors

Bud Smith: Bud is a computer book author with over ten years of publishing experience. *Creating Web Pages For Dummies,* 5th Edition, is one of a dozen books Bud has written; his IDG Books Worldwide titles include *AutoCAD For Dummies* and the upcoming *Internet Marketing For Dummies.* In addition to writing books, Bud has been a computer magazine editor and product marketing manager.

Bud got his start with computers in 1983, when he left a promising career as a welder for a stint as a data-entry clerk. Bud then moved to Silicon Valley to join a startup company, followed by work for Intel, IBM, Apple, and AltaVista. His work and interests led him to acquire a degree from the University of San Francisco in Information Systems Management.

Arthur Bebak: Arthur received a degree in Computer Engineering at the University of Illinois, which he attended on a fencing scholarship. He has designed mainframes, managed large engineering projects, and studied business administration. Arthur is founder of Netsurfer Communications, Inc., a highly successful electronic publishing company. Arthur has done a lot of writing, which has led to his current "surprising" (though only to him) role as coauthor of this book.

At Netsurfer, Arthur oversees a large staff of people who create Web sites for numerous clients. They also write, edit, and publish several Web-based electronic magazines, popularly known as "e-zines."

ABOUT IDG BOOKS WORLDWIDE

Welcome to the world of IDG Books Worldwide.

IDG Books Worldwide, Inc., is a subsidiary of International Data Group, the world's largest publisher of computer-related information and the leading global provider of information services on information technology. IDG was founded more than 30 years ago by Patrick J. McGovern and now employs more than 9,000 people worldwide. IDG publishes more than 290 computer publications in over 75 countries. More than 90 million people read one or more IDG publications each month.

Launched in 1990, IDG Books Worldwide is today the #1 publisher of best-selling computer books in the United States. We are proud to have received eight awards from the Computer Press Association in recognition of editorial excellence and three from Computer Currents' First Annual Readers' Choice Awards. Our best-selling *...For Dummies*® series has more than 50 million copies in print with translations in 31 languages. IDG Books Worldwide, through a joint venture with IDG's Hi-Tech Beijing, became the first U.S. publisher to publish a computer book in the People's Republic of China. In record time, IDG Books Worldwide has become the first choice for millions of readers around the world who want to learn how to better manage their businesses.

Our mission is simple: Every one of our books is designed to bring extra value and skill-building instructions to the reader. Our books are written by experts who understand and care about our readers. The knowledge base of our editorial staff comes from years of experience in publishing, education, and journalism — experience we use to produce books to carry us into the new millennium. In short, we care about books, so we attract the best people. We devote special attention to details such as audience, interior design, use of icons, and illustrations. And because we use an efficient process of authoring, editing, and desktop publishing our books electronically, we can spend more time ensuring superior content and less time on the technicalities of making books.

You can count on our commitment to deliver high-quality books at competitive prices on topics you want to read about. At IDG Books Worldwide, we continue in the IDG tradition of delivering quality for more than 30 years. You'll find no better book on a subject than one from IDG Books Worldwide.

John Kilcullen
Chairman and CEO
IDG Books Worldwide, Inc.

Eighth Annual Computer Press Awards ≳1992

Ninth Annual Computer Press Awards ≳1993

Tenth Annual Computer Press Awards ≳1994

Eleventh Annual Computer Press Awards ≳1995

IDG is the world's leading IT media, research and exposition company. Founded in 1964, IDG had 1997 revenues of $2.05 billion and has more than 9,000 employees worldwide. IDG offers the widest range of media options that reach IT buyers in 75 countries representing 95% of worldwide IT spending. IDG's diverse product and services portfolio spans six key areas including print publishing, online publishing, expositions and conferences, market research, education and training, and global marketing services. More than 90 million people read one or more of IDG's 290 magazines and newspapers, including IDG's leading global brands — Computerworld, PC World, Network World, Macworld and the Channel World family of publications. IDG Books Worldwide is one of the fastest-growing computer book publishers in the world, with more than 700 titles in 36 languages. The "...For Dummies®" series alone has more than 50 million copies in print. IDG offers online users the largest network of technology-specific Web sites around the world through IDG.net (http://www.idg.net), which comprises more than 225 targeted Web sites in 55 countries worldwide. International Data Corporation (IDC) is the world's largest provider of information technology data, analysis and consulting, with research centers in over 41 countries and more than 400 research analysts worldwide. IDG World Expo is a leading producer of more than 168 globally branded conferences and expositions in 35 countries including E3 (Electronic Entertainment Expo), Macworld Expo, ComNet, Windows World Expo, ICE (Internet Commerce Expo), Agenda, DEMO, and Spotlight. IDG's training subsidiary, ExecuTrain, is the world's largest computer training company, with more than 230 locations worldwide and 785 training courses. IDG Marketing Services helps industry-leading IT companies build international brand recognition by developing global integrated marketing programs via IDG's print, online and exposition products worldwide. Further information about the company can be found at www.idg.com.   1/26/00

Authors' Acknowledgments

The authors thank Steve Hayes, acquisitions editor, and the staff that helped produce this book: Colleen Esterline, project editor; Mike Lerch, technical editor, as well as the many people responsible for page layout, proofreading, indexing, and graphic art.

The Web was built more for love than money, and that tradition was continued by the many people who generously gave their time and support for this book. We especially thank the providers of Web tools who supplied us with an excellent set of programs for the CD-ROM and the Web authors who agreed to let us use their sites for the figures in this book.

Publisher's Acknowledgments

We're proud of this book; please register your comments through our IDG Books Worldwide Online Registration Form located at `http://my2cents.dummies.com`.

Some of the people who helped bring this book to market include the following:

Acquisitions, Editorial, and Media Development

Project Editor: Colleen Williams Esterline

> *(Previous Editions: Kathy Cox, Jeanne S. Criswell)*

Acquisitions Editor: Steven H. Hayes

Proof Editors: Teresa Artman, Dwight Ramsey

Technical Editor: Michael Lerch

Permissions Editor: Carmen Krikorian

Associate Media Development Specialist: Megan Decraene

Editorial Manager, Freelance: Constance Carlisle

Media Development Manager: Heather Heath Dismore

Editorial Assistant: Candace Nicholson

Production

Project Coordinator: Kristin Nash

Layout and Graphics: Joe Bucki, Barry Offringa, Tracy K. Oliver, Erin Zeltner

Proofreaders: Susan Moritz, Charles Spencer York Production Services, Inc.

Indexer: York Production Services, Inc.

Special Help
Beth Parlon

General and Administrative

IDG Books Worldwide, Inc.: John Kilcullen, CEO

IDG Books Technology Publishing Group: Richard Swadley, Senior Vice President and Publisher; Walter R. Bruce III, Vice President and Publisher; Joseph Wikert, Vice President and Publisher; Mary Bednarek, Vice President and Director, Product Development; Andy Cummings, Publishing Director, General User Group; Mary C. Corder, Editorial Director; Barry Pruett, Publishing Director

IDG Books Consumer Publishing Group: Roland Elgey, Senior Vice President and Publisher; Kathleen A. Welton, Vice President and Publisher; Kevin Thornton, Acquisitions Manager; Kristin A. Cocks, Editorial Director

IDG Books Internet Publishing Group: Brenda McLaughlin, Senior Vice President and Publisher; Sofia Marchant, Online Marketing Manager

IDG Books Production for Branded Press: Debbie Stailey, Director of Production; Cindy L. Phipps, Manager of Project Coordination, Production Proofreading, and Indexing; Tony Augsburger, Manager of Prepress, Reprints, and Systems; Laura Carpenter, Production Control Manager; Shelley Lea, Supervisor of Graphics and Design; Debbie J. Gates, Production Systems Specialist; Robert Springer, Supervisor of Proofreading; Trudy Coler, Page Layout Manager; Troy Barnes, Page Layout Supervisor, Kathie Schutte, Senior Page Layout Supervisor; Michael Sullivan, Production Supervisor

Packaging and Book Design: Patty Page, Manager, Promotions Marketing

◆

The publisher would like to give special thanks to Patrick J. McGovern, without whom this book would not have been possible.

◆

Contents at a Glance

Cartoons at a Glance

By Rich Tennant

page 7

page 161

page 105

page 49

page 289

page 203

page 277

Fax: 978-546-7747
E-mail: richtennant@the5thwave.com
World Wide Web: www.the5thwave.com

Table of Contents

Foreword

If you're reading this book, chances are you fall into one of three categories.

The Webophile. You're convinced that creating a Web site can help you win friends, influence people, find true love, improve your business, and get that nasty marmalade stain out of your favorite fez. You may even have made a few tentative attempts to design your own Web pages, but you still think HTML stands for "Hard To Master Lingo." Now you're sitting in front of your computer hoping this Foreword doesn't ramble on much longer so that you can get to the good stuff.

The Browser. You're thumbing through this book in your favorite bookstore. Perhaps someone else bought the book for you as a gift. Or maybe you actually plunked down the money, even though you aren't yet convinced this book will help you lose 30 pounds and build a Web site while you're at it. Unfortunately, you were voted "Most Likely to Remain Passive" in your high school yearbook. Creating Web pages sounds like fun (everyone's doing it), but you're not quite sure how or why to build a Web site yourself.

The Webophobe. You feel like roadkill on the information super-highway. You may be accustomed to using a computer and even to surfing the Internet, but the thought of designing your own Web pages fills you with inexplicable dread. Sure, your propeller-head friends have Web sites, but you don't have a Ph.D. in computer science and quantum neurophysics. And anyway, what could you possibly put out on the Web that other people would want to read?

So, for whom is this appropriate? All of you.

Regardless of your level of computer expertise, you can benefit from becoming a Web publisher. Users of my *Bare Bones Guide to HTML* — a concise index of the language used to create Web pages — often ask why they should invest time and effort in publishing a Web site. Why spend time fiddling around with some arcane computer codes just to stick a bunch of flashing doodads around a name and send it over the Internet?

Because you can do so many things, and it's so easy.

The Web is the most sophisticated, most open, and simplest publishing medium ever created. This book shows you just how easy creating Web pages can be. Here I offer a few reasons why you may want to do so.

The Web is your platform to say or show whatever you want to the millions of people with access to the global Internet. You can talk about yourself or your business. You can publish a short story or a collection of jokes. You can show pictures of your dog or of your company's latest product (available through this limited-time offer for the low, low price of only $19.95 plus shipping and handling!). You can display your groundbreaking work in Jell-O sculpture to an adoring public. Your own imagination is the only limit to what you can put on the Web.

The Web is an endless set of criss-crossing interconnections between an ever-growing number of points, and a community in the truest sense of the word. With over 100 million Internet users and counting, the Web is the world's largest community. Unlike most communities, this one isn't limited by geography, age, race, or anything else.

In short, the Web brings people together. By creating your own site on the Web, you can participate in this process. No matter what you're interested in, if you design good Web pages about it and publicize the pages well, lots of people with similar interests will visit. You may be the only person in your town lobbying for the return of New Coke, and 99.9 percent of the Internet population may disagree with you. Normally, in that situation, you would wind up a troubled loner. But one-tenth of one percent of the people on the Internet still means tens of thousands of people who can get to your Web pages with a click of a mouse. You don't need special permission or qualifications, and you don't need millions of dollars of venture capital and equipment to spread your message to the far corners of the Earth. All you need is a bit of knowledge about how the Web works and how to design Web pages.

Despite tremendous growth in recent years, the Web still has as much space for new Web pages as people with Internet access may require. No one else has quite the same interests, ideas, and talents as you do, so no one else will create the same Web page as you. As you move into the world of Web publishing, you'll find that, just like you, thousands and thousands of people are discovering how to create Web pages, and they're often happy to share their ideas and experiences. The most important thing is to take the plunge and get started.

Good luck and have fun!

Kevin Werbach

(Kevin Werbach is the managing editor of Release 1.0, *an executive newsletter that explores emerging technologies and the convergence of computing and communications. Previously he served as Counsel for New Technology Policy at the Federal Communications Commission. He is the author of* The Bare Bones Guide to HTML, *a popular Web site that is a resource for Web authoring. For more about* The Bare Bones Guide to HTML, *see Appendix C. Kevin can be reached at* kevin@werbach.com.*)*

Introduction

*I*t may be hard to remember, or it may seem like only yesterday, but just years ago, the personal computer was introduced. The rise and rise *and rise* of the personal computer — with maybe an occasional stumble but never a real fall — seemed certain to be the most important social and technological event leading into the new millennium. From Wozniak and Jobs's Apple II to Bill Gates's Windows 98, it may have seemed as though nothing could ever be bigger, or more life-changing and important, than PCs.

But, people do talk. In fact, talking is one of the main things that people are all about, and in the beginning, the personal computer didn't let you interact with others. However, first with modems, and then with networks, and finally through their combination and culmination in the Internet, personal computers became the tools that opened up a new medium of communication. The most visible, graphical, and fastest-growing part of the Internet is the World Wide Web. Now communication, not computation, is the story. Computers are still important but mostly as the means to an end; the end result is further enabling people to interact.

If the most exciting channel of communication is the Web, the means of communication is the Web page. Ordinary people demonstrate amazing energy and imagination in creating and publishing diverse Web home pages. And although ordinary people have a *desire* to create Web pages, businesses have a *need* to set up shop on the Web. So the rush to the Web is on, often with the same people expressing themselves personally on one Web page and commercially on another.

So you want to be there, too. "But," you ask, "isn't it difficult, expensive, and complicated?" Not any more. As the Web has grown, easy ways to get on the Web have appeared. And we discuss the best of these ways in the pages of this book.

About This Book

It's *about* 370 pages.

Seriously, what do you find here? Almost every easy way to get published on the Web that we could find or think of. Plus the information you need to go beyond your first Web page and create a multipage personal or business Web site. And tools — which we describe in the book or provide as demos or in full versions on the CD-ROM — to help you go as far as you want to go in creating a Web site.

Foolish Assumptions

Lots of good information is in this book, but no one is going to read all of it — except our long-suffering editor. That's because we cover Web page topics from beginning through intermediate levels, including how to publish a Web page via Web-based services and the major online services, how to use half a dozen different tools, and some Mac-specific and Windows-specific stuff. No one needs to know all of that! But anyone who wants to get a Web page up on the Web does need to know some of it.

But what do *you* need? We assume, for purposes of this book, that you have probably used the Web before and that you want to create a Web page. We further assume that you are not yet a Web author or are fairly new to the process. To use the information in this book, you need access to a personal computer running Mac OS or Windows, and you need access to the Web — either through an online service or a direct Internet service provider (ISP). You should be running a Web browser such as Microsoft Internet Explorer, Netscape Navigator, or a browser provided by an online service. If you have a UNIX system and an Internet connection, much of this book will work for you, but you won't have access to any of the online service or Web page creation tools that we describe, except those available directly on the Web.

If you don't have Web access from your personal computer, see Appendix B for a list of service providers who can help you get it. (If you're looking for the least expensive way to get started, see Chapter 15 for information about WebTV.) You should already have spent some time surfing the Web, or be willing to do so as you gather information and examples for your Web page. In other words, if you're wired, or willing to get wired, you're in. With that, the door to this book is open to you, whether you want to create your first Web page or add new features to one you already have.

 The figures in this book show up-to-date Macintosh and Windows screen shots. We wrote the instructions and steps in this book to work equally well for the Macintosh and Windows.

Jump around in the book and go straight to information that you need. Later, you can back up and read something that interests you, page through the tools sections, try using one of the tools on the CD-ROM, and then go look at something on the *Creating Web Pages For Dummies* home page (created by one of the authors) at the following address:

```
www.netsurf.com/cwpfd
```

CD (-ROM) for Me, See?

The CD-ROM that comes with this book is a rich source of software for creating World Wide Web pages. You can find plenty of software for either Macintosh or Windows. For details about what's on the CD-ROM, see Appendix E. For details about how to use specific programs, see the chapters and sections of this book. For information on how to install the software on the CD-ROM, see the instructions in Appendix E.

Conventions Used in This Book

When our publisher first told us that this book was going to have *conventions*, we got out our silly hats and our Republican and Democratic paraphernalia, but apparently she just meant that we had to be consistent. The conventions in this book are standard ways of communicating specific types of information, such as instructions and steps. (One example of a convention is the use of italics for newly introduced words, as with the word "conventions" in the first sentence of this paragraph.)

Here are the conventions for this book:

- Things that you, the reader, are asked to type are shown in **bold.**

- New terms are printed in *italics.*

- Information used in specific ways is formatted in a specific typeface. In this book, one of the most common kind of information displayed this way is HTML *tags;* that is, formatting information used to create Web pages (see Appendix A for a more complete definition). An example of a tag is `<TITLE>`.

   We also use a special typeface for *URLs* (Uniform Resource Locators), which are the addresses used to specify the location of Web pages. For example, the URL for IDG Books' Dummies Press is as follows:

   `www.dummies.com`

- The Web is fast-paced and evolving. Some of the URLs listed throughout this book may have changed, may have become inaccessible, or may not be supported through your local Internet service provider.

- Representative browser versions appear among the figures.

- Menu selections look like this: File⇨Save. This particular example means that you choose the File menu and then choose the Save option.

- Related, brief pieces of information are displayed in bulleted lists, such as the bulleted list that you're reading right now.

> ✔ Numbered lists are used for instructions that must be followed in a particular sequence. This book has many sequential steps that tell you just how to perform the different tasks that, when taken together, can make you a successful Web author.
>
> To make the steps brief and easy to follow, we use a specific way of telling you what to do. We don't use a lot of formatting because of the need to provide instructions that work equally well on the Macintosh and Windows. Here's an example of a set of steps:
>
> **1. Start your Web browser.**
>
> **2. Go to the Web site**
>
> ```
> www.tryfreestuff.com
> ```
>
> *Note:* This is not a real site, just an example.
>
> **3. Click the link that matches the type of computer you have: Macintosh, PC, or UNIX.**
>
> In the chapters in Part V that cover specific Web authoring tools, we provide general steps for tasks, such as formatting a word or phrase, followed by the details that show how to create a specific example illustrated in that chapter's figures. In this way, you have access to both general procedures and specific examples.

Part-y Time: How This Book Is Organized

We wrote this book to a carefully plotted, precise, *unvarying* plan, with the predictable and predicted result: the book you're holding in your hands now. And the CD-ROM? Same thing.

Wait a second. Isn't it true that the Web is changing every day, that Web sites appear and disappear like so many jacks-in-the-box — or whack-a-moles, if that's a more familiar example to you — and that Web companies go from opening their doors to public stock offerings — and sometimes back — in weeks? So, what was that about a plan?

Well, okay, we did change things a little along the way. Maybe a lot. But we *did* have a plan behind the book, even if it was finalized in a conference call at 5:00 this morning. The following sections explain the parts that make up the book.

Part I: Get Started on Your Web Page

One of the hardest "parts" — no pun intended — of getting into any new area is learning how things work and all the little "of course" bits of information that turn into gotchas when you try to do something new. This Part gives you a clear and concise introduction to the basics of Web publishing. You'll save hours by getting a clear idea of what's possible and how to get started.

Part II: Build a Web Page in a Day

You bought this book to get a Web page up and running. This Part tells you how to do exactly that! Use GeoCities to create your first Web page in a few hours. The cost: free for this Web-based service. The reward: You'll be telling friends your Web address tomorrow!

Or, are you looking for an online service that can help with Web publishing? Want to use your existing account with America Online or CompuServe to get a Web page up fast? This Part is the answer. Use it to take full advantage of the tools and support built into top online services. There's no additional cost beyond the normal monthly bill for your online service!

Part III: Better, Stronger, Faster Pages

At some point in your Web publishing adventure, you may want to learn just a bit of HTML, the underlying language of Web pages. We make it very, very easy to get off to a strong start. Then you add graphics and multimedia and publish your full-featured Web pages. This part shows how to get to the next level of coolness with simple but powerful additions to your Web pages.

Part IV: Sites for Sore Eyes

People who start with a simple Web page like to build it into a Web site, and most businesses today need a respectable presence on the Web; but how do you create a site that's attractive and informative without spending too much time or money? This part shows you how to build up and publish your Web site quickly and easily.

Part V: Web Publishing Tools

If you're creating and maintaining a multipage Web site, and you really want the most creative capabilities with the least exposure to HTML, you should consider one of the Web publishing tools that are transforming Web page authoring. Part V introduces the cream of the crop of full-featured, easy-to-use Web authoring tools, as well as information about Web publishing with and for WebTV.

Part VI: The Part of Tens

A Top Ten list is a great way to make complex information fun and easy to remember. Our Top Ten lists show you some DO's and DON'Ts of Web publishing.

Part VII: Appendixes

Appendixes in books are usually like appendixes in people: funny little things that get taken out of the patient in a hurry if they act up. But for this book, we pack in great information that can really help you. In Appendix A, a complete glossary defines the Web and Web publishing terms that may be confusing to you. In other appendixes, you see information about Internet service providers and Web page developer resources, including a guide to the CD-ROM that comes with this book.

Icons Used in This Book

Tells what is on the accompanying CD-ROM.

Marks information that you need to keep in mind as you work.

Points to things you may want to know but don't necessarily need to know. You can skip these and read the text, skip the text and read these, or both.

Flags specific information that may not fit in a step or description but that helps you create better Web pages.

Warns you of effects that take a long time to appear.

Points out things that may cause problems.

Part I

Get Started on Your Web Page

The 5th Wave — By Rich Tennant

MIDTOWN

WHERE'S THE DANG DOOR?!

WebSite DESIGN Co.

C'mon in!

OUR AWARDS

In this part . . .

This part orients you to the key ideas behind the Web and Web publishing. It also helps you plan your initial Web page for quick success.

Chapter 1

Web Publishing Basics

*T*he Internet and the World Wide Web have such a high profile that almost everyone knows what they are. But to do a proper job of publishing on the Web, you need to know more than the casual Net user. In this chapter, we map out the territory that you, as a Web publisher, are about to enter. You can start Web publishing without most of the information in this chapter simply by following the steps we provide in this book. However, knowing the basics makes it easier to go beyond the steps and create a Web page that really does what you need it to do.

If you can't wait to get started with Web publishing, go straight to the "Seven Steps to Successful Web Publishing" section later in this chapter.

The Internet Begets the Web

Many people think that the Web seems to have burst out of its host, the Internet, and taken over. The fact is, however, that the rest of the Internet is alive and well. To understand the Web, you need at least a basic understanding of the Internet.

What the heck is the Internet?

The *Internet* is a giant computer network that connects other computer net-works. More and more of the world's computer networks are being connected to it. Think of the Internet as a giant octopus with a million tentacles. Each tentacle grasps another smaller octopus — that is, the smaller networks con-nected by the Internet. At the end of each tentacle is a single PC.

Networks support different kinds of uses called *services*. The Internet hosts several different services; the one used by the most people is *e-mail*. Just a few years ago, you couldn't send e-mail to someone unless both you and the recipient were on the same online service such as CompuServe or MCI Mail. But with the Internet, you can send a message to anyone on any online ser-vice or on any other network connected to the Internet.

In addition to e-mail, some other popular Internet services are FTP and Gopher. *FTP* is not a misspelling of the name of a flower delivery service; it stands for *File Transfer Protocol,* which is a method for transferring files from one com-puter to another. You use FTP for a few of the procedures in this book. *Gopher* is a steward on *The Love Boat,* an old TV show — whoops, sorry, wrong book. Gopher is another relatively well-known Internet service and is sort of a precur-sor to the Web. It allows text searches, like the Web, but does not have built-in support for graphics. We don't use Gopher in this book.

The Internet accesses different resources that are stored within different kinds of services by using a special kind of address called a *URL (Uniform Resource Locator* — which sounds like something the Armed Forces invented to track down clothes!). The address that you type to get to a Web page is a URL. For example, `www.netsurf.com` is the URL for Arthur's Netsurfer Communications Web site. The URL consists of the three following parts, which are shown in Figure 1-1:

> ✔ The *protocol* is the name of the communications language that the URL uses: HTTP (HyperText Transfer Protocol, used on the Web), FTP, Gopher, and so on.
>
> ✔ The *domain name* is the logical name of the server that the file is on.
>
> ✔ The *pathname* tells how to find the file you want to retrieve.

Figure 1-1:
URLy to
Web, URLy
to rise.

◄—Protocol—►   ◄—Domain name—►   ◄—Pathname—►
http://   www.server.com/   folder/filename.ext

What the heck is the World Wide Web?

The *World Wide Web,* now approaching its first decade of use, is the newest of the widely popular services on the Internet. The Web combines text, graphics, multimedia, and links between files to create a giant "web" of easily accessible information.

How to picture the Web? Imagine laying a single copy of every magazine in the world on the floor of a huge building. Imagine that pieces of string connect specific locations in each magazine to relevant information in other magazines. The result — a giant "web" of text and graphics — pretty much represents what the World Wide Web is like. People who can move smoothly through that web — that is, through the Web — are empowered. People who can add their own information to the Web and tie the information to other related material are *very* empowered. The purpose of this book is to help you become very empowered.

The Web has several key features that make it popular. Each document on the Web, a *Web page,* is based on a text file. Just as e-mail is made up of text files, so are the basic underpinnings of the Web, which makes it easy to create, edit, and transmit Web pages. But the Web is flexible; you can include a graphics or multimedia file in a Web page by creating a link to it. You can tie in small programs by referencing them from within the Web page. And you can link the page to other Web pages.

The Web continues to be the most popular and fastest-growing service on the Internet. Why? Because the Web is graphical and easy to use and because it has so much great stuff on it. And why does it have so much great stuff on it? Because publishing on the Web is surprisingly easy, as we show you throughout this book.

Getting Webbed

This book talks a lot about the Web but doesn't discuss how to get on it. And even if you're on the Web already, perhaps through a connection at work, you may also want to get on the Web from home. How do you do that?

The quickest and easiest way to get on the Web is to use the MindSpring Web access software included on this book's CD-ROM. You can also use a proprietary online service; America Online (AOL) is by far the largest. Both services have phone support people to help you get connected, and the Web and AOL's proprietary forums each have thousands of users in online forums who are eager to help you understand the Web.

I link, therefore I am

The most exciting features of the Web are based on *linking* — that is, clicking a specific spot on a Web page to see a graphic, hear a sound file, or jump to another page. For example, from a Web page about the United Nations, you can view images of flags from countries around the world, hear people say "hello" in their own languages, or jump to additional information on related topics, such as other international organizations or worldwide news.

How does this magic work? A Web page is stored on a special kind of computer called a *Web server.* A Web server is not to be confused with a *Web surfer,* the name for someone who uses the Web — though both surfers and servers can wipe out spectacularly! A Web server is a computer that is connected to the Internet and can answer requests made in a particular communications language, or *protocol,* called HTTP.

When you use the Web, your machine is acting as a *Web client,* a machine that retrieves information from the Web. When you access a Web page, your machine fires off a request over the Internet for a Web file specified by an address, or URL. Your machine connects to the server that has the Web file. (So every time you get another file from the Web, even a little bitty graphic, the process is called a *connection.*) The Web finds the file and downloads it over the Internet to your machine. Your *Web browser* (the program used to look at World Wide Web documents) then displays the file. This request/receive cycle, shown in Figure 1-2, is repeated every time you surf the Web.

Access several Web pages and watch the process of downloading the text and graphics in each site. Each file downloads separately; you can watch the contents of the Web page fill in as each graphic or multimedia file appears in turn.

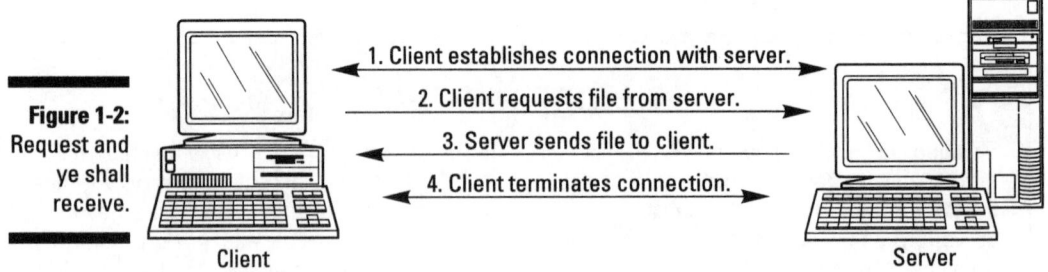

Figure 1-2:
Request and
ye shall
receive.

1. Client establishes connection with server.

2. Client requests file from server.

3. Server sends file to client.

4. Client terminates connection.

Client

Server

Being a Player on the Stage of the World Wide Web

As a World Wide Web user, you're part of the audience for a constantly changing drama. After you put your own page on the World Wide Web, you're actually one of the players in the drama. To play your part correctly, you need to know a bit about the other *dramatis personae* that make the Web work.

Getting to know the cast of characters

GIFs and JPEGs and Web pages, oh my!

The Web is so new that people can't even completely agree on how to define it. So in the list that follows, we define a few basic terms that you need to understand to become a Web publisher. In the process of reading the definitions, you find out a little more about how the Web works. Although people don't yet completely agree on how to talk about the Web, most accept the following definitions:

- **Web page.** A text document on the Web that includes formatting information and pointers to graphics files, multimedia files, and other Web pages.

- **Home page.** A Web page that serves as a Web site's entryway.

- **Web site.** A home page plus (optionally) additional pages. You usually access these additional pages from the home page.

- **Browser.** A program, such as Microsoft Internet Explorer or Netscape Navigator, that's used to look at World Wide Web documents.

- **Search engine.** Web-based services that help you find things you're looking for. (The Web is so popular that finding what you want among the millions of Web pages online is a big problem.) The authors' favorite search engines include Yahoo!, which has a hierarchical listing of many Web sites, and AltaVista, which has powerful basic and advanced text and image search features. (Disclosure: One of the authors likes AltaVista so much, he works there.) You can find these search engines at the following URLs:

  ```
  www.yahoo.com
  www.altavista.com
  ```

- **Inline image.** A graphic that's displayed as part of a Web page.

✔ **Downloadable image.** A graphic that you download and display by clicking a link. Figure 1-3 shows a Web page from Vigra, a San Diego-based division of VisiCom Laboratories. This home page has both an inline image and a downloadable image, which is available by clicking the underlined words. Downloadable images, once common, are now generally used only if an image is very large and detailed.

✔ **GIFs and JPEGs.** The two common types of graphic files on the Web. GIF files (known as *GIFs* and pronounced "jiffs" by some and "giffs" by others) are more common and easier to create. JPEG files (known as *JPEGs* and pronounced "jay-pegs") are more compressed and can usually produce the same size image while taking up less disk space than GIFs. All currently available browsers that support graphics support GIFs and JPEGs as inline images that you can view embedded in the Web page.

If everything in the preceding list seems like just a bunch of words, stop reading and surf around the Web a little bit; look for examples of the terms used in the list. They are easy to find! You can even look up the terms with a search engine by using the search engine URLs above.

Inline image   Downloaded image

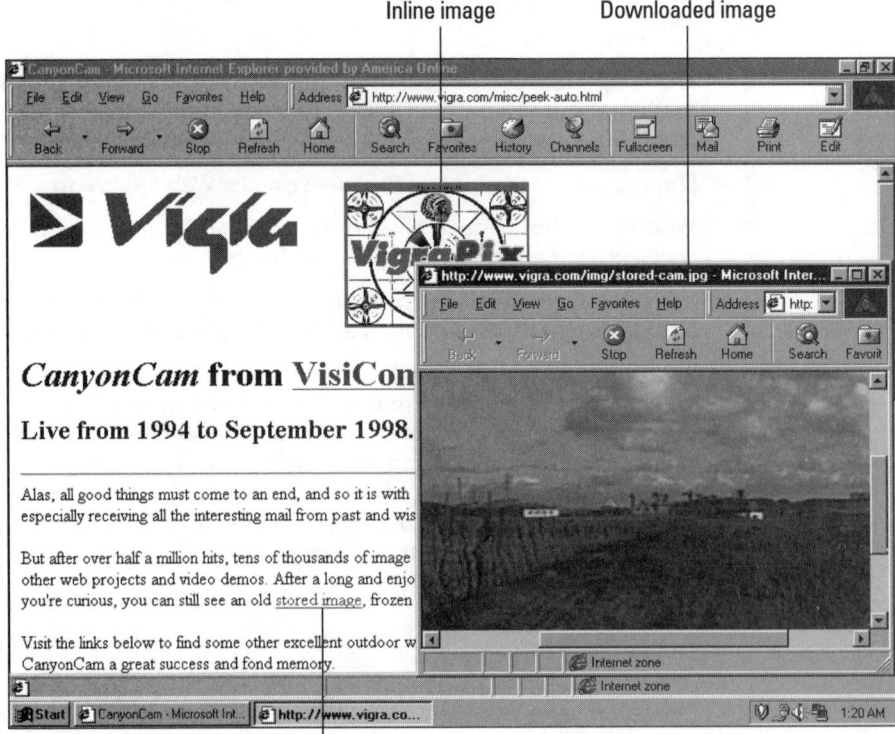

Figure 1-3:
Image-ining
a home
page of
your own.

Downloadable image

When the first edition of this book appeared in 1995, many users had slow computers and slow Internet connections, and therefore used text-only Web browsers that didn't even display graphics, or kept the graphics capability turned off in their Web browsers. While almost all computer users today have graphics capability in their Web setups, new devices have sprung up that have limited abilities — from WebTV, which uses a TV screen as a display, to Palm Pilot-type handhelds and even Web-ready cell phones. Like the old text-only browsers, these devices benefit greatly from simple, clear Web pages that make their point fast, and with text rather than graphics wherever possible.

Examining the HTML script

We keep saying that a Web page is a text document that almost always includes formatting information and links to other files. But how is that special formatting and linking information stored in the text document? It's stored in *tags,* special strings of text within the document that are marked by <angle brackets> on either side. The format of these tags and what each tag means are determined by a specification called *HTML,* or *HyperText Markup Language*. You'll find that having a basic understanding of how HTML works is worthwhile before creating your own Web page, whether you use a Web page creation tool that hides HTML from you most of the time, or whether you work directly in HTML and type in the tags yourself.

If you want to see an example of HTML code for a simple Web page — including formatting, an inline image, and a link — see the Cheat Sheet at the front of this book.

Take a closer look at the term for which HTML is an acronym, HyperText Markup Language. You may already know that hypertext is text that has links in it. A *link* is just a connection to another document. So far, so good. But what's a *markup language*? (It's not that confusing language that car dealers speak when they decide how high to jack up the price!) A markup language is simply a way to put information about a document — for example, information about hypertext links and formatting — in the document itself. Markup languages often use *tags* — labels placed within text that give display instructions. So HyperText Markup Language — HTML — is a specific way of using tags to convey information about a document.

Most tags in HTML come in pairs: One starts a change and the other ends it. In the following sample sentence, the first tag, ⟨B⟩, means start displaying text in a **bold** typeface; the second tag, ⟨/B⟩, means stop using bold.

Here's how the sentence looks when "marked up" with HTML tags:

```
That's a <B>bad</B> idea.
```

Here's how the sentence looks when displayed on-screen:

```
That's a bad idea.
```

The browser reads the original, text-only sentence — That's a <B>bad </B> idea. — and says to itself, "I'll display That's a, turn bold on, display bad, turn bold off, and display idea." The person who created the original sentence puts in the HTML tags, the browser interprets them, and the user only sees the effect — in this case, the word bad displayed in boldface type.

The <B> and </B> tags are *formatting tags* that describe how a browser displays text. The other kind of tag in HTML is the *linking tag*. Linking tags specify outside information to be brought into a document. Here's some complicated-looking HTML text that shows examples of formatting and linking tags:

```
To learn about <I>Pokemon</I>, the "pocket monsters" so
popular with kids today, go to the official Web site for
<A HREF="http://www.pokemon.com">Pokemon</A>.
```

The text appears on-screen as follows:

```
To learn about Pokemon, the "pocket monsters" so popular with
kids today, go to the official Web site for Pokemon.
```

The <I> and </I> formatting tags specify that the word Pokemon is to be displayed in italics. The <A> and </A> linking tags specify that Pokemon is displayed as an *anchor* — that is, the starting point of a link. On most browsers, as here, anchors are underlined. So what does the extra text — HREF="http://www.pokemon.com" — inside the <A> tag mean? HREF is short for *Hypertext REFerence*. If you click the anchor, your browser looks for the URL that serves as the hypertext reference, which in this case is the Pokemon Web page address that appears after the equals sign.

Other tags work the same way: They tell the browser either how to format text or where to look for more information. We go into further excruciating detail about what the most commonly used tags do in Chapter 7.

The idea of a machine or procedure that reads a piece of input, uses that input to make a decision, carries out the decision, and then reads some more input is centuries old and has been thoroughly studied. Such a machine or program — a browser, for example — is called a *finite automaton*. (Pronounced to rhyme with "flynight ought-omaton.") Try dropping that term into your conversation the next time the Web comes up!

Building the set with image maps

Two of the most important elements that affect what you can do with the Web are image maps and forms.

An *image map,* or *clickable image map,* is a graphic that has hot spots built into it. A *hot spot* is an area inside a graphic that acts as a link to another URL, the same way that the underlined text in a Web page acts as a link. These hot spots do different things when you click them. Clicking a hot spot usually invokes a URL, which causes the user to go to a different page. Used this way, an image map can serve as a map or guide to different parts of the Web. The Apple home page, shown in Figure 1-4, is an example of this kind of clickable image map. To paraphrase Buckaroo Banzai: Wherever you click, there you are.

Image maps are hard to create, and users who turn off graphics in their browsers while surfing the Web can't see them. But image maps are very attractive and easy to use. Chapter 8 describes how to create a simple image map.

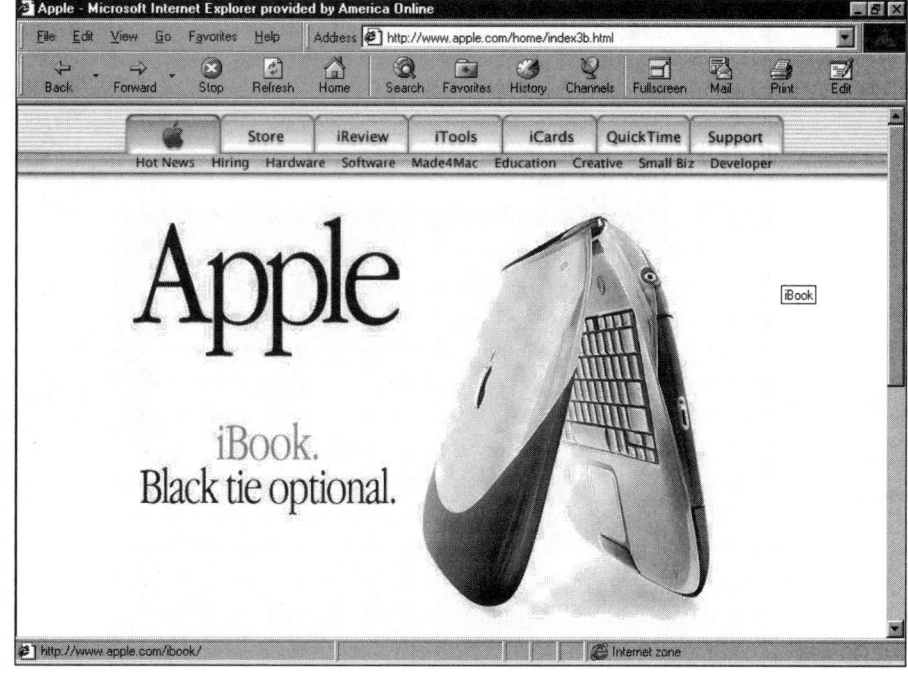

Figure 1-4:
An Apple
with (hot)
spots —
including
each of the
tabs across
the top.

A *form* is just what the name implies: a place where a user can enter data, such as name, address, and telephone number. Figure 1-5 shows a form used by the Monster job search database from TMP Worldwide. On the part of the form shown in the figure, you enter data by clicking your choice from a scrolling list.

The form has elements for entering data and for choosing from a list of predetermined options. Although forms are easy to set up in a Web page, the Web page doesn't automatically know how to handle the data that is entered in the form. You have to write a computer program or use some other kind of tool to receive the data and act on it. Because of this added level of complexity, we mostly ignore forms in this book, but they're an important element in some Web sites.

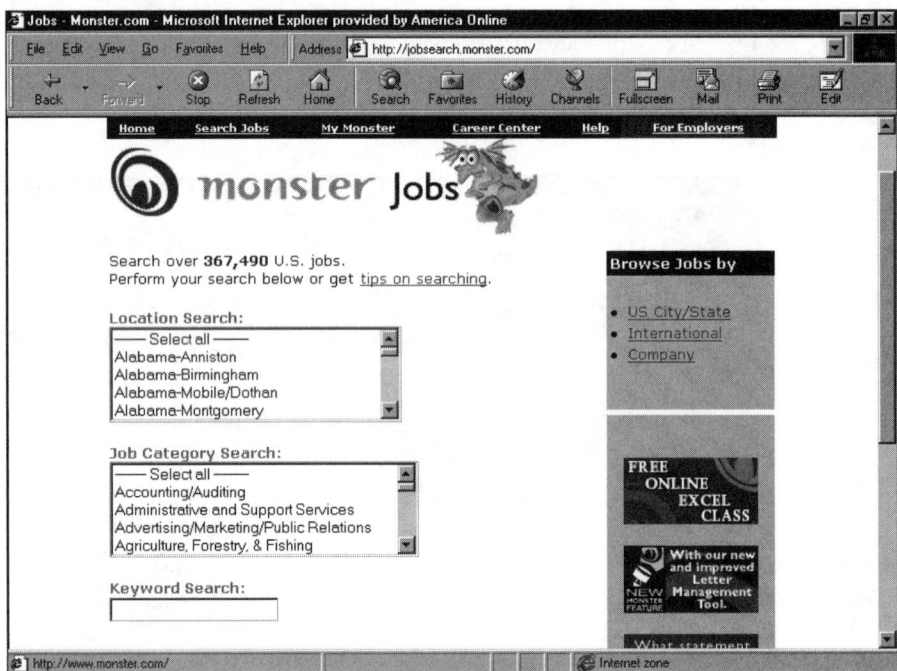

Figure 1-5:
A Web
page form.

Seeing HTML

When Tim Berners-Lee invented HTML at CERN (the European particle physics research facility) a few years ago, he probably never imagined that so many people would be interested in seeing it. Today, most browsers include a command that enables you to see the actual HTML source that makes the page look and work the way it does (see the figure in this sidebar for an example).

For example, in Internet Explorer, choose View⇨Source to view the underlying HTML file. You see all the HTML tags that make the Web page look and act the way it does.

Once you open the HTML file, you can edit the text and the HTML tags, save the file, and then open the file again in your browser to see how it looks with the HTML changes. In Internet Explorer, choose File⇨Open.

Editing a Web page that you've saved on your hard disk doesn't change the page stored on the Web; only the local copy stored on your hard disk changes.

```
                          (untitled)
<HEAD>
<TITLE>Version 2.0b1-95279</TITLE>
</HEAD>
<BODY BGCOLOR="#C0C0C0" TEXT="#000000"
 LINK="#0000EE" VLINK="#551A8B" ALINK="#FF0000">
<TABLE CELLPADDING=3 WIDTH="100%">
<TR>
 <TD ALIGN=CENTER><A HREF="about:authors"><IMG ISMAP SRC="about:logo" ALT=""
border=0></A></TD>
<TD>
 <CENTER>
 <B><FONT size=5>Netscape Navigator
    <SUP><FONT SIZE="-1">(TM)</FONT></SUP></FONT><BR>
<FONT size=4>Version 2.0b1</BR></FONT></B>
Copyright &copy 1994-1995 Netscape Communications Corporation,
All rights reserved.
</CENTER>
<P>
<FONT size=2>
This software is subject to the license agreement set forth in the
<A HREF="about:license">license</A>. Please read and agree to all
terms before using this software.
<P>
Report any problems through the
<A HREF="http://cgi.netscape.com/cgi-bin/auto_bug.cgi">
```

Advances in HTML

Since the Web first became widely (and wildly) popular in the mid-1990s, several advances in HTML have taken place. These advances build on the solid base of the original HTML specification and add new capabilities. However, they also make HTML much more complicated and add many more issues for those who design Web pages.

The biggest changes are the additions of tables, frames, and Dynamic HTML. *Tables* not only display information in table form, but also are used to help precisely position text and graphics. Tables are widely used. *Frames* allow a Web page to be divided up into independently controlled sections. They are somewhat widely used, but not as popular as tables. And *Dynamic*

HTML, a new addition to the original HTML specification, allows moving elements to be included in a Web page, among other changes. Dynamic HTML is not yet widely used.

What all these features have in common is that they add a great deal of complexity to your Web pages, if you use them, and they aren't usable by all the Web browsers out there. (Tables come close to this ideal.) We describe how and when to use these advanced features in Chapter 7 (tables and frames) and Chapter 9 (Dynamic HTML). However, you can go far with the basic HTML specification that is usable by all browsers, so we stick with that version in nearly all of this book.

Putting Your Name in Lights on the Web

You already know that the Web is a great and exciting thing, and you want to be part of the excitement by publishing your own Web page. But you may run into a few potholes on the road to fame and fortune on the Web. What does it take to be a Web publisher? You find out in this section.

Stumbling blocks on the Web

For all its great things, the Web has some problems from the point of view of a publisher:

- **Differences in browsers.** Different browsers, such as different versions of Internet Explorer or Netscape Navigator, display the same HTML tags differently. And some browsers support newer or nonstandard tags, so pages displayed in them look better — or at least different — than they look on other browsers. This inconsistency can drive you to distraction.

- **Faster and slower connections.** Some users have fast network connections to the Web, whereas many home users dawdle along at 28.8 Kbps — ten times slower than a typical corporate connection. So a graphics-rich page that comes up fast on one machine downloads *very* *s-l-o-w-l-y* on another.

✔ **Those darn users.** Users have different screen sizes, and they can reconfigure their browsers to use different fonts, different window sizes, and so on. So even users who connect to the Web through the same network and run the same browser can see the same Web page quite differently.

✔ **Getting on a server.** For your Web pages to show up on the Web, they have to be on a Web server. This means that you have to find either a volunteer or a vendor with a Web server and some hard disk space to spare. Luckily, space for a small Web site is usually either free or cheap, but finding server space and getting your files to the server can be a big hassle.

The first three problems are related to inconsistencies in the Web, and you may have run into them as a user looking at different Web pages. Now that you're a beginning Web publisher, the answer to all these problems is the same: Keep it simple! In this book, we use simple Web page layouts and stick almost completely to the basic HTML features available in all browsers.

The problem of getting your Web page on the server is a little different — the kind of hurdle that can stop neophytes cold, but one that experienced users clear with ease. In the next few chapters, we show you enough varied server solutions to meet any needs — and some of the solutions are even free!

Kirk versus Spock in Web publishing

Reading this book is going to make you a Web publisher — anyone who puts up even a single, simple home page is a publisher on the World Wide Web. Congratulations in advance!

You can take two approaches to this role: the spontaneous approach favored by someone like Captain Kirk, the risk-taking leader of the Starship *Enterprise,* or the careful approach favored by the more logical Mr. Spock. The spontaneous Captain Kirk approach can be summarized in the popular Nike slogan "Just Do It." You can get a simple page up on the Web with just a few hours of work, and without paying any money, simply by following the instructions in this book.

In contrast to Captain Kirk's quick-and-dirty approach, Mr. Spock's more logical method requires you to do the following:

✔ Set goals for your Web site.

✔ Plan the contents of your site to meet those goals.

- ✔ Storyboard your site to specify what's on each Web page and how the pages fit together.
- ✔ Compare your planned site to similar or competing sites and revise your plans accordingly.
- ✔ Create your site on your own machine first and test it thoroughly.
- ✔ Carefully choose a Web service provider that will do the best job of hosting your site.
- ✔ Get your site up on the Web and begin an ongoing cycle of testing and revision.

Whew! That's a lot of Tribble — I mean, a lot of trouble!

Either the spontaneous or the careful approach is just fine, but you should match your approach to what you want to do on the Web. We recommend that you try the spontaneous approach first. Don't put out a great deal of effort, and don't use your initial page to try to start a Web-based business empire. Just create a personal or business home page that says something about you or your organization.

If you don't own or run your organization, make sure that you have the permission you need before putting up a Web page that represents the organization. Otherwise, you could find yourself on an unexpected, rapid transition off your current career path. (The Monster job search database we mention earlier in this chapter is a great help in looking for a new job!)

If that one page is all you ever publish on the Web, fine. A lot of the fun of being on the Web is seeing the Web pages created by individuals who are just trying to have fun and share their interests. Whether you go on to create a Web presence for a business or even create a Web-based business of your own, the experience that you get when you "just do it" may prove invaluable. Table 1-1 suggests when to use the careful versus the spontaneous approach to Web publishing.

Table 1-1	The Kirk (Spontaneous) and Spock (Careful) Approaches to Web Publishing				
	Have Fun	*Learn Now for Advanced Work Later*	*Small Business Web Presence*	*Larger Business Web Presence*	*Web-Based Business*
Spontaneous	X	X	X		
Careful			X	X	X

Seven Steps to Successful Web Publishing

Once you understand the different parts that make up the Web, you're ready to become a Web page publisher. Here, we break into steps the process of becoming a publisher on the Web:

1. **Create your HTML-tagged text files.**
2. **Create or otherwise obtain graphics files.**
3. **Put links to graphics files and to other Web pages into your HTML files.**
4. **Test your soon-to-be Web site on your own machine.**
5. **Find Web server space.**
6. **Transfer your files to the Web server, thus creating your Web site.**
7. **Check that your new Web site works the way you want it to work.**

Although these steps sound simple, they can become complicated. In fact, some people make a good living handling just parts of each of these steps. The "simple" step of creating your HTML files, for example, includes deciding what you want to say; deciding how you want your page to look; choosing whether to use HTML directly or use an HTML editing tool; figuring out HTML, the HTML editing tool, or both; and more. The different parts of this process are the reasons for most of the chapters in this book.

Making simple things simple

If all you want to do is create a simple "I exist" Web page, either for yourself or for your business, you shouldn't have to go through the rigmarole of figuring out HTML or a tool, finding server space, and so on. Part II describes easy ways to get on the Web. Chapter 3 and Chapter 4 describe some of the many free services for putting a simple personal page on the Web. GeoCities (Chapter 3), the Web's biggest personal Web page publishing site, provides free server space and tools for creating personal Web pages to get you published on the Web quickly. America Online (Chapter 5), the largest online service in the world, and CompuServe (Chapter 6), its less expensive cousin, include free Web publishing services as well.

To see how easy it is to publish on the Web, just turn to Chapter 3, 4, 5, or 6 and get started. You'll be a Web publisher with just an hour or two of effort.

Making difficult things possible

The free services and online services we describe in this book differ in how far they allow you to go without outgrowing the free Web site. If your site gets too large or gets too much traffic, at some point these services will probably ask you to start paying for the site. Also, you may want a new site with your own easy-to-find URL, especially if your site represents a business. And if you know from the start that you want to create a relatively large or busy Web site, to go with your real-world business or personal activities or to start something exciting online, you may want to start planning now for something that goes beyond the limited support available for a free Web site.

The rest of Part I describes the basic strategy you can follow to get your first site up on the Web. Part II tells you how to create your initial site on a free Web-based service or an online service.

After Part II, this book is all about creating or expanding your Web site so that it's right up there with some of the most interesting and attractive sites on the Web. But we've said it before, and we'll say it again: Even if you want to do something big on the Web, it's well worth getting some hands-on experience by first creating a personal or simple business Web page by using one of the free approaches mentioned in this Part.

Chapter 2
Your Web Publishing Strategy

- -

In This Chapter

▶ Using Web page design guidelines

▶ Reviewing four types of Web pages: personal, topical, commercial, and entertainment

▶ Creating your Web publishing strategy

- -

Creating an initial Web page is easy, especially if you use the Web page creation services we describe in Part II. But creating a good Web page or a multipage Web site is more work. Doing the extra work is what makes you a real Web publisher — someone who can go beyond saying "I've done that" to actually creating a Web page that gets a point across, helps people, and contributes something positive to the Web.

If you're a person who gets all your ducks in a row before proceeding — a Spock, as we say in Chapter 1 — or you want to create a more advanced Web site, read this chapter in its entirety before creating your first Web page. But, if you're more spontaneous — more a Kirk type — or are just in a hurry, we suggest that you go to Chapters 3 and 4 and use the instructions you find there to create your first Web home page right away. Then come back to this chapter and the other chapters in this book for the information you need to make your Web page something to be proud of.

This chapter condenses our experience in paper publishing and Web publishing down to a few principles and steps that can make your early Web work a success and can lay the foundation for making your page even better in the future. Follow these guidelines to get your message across more effectively.

Web Page Guidelines

A Web page or Web site is basically a publication, though an interactive one. Thinking through a few simple principles now, before you start, will help make your Web page much more interesting and useful to the people who see it. Or you can revisit this section after you put up your initial Web home page and use these guidelines to revise your page and make it even more interesting and useful!

Ask "Why am I doing this?"

We talk soon about the purpose of the Web page itself. But a good question to ask yourself going in is "Why am I doing this?" (As you do more and more work on your page, your answer to this question may come to have some degree of profanity in it!) That is, why are you creating the page, and not having someone else create it for you? The answer helps you determine some important things about the page. The following list details the most common reasons for creating a Web page or Web site:

- ✔ **For work.** More and more people are being asked to create Web pages and Web sites as part of their jobs; for example, they use the Web to communicate with people inside or outside their companies. But unless you plan to be a full-time Webmaster, you need to balance the time you spend developing your pages with the time you spend on the other demands of your job. Be modest in your initial goals, and plan to find out more about Web publishing so that you can keep your pages useful and interesting by building on what you previously created. Be sure to keep records of each step in creating and modifying your Web pages — just a brief line or two of text for each major change in a project file is all you need — so that you — or the person who takes over for you — can refer to the records later.

- ✔ **For fun.** Fun sites are a good thing, and they are a lot of what makes the Web worthwhile. But if you create your site for fun, you may find time to work on it only after you spend time on other things, such as work, school, or time with friends and family. So don't be too ambitious in your initial plans, or you may take quite a while to finish and publish your page.

- ✔ **As a career move.** So you want to be a full-time, or nearly full-time, Webmaster; or you want, in some other way, to make the Internet or Web part of your career. In this kind of situation, you can afford to plan an ambitious Web site that uses advanced tools, tracks use, and otherwise gets close to the cutting edge of the Web. To gain experience, create your initial Web page by using the accessible and broad-based tools and approaches we describe in this book. Then take your page closer to the cutting edge by using the more advanced techniques described and taught elsewhere, such as the JavaScript programs described in *JavaScript For Dummies,* 2nd Edition, by Emily A. Vander Veer (IDG Books Worldwide, Inc.).

- ✔ **Who knows?** To mimic a line from the film *Risky Business,* sometimes in life you just have to say, "What the heck." You may not have a specific reason for publishing on the Web, but that shouldn't stop you. You may figure out a good reason after you have a little Web experience under your belt. Start simple, so you can score an early success in getting a basic Web page up, and then go from there.

Web terms to know

As in Chapter 1, we want to clear up, and also reemphasize, how we define and use some Web terms:

✔ **Web page.** A text document that is published on a Web server, has HTML tags in it, almost always includes hypertext links, and often includes graphics. When you click the Forward and Back buttons in your Web browser, you move chronologically through the Web pages that you already visited.

✔ **Web site.** A collection of Web pages that share a common theme and purpose and that users generally access through the site's home page. Some Web sites have only

a home page; others have many pages and even multiple home pages.

✔ **Home page.** The Web page that people generally access first within a Web site. You let people know the URL (address) of your home page and try to get other Web page creators to provide links to it. Your home page is your Web site's starting page and contains links to other pages in your site.

✔ **Site versus page.** You can use these terms almost interchangeably, as we do in this book. Just remember that a Web site can have more than one Web page in it.

Don't spend too much time on design

Designing a Web page is unlike designing any other kind of publication, because you don't have as much control over the look and feel of Web pages as you do with other types of publications. Modem and network connection speeds, browsers, screen sizes, and font and other settings within a browser vary so much that users can have very different experiences with your Web page.

Web page creators often use HTML as a page-layout system, but the goal of HTML is to mark the documents in functional bits. For example, you mark a piece of text as a headline to indicate that it's significant, not to specify exactly how it appears on-screen. This is an underlying principle of using HTML. Remember that you use HTML to describe the function of different parts of your document; the HTML tags control the structure of your document and enable search engines and Web "spider" programs to help users find your Web page. Web browsers and user-specified settings determine exactly how your document appears on-screen.

With the latest versions of HTML, it's possible to control more aspects of your Web page's appearance. Advanced sites such as AltaVista, the site where one of the authors works, use many different aspects of HTML as well as the programming language JavaScript to create dense, rich layouts more like a magazine than a typical Web page. However, many aspects of the newest versions of HTML are not yet standard across different Web browsers. In this book we stick with HTML 4.0, which works the same way for nearly all Web users.

Most Web publishing strategy leads to a single, bottom-line conclusion: Keep your design simple and don't spend too much time on it initially. Then build it up as you find out more about Web publishing generally and more about how people use your page specifically.

Put your work on the panel

The Web can seem pretty neat to a writer who is accustomed to creating work that's printed. Unlike printed pages, Web browsers have scroll bars that enable you to create a page that's as long as you want it to be — just like an old-fashioned scroll. But when you design a Web page, more is less. The more you put on a page, the less likely someone will look at all of it!

Instead of thinking of your Web page as an infinitely extendable page, think of it as a series of panels, such as those in a comic strip. Each panel is the size of the browser window on the user's screen. Upon arriving at your Web site, a user sees the initial panel — the top part of your home page. The next action the user takes — scrolling down, clicking a link, or hitting the Back button on the browser — depends entirely on the user's reaction to that initial panel. Similarly, the user first experiences every link destination in your Web site as a panel and then decides what to do next based on what's in that panel. Figure 2-1 uses this idea in creating an initial screen that's interesting and informative to the user.

Users always see the top portion of each Web page as a panel. If you provide links to a spot within a page, users also experience the area around each link destination — the spot they arrive at when they click the link — as a panel, too.

As an example, think of most of the big corporate Web sites you see. Many have a graphic that fills much of the top of the site's home page. Why? To make a good impression in that first panel that the user sees. Poorly designed Web pages tend to start with text at the top and just keep going, ignoring the notion that the user, upon seeing all that text, may immediately go somewhere else.

As you design and test your Web site, think of each panel that the user sees and what actions the user may choose next. Which choice in each panel looks most interesting? What do you want the user to do? What would you do if you were the user? Then have a few friends try your site. Which path do they follow through — or out of — your site, and why? Finding the answers to these questions, and revising your site accordingly, can place you way ahead of most Web publishers.

Surf around some of your favorite Web sites. What brings you back to them? Can you easily access the information you want? Do you enjoy the site as a whole, or do you just check one or two things before leaving? Keep your answers in mind when you design your own site.

Big issues for big sites

This book focuses on the needs of people who create a single Web page or a small Web site, and who do so on their own. Larger sites, or sites that need to be put up quickly or changed rapidly, need to have additional people working on them.

If you want to create a larger site down the road, start thinking now about what resources may be available to put into it. How many people in your company or other organization work on advertising, public relations, and marketing? How many people question whether those jobs are real work? (Just kidding — the lead author, who's a marketer, wrote that!)

You may reasonably expect your company to re-target some fraction of its advertising, marketing, and PR resources to support a presence on the Web. And what about sales? As Web-based business transactions take off, some portion of a company's sales effort becomes Web-based, necessitating a suitable up-front commitment to bring returns down the road.

Or your company may already suffer from Web burnout. Classic symptoms of Web burnout include massive early investment to create a beautiful site, months of failure to update or maintain the site, followed by finger-pointing about who wasted all that money. Usually the problem is that no one set goals for the site, so no one managed the site's design and construction with those specific goals in mind. Companies often designate too few financial and human resources for maintenance and improvement of the site. If this has happened in your company, you know the problems that result, so be sure to establish clear goals for your own Web efforts.

The most important element in adopting any new technology for business is a successful pilot project. As someone creating a smallish Web site, you're developing important skills and knowledge about the all-important intersection of your business's needs with the Web's opportunities. Set specific goals, strive to meet them, and record both your problems and your successes. By doing so, you position yourself to justify further investment of resources as the Web grows in importance for your company.

Put the good stuff first

Imagine the Web as a giant magazine rack and the person surfing the Web as someone scanning the front covers of all those magazines. People who see your Web page decide whether to stay at your site or go elsewhere based largely on what they see when your page first comes up.

If your purpose is to provide information or links, put that information first or, at most, one click away. For example, to create a site that provides information about your company, make getting the contact information — your company name, address, phone number, and fax number — easy for people. To create a personal site that is attractive to potential employers, make clear what employment field you're in and make your résumé easy to access.

If your purpose is to draw people into your site to entertain them, educate them, or expose them to messages from advertisers — or to do all of these things at once — then the first part of the page should make a strong impression and invite the user to go further into your site. To make a good first impression, consider placing a clickable image map on your home page, but carefully weigh its effectiveness against the time it takes to download. (See Chapter 1 for a definition of a clickable image map and Chapter 7 for a description of how to create one.) Figure 2-1 shows the Kaua'i Exotix Web page, certainly one that catches your attention, located at the following URL:

www.besttropicals.com

But, like the Kauai Exotix Web page, your home page also should help people who seek a quick "hit" of information; they're more likely to come back later if you don't waste their time during their first quick visit.

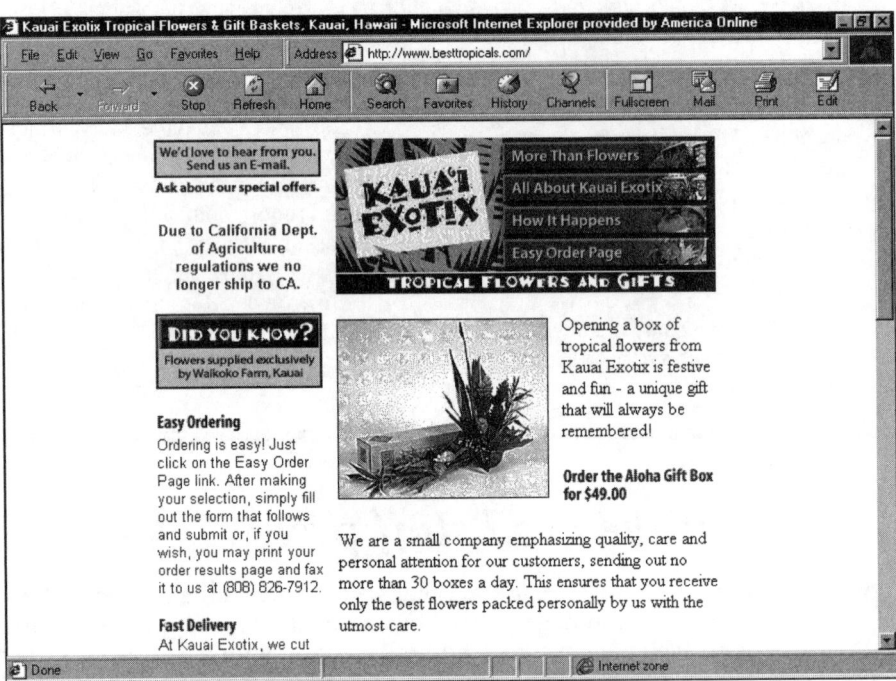

Figure 2-1:
Buds for
your buds.

Think twice about download times

Putting lots of graphics in your pages is time-intensive for you because creating or finding good graphics and then placing them takes a great deal of time and effort. Graphics are also time-intensive for those who surf your site. So plan to use spot graphics (small images that download quickly) at first and think twice before creating large clickable image maps or attractive opening graphics such as those you find on the Netscape, Apple, and SGI (Silicon Graphics, Inc.) sites.

You may find a good deal of coverage in the computer press, and even in mainstream newspapers and newsmagazines, about ongoing efforts to make faster access available to ordinary users. But for all the talk about ISDN, cable modems, satellite downloads, Digital Subscriber Line (DSL), and other advanced techniques, most users are still on 56 Kbps or slower modems. So ignore the hype — the speed at which the average person accesses the Web is creeping upward slowly, not leaping ahead. For now, be conservative in how much data you put in each page, and test the download times of your pages over a modem-based connection before you publish them.

Know your audience

According to Web researchers, Web users overwhelmingly speak English as either a first or second language. Consequently, the great majority of Web content, Web creation tools, and Web browsers use the English language. Even ten years after the birth of the Web — in Europe — North America is still the "center of gravity" for Web access. This will gradually change as other countries catch up to Web penetration in the U.S.

Why are people online? Surveys indicate that the top reasons people use the Web are for information-gathering, entertainment, education, work, "time-wasting," and shopping. Which of these purposes do you intend for your site to serve? How do you appeal to these people? How do you help them find you? The answers to these questions will help you enhance the appeal and usefulness of your site.

Finally, what kind of browsers are your users running? Surveys indicate that over 80 percent of Web users run Microsoft Internet Explorer; nearly all the rest use Netscape Navigator. Both of these browsers, and most others that make up the remaining user base, support graphics and tables, and nearly all users run their browsers with graphics turned on (which doesn't mean that they appreciate waiting for complex images to load — unless those images are pretty cool!).

For more details about who's online, what they do there, and what it means to you if you're creating a business Web site, see *Marketing Online For Dummies*, by Frank Catalano and Bud Smith (IDG Books Worldwide, Inc.).

Use text bites

As we mention earlier in this chapter, when preparing a Web site, less is more. Saying something with less text makes users more likely to read and remember it. A *text bite* is like a sound bite — it's a short, clearly written piece of text that makes a single point.

Although you can overuse text bites, they are very important in Web page design. Text bites help you convey as much information as possible in the limited amount of time users spend looking at each Web page. And they help you balance the basic elements of Web page design: text, links, and graphics.

If you want to put long documents on the Web, consider rewriting them as a series of text bites. If rewriting them isn't a good idea, at least provide short, clearly written blocks of text that present navigational information for your Web site and introductory and summary information for the documents themselves. Put this information at the beginning and end of long documents. Add headers to break up the flow of text and provide pointers to key areas. Without such guidance, users may well give up in frustration without reaching the information they're looking for.

Consider using non-English Web pages

One of the most limiting factors to the spread of the World Wide Web is that it's nearly all in English. This situation is changing; already some sites, such as the AltaVista search engine, offer their services in other languages. But the amount of non-English content is small compared to the size of the Web.

To create Web pages, you need to know enough English to figure out and use HTML and Web tools. But what about your audience?

First, find out how many people in your target audience speak a specific language and how many of them have access to the Web. Then consider the cost of translating your content into each language that you're interested in. Compare that cost to the size of the potential audience.

Be optimistic; having native-language content really distinguishes your site. At this point in the Web's growth, you're better off having the Web's best list of movies in Farsi (Iran's predominant language) than yet another list of movies in English.

At the least, if you have printed materials already translated into other languages, either put those materials on the Web or publicize them there. In some languages and some areas of information needs, using non-English languages on the Web offers the same kind of ground-floor opportunity that the Web as a whole offered when its popularity started several years ago.

What about hiring out your Web work?

If you work in a large organization, you or your boss may consider hiring out all the Web work for your company. This is a bad idea. Although using consultants to help introduce and use new technology is a good idea, developing a reasonable amount of expertise in-house is also a good idea. So don't hire out the entire process; have a mix of employees and contractors working on your company's Web site. A good way for you to get the necessary experience to be a useful member of such a team is to create a couple of small Web sites yourself.

Look at sites you like

Look at sites you like and at sites whose purposes are similar to your own. What's good about them? What's not? Imitate successful elements — without copying, which would be a violation of copyright laws — and avoid unsuccessful ones. As the development of your site progresses, keep checking it against the sites you previously identified and widen your search to get additional ideas — on what not to do as well as on what to do.

Very few original ideas exist on the Web, and your initial site is likely to contain one or two new ideas at best. The rest of your site may echo things readers have already seen, and you're better off if your site brings to mind other good sites, rather than bad ones. (But be careful. If you start yelling "Bad! Bad site!" at your computer screen and swatting it with a rolled-up newspaper, you may not be allowed around sharp objects much longer.)

Plan for ongoing improvements

As you plan and implement your Web site, you will, no doubt, find yourself creating a "To Do" list of things that you can't fit into the original site but want to add later, when time allows. (Creating this list for later use is great protection against trying to create a supersite right off the bat, getting stuck in the creation process, and never getting to a point where you can actually publish.) This list is the start of a plan for ongoing improvements.

Some things that you put in a Web site need to be kept current. For example, if your business Web page shows your company's quarterly results, be ready to update it quickly when the next quarter's results come out. If it lists company officers, update it as soon as a change takes place. (Unless you're one of the people changed — then it's your successor's problem!)

Web site information that is obviously out of date is one of the best ways to leave a bad impression of you or your company overall and to steer visitors away from your Web site.

Not only do you want to update the Web site, you want to avoid using "Under Construction" signs and otherwise apologizing for things that aren't there yet. Everything on the Web is under construction, which is half the fun of using the Web and creating pages for it in the first place. You get only one chance to make a first impression, and an "Under Construction" sign doesn't count in your favor.

Be sure to give users a place to see the progress of your Web page and find out about your plans for it. Some sites have a "What's New" page to describe recent additions, and such a page would also be a good point to describe your plans for expansion. Avoid giving specific dates unless you're very sure of them. Be sure to convey excitement about what you already have up and what you're planning to add, not embarrassment about what's missing.

Decide how you define success

Before you design and create your Web page, define what you believe will make it a success. For an initial effort, simply putting up something on the Web that clearly conveys basic information is probably enough. For follow-up work, get more specific. Are you trying to reach a certain number of people or type of people? Will measuring *hits* — the number of times that people access some piece of your site — be enough, or do you need some other measure of response, such as having people send e-mail or call an 800 number? Do you want to create a cutting-edge site in terms of bell-and-whistle features like fancy graphics and animation — and if so, are you willing to invest the time and money to make this happen? Talk to people who do advertising and marketing in the real world, as well as to people who work on the Web, and get a sense of what goals they set and how they measure success in meeting their goals.

Types of Web Sites

The Web offers examples of nearly every communications strategy known to humanity, successful or not. But not every example will apply to your situation. For one thing, the resources of different Web publishers vary tremendously. For another, several different types of Web sites exist, and not every lesson learned in creating or inspecting one type of Web site applies to the others.

The major types of Web pages are personal, topical, commercial, and entertainment sites. In the next sections, we describe some of the specific considerations that apply to each type of Web page and not to the others. Decide in advance what type of Web page you want to create. When you look on the Web for examples of what to emulate and what to avoid, focus mainly on pages of the type that you want to create; examples from other genres are as likely to be misleading as helpful. Don't be afraid to integrate elements of one type of page into another; just make sure that in doing so, you're helping to meet the overall purpose(s) of your Web site, instead of detracting from it.

Personal sites

Personal Web sites can have many goals. Often, your goal is simply to share something about yourself with coworkers, friends, family, and others. Personal Web pages are a great way for people to find out about others with similar interests and for people in one culture to find out about other cultures. A representative example of an initial home page is the personal home page shown in Figure 2-2. (A simple home page that already has a counter — pretty cool!) See it at

`www.geocities.com/Athens/Olympus/5648`

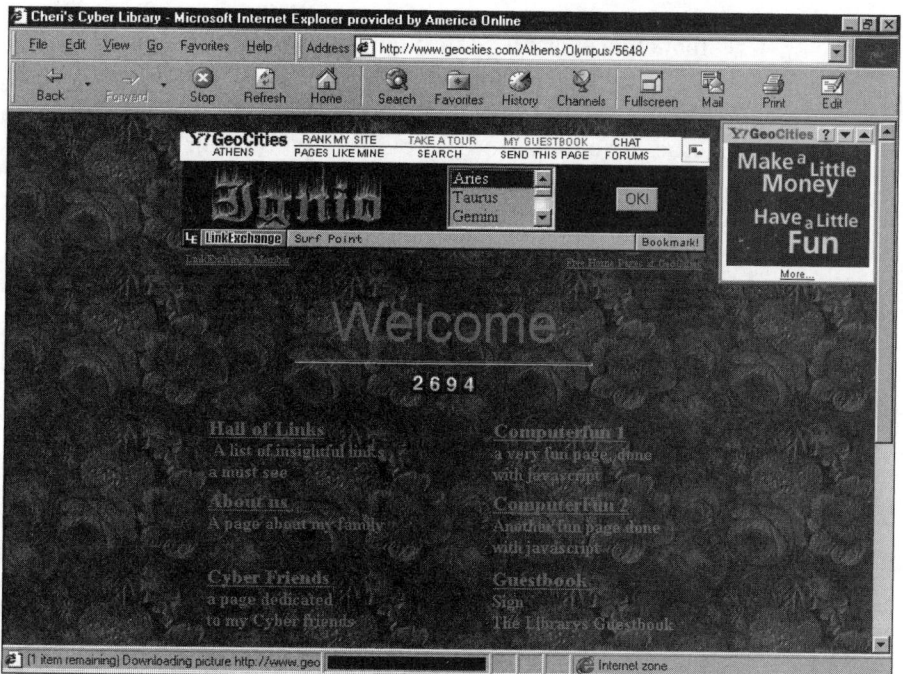

Figure 2-2:
Hurry up and become the next visitor.

Designed by Cheri Elliott and her son Joe (also known as Silent Dragon)

Creating a personal Web site is a great deal of fun and great practice for other work. But personal Web sites are often left without additions or updates after the initial thrill of creating and publishing them fades. Be different — add to your Web site today! To the extent that personal Web sites evolve, creators tend to add more information about a single key interest, in which case the pages may become topical Web sites, or they add more information about professional goals and accomplishments, in which case the pages resemble commercial Web sites.

Following a few simple rules helps make your personal Web site more fun and less work:

- **What's on first?** No, no. What's on second. . . . The first panel, or screenful, of your personal Web site's home page should make the main point of the site clear. If the main point is just "you," the first screenful should have links to Web pages about some of the things about "you" that are in your site. If the point is a topical interest, business interest, or professional self-promotion, you should make that clear, too.

- **Keep it simple.** Start with modest goals and get something up on the Web; then create a "To Do" list of ways in which to extend your site. Consider spinning off commercial and topical pages that reflect your desires and interests, each page with its own access point, rather than funneling everything through your personal home page.

- **Provide lots of links.** One of the best ways to share your interests is to share information about Web sites that you like, as well as books and other resources. You can put this list on your home page or make it a separate page that's part of your personal Web site. If you develop a thorough, carefully updated list of links for a specific interest area, you create a very valuable resource for others.

- **Consider your privacy.** A Web page is just like a billboard — except that 30 million or more people can see it, not just a few thousand. Don't put anything up on your Web page that you wouldn't want on a billboard. And think twice before putting up information about your kids, especially pictures; there are weirdos in cyberspace, too.

Topical sites

That's "topical," not "tropical." (See the Kaua'i Exotix home page earlier in this chapter for an example of the latter.) A *topical home page* is a resource on a specific topic. A topic can be an interest or volunteer group to which the author belongs, in which case the page may grow over time into something much like a commercial Web site. (Creating a Web site for a group is a tremendous contribution that you can make, but watch what you may be getting yourself into!) Or it can be about any interest, cause, concern, obsession, or flight of fancy that you have. In this sense, the Web is like an out-of-control vanity press, allowing anyone to go on and on about anything — sometimes offering something of great value, oftentimes not.

The best-supported topical interest area on the Web is on Web publishing itself. One such topical site is the Useless Pages page shown in Figure 2-3, which started as a pet project of one of the talented employees of Primus Consulting, Inc. (The fun part is to guess which of the Useless Pages were intentionally designed badly just to get on the Useless Pages list!) Check out this site at

```
www.go2net.com/useless
```

Making a second career out of maintaining and extending a topical Web site is easy, but the pay is usually nil. This is especially true if you create a Web site for an interest or volunteer group that is, of course, delighted to be on the Web — and, by the way, will have just a few little ideas of additional things that they'd like to see you put on the site, then a few more, then a few more. . . . Here are some things to consider when you create a topical Web site:

- ✔ **What's on first?** As with a personal Web page, the title of a topical Web page and the first screen need to make unmistakably clear the topic that the page covers. And, to the extent possible, it must describe what resources the Web site offers about the topic.

- ✔ **Keep focused.** A topical Web site loses value if it goes beyond a single topic. How many of the people who share your love for Thai cooking also share your abiding interest in rotifers? (Which are too small to use in most recipes.) If you have two interests that you want to share on the Web, consider creating separate sites.

- ✔ **Create a succession plan.** If your Web site grows beyond your capacity to maintain and extend it properly, find someone to help out or to take it over. The first person you should ask about taking over is anyone who's complaining that you're not extending the site fast enough! If your site supports a specific organization, people in that organization are the logical ones to take over the site. Decide what role you can handle and then ask for help in doing the rest.

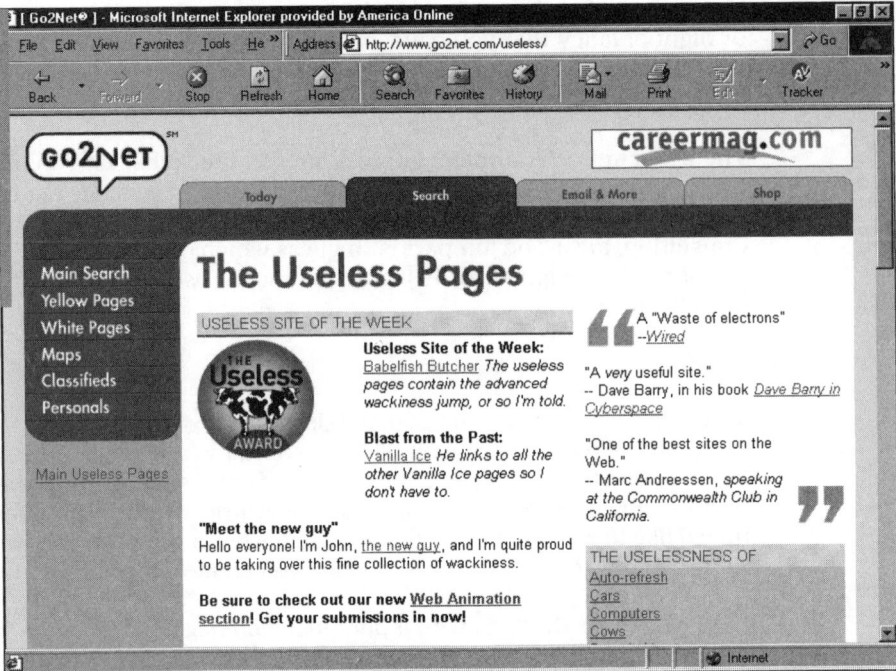

Figure 2-3: A unique take on Web publishing.

Are personal Web sites still relevant?

Recently, a tremendous amount of interest has developed in Web-based commerce, corporate intranets for internal company communications, and extranets for private communications between organizations. Personal Web sites have gotten somewhat lost in the shuffle as well-funded corporate sites get all the attention. Never fear; personal Web sites are still fun and easy to create. And did we mention that they're fun?

GeoCities, which we describe in detail in Chapter 3, pioneered the free hosting of personal Web pages; and its Web site consistently ranks among the Top Ten most-visited Web sites — an enviable distinction indeed. Another such service, Homestead, is not as large but is growing very quickly. Personal Web pages on other sites continue to proliferate as well.

Part of what's driving the continuing interest in personal Web pages is that more and more people all over the world have access to the Web. The chances are better than ever that a high percentage of your friends, family, and colleagues can visit and appreciate your site. So don't be put off by the tremendous growth of business on the Web. The personal and fun side is growing, too; it's just getting less media attention than the commercial side.

Commercial sites

Business Web sites, also known as commercial sites, constitute the 50,000-pound gorilla of the Web, with a tremendous amount of time, energy, and money devoted to them. Business Web sites cover a wide range of styles because their goals and the expertise and resources behind them vary so much. This book provides enough information for you to create a competent "Web presence" site with several pages of contact and company information. But even these kinds of sites vary quite a bit, and you need to be sure that your company's page is well executed. Figure 2-4 shows the Netsurfer home page created by Arthur's business.

Go surf around the Netsurfer site to see what a site designed and implemented by one of the authors (Arthur Bebak) looks like.

    www.netsurf.com

The first question to ask about a business Web site is "Who can access it?" Some sites are intended for the World Wide Web and everyone on it; others are on the World Wide Web but are password-protected or otherwise restricted in access; still others are on private networks and inaccessible to outsiders. These inaccessible networks are "behind the firewall," as we explain in Chapter 1. Any Web page that isn't accessible to everyone is considered an internal or private Web page, even if the list of people who can access it includes thousands of people.

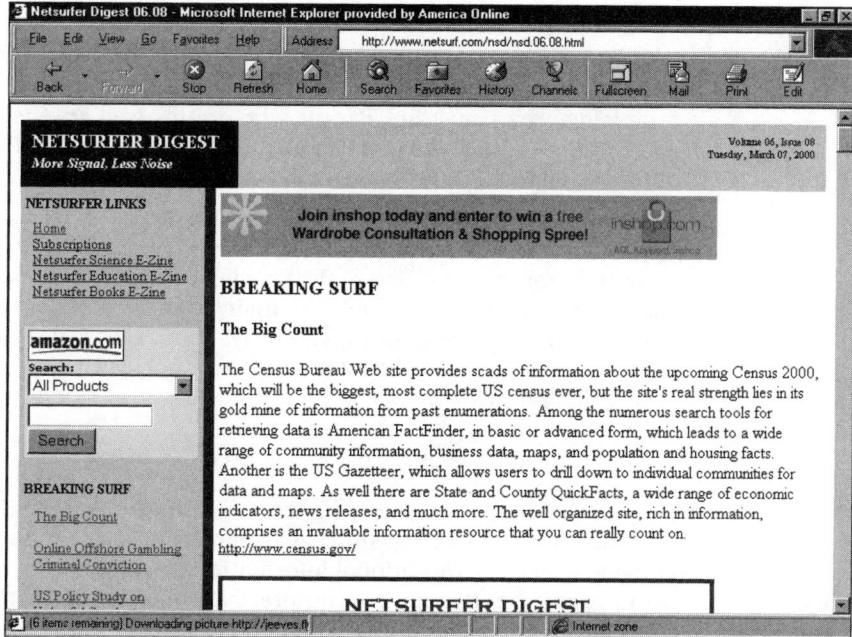

Figure 2-4:
The
Netsurfer
Communica
-tions motto:
More signal,
less noise.

Despite the wide variety of business Web sites, following just a few rules can help you create a page that meets your goals:

- ✔ **What's on first?** A business Web page should make the name and purpose(s) of your business immediately clear. Also, the site should provide information on how to contact your business and what resources the site offers.

- ✔ **Get permission.** Unless you own the business, you should ask for permission before putting a company page on the open Web. If you don't, someone may give you a hard time after you publish, to the point that you wish you'd gotten permission or hadn't published at all. For internal pages on your company's intranet, you may not need permission. Make sure that you have any permissions that you need before you publish your Web page.

- ✔ **Inside or outside the firewall?** Deciding who gets access is tricky. For example, a small amount of otherwise confidential information can make a site more valuable, but the presence of confidential information also prevents you from opening up the entire site to the broader public — including people who may benefit from it. Implementing access decisions can also be difficult. Investigate how to password-protect a site, or ask a network administrator at your company whether you can physically control access. For instance, you may be able to prevent access based on what network the user connects from.

- ✔ **Find experts.** It's likely that businesses similar to yours — or even coworkers, if you're in a large company — have Web sites that have a purpose similar to yours. Look to the creators of those sites for guidance and inspiration.

- ✔ **Pursue uniqueness.** Who wants to be a clone? Find specific ways to make your site different from — and better than — others, without compromising broad usability. People who do this well are the ones you see getting "Cool Site of the Day" and similar tokens of recognition from other Web users.

- ✔ **Monitor usage.** Investing time, energy, and money in a business Web site requires a trade-off among the Web site and other things that those resources could go to. One of the crucial questions you may need to answer in order to justify Web site maintenance or expansion is how much use the site gets. Investigate ways to measure the use of your site. A good way to start is a basic hit counter, such as the free one you can find at the following URL:

```
fastcounter.linkexchange.com
```

- ✔ **Seek out additional resources.** This book focuses on hands-on creation of simple personal and business Web sites. For a larger business site, you need access to additional information to help you with the planning, hosting, and maintenance of the site. Consider purchasing *HTML 4 For Dummies,* 2nd Edition, by Ed Tittel and Natanya Pitts, for more information on the HTML specification, and *Marketing Online For Dummies,* by Frank Catalano and Bud Smith (both books from IDG Books Worldwide, Inc.), for more information on planning and creating a business Web site with a marketing bent.

Having a Web site that's too obviously "handmade," rather than professionally created, can be embarrassing for a business. However, many sites are going "back to the future" with a simple, clean look that's light on graphics. So how do you decide whether to make your "look" fancy or simple? The best way to get a quick "reality check" is to look at some competitors' Web sites and make sure that your initial site looks about as good as theirs. And remember that the most embarrassing thing is having no site at all.

Entertainment sites

Entertainment is one of the top three reasons that people use the Web, and the number of entertainment sites is growing. Humorous pages and services such as multiuser dungeons (MUDs) and shared games on online services are now expanding onto the Web. Figure 2-5 shows Ancient Anguish, an interesting adventure MUD that was developed starting in 1992, which does indeed make it ancient in Web terms. You can become anguished, too, at the following URL:

```
www.anguish.org
```

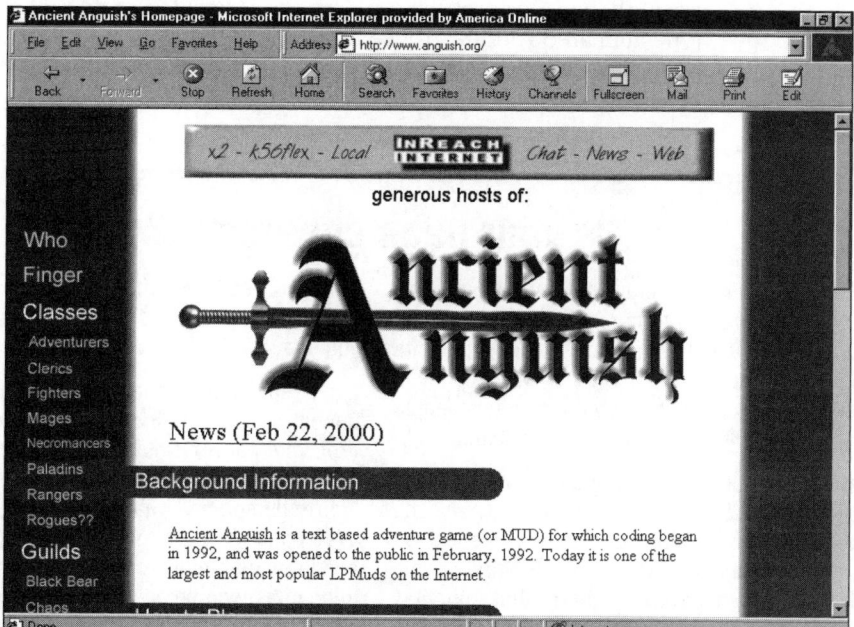

Figure 2-5:
May your
only anguish
be ancient!

A MUD is an agreed-upon environment in which users interact. It can be anything from a medieval adventure to a shared experiment in running a fictitious country. So if someone tells you he spent the morning "wandering around in the MUD," you may have to look at his shoes to determine which kind of mud (or MUD) he means.

Entertainment sites are usually for more than "just" entertainment. For one thing, many include advertising or intend to at some point down the road. Ad sales and advertising support for sites are among the trickiest issues on the Web, because in its early years the Internet was a noncommercial environment. Educational elements are often included in the entertainment mix, covertly or overtly. These complicating factors, and the high expectations that people have of entertainment sites, can make these sites some of the most demanding ones to create. Here are a few suggestions for creating entertainment sites:

- ✔ **Don't start here.** Don't try to figure out Web publishing by creating an entertainment site. It's a very demanding task. Try another type first and edge your way into entertainment.

- ✔ **Keep it fresh.** How funny is a joke the second time you hear it? You have to either rapidly update the content or allow participants to provide the content through their interaction with one another — neither option is easy.

- ✔ **Push the technology.** Interactivity is also key to entertainment, which means going beyond HTML and static graphics. You need to figure out and use at least one advanced Web technology to make a fresh and interesting entertainment Web site.

- ✔ **Let the technology push you.** The technology can give you ideas that are in themselves pretty funny. Try using Java to create a Three Stooges-type animated routine, or use ActiveX to create a virtual reality environment that includes funhouse mirrors. (We describe both Java and ActiveX in Chapter 9.)

Is your page cybersmut?

For most Web page publishers, the best policy with respect to putting anything potentially offensive in your Web pages is to keep your site clean. The use of gratuitous sex and violence in your Web pages will simply put off many people and put the Web site itself in a bad light.

But what if the sex or violence is not gratuitous and is actually central to your point? Then send the authors your URL so that we can see it for ourselves, and be sure to make the first page a home page that warns readers that they may find your content offensive. That lets them gracefully opt out before they view whatever you show.

Even that enlightened approach may not be enough, however. Some Web server owners will drop your page if it violates their rules, and several countries have laws that may directly or indirectly specify what can and can't be on a Web page. Be sure to find out about the rules and laws that apply to you before you put anything questionable on your Web page.

The ...For Dummies Way to Web Publishing

Getting an initial Web page up on the Web is easy, but making a good, useful Web site is more work. For anything beyond an initial home page, we highly suggest the following decision-making process:

- Determine the purpose of your site.
- Decide the structure of your site.
- Decide the layout of your pages.
- Decide what links to use between pages in your site.
- Decide what links to external Web sites to include.
- Create the text for your pages.
- Convert the content to HTML.
- Create the graphical elements in your pages.
- Test your site.
- Put your content on a Web server.
- Publicize your site.
- Bask in the glory of being a Web publisher. (Then start again at the first step. . . .)

These detailed steps fall into three larger categories: planning your site, creating the content for your site, and publishing your site. Though most information about Web publishing focuses on the content-creation part in general, and HTML authoring in particular, all parts of the process are important. For a good, more advanced book that includes design information, pick up *Creating Cool HTML 4 Web Pages,* by Dave Taylor (IDG Books Worldwide, Inc.).

Plan your Web site

The only tools you need for this part of the Web publishing process are Web access, for doing research, and either a word processing and drawing program, or a pencil and paper — whichever is more comfortable — for sketching your plans and taking notes. A few extra hours up front can save you a great deal of time later and help you produce a better Web page. Yet the planning step is the most frequently overlooked part of the Web publishing process. To plan your Web site, follow these steps:

1. Determine the purpose of your site.

Decide which type of site you want to create: personal, topical, commercial, or comical. (We could also call the last two "business" and "entertainment," but those don't rhyme.)

We describe each type of site, and some specifics about how to design each type, earlier in this chapter. See those specifics, research existing sites, and research other media that serve the same purpose (magazines, brochures — even television). Ask what about your material, or about the Web, makes the Web a good way to get your material out. Think some more about your own needs and interests. Then write a few goals for your initial site and for later versions of it.

2. Decide on the structure of your site and the layout of your pages.

The structure of your site can help guide readers to the parts that interest them most. The layout of your site's Web pages can make them more useful, more interesting, or more entertaining, whichever is their purpose. Here are a few general rules:

- Decide how many pages to have and how they link to each other.

- Put the purpose of your site near the top of your home page.

- Indicate the purpose of additional pages near the top of each page.

- Use headers, bullets, icons, and other graphical or emphasis elements to highlight key points.

- Think about what graphics you need. Start the process of generating or obtaining them.

- Use summary elements, such as a table of contents and Frequently Asked Questions (FAQs).

- Put navigational elements — links from your home page to other pages in your site, and from other pages back to the home page — in a consistent spot at the top or bottom of each page.

3. Decide which links to include.

A Web page that has no links is generally pretty boring. You already decided in Step 2 which links to include between the pages in your site. Now think about what links to include from your pages out to other sites. What links make sense? What links are fun? Use Web search engines such as AltaVista (www.altavista.com) to search the Web and find suitable links (see Figure 2-6). Then check the links and cut the list down to the personally significant ones, not just a laundry list. (Unless you're making a list of laundries!) Create a place to save links that you run into while using the Web so that they're available for you to use in future versions of your pages.

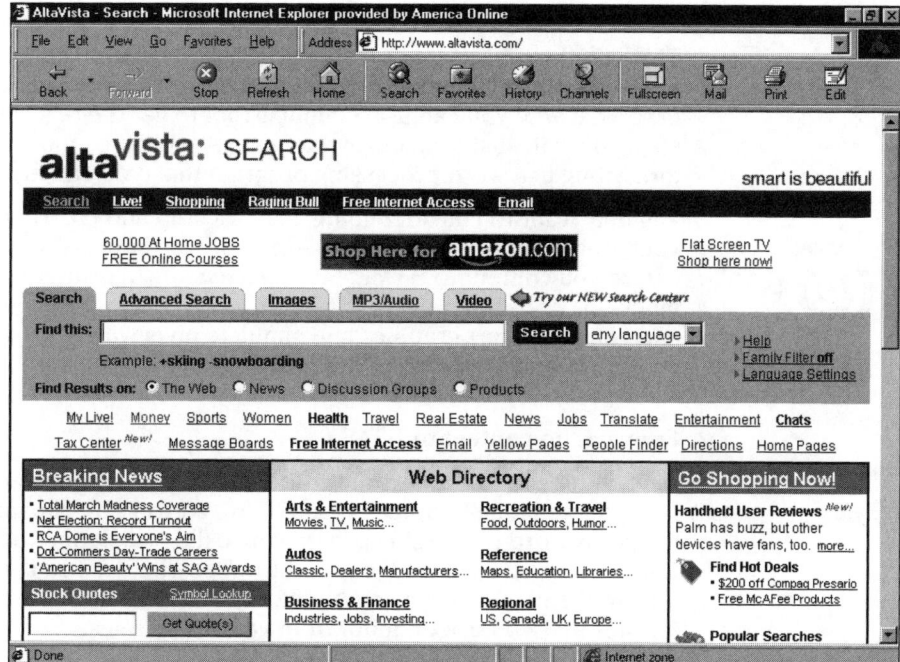

Figure 2-6:
The
AltaVista
scene.

Now think some more. Do the links that you're including fit the purpose of your page? How can you organize them? Should you group sets of key links together? Are some of the links repetitive or superfluous? Getting your links right makes your site more useful. And although no one likes to be left behind, which is what happens to you when people click an outbound link in one of your pages, a good set of links can, paradoxically, make users more likely to return to your site in the future.

Create the content

Creating content is the part of the Web publishing process where tools come in. You need tools to create HTML-tagged text (or a word processing program or text editor if you want to work in HTML directly) and graphics tools to create graphics and convert them to one of the common Web formats, GIF or JPEG. (Yes, you can use other file formats for Web graphics, but, as we say in Chapter 1, GIF and JPEG are the most widely supported.) For simple sites, one person can do all the work (but it will be a lot of work); for creating and maintaining larger sites, you need a team of people, often including consultants who have HTML expertise or other skills.

1. **Create the text for your pages.**

   The best thing to do here, if you're new to Web publishing, is to work in a word processing program without putting in HTML tags, at least at first. That way you can use a familiar tool to get the text right and to spell-check it. Just remember that you can achieve much more precise formatting in a word processing program than you can in a Web page.

   You may want to consider going an extra step and creating a "dummy" of your Web site — pun intended — in your word processing program before you commit to HTML. Making a *dummy* (a printer's term for a mock-up of a printed page) is a good way to plan what's on each page, and you can insert graphics and simulate links with underlines and colors. Compare this model to relevant Web sites you admire and see what changes you want to make.

2. **Convert the content to HTML.**

   Next, you need to convert the content to HTML. You can add the HTML tags yourself (see Chapter 7), use HTML conversion capabilities built into your word processing program, use file translation tools (see Chapter 12), or use a Web page editor (see Chapters 13 through 16). You may well end up using a combination of methods for new content and for files that you use or adapt from various sources.

   Read Chapter 7 to find out how HTML works. Even if you use a Web authoring tool to create your Web page and don't put in the HTML tags yourself, knowing what is and isn't possible in basic HTML saves a great deal of time and effort in the overall publishing process.

3. **Create the graphical elements in your pages.**

   Graphical elements include not only photos and computer-generated images but also mastheads, separator bars, and icons. This is also the time to create multimedia elements, such as sounds or video clips, if you really want to push the envelope. We cover all of these elements in Chapters 8 and 9.

Publish your Web site

Putting your site on the Web — either an intranet or the open World Wide Web — is the most exciting part of the Web publishing process. (But watch out! Your excitement may quickly turn to anxiety as you think of people actually looking at your carefully crafted baby.) For this part of the process, you don't need any tools, except possibly an FTP (File Transfer Protocol) program to move your files to the Web server. Usually, whoever is providing your Web hosting service supports this process.

First bring the elements of your site together, then test it on your local machine, and finally publish it! Here are the steps for publishing (or republishing) your site:

1. **Put it all together and test it.**

   Check that you have all the content and links in the places that you want them and then test each Web page and the entire site. On your own machine, you can use a Web browser not only to see what your pages look like but also to follow links from your site to other sites; then you can use the Back button on your browser to return. (The only thing missing is that the people who eventually surf your site can't get to it until it's actually published on a Web server.) We describe in detail this testing process and the other stages of publishing your Web site in Chapter 11.

2. **Put your content on a Web server.**

   This is when it gets real. After you get your pages on the server, test them again. Especially, test all the links to make sure that they really go somewhere; remember, nothing is more frustrating than clicking on a broken link.

3. **Publicize your site.**

   Get some users onto your site. Tell your friends, use Web resources, and, especially, get related Web sites to put in links to your site. Offer some kind of reward for feedback on your site — even if it's just taking that person's site off your "bad HTML examples" list! (For more detail on this part of the process, and the entire Web publishing process, see Chapter 11.)

4. **Bask in the glory of being a Web publisher.**

   Having a Web site up and running is something to be proud of. Sit and enjoy it for a while.

After you get your site on the Web, you'll experience a brief moment of elation, and then feel concern as you think of all the things you wanted to do with the site before you ran out of time. Then you'll click around your site and realize that something doesn't look quite as good as you wanted. You may compare your site with others and decide to add new features. Back to square one!

To HTML or not to HTML?

In the early days of the Web, it was really difficult to create a decent Web page without knowing at least some HTML. Now, it has become easy.

The free services we describe in Chapter 3 (GeoCities) and Chapter 5 (America Online) combine templates, graphical tools, and free Web server space to allow you to publish your first Web page without using HTML. These tools also automatically transfer your files for you, so you don't have to worry about the file transfer process. This makes getting your first Web page up really easy.

If you have an Internet Service Provider (ISP) who isn't AOL, but who does offer free Web publishing tools, we still suggest using GeoCities to get your initial Web page up; GeoCities has a strong set of tools for beginners. Then you can consider using your ISP's tools to take your site to the next step.

Once you've achieved initial success, use the later chapters in this book to create a more robust Web site and to use any number of different hosting options. That may include learning enough HTML (as described in Chapter 7) to allow you to fine-tune your own Web pages.

Part II

Build a Web Page in a Day

The 5th Wave   By Rich Tennant

"Just how accurately should my Web site reflect my place of business?"

In this part . . .

Use this part to create your first Web page in an hour or two, using free Web publishing services provided by GeoCities or free online Web publishing tools provided by America Online and CompuServe. Your out-of-pocket cost: free for the Web-based services, or included in the usual cost of your online service. Your reward: being able to tell your friends and colleagues your Web address tomorrow!

Chapter 3

Going Worldwide with GeoCities

● ●

In This Chapter

▶ Using GeoCities for a personal Web page

▶ Getting registered

▶ Setting up

▶ Putting the wizard to work

● ●

*G*etting your first page up on the Web seems like a tall order. So it may be hard to believe just how easy it is to get started. With the free Web-based publishing services we describe in this chapter and the next, you can have your first Web page up within a couple of hours — at no cost. You don't have to figure out everything about HTML, you don't have to deal with typical publishing complexities, and did we mention that you don't have to pay anything?

If you're a member of America Online (AOL) or CompuServe, you can use free Web publishing tools available from these services to get a Web page up quickly and easily, as we describe in Chapters 4, 5, and 6. These services have the advantage of built-in support for your Web page efforts from the same help resources — including your fellow online service members — that you're already familiar with. So if you're a member of America Online or CompuServe, consider starting your Web page creation effort with the next chapter.

If not, though, you have an alternative that's just as good: Yahoo!'s GeoCities site. GeoCities is the most popular site for free personal Web page publishing and has offered this service for more than five years. Since its inception, GeoCities has hosted the creation of more than 4,000,000 — yes, that's four *million* — personal Web page sites, with thousands of new sites currently added each day. And now that GeoCities has been acquired by Yahoo!, it has the resources to keep on growing for quite a while to come.

GeoCities' high level of popularity means that their service is extremely popular with visitors as well as publishers. It also means that their advertising-supported, self-publishing model is so successful that it's likely to be around for a long time to come. (Other services featured in earlier editions of this book have since disappeared, a testament to the rapid rate of change on the Web.)

Follow the instructions in this chapter to become a publisher on GeoCities. You can be a Web publisher in less time than most people take to start thinking hard about how to get their first home page published on the Web.

Start with a Personal Web Page

Putting up a personal Web page accomplishes a lot of things. For one, it's fun. Millions of people have gotten a real kick out of sharing information about themselves and their interests with their fellow Web users. Many personal Web pages that initially start out quite simple evolve into large and popular Web sites focused on topics of any imaginable sort. As the number of Web users increases, more and more of your colleagues, family, and friends can see your Web page, as can (of course) tens of millions of complete strangers.

Creating a personal Web page is also very valuable in helping you find out how to publish on the Web. Until you publish something on the Web, you may find the notion that you can actually do it hard to believe. After you put up your first Web page, you may find the notion that anything can stop you from doing it again hard to believe! The initial success of getting up your personal Web page will spill over into all your future Web efforts.

Now, you may feel that you should start out with a business Web site, a home page for a nonprofit organization, or something similarly serious. But the business or serious approach has a couple of problems:

- The "barriers to entry" — if we may use a marketing term — for a site that represents an organization are much higher because you're taking on a more complex task.

- For a more serious site, the quality of your work has much more impact because you're representing a larger cause than just your personal interests. So your fear of failure is greater. And you're undertaking this important task with no background and no experience.

- Finally, Web space for business sites almost always costs money. So you have a buying decision to make before you can even get started — yet another barrier.

So get on the Web first with a simple, personal Web page. Discover something new, have some fun, and prepare now for more ambitious endeavors later. And GeoCities is just the place to do it.

To see what other people have done with their personal Web sites, visit GeoCities right now:

```
www.geocities.com
```

Figure 3-1 shows the initial home page for GeoCities. Yahoo!, after buying GeoCities, put their name on the pages too, but didn't change the basic workings of the site. (Don't be alarmed if you see something slightly different for the home page; GeoCities, like any popular Web site, often updates its home page. Even if the GeoCities home page has changed, the instructions in this chapter are likely to still be valid.)

GeoCities initially organized the Web pages that users created into *neighborhoods,* with each neighborhood hosting home pages from people with a specific set of shared interests. However, Yahoo! has stopped supporting the neighborhoods idea; only people who created Web pages on GeoCities in the 1990s can still use them. As a new GeoCities user, you'll get a Web address based on the Yahoo! user ID that you get when you first visit GeoCities.

Figure 3-1: GeoCities is the home of more than four million personal Web pages.

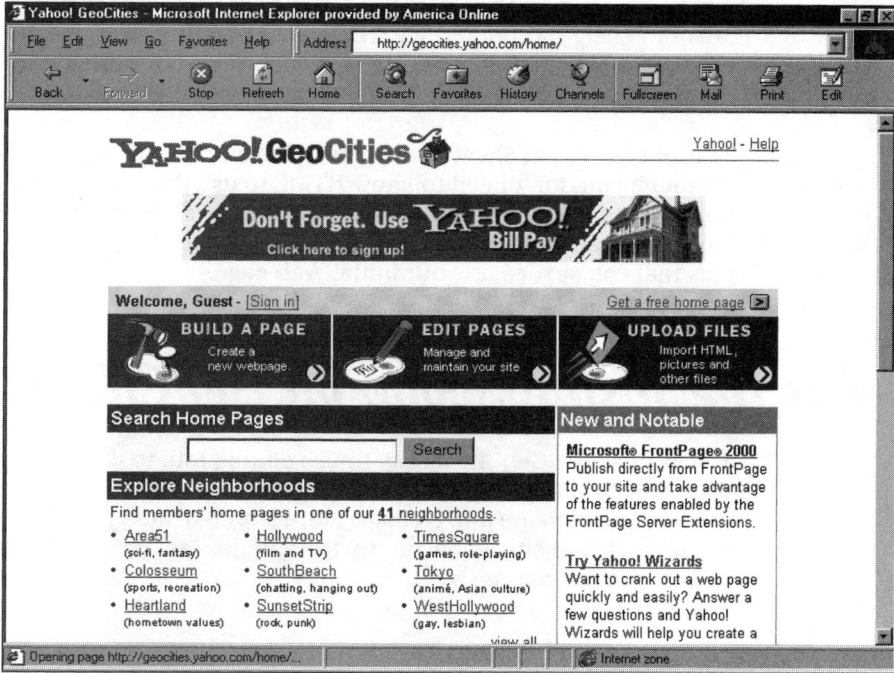

Web tools versus Web services

A Web publishing tool, such as a text editor, is a program that helps you prepare content for the Web. A Web publishing service is a support function that handles part of the process of Web publishing for you, such as hosting your Web page(s) on a server. The Web publishing services we describe in this chapter also include online tools for preparing your Web page(s), but the free Web page hosting they provide is most notable, so we refer to them as services rather than tools.

Your Web page's Web address will be in the following form:

```
www.geocities.com/youruserid
```

This is simpler than the Web addresses that GeoCities used to give people, which included the name of the neighborhood the user chose as well as a specific site number.

When you first visit GeoCities, tour the GeoCities neighborhoods and use the Search function on the GeoCities home page to find GeoCities Web pages that are not in neighborhoods. See what other people have done; look at some pages that are still initial efforts, and then see what others have done with their Web pages to spruce up the place after they first arrived!

Tear out the Cheat Sheet at the front of this book and tape it to the wall! Although you don't need to know HTML to use the services we describe in this chapter, knowing a little bit of HTML can help you make your initial page look better. See the Top Ten list in Chapter 7 and the Cheat Sheet for a list of tags that can spruce up your initial Web page.

Get the Inside Scoop on GeoCities

You can use the GeoCities easy-to-use editing tool to create a simple home page quickly and easily. You can then use HTML, FTP (see Chapter 1), and other tools to create and transfer more sophisticated pages to build almost any kind of Web site you want, up to 15MB in size. But you have to keep in mind these restrictions:

✔ **Not for your business.** You can't use this free Web page service for a business home page, although you can mention your business on your free personal home page. (Some people use their free personal Web pages to "mention" their businesses an awful lot.) That means you can't sell products or services, advertise, conduct raffles, or display advertising or sponsorship banners. You can, however, use Yahoo!-supported partnership programs that allow you to get paid for books, music, and other goods sold on your site. For details on what you can't do, check the Terms of Service at

```
docs.yahoo.com/info/terms/geoterms.html
```

If you do want a business Web site, and want a very easy-to-use way to get started within the Yahoo! framework, try Yahoo! Site at site.yahoo.com. To learn more about this and other business site options, see Chapter 10.

✔ **No monkey business.** Yahoo! imposes restrictions on what you can publish; obscenity, harmful or abusive content, libel, and invasion of privacy are prohibited, among other things. Check the Terms of Service for details.

✔ **No more than 15MB.** All your Web files together must occupy no more than 15MB of disk space, which is about 15,000 pages of text or about 100 large, quarter-screen graphics. This restriction is not a problem for single Web pages, because only one Web page is almost certainly well below the limit. If you expand your Web page into a multi-page site and the limit becomes a problem for you, you can get 10MB more of disk space and other goodies as part of the GeoPlus program for $4.95 a month. See

```
geocities.yahoo.com/geoplus
```

✔ **No guarantees.** Yahoo! doesn't guarantee that it will continue to provide free Web page service in the future. (The company has to include this disclaimer to protect itself from unanticipated events, but all indications are that it does indeed plan to continue this free service for quite a while.) If Yahoo! does stop offering GeoCities, or even if you just find another hosting site you like better, you can always set up shop there instead. For now, the point is to take advantage of a very valuable opportunity.

Unlike a business that charges for products or services, any nonprofit organization or anyone offering a free public service is likely to find GeoCities a great place to get started.

GeoCities or online service?

If you are a user of an online service such as America Online, you have the option of creating a free personal Web page on GeoCities, on your online service, or on both. We recommend that online service users put their first Web page on their online service. Why?

The first and foremost reason is support. Online services are great sources of help for all kinds of online concerns, not the least of which is getting your first Web page up and running. You can easily get a lot of help from your fellow members and from the support personnel of your online service.

Second is familiarity. You're already familiar with your online service. You're more able to take advantage of its free services than the services

in any other kind of setup, even one as friendly and open as GeoCities.

Third is community. Online services try to foster a sense of community, as does Yahoo! with GeoCities. If you're a person who values this feeling, you probably have already developed it within your online service; you may as well take advantage of the community that you're already paying for!

So if you're an AOL user, go to the next chapter and follow the instructions for creating and hosting a free Web page. If not, you don't need to join an online service just to get free Web hosting service; GeoCities is fast, easy, and fun.

Plan Before You Begin

Putting up your home page on GeoCities takes only an hour or two — not bad for getting a free Web page set up, hosted, and published! Even so, doing a few things before you begin makes the process easier, more pleasant, and more productive:

- ✓ **Visit GeoCities Web pages.** GeoCities does a good job of helping you get your initial Web page up, but don't you want to see what others have done before you get started? Use the Search function to find Web pages related to your interests. To see what older sites look like, started before Yahoo! revamped the site, look in Neighborhoods that relate to your interests to see what people have done within them.

- ✓ **Find out more about GeoCities in general by clicking and navigating around GeoCities-related Web pages in the Yahoo! Web site.** You can discover a lot about GeoCities by clicking around and reading press releases, the Terms of Service, and so on. One thing you may not discover is how Yahoo! can afford to give away free Web space through GeoCities. The answer is that free Web pages are a powerful way for sites like Yahoo! to attract and retain users for their other services. Also, Yahoo! places advertising on Web pages built in GeoCities; this means that Yahoo! makes a few cents every time someone (including you) looks at your home page.

✓ **Look for the URLs of your favorite Web sites.** Many GeoCities templates let you list links to several of your favorite Web sites — but to link to them, you need the URLs. Surf around the Web and find the URLs of six sites that reflect your interests. (The more obscure your favorites are, the better!)

✓ **Use a word processing program or a few pieces of notebook paper to plan your initial Web page.** (Use the paper for drawing only — neither origami nor paper airplanes translate well to the Web.) Just rough out what text you want to put in and what URLs to include. Then you can be ready to focus on the mechanics of getting the Web page right.

✓ **Scan a picture.** Many personal Web pages look much better with a picture — of you, or of something relating to the topic you're interested in. Scan in a picture of yourself and use an image editing program such as Photoshop to save it in a Web-ready format such as GIF or JPEG. (For more on graphics for the Web, see Chapter 8.) If you lack appropriate software, go to a copy shop that rents scanners and time on personal computers with appropriate software, such as Kinko's. Or ask your photo developer to put your pictures on disk; several nationwide chains do this, including K-Mart and Walgreen.

Get Registered

The steps you need to follow to sign up for a GeoCities Web page may change after we complete this book. If so, go to geocities.yahoo.com/ budsmithidg for updated instructions.

If you do not live in one of the 50 states, click on the link Non-US Sign up form. You will be given a slightly different page than the one for U.S. residents. We wrote the following instructions so as to apply to either form.

The first step in setting up your GeoCities Web page is to apply for a Yahoo! user ID number. This user ID will enable you to use a variety of services on Yahoo! and, if you're not careful, to receive e-mail solicitations you don't really want. Follow these steps to set up your Yahoo! user ID and start using GeoCities:

1. **Open your Web browser.**

   The GeoCities Web site works with any browser.

2. **Go to www.geocities.com.**

   The screen shown in Figure 3-1, or something very much like it, appears.

3. **If you are currently signed in as a member of Yahoo!, skip the rest of the steps in this section.**

If you are a member of Yahoo! but are not currently signed in, sign in by entering your Yahoo! ID and Password under the header, **Member Sign In**, and then clicking **Sign In**. Then skip the rest of the steps in this section.

If you are not yet a member of Yahoo!, click on the Sign In link in the upper-left corner of the browser window.

The Welcome to Yahoo! GeoCities screen appears.

4. Click on the Sign Me Up! link.

The Sign up Now screen appears, as shown in Figure 3-2.

5. Enter your desired Yahoo! ID and password.

It's pretty unlikely that any Yahoo! ID that you would find desirable, like your first name and last name ("budsmith" for one of the authors), or your favorite sports team ("sfgiants," for instance), is available — one of Yahoo!'s existing tens of millions of users probably already got it. To save yourself a bunch of retries, pick a user name that makes sense, but is likely to be unique. Try to make it memorable, too — your home page's URL will be in the form `www.geocities.com/`, followed by your Yahoo! ID.

Figure 3-2:
Sign me
up for
GeoCities.

For your password, use three or more characters.

6. **Enter information in case you forget your password.**

Use the pull-down menu to select a question that Yahoo! will prompt you with if you forget your password. Enter your answer, your birthday (with a four-digit year, such as 1978), and your current e-mail address. (Enter your real birthday — "Always tell the truth, so you don't have to try to remember what you told people.")

"He tried, but he couldn't do it" — despite our best efforts, we were unable to get GeoCities to accept a Yahoo! e-mail address as the e-mail address of record for a GeoCities Web page. You will have to use a different e-mail account, not a Yahoo.com account. You can get a new, free e-mail account at `www.hotmail.com` (the most popular source for free e-mail), or any of several other sites on the Web.

7. **Enter your personal account information.**

For the United States, enter your zip code; outside the United States, enter your country and your primary language (about a dozen languages are supported at this writing). Then enter your gender, occupation, and industry. (These fields are the same for U.S. and non-U.S. residents.)

Be sure to uncheck the checkbox, Contact me from time to time about specials and new products, unless you want to receive advertising e-mail from Yahoo! and its partners. Many Web sites have agreed to present boxes such as this one with the option unchecked, so that only users who click on the box to put a check in it will receive such e-mail messages. At this writing, though, Yahoo! is still following the more invasive policy of presenting the box to you checked and forcing you to make the effort to uncheck it. See the sidebar, "Yahoo! for privacy?," for more.

8. **If you want to, indicate areas of interest to you.**

You have the option of clicking on areas of interest to you by putting a check in each relevant checkbox. This helps Yahoo! and its partners target e-mail they send you, ads they put on Web pages that you view, and otherwise personalize their marketing efforts to you.

9. **If you want to read the GeoCities' Terms of Service, right-click on the link to open them in a separate window. Otherwise, or after you're done, click the Submit this Form button.**

If you click on this link with a regular mouse click, the GeoCities' Terms of Service replace your current browser window contents — and when you click the Back button in the browser window to return to the signup screen, everything you entered so far will be gone! If you make this mistake — which is all too easy to do — repeat Steps 5 through 7.

Once you click Submit this Form, you'll be taken to a new Web page, titled About Your Home Page. Read all about it in the next section.

If you look closely at the top of your Web browser window when you first log into GeoCities, you see that the Web address www.geocities.com is automatically remapped to geocities.yahoo.com/home. Web sites often give simpler Web addresses to the public, but remap them to other internal Web addresses for their own convenience. You can continue to use the www.geocities.com address as a starting point for your own ease of use.

Tell Yahoo! About Your Home Page

Once you're signed in, GeoCities will ask you for some details about your page (see Figure 3-3). Here's where that planning we suggested that you do earlier in this chapter kicks in! Quickly tell GeoCities about your Web page:

1. **Describe your Web page.**

   Write a short description of your Web page. Be literate, accurate, and polite — GeoCities may use this description in any number of ways, including using it to help guide people who are searching for your Web page. Be sure to use relevant buzzwords like "rich," "creamy," and "strawberry" for a Web page about ice cream, or "Saturn," "Proteon," and "NASA" for a Web page about space exploration. You have 90 characters of space to work with.

2. **Choose a topic for your Web page.**

   Carefully choose a topic for your Web page. Yahoo! will display advertising relating to this topic on your page, so again, choose carefully. (The right kind of advertising can actually "ad" value to your page — pun intended.)

3. **Choose whether you want to receive e-mail about selling merchandise on your Web page through the Pages That Pay program.**

   Unless your site is about the evils of capitalism, we suggest you say yes to this one; it can't hurt to learn about ways to make money from your site.

4. **Click the Submit button.**

   A Congratulations Web page appears, as shown in Figure 3-4.

5. **Write down your Yahoo! ID and password and your new home page's Web address.**

   Yahoo! will send you an e-mail explaining steps to take to begin creating your Web page. In the next section, we'll start giving you our own take on the process.

6. **Click on the link, Build Your Page Now!.**

   The front page of the Yahoo! GeoCities Web site will appear, but this time with your user name in the upper-left corner and your Web page's URL in the upper right. Follow the steps in the next section to begin building your Web page.

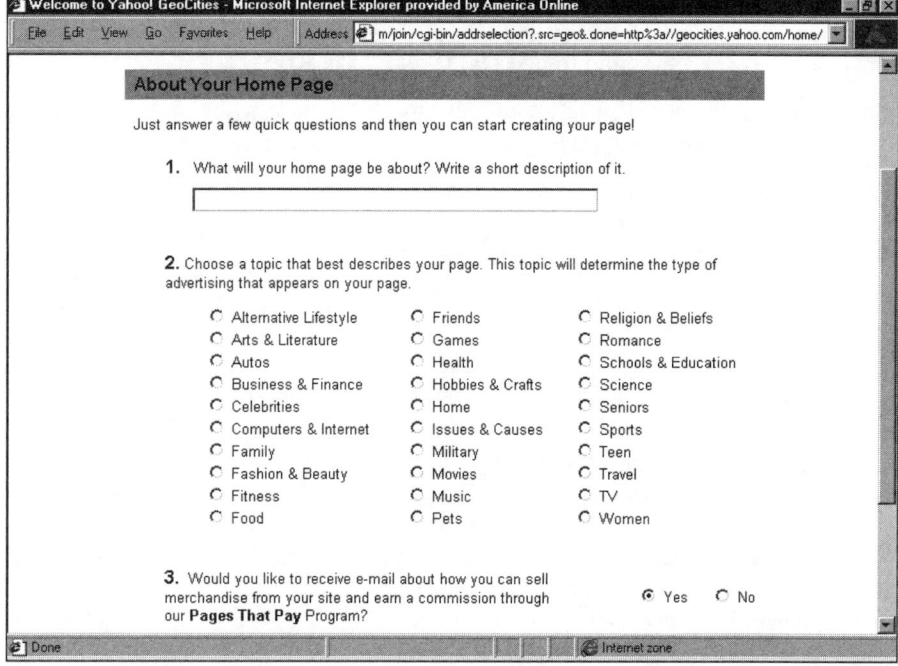

Figure 3-3:
Just tell
GeoCities
what you
see in the
inkblot.

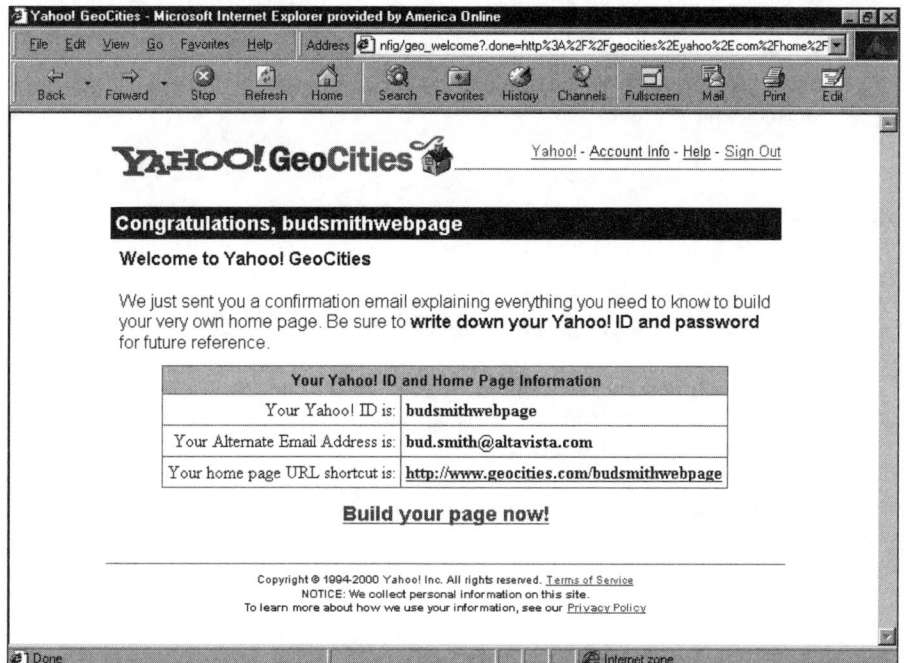

Figure 3-4:
When you
see this,
you're in.

Yahoo! for privacy?

Yahoo! follows certain policies relating to your privacy. Some of the highlights:

- **No opt-in guarantee.** Some Web sites now promise not to put you on e-mail lists unless you opt in — take some affirmative action, such as checking a checkbox, to put yourself in spam's way. Yahoo! doesn't do this, at this writing. So it's easy, when signing up for a Yahoo! service, to accidentally put yourself on an e-mail list that will then be used to send you advertising.

- **TRUSTe-certified.** Yahoo! is TRUSTe-certified. This means that Yahoo! has submitted a privacy statement to TRUSTe, an industry privacy organization. TRUSTe is not a strong organization at this point, but at least Yahoo!, through TRUSTe, has committed itself to a policy statement in writing.

- **Use of information.** Yahoo! uses the information you give it, and the information it gathers from the choices you make in using Yahoo!, to customize your Web-surfing experience to your interests and to send you customized e-mail.

- **Sharing with partners.** Yahoo! doesn't actually transfer data about you to partners without your permission. However, partners' agreements with Yahoo! may include access to you through Yahoo!.

- **Pages That Pay.** You can put advertising and buying opportunities for specific, Yahoo!-approved merchants on your GeoCities home page through the Pages That Pay program. If you do, your information will be shared with specific partners.

- **Third-party data.** Yahoo! does reserve the right to tie information it gathers about you to third-party data. The online advertising agency Doubleclick was much-criticized for its plans to do this, and marketers are still testing the limits of user tolerance for this kind of data integration.

- **Changing your information.** To change your account information, log into Yahoo! with your user ID and password, then go to `edit.my.yahoo.com/config/set_p rofile`. There, you can change your account preferences to stop receiving e-mail offers or update your personal information and preferences.

We're Off to See the Wizard

GeoCities has recently introduced a new feature, Yahoo! Wizards, for creating an initial Web page quickly and easily. Wizards are a good way to get your Web page off the ground.

Unlike many other Web page tools, you cannot enter HTML tags in the text within Yahoo! Wizards.

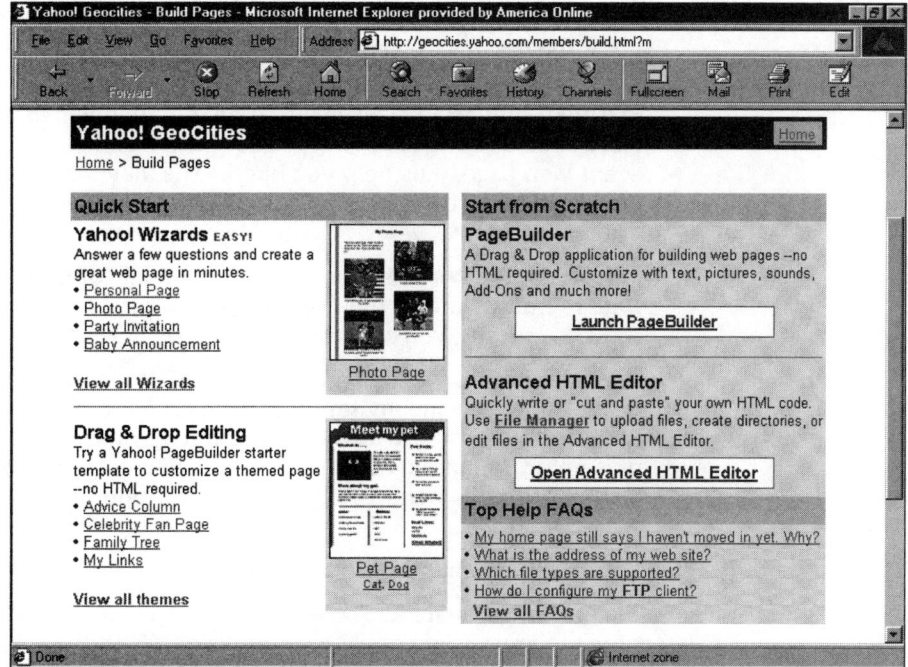

Figure 3-5:
We're off to
see the
(Page)
Wizards.

Use the Yahoo! Wizard to quickly create your initial Web page:

1. **From the front page of GeoCities, at** www.geocities.com, **make sure you're signed in (see above), then click Yahoo! PageWizards.**

   If you have not done so already, you'll have to become a registered Yahoo! user to proceed. To do so, see the instructions at the beginning of this chapter.

   If you're a registered user, the Yahoo! PageWizards page, part of which is shown in Figure 3-5, appears.

2. **Click the Personal Page link.**

   Getting the right wizard can save you a lot of time, so it's worth looking at as much information as possible before choosing. For the purposes of this chapter, we'll describe how to use the Personal Page Wizard; if you want to try a different wizard, roughly the same steps will apply, but you'll need to work around the differences.

   The choices, at this writing, are

   • **Photo Page.** If you have a bunch of digital photographs handy — or can get your local photo processor to convert your next roll to digital format — this is a fun choice to start out with.

- **Baby Announcement.** Great if you just had a little one; not much use otherwise. If you do this, make sure to include a picture! See Chapter 8 for details.

- **Birthday Invitation.** This is fun to do, but online invitation services such as eVite (www.evite.com) will also help you put up an event Web page, plus help you handle the inevitable e-mail messaging back and forth. Either this wizard or the eVite-type approach is a good option.

- **Personal Page Wizard.** This is the best choice for most people who want to quickly create their own page. You have four choices of color — and yes, you can replace the little stick figure with a picture.

- **Party Invitation.** As with a birthday invitation, this kind of page is fun to do, but online invitation services such as eVite (www.evite.com) will also help you put up an event Web page, plus help you handle the inevitable e-mail messaging back and forth. Either this wizard or the eVite-type approach is a good option.

3. **Click the link, Launch Yahoo! PageWizard.**

   The Build Your Personal Page screen, shown in Figure 3-6, will appear. It shows the ten areas that you'll be customizing: Your name, your image (or you can keep the stick figure!), your e-mail address, a brief personal description, a list of hobbies and interests, a list of favorite links (up to four), a description of family and family links, and a description of friends and friends' links.

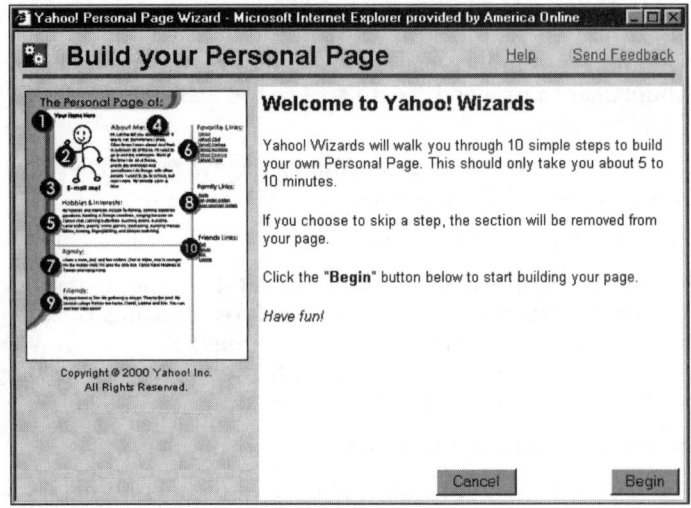

Figure 3-6: Ten items, ten minutes, one home page.

4. **Click on the Begin button.**

   A screen that allows you to choose a look for your page will appear: green, blue, yellow, or pink. Choose one.

5. **Click Next.**

   Now follow the onscreen prompts to enter contents for the ten areas of your new Web page:

   - **Name.** Enter your name as you want it to appear at the top of your Web page.

At any point in the wizard process, you can preview your page as you build it. Just click the Preview button where it's available. You can close the preview when you're done with it; don't close the underlying Personal Page Wizard browser window!

   - **Picture.** GeoCities allows you to pick any image from your hard disk in any of the following Windows formats: .jpg (JPEG), .gif (GIF), .tif (TIFF), .bmp (Windows BitMaP), or .png (Portable Network Graphics). See Chapter 8 for more on these formats and on obtaining images.

Don't publish an image you don't have rights to on your Web page. No sense in inviting a call from someone's lawyer.

   - **E-mail address.** Enter an e-mail address here for people to use to send you e-mail.

If you don't want to publish your work e-mail address, or heavily used personal e-mail address, on the Web — where it might be copied into spammers' lists — consider creating a Yahoo! e-mail account for the purpose of publication. Go to mail.yahoo.com to sign up; if you do create a new address, remember to check it.

   - **Description.** Enter a brief description of yourself. Leave out hobbies and interests; they're in the next section. You may want to include where you were born and live, what kind of work you do, and similar information. Don't give too much information, though; a scam artist can do wonders with your name, address, and mother's maiden name.

   - **Hobbies and interests.** Keep it brief, for now, but make it interesting; your hobbies and interests may be as individual to you as your fingerprint.

   - **Favorite links.** Include up to three favorite Web links, with brief descriptions. (Don't worry, you can add to the number of links later, using other tools.)

- **Family description.** Say something about your family — the one you came from, not just your kids. Emphasize anyone who has a personal Web page — or anyone who will be especially thrilled to see their name on the Web, such as kids. Again, be careful about giving too much detail that scam artists could use.

- **Family links.** You can link to family members' Web pages. If you don't know of any, just leave all the entries blank.

- **Friends description.** People love to read about themselves, so go into detail here. At least mention everyone who you intend to tell about the Web page. Also, mention any schools you went to.

- **Friends' links.** Again, link to friends' pages. (The companies your friends work for are an okay choice but not as interesting as their personal pages, unless your friends own their own companies.)

When you have entered all this information, the Wizard will ask if you want to make the page you've just created your home page, as shown in Figure 3-7.

6. **Choose whether to make your new Web page the home page of your site. Click Next.**

Click Yes; you can always move this page around within your site if you add more pages later. The Congratulations Web page will appear, as shown in Figure 3-8.

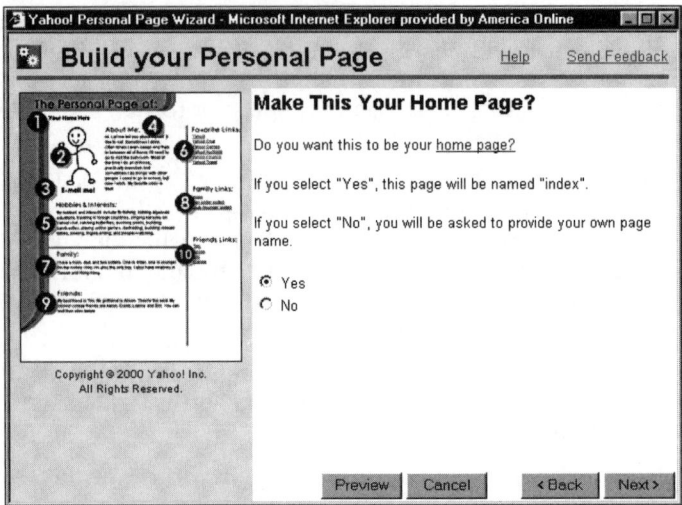

Figure 3-7:
Make your
new page
your home.

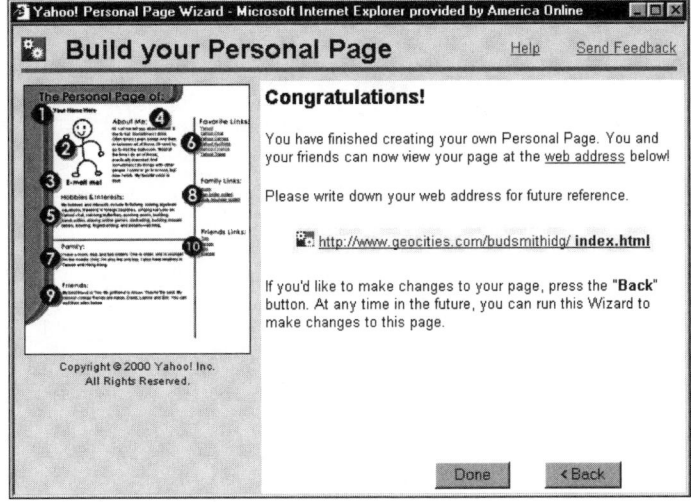

Figure 3-8:
Congratula-
tions are
in order!

If you do choose Yes, your Web page will be named index.htm, the name commonly used for the home page of a Web site. (By naming your page index.htm, your users don't have to type the page's specific name when they visit it.)

If you have not done so already, you'll have to become a registered Yahoo! user to proceed. To do so, see the instructions at the beginning of this chapter.

7. **Write down or save your Web address, and then click Done.**

Your new Web URL will appear in a window.

You will probably want to improve your Web page quite a bit from here, but you're off to a great start. See Chapter 10 for information on how to expand your initial Web page. But for now, send your new Web address to your friends, and take a well-deserved break!

Chapter 4

Using Online Services for Web Publishing

*A*lthough the easy-to-use, open, ungovernable World Wide Web may seem as though it is going to wipe out traditional, closed, monitored online services such as America Online, CompuServe, and The Microsoft Network (MSN), circumstances are not really working out that way. The online services are adapting quickly. They have become gateways to the Web, and in some cases offer easy-to-use Web publishing services that include hosting your Web page for free.

If you already use AOL or CompuServe, that service is probably the best place for you to start experimenting with Web publishing. You already know the interface, you can find online forums and discussion boards for Web publishing, and you can take advantage of the easy-to-use Web publishing features that these major services have scrambled to provide.

If you aren't an America Online or a CompuServe user, the quickest and cheapest way to get your first page up on the Web is to use GeoCities, the Web-based service we describe in Chapter 3. When you're ready to improve your Web site, your next step may be to subscribe to an online service. America Online, in particular, has strong features for intermediate Web publishing, including support for both Windows and Macintosh, 2MB or more of free server space, and (at the time of this writing) no restrictions on using free Web pages for business.

Note: Just like the Web, online services are always evolving. The information in this chapter is accurate at the time of this writing, but you need to check online for the latest info.

The Best Online Service

You certainly have freedom of choice when it comes to online services. And your choice truly is free — most online services offer free signup and a free trial period. You can try two or three services before making a long-term choice. Just remember to re-sign from any service that you stop using, or the $20 or so a month charge to your credit card will go on forever!

You also have the option of using a traditional Internet Service Provider (ISP) like MindSpring, for which you will find setup software on the *Creating Web Pages For Dummies* CD-ROM (see Appendix E). MindSpring has more and more built-in content and services, like America Online or CompuServe, but is really focused on open Internet and Web content and tools. Other ISPs vary in the amount of built-in content and services they offer.

In many areas you also have the ability to use a free ISP service like AltaVista FreeAccess. A free ISP service will give you a fast, free connection to the Internet, and few additional frills. But who needs them? If you like using the Internet and the Web for your information, chat, and so on, and a free ISP service is available in your area, you should seriously consider it.

With any ISP, you can use GeoCities (described in Chapter 3) or other free Web page publishing services to create your first Web page. With AOL or CompuServe, you also get the option of using built-in Web publishing services, as described in this chapter.

America Online is the biggest and best traditional online service. Because America Online is far bigger than any other online service — over 20 million users, about five times the number of the next competitor — it has more people to chat with online, more areas with existing content, and more people to support you. America Online service is also included with many Gateway computers; Gateway had to give AOL part of the company to get this deal.

America Online owns CompuServe; CompuServe has been positioned as the "value" service — a little less content, a little less service, for a little less money. You can get basic service using CompuServe 2000, the latest version of CompuServe, for $9.95 a month. Or you can buy a bundle that includes CompuServe 2000 service for so many dollars per month with a big discount on the computer — even a free computer. But if you want the most-used online service, America Online, it will cost you extra.

Many professional, trade, and interest groups have a home on one of the online services. Microsoft software support finds a natural home on MSN; AutoCAD has long provided support for its users on CompuServe; and America Online has a wide variety of consumer-oriented services, one example of which is the very popular NetNoir service spotlighting African-American culture. All three services are trying to provide the best features for children. If you have a specific professional or personal interest to pursue online, ask around to see whether one of the online services has a clear lead in content for your interest.

As for more general concerns, all three interfaces have a modern, relatively attractive GUI *(graphical user interface);* CompuServe 2000, the latest version, incorporates many features of America Online. The experience of using America Online also is increasingly marred by pop-up ads that you have to click to get rid of; these ad deals are worth tens of millions of dollars to America Online, Inc., but they are just as annoying as TV ads. (You can get rid of them if you take the time to change a couple of settings.) Figure 4-1 shows the clean and attractive interface of America Online, but watch out for those pop-up ads. Figure 4-2 shows the improved interface of CompuServe 2000; Figure 4-3 shows the revamped interface of MSN, which is simply a Web page available to any Internet user.

The examples show the versions for Windows. The Macintosh offerings on the Big Three tend to lag behind the versions for Windows, and MSN Internet Access doesn't work with the Macintosh or even with Windows 3.1. Many Macintosh owners choose America Online, which got an early start with Macintosh users (America Online's software is based on work Apple did for its own defunct online service). However, Apple recently announced a deal with Mindspring with special features for Macintosh users.

So what's the best online service for budding Web publishers (no pun intended)? If you already use one, you should probably stick with it when pursuing your Web publishing efforts. Figuring out a new service is a big hassle, and CompuServe and AOL both have decent Web publishing support. You always have the option of using GeoCities or a competing Web-based publishing site (see Chapter 3).

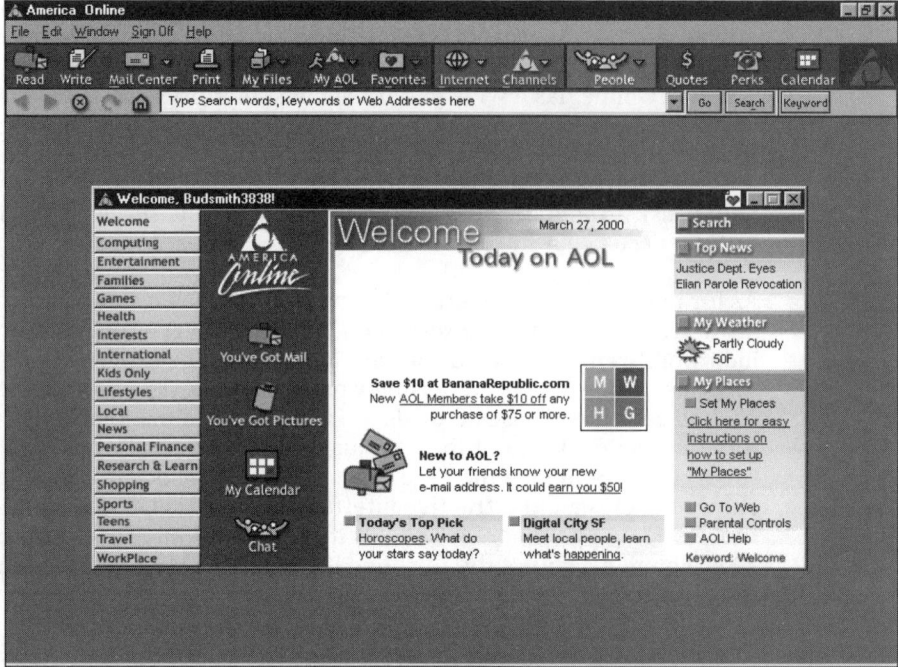

Figure 4-1:
America
Online is
easy for
everyone
to use.

Figure 4-2:
CompuServe
gets more
GUI with
time.

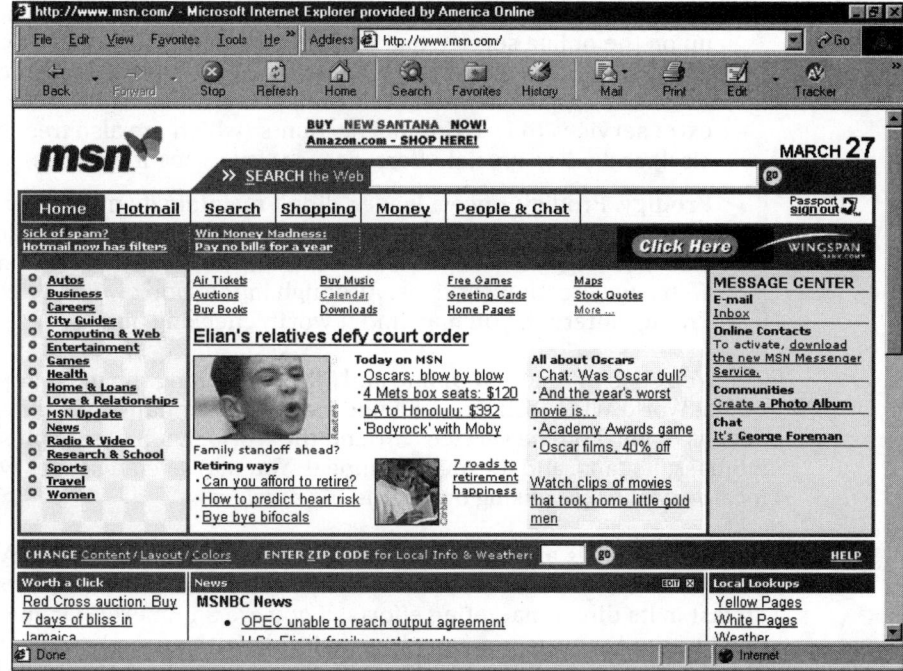

Figure 4-3:
MSN
Internet
Access —
part online
service,
part ISP.

But if you have not yet chosen an online service, or have been considering switching, here are the high points — and low points, where applicable — of each service:

✔ **America Online.** So far, the market consistently votes most strongly for America Online, making it the largest and fastest growing of the services now with over 20 million users. It has recently launched Version 5.0, Internet access, e-mail, and Web publishing. America Online also has the most Macintosh users and Mac-related content of the major services. America Online has in the past suffered from growth-related problems, such as users complaining about difficulty signing on, performance problems, and even billing problems. AOL works hard to address these concerns, but joining the leader may cause you occasional performance anxiety. You can find current information about the services and download client software from www.aol.com.

✔ **CompuServe.** For business, CompuServe may still be a good choice. It has a vast array of business-oriented services and millions of business-oriented users, who help each other with both general and industry-specific questions, as well as robust offerings in other areas. However, more and more such support is moving to the open Web. With CompuServe being repositioned as a value service, price may be the main attraction for CompuServe. You can find current information about the services and download client software from www.compuserve.com.

✔ **The Microsoft Network/MSN Internet Access.** Microsoft basically gave up on the online service market and relaunched The Microsoft Network as MSN Internet Access. MSN Internet Access uses the Internet Explorer browser and the msn.com Web site as its entire user interface and limits extra services to free Hotmail accounts (which are also free to anyone else!) and a few special offers. See `www.msn.com` for details.

✔ **Prodigy.** Prodigy, once a leader, didn't maintain its momentum and growth while going through a change of ownership and a change of focus. Prodigy relaunched itself as Prodigy Internet and has introduced Web page creation services. Although in this book we don't cover Prodigy Internet, you may find it worth checking out.

The Web sites of America Online and MSN are among the most popular sites on the World Wide Web. You can find many smaller national services and dozens of local online services around the world. Each has its pluses and minuses, its fans, and its specific appeal. You may even discover worthwhile local services by cruising one of the big services.

America Online is an aggressive marketing machine. So now that America Online owns CompuServe, don't be surprised if CompuServe starts to catch up fast in its direct marketing efforts. If you are an America Online user and don't want to receive pop-up ads, e-mail solicitations, and even solicitors' phone calls at your home or office, go to keyword Marketing Preferences and change the appropriate options.

Some services offer language-specific support. If you want to work in a language other than English, ask users who have experience using your preferred language about available services.

Checking newsgroups for the real deal

For user feedback on online services, you may want to check Usenet newsgroups, which you may have access to at school or at work. Newsgroups are discussion groups, hosted on the Internet, that allow people to discuss shared interests. Web browsers often include the capability to read Usenet newsgroups, and the online services offer Usenet access along with Web access. Try the following newsgroups:

✔ `alt.online-service.america-online`

✔ `alt.online-service.compuserve`

✔ `alt.online-service.microsoft`

The Best Web Access

The major online services all offer Web access, but what's offered varies dramatically. In general, if all you want is Web access, you may be better off with an Internet service provider (ISP), a company that provides direct access to the Internet and that may well be cheaper, have better browser support, or offer more reliable access than the major online services. However, Web access through the major online services offers some shared good points:

- ✔ **For occasional use, online services are cheap.** If you use the Web only a few hours a month, online services offer base rates lower than almost any ISP — as little as $5 a month or less for three hours of use. The typical rate for online services and ISPs is $20 a month or more for unlimited use, though more and more cheaper prices exist.

- ✔ **Access is easy and reliable.** You can get to the Web by using the same phone numbers and access techniques that you use for the online service. If you have trouble getting a connection, you also can call an 800 number for help. If you travel a great deal or need backup Web access in addition to that offered by an ISP, easy, reliable access alone can make the online service worthwhile.

- ✔ **You can find plenty of online support.** Given the difficulties you may encounter in figuring out how to use the Web and publish on it, who wouldn't want a few million friends online to help out? All the online services offer support for Web use and Web publishing. Online forums can tell you what to do, point you to good sites, and more. Online technical support helps you get beyond Web problems and problems with the online service itself.

- ✔ **Online services offer Web server mirroring.** Online services can *mirror* popular Web sites; that is, online services can keep a copy of the site on their own servers and offer simultaneous support of more users and faster access than can be provided over the open Web.

However, the online services also share some Web access problems:

- ✔ **Lack of choice.** Online services can lock you into a specific browser, usually Microsoft Internet Explorer. If you want to use Netscape Navigator, you may be able to, but only by doing extra setup work — and then you have a harder time getting questions about how to use your browser answered by your fellow online service users, who will tend to be Internet Explorer users.

- ✔ **Slow access.** As we note previously, access to some popular pages can be faster through an online service than through the open Web. But although some pages are cached on the online service's computers for faster access, those that aren't have extra overhead; the online service has to go get them for you from the Internet and then provide them to you, adding an extra step to the process of retrieving the pages.

✔ **Like using training wheels.** Remember how free you felt when your parents finally took the training wheels off of your first bike? Having the interface of your online service take screen space away from your Web browser, having access to online newsgroups restricted by the online service, and switching back and forth between the "look and feel" of your online service and your accustomed browser may irritate you when compared to feeling the open air of the unregulated Internet.

Along with their common pluses and minuses for Web access, online services also have their own specific pluses and minuses:

✔ **America Online.** For most users, America Online has the best combination of online service features and Internet features. (It has been named the Editor's Choice by *PC Magazine*.) Figure 4-4 shows America Online 5.0 with Internet Explorer 5.0, America Online's built-in Web browser, running. (You have to upgrade to Version 5.0 to use the newest version of America Online's Web publishing features.) But when you run your Web browser within America Online, you lose some screen space to AOL's menu bar and icons.

✔ **CompuServe.** CompuServe now has direct Web access from within CompuServe, and the CompuServe service itself is made up of Web pages. Like America Online, CompuServe has also won the *PC Magazine* Editor's Choice award. CompuServe was the first online service to have a Back button — which works like the Back button in your browser — within the CompuServe service itself.

✔ **The Microsoft Network.** MSN Internet Access is only available on 32-bit Windows (that's Windows 95, Windows 98, Windows NT, or Windows 2000) and forces you to use Microsoft's Internet Explorer browser. The Microsoft Network isn't a full "online service" in the traditional sense, but MSN Internet Access may be a good choice as an ISP.

Many Web users start with an online service and then move to an Internet service provider after they get going. We recommend that you use America Online or CompuServe to get started, or for occasional use, and then consider moving up to an ISP, which can be cheaper as you increase your time on the Internet.

Figure 4-4:
America
Online —
best for
Web?

The Best Web Publishing Support

Online services are a good place to start your initial Web publishing efforts: low prices, good tools, lots of support — kind of like running downhill with a tailwind. Now that America Online, CompuServe, and The Microsoft Network are increasingly integrated with the Web, Web publishing is the cutting edge of Web-related functionality for the services to offer. America Online and CompuServe offer the following:

- ✔ **No extra charge for Web page authoring.** America Online and CompuServe both offer free support for Web page authoring; you pay only the normal access charges for creating and viewing your page and other Web pages.

- ✔ **Easy Web page authoring tools.** America Online and CompuServe offer easy-to-use, fill-in-the-blank tools that help you quickly create an initial Web page. AOL has an easy-to-use, Web-based service; CompuServe has a somewhat more powerful, but more complex, stand-alone HTML editor.

✔ **Free Web server space.** One of the biggest problems in creating an initial Web page is getting space on a Web server. America Online and CompuServe both offer free Web server space for personal home pages; America Online offers free space for business pages as well.

✔ **No file transfer hassle.** Getting your files onto a Web server is often a pain; the online services' easy-to-use Web page authoring tools can make getting your information online easy.

✔ **Upgrading to HTML tools.** The online services enable you to use separate HTML tools, such as the ones we describe in Part V, to create your own custom Web page and then to transfer your files to their server for free hosting.

The online services are rapidly developing their Web support in general and their Web publishing support in particular, so check updates on Web services before making a final decision about which online service to use.

Each online service has different specific features and restrictions on your Web pages. At this writing, the policies and offerings of the top online services are as follows:

✔ **America Online.** Up to 2MB of free Web server space per screen name — and you can have up to seven screen names per account. More good news: AOL has a very easy-to-use tool called 1-2-3 Publish, and a more capable tool called Easy Designer, both integrated into the service. Also, America Online is the only major online service that enables you to use your free server space to put up business Web pages.

✔ **CompuServe.** CompuServe 4.0 offers a powerful, flexible tool called Home Page Wizard for creating Web pages and a separate Publishing Wizard for getting pages onto the Web. You get up to 5MB of free server space for personal Web pages. Although powerful, the Home Page Wizard/Publishing Wizard combination is somewhat complex. CompuServe 2000, the newer version of CompuServe, gives you free access to Trellix Web, a Web publishing tool. Whichever version of CompuServe and CompuServe Web publishing tools you use, you can use the free service to mention or describe a business but not to promote it; you can't do an all-business Web page. For business pages, you have to pay additional charges.

✔ **MSN.** MSN doesn't really do anything special for you when it comes to Web publishing — and if you look around the Web, you'll find that many Web pages on free, Web-based services such as GeoCities (see Chapter 3) are created by MSN members. Basically, as an MSN user, you're on your own.

Using an Internet service provider

Internet service providers offer complete Internet and Web access, usually for a moderate price for a large number of hours. Although some ISPs provide only local service, do little to get users set up, and offer poor connections, an increasing number of "best of breed" ISPs offer nationwide or even international service, easy setup, and robust connections, including 56K, DSL, or ISDN access for faster performance. (*56K* is a newly standardized modem technology that offers faster access; *DSL,* or *Digital Subscriber Line,* is an improved kind of service over existing phone lines; *Integrated Services Digital Network,* or *ISDN,* is a different kind of improved phone service.) Although covering the entire range of ISPs is beyond the scope of this book, the following are a few of the top ones in terms of breadth of service and ease of use:

✔ **MindSpring.** Recent winner of the *PC World* Best Internet Service Provider award, MindSpring is a popular ISP; unlimited Internet access and 5MB of space for your home page are available for $19.95 a month. MindSpring access software is available free on the *Creating Web Pages For Dummies* CD-ROM (see Appendix E).

✔ **MCI WorldCom.** Internet access for $16.95 a month, which includes a special offer for MCI phone service. Connections are robust and available nationwide, as one might expect from MCI, and Netscape is the browser provided.

✔ **UUNet.** As a longtime leader in Internet access and a Best ISP winner from *PC Week* magazine, UUNet provides good connections in many countries around the world for a $25 startup fee plus $24.95 a month for 150 hours of access, $2 an hour thereafter. The fact that UUNet requires a startup fee, where others offer periodic specials with several months' service for little or no money, might show that UUNet is less interested in getting lots of individual users onto their service. Personal Web access is not their only business; UUNet sells access to other ISPs as well.

✔ **AltaVista FreeAccess.** AltaVista, a Top Ten worldwide Web site that employs one of the authors (Smith), offers a free ISP service called AltaVista FreeAccess. At this writing, this service is available in the United States, Canada, and England. In exchange for giving up a small amount of screen space for an ad area, you get a fast (56K), free connection to the Internet, including e-mail.

Also, if you buy Netscape Navigator over the counter as a boxed, retail product, you get a free setup program that enables you to easily choose an ISP. When we checked, the product was available for under $20, and you could choose from internetMCI, NetCom, and UUNet Technologies. Internet Explorer is also available as a boxed product with Internet access. You can just buy Netscape Navigator or Internet Explorer, choose an Internet service provider, and be in business! If all you want is Web access, the Netscape Navigator or Internet Explorer retail product is a good choice.

For Mac owners, Apple offers special deals for online access in cooperation with MindSpring.

Note: Specific prices and "deals" are subject to change, as is international availability of these and other Internet services.

ISPs make a great deal of money from users who pay a flat fee of $20 or so and then log on for only a few hours a month. If you're going to use the Internet and the Web for only a few hours a month, consider one of the low-cost plans available through an online service or free Internet access providers.

What's a Mac user to do?

Two words: Get AOL. America Online has robust Macintosh support, including full cross-platform support for easy Web publishing. CompuServe doesn't support an easy-to-use Web publishing tool on the Macintosh, only on Windows. (Mac users have access to free Web server space, but no easy-to-use publishing tool.) The Microsoft Network doesn't support the Macintosh at all! So if you are a Mac user who wants an online service that supports your Web publishing efforts, get America Online.

Publishing your Web page online

In the following chapters, we describe how to use the easy-to-use Web page tools and free Web server space from America Online and CompuServe. The descriptions include the following:

- Overall capabilities of each service's Web publishing tools

- Steps for creating and publishing a simple personal home page — with a personal description, favorite URLs, and a photo or other image — by using the online service's easy-to-use Web publishing tools

- Steps for copying text from your word processing program or text editor to the Web publishing tool

The descriptions in this Part are only the steps for *creating* your Web page; for ideas on how to *design* it, see Chapter 2. The descriptions in this chapter also don't describe the tools that each online service has for transferring HTML-tagged text and other Web files created with other tools to its Web servers; for information on this more advanced topic, see the instructions available on each online service. The descriptions here represent just the beginning of the Web publishing resources on each major online service. After you create your initial home page, use the rest of this book and the online service itself for further help, support, and ideas.

All the publishing services we describe in this book enable you to include HTML commands in your text. For a description of key HTML commands, see the Cheat Sheet and Chapter 7. (Feeling restless? Tear out the Cheat Sheet and tape it to the wall in front of you, where you can see it!)

Chapter 5

Get Your Web Page Online with AOL

● ●

In This Chapter

▶ Finding what AOL offers

▶ Choosing your publishing tool

▶ Getting started with 1-2-3 Publish

● ●

*A*merica Online is an amazing success story — and by far the leading Internet service provider in the world. It also offers solid Web publishing services, backed by a strong online community that can help you publish your first Web page and then steadily improve it.

If you're not an America Online user, GeoCities (described in Chapter 3) is an excellent choice. Anyone with Web access can use GeoCities. But if you're an America Online user, you have a choice between America Online's built-in services and GeoCities. We suggest that you start with AOL if you have that choice.

Why? The answer isn't really that AOL's tools are better; they're roughly equivalent to the GeoCities tools. The difference is community. Most AOL users spend more time in AOL's online forums than on the open Web. And in those open forums you can quickly get answers to your questions about using AOL's tools to get your initial Web page up, then improve it from there.

If you're already an America Online user and are still on Version 3.0 or 4.0 of the service, do upgrade to Version 5.0 before proceeding. All it will cost you is a little time, and you'll get access to the Web publishing capabilities described in this chapter.

Use this chapter to get started with the America Online tools and create your first Web page. Then use the more advanced information later in this book and the online forums in America Online to push your page to the next level.

What AOL Offers

America Online has several parts to its Web publishing service:

- **1-2-3 Publish.** 1-2-3 Publish lets you use a template to quickly create your first Web page. It removes most of the initial barriers to getting a Web page up quickly and easily. It doesn't let you create your own custom Web page design or work in HTML.

- **Easy Designer.** Easy Designer is the next step up from 1-2-3 Publish. It lets you drag and drop text and images, and use HTML to extend the capabilities of your page. (Easy Designer replaces the old Personal Publisher and Personal Publisher 3 services from previous versions of the AOL software.)

- **Verio services.** AOL has integrated Web hosting services from Verio, a major Web hosting provider, into its offering. The good news for you is that you get some Verio services free, and others at a discount, by accessing them through AOL.

We recommend that you use 1-2-3 Publish to get that all-important first Web page up, then continue editing your Web page with Easy Designer. The next section tells you how to create your first Web page with 1-2-3 Publish; it should take 30 minutes or less. If you already know something about Web page creation and want to go straight to a more challenging environment, try Easy Designer first.

America Online gives you 2MB of Web server space for each AOL screen name you have. Nothing prevents you from creating up to six additional screen names for yourself, putting up 2MB of Web files for each screen name, and then tying all the files together through the judicious use of links between Web pages. (Just don't tell AOL we told you so!)

Choose Your Tool

America Online has a tremendous amount of content and services, and it can sometimes be hard to find what you want — or to choose from among several options when they're offered. Follow these steps to get to the right Web publishing tool for you:

1. **Start America Online.**

   The Welcome screen will appear, as shown in Figure 5-1.

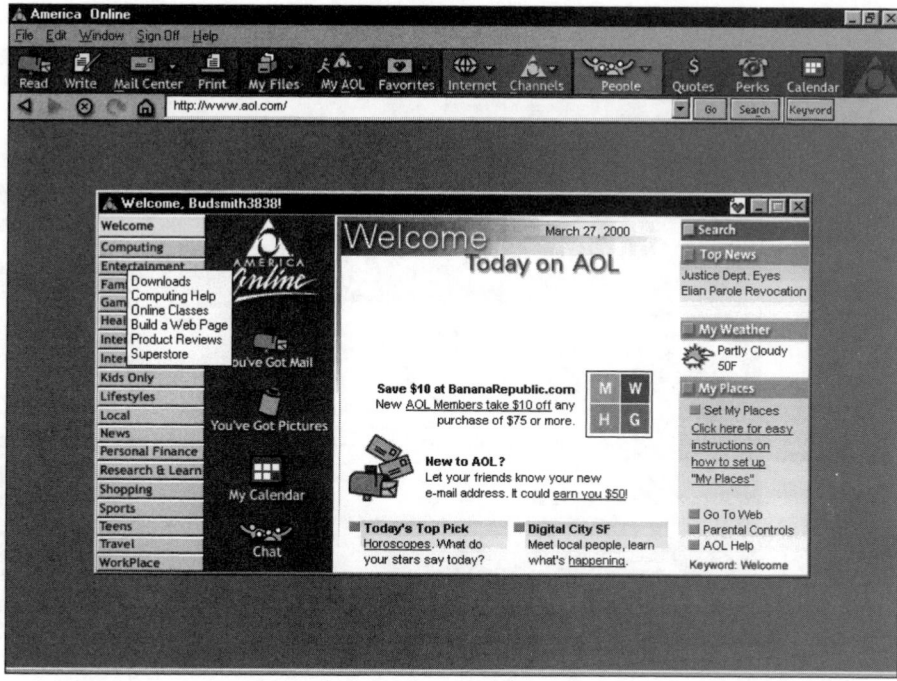

Figure 5-1:
Build your
Web page in
the handy
Computing
section.

2. Click on the Computing channel.

The AOL Computing channel, consisting largely of CNET content, appears. (CNET is a major Web site for computing content and a partner of AOL.)

3. Click on Build Your Web Page in the lower area of the screen.

The AOL Computing Build Your Web Page area appears, as shown in Figure 5-2.

From this point, you can choose 1-2-3 Publish, the very easy-to-use tool that helps you put a Web page up fast, or Easy Designer, a more flexible tool that helps you do more with your Web page. Easy Designer can work with Web pages that you create initially in 1-2-3 Publish.

We recommend that you use 1-2-3 Publish to get that all-important first Web page up, then continue editing your Web page with Easy Designer. The next section tells you how to create your first Web page with 1-2-3 Publish. If you already know something about Web page creation and want to get straight to a more challenging environment, skip ahead to the section on Easy Designer.

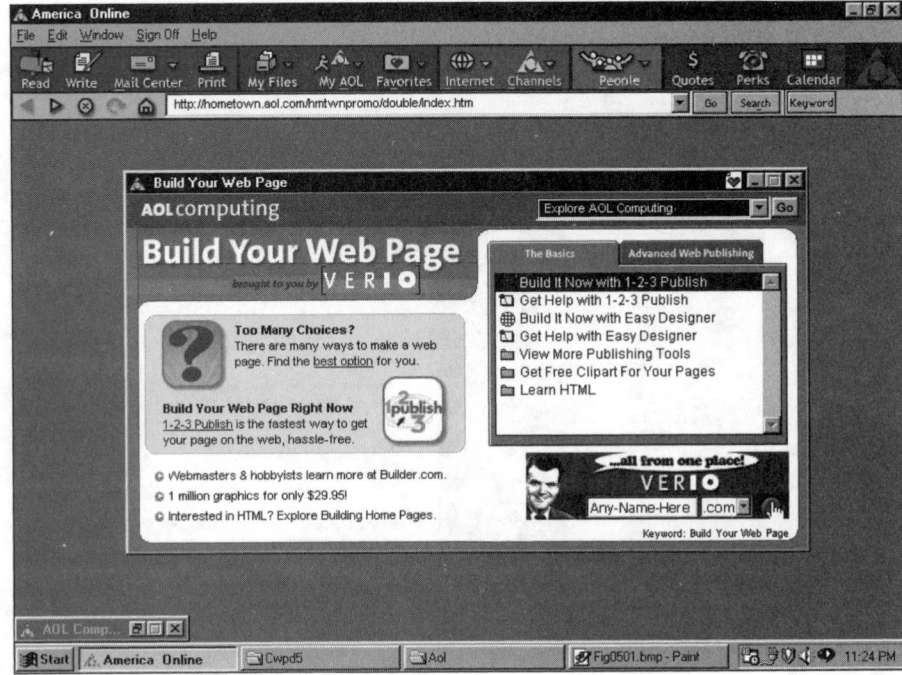

Figure 5-2:
AOL gives
you a
toolbox full
of ways
to start.

Get a Start with 1-2-3 Publish

1-2-3 Publish offers the best of both worlds: an easy-to-use tool that isn't limiting, because you can use Easy Designer to improve your initial page. First, get to the Build Your Web Page screen, as described in the previous section. Then follow these steps to create your first Web page with 1-2-3 Publish:

1. **From the Build Your Web Page screen in AOL, double-click on the words Build It Now with 1-2-3 Publish.**

   The 1-2-3 Publish starting screen appears, as shown in Figure 5-3.

2. **Scroll down and examine all the different templates.**

   You can use one of the top-level templates or one of the more specific templates farther down for your first Web page.

3. **Click on the template you want to use.**

   A page with a series of steps will appear, as shown in Figure 5-4. These steps are the same for all the templates, but some of the details are different. For instance, the content areas are different for different Web pages.

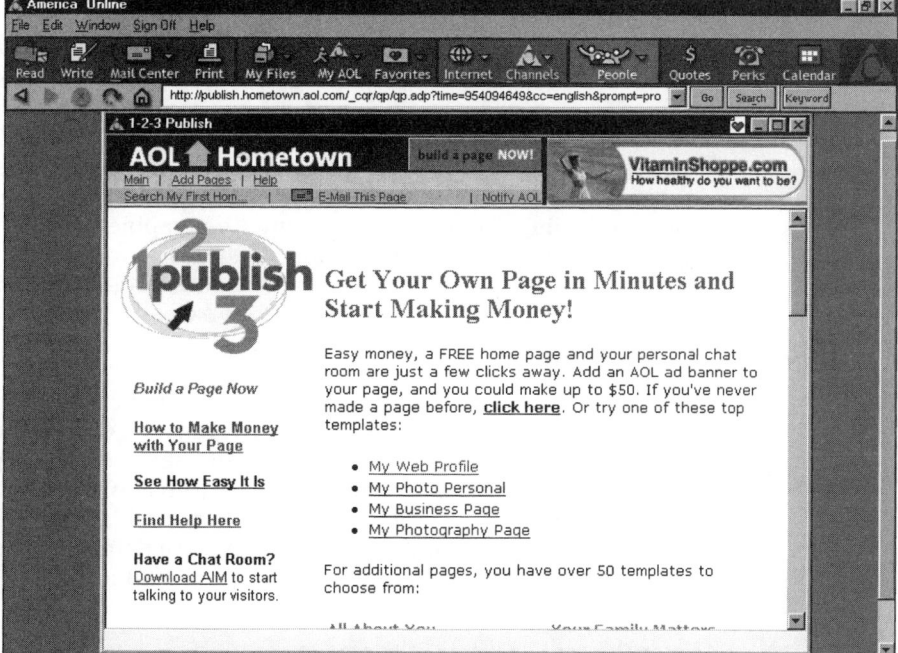

Figure 5-3:
1-2-3
Publish
even lets
you make
money.

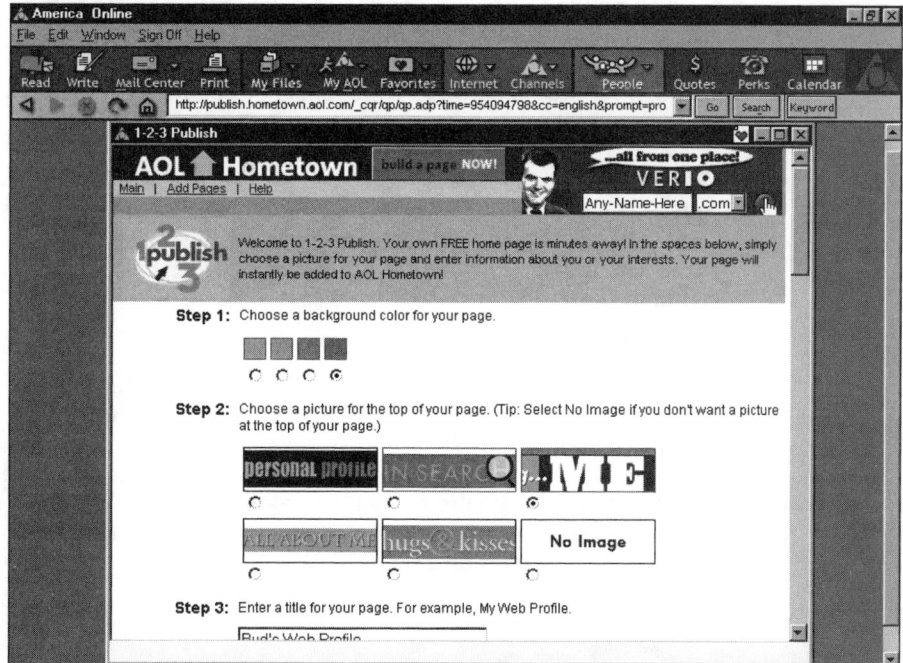

Figure 5-4:
You're just a
few steps
away from
your Web
page.

4. Set up the overall look of the page.

Step 1 is to select the background color for your page. For Step 2, choose a picture for the top of the page (the pictures you have to choose from vary depending on your template). In Step 3, choose a title for your page. If you have your own picture on your hard disk, you can choose that too; AOL will automatically upload it and include it in your Web page. (This is a very easy way to do something that can be tricky if you aren't using a template.) Make sure the graphic you choose in Step 2, the title you enter, and the image you select go well together; you can choose No Image in Step 2 if the title you enter and the picture you upload are all you want at the top of your page.

5. Choose a divider.

This is a very important choice, because the divider between sections has a surprisingly strong effect on the overall look of your Web page, and most of the choices offered are kind of cheesy looking, IMHO. ("In My Humble Opinion" — a commonly used Web abbreviation that usually appears near opinions that are anything but humble) You can choose "No Divider" to avoid problems. If you do use a divider, make sure it isn't the same color as your background, or it will tend to disappear into the background.

6. Enter the text sections of the page.

Here's where you get creative. (Hopefully not too creative, if you're creating a resume or other fact-based page!) Enter a title and basic facts about you, your interests, your hobbies, your friends, or more specific topics such as your work history. Don't spend too much time at first, though — you can always come back and change the contents later.

7. Enter your links.

This is a key part of many Web pages. Your favorite links are like your gift to the Web community, giving people who share your interests quick access to the most valuable resources you've found. Enter Web pages that you like and use a lot and that other people might not already be familiar with.

8. Keep or eliminate "special features."

The "special features" are AOL's way to get your Web page to advance its interests. You can include an ad banner in your Web page to induce people to sign up for AOL, and you can include access to AOL Instant Messenger (AIM) in your page. We recommend that you not include the ad banner — you're more likely to irritate people than to make big bucks — and that you only include Instant Messenger access if you're already an AIM user and really, really want a lot more people to contact you.

All about the Benjamins?

AOL offers you the opportunity to make money for including an AOL ad banner in your page. The idea is that, whenever someone visits your Web page, they'll see an ad banner inviting them to join AOL. If they do so, and stay 90 days or more, AOL will pay you "up to" $50. (That's two-and-a-half "benjamins," or U.S. $20 bills.) Don't do it! First of all, AOL doesn't define what "up to" $50 means, so who knows what the offer really means. More importantly, many Web users feel besieged by advertising on the Web. Don't add to the clutter and annoy the friends and family who will probably be your first Web page visitors by including an ad with your first Web page.

   9. **Click the Preview My Page button.**

   Your Web page will appear! It has a special box at the top that allows you to go back and change the page (by clicking Modify) or save it to the Web (by clicking Save). Figure 5-5 shows the very simple Web page one of the authors created as an example.

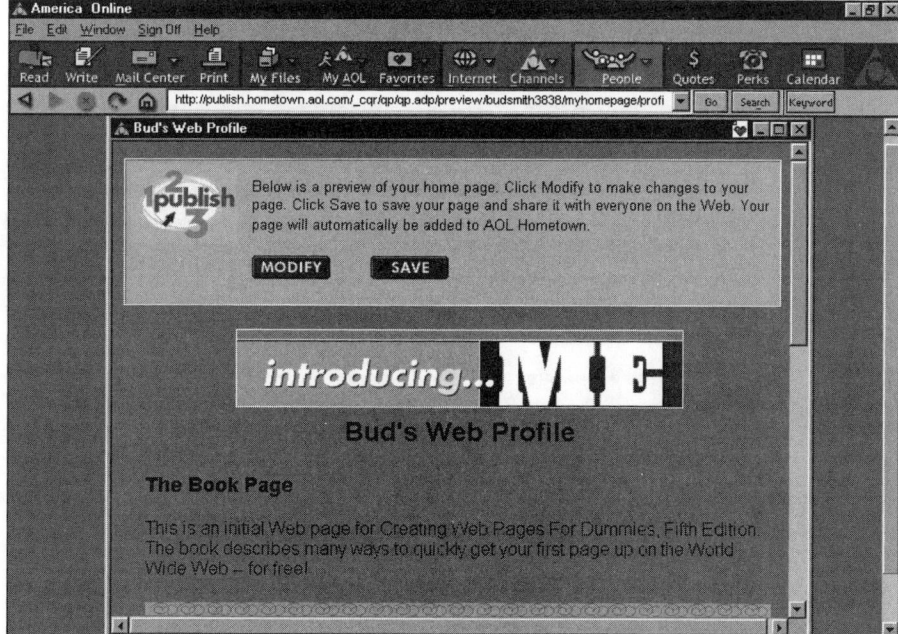

Figure 5-5: It's easy to preview and modify your Web page as many times as you want.

10. **Continue to modify and preview your page until it's ready, and then choose Save.**

    Your Web page will be published on the Web! You'll see a Congratulations page, as shown in Figure 5-6, and the Web address of your new page. Write it down or save it in a safe place. Tell your friends!

    You can also make other changes, such as moving your Web page to a different area within AOL's home page categories. Click around on the Congratulations page and investigate the different options.

11. **To modify your page in the future, go to it and then click the 1-2-3 Publish link at the bottom.**

    You'll be returned to 1-2-3 Publish and be able to modify your page.

Click on the link for your home page to make it appear in a Web browser window. Then click the Favorites icon at the top of the AOL screen. Choose Add Top Window to Favorite Places, and you'll always be able to return to your Web page again.

After you take your page as far as you can with 1-2-3 Publish — which may take a while, because the tool is pretty capable — you can move up to Easy Designer. Easy Designer allows you much more flexibility in the content and layout of your Web page, with drag-and-drop editing and placement of text and graphics.

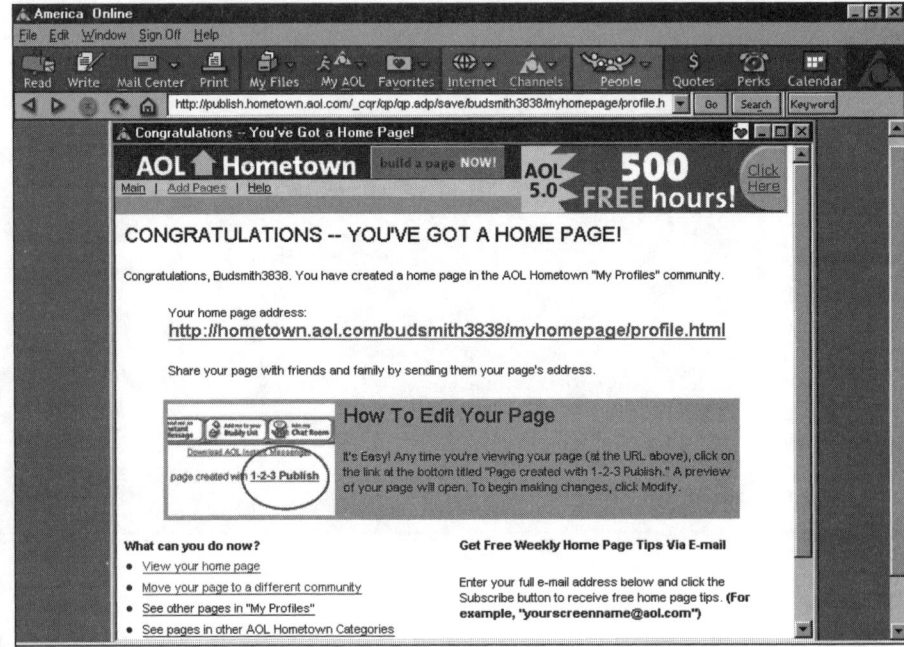

Figure 5-6: AOL gives you your URL and more ways to change your page.

Just use the steps at the beginning of this chapter to choose a tool, but choose Easy Designer instead of 1-2-3 Publish. You can use the Web page you developed with 1-2-3 Publish as your starting point for work in Easy Designer.

Once you edit a page in Easy Designer, you can no longer edit it further in 1-2-3 Publish. So be sure you've taken your Web page as far as you want to in 1-2-3 Publish before editing it with Easy Designer.

Chapter 6

Get Your Web Page Served
with CompuServe

In This Chapter

▶ Figure out the best CompuServe version for you

▶ Publish with the tools in CompuServe 4.0

▶ Download Trellix Web for CompuServe 2000

CompuServe was once the leading online service, with a special focus on business use. Many companies put their entire online presence on CompuServe. However, America Online bypassed CompuServe — first in users, then in features. At the same time, much of the product support once found on CompuServe moved to the Web, reducing CompuServe's edge. America Online finally bought CompuServe several years ago.

This means America Online has two major online services, AOL and CompuServe. The company has now positioned CompuServe as the lower-cost, "value" service, and AOL as the premium service. And the company has gradually moved CompuServe's functionality to be more like America Online's in key areas.

In this chapter we give complete instructions for publishing a Web page using either of the two major versions of CompuServe, CompuServe 4.0 and CompuServe 2000. Choose the instructions that fit your version and get started!

CompuServe: Version on Confusion

The biggest change in the CompuServe world is represented by CompuServe 2000, the new version of CompuServe. CompuServe 2000 uses much the same access network as America Online, and its appearance is also much like America Online's. It offers different Web publishing capabilities than AOL or older versions of CompuServe.

Many existing CompuServe users feel they can't upgrade to CompuServe 2000 because it requires upgrading users to get a new user name and e-mail address — the last thing many users, who have given their e-mail address to dozens or even hundreds of friends and business contacts, want to do. CompuServe 2000 is also not available on all the systems, such as the Macintosh and older versions of Windows, that can run earlier versions of CompuServe. And some users just plain like the older version — including its fairly robust Web publishing tools — and see no reason to upgrade to the newer one.

So the CompuServe user base is split between previous versions of CompuServe and CompuServe 2000 — and we can't just advise those of you who are on previous versions to upgrade, because you may have good reason not to. So, we're going to cover all bases. This chapter covers both CompuServe 4.0 and CompuServe 2000. That way you can use the Web publishing services in CompuServe 4.0 if you need to, and don't have to upgrade to CompuServe 2000 just for Web publishing.

You can use the CompuServe 4.0 publishing tools from within CompuServe 2000. Just go to the following URL:

```
ourworld.compuserve.com
```

Earn Your Web Presence with CompuServe 4.0

If you're still using CompuServe 4.0, you've probably been with CompuServe a long time — because CompuServe 2000 has been the only version you can get for Windows 95 or Windows 98 for over a year — and may know it fairly well. Use the forums on CompuServe to ask around about what other CompuServe users have been able to accomplish on the Web, and what barriers they've encountered, before you start.

CompuServe 4.0 offers its users 5MB of free Web server space for their Web pages. Like America Online, CompuServe 4.0 has several parts to its Web authoring support. But unlike America Online, CompuServe 4.0 doesn't have one integrated, easy-to-use, Web-based service that enables you to create and publish a home page in a single operation. The parts of CompuServe's Web authoring services are

✔ **Home Page Wizard.** Home Page Wizard is a stand-alone tool that runs outside CompuServe and creates HTML-tagged text. Home Page Wizard may not meet all your needs, and over a year after its introduction, the program is still stuck at Version 1.0. However, Home Page Wizard is free, well-supported by CompuServe and its users, and worth trying. (Be sure to check CompuServe forums for recommendations from other users about other tools that may better suit your purposes.)

> ✔ **Publishing Wizard.** Publishing Wizard takes HTML output from Home Page Wizard or other HTML editors and other Web files, such as GIF and JPEG graphics files, and places them on the CompuServe Web servers for you. You have up to 5MB of free server space for your personal Web site.

Mac users can use Publishing Wizard but not Home Page Wizard; the Home Page Wizard software is not made available for the Macintosh. To download the Macintosh version of the Publishing Wizard, press ⌘+K to enter a keyword, and then type **MACPUBWIZ**. Use a tool like Netscape Composer (see Chapter 14) to create your page, then use the Macintosh Publishing Wizard to get it on the Web.

Unlike other online services and unlike the easy-to-use, free Web-based services we describe in Chapter 4, CompuServe's Web page creation tool is stand-alone software that you run from your hard drive. In this way, it's more like the HTML editing tools we mention in Part V of this book. Home Page Wizard is both more powerful and potentially more confusing than the Web-based services. But never fear, ...*For Dummies* is here! To get a simple home page up quickly and easily, just follow these instructions, which we divide into groups of steps to make them a little easier to follow.

CompuServe has an offering called BusinessWeb that supports many desirable Web publishing features, but at this writing it's expensive at $50 for setup and $79 a month (which includes the cost of a regular CompuServe account). To find out more, go to businessweb.csi.com.

Grab the software you need

First, get the Home Page Wizard and Publishing Wizard onto your hard disk. (Skip these steps if you already have the programs, but go ahead and grab them if you're not sure whether you have the latest and greatest versions. Why use software that has old, familiar bugs when you can use software that has new, fresh ones?)

1. **Sign on to CompuServe.**
2. **Click the Go button.**

   The Go dialog box appears.

3. **Type in** Ourworld **and press Return.**

   The Our World page appears.

4. **Click the Download Publishing Utilities button.**

   The Download page appears.

5. **Click the Download Windows 3.1 Publisher link.**

   The Author Tools Web page appears.

Click the Download Windows 3.1 Publisher link even if you are a Windows 95, Windows 98, or Windows NT user. The Home Page Wizard works on all these versions of Windows but is only available by choosing the Windows 3.1 Publisher button.

6. **Click the option, Download Home Page Wizard (with Publisher).**

   The license agreement appears.

7. **Choose the option, Retrieve.**

   The Save As dialog box appears.

8. **Open the folder you want the program to download to, and then click Save.**

   The compressed file with the Home Page Wizard downloads to your computer. The file is about 1MB in size and takes about ten minutes to download using a 28.8 Kbps modem.

9. **After the download completes, shut down CompuServe.**

   For a while, you're going to use the Home Page Wizard, which is a separate program that doesn't require CompuServe. So you may as well shut down CompuServe while you work on your Web page. (Exception: You may want to leave CompuServe running while building your home page, if you want to use CompuServe to surf the Web to find graphics files, favorite links, and so on.)

Install the Home Page Wizard

With the Home Page Wizard downloaded, you install the program so you can run it. Here's how to get going:

1. **Find the file HPWIZ.EXE. Double-click it to start the installation.**

   Use the Windows Find function (Start⇨Find⇨Files or Folders) to find the file. Then double-click the icon to run the program.

2. **Click OK in response to the self-extractor message and then click Unzip to decompress the file. Click OK to acknowledge that the files decompressed successfully.**

   The file self-extracts.

3. **Install the Home Page Wizard and the Publishing Wizard.**

   A Windows installation wizard sets up, then prompts you through the process of installing these other wizards. Before running the program, be sure to review the ReadMe file; it may have helpful information. Don't start the Home Page Wizard for a moment, though; we do that in the next section.

Follow the installation program's recommendation to quit all other programs before installing, even though doing so means that you may have to disconnect from CompuServe. If you don't follow this recommendation, and something goes wrong while setting up the Home Page Wizard, you may lie awake nights wondering whether the problem occurred because you didn't follow this recommendation.

Put the wizard to work

With the Home Page Wizard downloaded and installed, you can finally start creating your home page:

1. **Choose Start⇨Programs⇨CompuServe⇨Homepage Wizard.**

   The Welcome to the Home Page Wizard screen appears (see Figure 6-1).

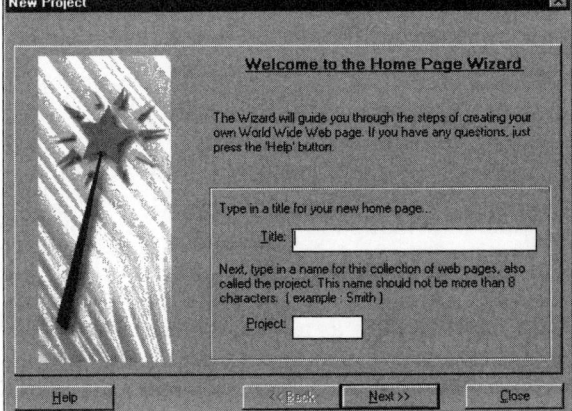

Figure 6-1: Welcome to the CompuServe Home Page Wizard.

2. **Enter the title of your home page.**

   The title appears in the title bar of most browsers and is also used by Web search engines to find your Web page.

3. **Enter a name of up to eight characters for this project.**

   A project is the same thing that we call a Web site in this book: one or more Web pages, accessed through a single home page that the user goes to first and that gives access to the rest of the site. You can save multiple projects on your hard disk, but you can publish only one at a time on the Web.

   The project name doesn't appear on your Web page. The Home Page Wizard names a subfolder after your project and places Web pages for that project as separate files in the subfolder.

Create your first Web page in one project and then work on a replacement in a separate project. When the new project is complete, you can replace the original Web page with the new one and keep the first Web page available as a backup in case of problems.

4. **Click the Next button.**

The Personal Information window appears.

5. **Enter your personal information.**

Some fields in the personal information area are required, and some are optional. You don't have to display this information in your Web page (see Step 6). The information that you enter is available for use in future projects as well.

Personal information that you can enter includes

- **First name:** Required

- **Middle initial:** Optional

- **Last name:** Required

- **City:** Required

- **State/Province:** Optional

- **Country:** Required

- **Occupation:** Optional. Enter as a noun or noun phrase — for example, welder, carpenter, or real estate salesperson. (If you include your personal information in your home page, your occupation is inserted into a predefined sentence, and a noun works best in that sentence.)

- **Hobbies:** Optional. Enter as a noun or noun phrase or a list of nouns — for example, stamp collecting, Elvis impersonation, rock climbing, Elvis sightings, rock collecting, and sighting Elvis impersonators. (If you include your personal information in your home page, your hobbies are inserted into a predefined sentence, and nouns work best in that sentence.)

Do not capitalize the first letters of your occupation and your hobbies. If you do, they look strange when CompuServe displays them on your home page in sentence form.

- **E-mail address:** Optional. CompuServe asks you to enter your CompuServe User ID followed by @compuserve.com. You can probably get away with using a different e-mail address if you prefer.

6. **To include your personal information in your home page, leave the checkbox named Use Personal Information in Home Page checked. To exclude your personal information, clear the checkbox.**

If you include your personal information, it appears in the following
format:

```
Hello! My name is <First name> <MI> <Last name> and I
       live in <City>, <State/Province>, <Country>. I am
       a <Occupation> and enjoy <Hobbies>.
```

If your personal information comes out looking good the first time, congratulations! If not, you have to go back and change the word order and
capitalization in entries such as your list of hobbies.

7. **Click the Next button.**

8. **Choose a radio button — Blank Page or Template. If you choose
   Template, highlight one of the choices: Career, Fun, or Nature.**

9. **Click Finish.**

   A preview of your home page appears. See Figure 6-2 for an example
   made by using the Fun template.

Figure 6-2:
A fun home
page from
the Home
Page
Wizard.

Gussy up your home page

The steps in the previous sections help you create a very simple, basic home
page. In this section, you enter the part of the Home Page Wizard that has
many options for improving your page. The nice thing is that you can publish
your page at any point, come back to it, improve it some more, and republish
it as many times as you want. If you aren't already in Home Page Wizard, start
it now. Then follow these steps to add a few features to your basic page:

1. **Click the Close button to close the Tip of the Day, if it appears.**

2. **Inspect the options available for your home page (refer to Figure 6-2 for an example).**

   The buttons across the top of the Home Page Wizard editing window make many options available:

   • **Headline.** Insert or edit a headline. Choose a headline style from Headline 1 (largest) to Headline 6 (smallest).

   • **Text.** Insert or edit text. Choose text styles: centered, preformatted (use existing line breaks and a nonproportional font), or bulleted.

   • **Image.** Insert an image. Browse your hard disk to find images. Enter alternate text for an image. Set an image's size. Center an image.

   Alternate text for an image is text that appears if users have graphics display turned off in their browsers. Many users with slow connections turn the graphics display off for speed, so providing a text description of the image helps them decide whether to download it.

   • **Lines.** Insert or edit a horizontal line. Choose its dimensions and alignment: left, center, or right.

   • **External link.** Insert or edit a link to an Internet location, such as a Web URL. Center the link, or place it in a bulleted list.

   • **Internal link.** Insert or edit a link to another page within your current Web project. Create a new page to link to. Center the link, or place it in a bulleted list.

   • **E-mail.** Insert or edit a link to an e-mail address. Center the link, or place it in a bulleted list.

   • **Background.** Change page properties such as the background pattern, link color, or text color.

   • **Test.** Automatically open your page in any browser that you have on your hard disk. (You have to use the Browse button to find each browser the first time you use it; then it is added to a list within the dialog box.)

   • **Publish.** Start the Home Page Publishing Wizard, which publishes your Web project on the World Wide Web.

3. **Edit items on your home page.**

   To edit any of the items you have already put on your home page, double-click the item. An appropriate editing box opens, and you can make the appropriate changes. For example, if you double-click a line of text, a text editor opens. You can change the text and change its style. Then click OK to place the revised text back in your Web page.

4. **Delete items from your home page.**

   To delete any of the items you have already put on your home page, click the item to select it. Then press the Delete key, Ctrl+X, or the Backspace key to delete the item. To undo the deletion, press Ctrl+Z or choose Edit⇨Undo.

5. **Add items to your home page.**

   To add any item to your home page, click the page to put the insertion point wherever you want the new item. Then click the button that's appropriate for what you want to insert: Headline, Text, Image, and so on. An appropriate editing box appears, and you can enter the text you want, select an image, or whatever, and then you can pick appropriate style options.

6. **Continue editing, deleting, and adding items. Drag items around to rearrange their location.**

   Continue working on your home page until it seems ready to publish.

7. **Test your home page.**

   To test your home page in other browsers on your hard disk, click the Test button. Select a browser on your hard disk to add to the list of browsers. Then open your page in each browser and see how it looks. Make any changes necessary so that your home page works well in all browsers.

8. **Publish.**

   When you're ready to put your home page on the Web, log on to CompuServe, then click the Publish button. The Publishing Wizard starts.

Here are some tips that you can use to create or improve your Web home page:

✔ The first forum on CompuServe to go to for help with Web page authoring is the Internet Resources Forum.

✔ If you switch to another program while using the Home Page Wizard, the other program may appear after you click Finish. Press Alt+Tab to cycle among programs and return to the Home Page Wizard.

✔ To publish the Web page that you created, you must use the Publishing Wizard. This tool works with any HTML-tagged text (not just output from the Home Page Wizard).

Publish your page with the Publishing Wizard

The Publishing Wizard publishes any HTML files you have created, either in the Home Page Wizard or elsewhere, and puts them up on CompuServe's servers. These steps describe how to use the Publishing Wizard to get your initial Web site up on the Web.

Before you start the Publishing Wizard, log on to CompuServe. Keep checking that your connection doesn't drop while entering info in Publishing Wizard. Why do this? At this writing, the Publishing Wizard can't make a connection itself but needs to have one provided for it — and you must start the connection before you start Publishing Wizard. If you start Publishing Wizard first, you have to close the program or even reboot before opening a connection, restarting Publishing Wizard, and completing the file transfer.

1. **Log on to CompuServe if needed, and then start the Publishing Wizard.**

   If you came to these steps directly from the previous ones, the Publishing Wizard is running already. Otherwise, find the Home Page Wizard, start it, and click the Publish button to start the Publishing Wizard.

2. **Click Next.**

3. **Click the Upload Files radio button, then click Next.**

4. **Enter personal information — Name, City, and so on. Then click Next.**

   If you previously entered this information in the Home Page Wizard, it appears. If not, enter it now; it's only for use by CompuServe, not for display. If Country doesn't appear, choose one from the drop-down list.

   Tips for Americans: America is listed as United States of America and is near the end of the list — a few entries after Tuvalu and a few before Vatican City State (Holy See). You also see a separate entry for United States Minor Outlying, which we assume means U.S. dependencies that are not part of the 50 states.

5. **Enter directory information such as occupation (optional). Then click Next.**

   If you previously entered this information in the Home Page Wizard, it appears. If not, you can enter it now so that other Web users can find your Web page more easily.

6. **Check or enter your CompuServe account information. Then click Next.**

When it comes time to enter your CompuServe ID, enter your numeric CompuServe account number, using a comma in the middle; your text user ID won't work here, and neither will your numeric ID with a period in the middle.

7. **Click Next to publish.**

CompuServe connects to the Publishing Server.

If you didn't follow the tip about having CompuServe connected while using the Publishing Wizard, you may get a connection error when connecting to the Publishing Server. We got around this error by restarting our machine, starting CompuServe, and then starting the Publishing Wizard. We had to go through the previous steps again, plus identify our Web page files, and then we could upload successfully.

8. **If you have not yet created a CompuServe Personal Address, CompuServe prompts you to create one.**

A Personal Address is a name that you can use on CompuServe in addition to the numeric user ID that all users get when they sign up. The Suggest button prompts you with some suggested names. Enter a suggested personal address, such as Firstname_Lastname, and then click Next.

CompuServe registers your personal address.

9. **CompuServe uploads your Web site and then provides you with its URL. Write down the URL, which is in the form:**

```
http://ourworld.compuserve.com/homepages/
  <personal address>
```

Share your home page URL with your friends!

10. **Click the View Page button to see your page.**

11. **CompuServe may prompt you for a browser. Choose a browser from the drop-down list; if you have not already used a browser with CompuServe, you have to find one by using the Open dialog box.**

Congratulations — CompuServe opens your home page!

To see other CompuServe members' home pages — over 100,000 of them — surf over to the CompuServe personal Web pages home page at

```
ourworld.compuserve.com
```

Join Ourworld with CompuServe 2000

CompuServe 2000 has a "leveraged" solution to the challenge of providing Web page functionality to their users: a free copy of Trellix Web, a third-party program available from ZDNet, with free Web publishing privileges on CompuServe 2000.

"Leveraged" means "taking advantage of someone else's capabilities;" in this case, it has been used to an extreme. The powers that be at CompuServe — that is, AOL Time Warner — have not even bothered to include the Trellix Web download directly in CompuServe 2000. Instead, they send you off to ZDNet to get it.

(We once heard "leverage" used this way on a visit to New York. A friend of ours left a small tip, in quarters, after a fancy lunch. The waitress chased him outside to his cab, threw the quarters at him, and said "Go leverage yourself!")

 ZDNet is one of the most popular Web sites around, famous for its computing- and Internet-related content derived from Ziff-Davis magazines such as *PC Magazine* and *FamilyPC*. It includes the second-most-popular file downloading site on the Web — CNET's download.com site is significantly more popular, to ZDNet's ongoing chagrin. To visit the ZDNet download area, go to hotfiles.com.

You have to go outside of CompuServe 2000 to ZDNet to get Trellix Web. Follow these steps:

1. **Log on to CompuServe.**

2. **In the address area at the top of the screen, type** Ourworld. **Click Go.**

   The CompuServe Our World area will appear.

3. **Click Build Your Page.**

   The Build Your Page page will appear.

4. **Click on the link for Trellix Web.**

   The CompuServe Trellix area will appear, as shown in Figure 6-3.

5. **Click DOWNLOAD Trellix Web.**

   The Trellix Web registration area appears.

6. **Enter your name and e-mail address and, if you wish, your phone number.**

   Your phone number is optional.

Figure 6-3:
CompuServe
2000 has a
deal with
Trellix Web.

7. Click the Submit button.

A ZDNet download page with Trellix Web appears.

8. Click the Download Now button.

Trellix Web will be downloaded to your computer.

Trellix Web is a separate application with its own publishing instructions. Follow the instructions in the program to create and publish your initial CompuServe Web site.

Part III
Better, Stronger, Faster Pages

The 5th Wave   By Rich Tennant

"Hold your horses. It takes time to build a home page for someone your size."

In this part . . .

After you get your initial Web page up, you no doubt want to improve it. To do this you need to know some of the basics about HTML (HyperText Markup Language), the specification from which Web pages are built. Then you can tweak your page's underlying HTML code, add graphics and multimedia, and generally make it a happening place to be on the Web. This part shows you how to make your page really good.

Chapter 7

Just Enough HTML

Knowing a little HTML is a *good* thing. HTML is the code that connects the text content of your Web page and the graphics, links, and appearance users see in a Web browser.

You can add HTML tags, the formatting and linking elements we describe in Chapter 1, to regular text to create your own Web documents in any text editor or word processing program. Or you can use a Web editing tool that hides from you the gory details of HTML tags. This chapter gives you enough background to know what you're seeing when you look at text that includes HTML tags and to make a few changes if you need to.

Trying to figure out a lot of HTML right away is a *bad* thing. Spending hours and hours going over all the details of HTML is likely to slow your sprint to becoming a Web publisher. And becoming a Web publisher quickly can be a *good* thing. So don't let a bad thing get in the way of a good thing; use this chapter to find out just enough about HTML to help you create some basic pages and get them on the Web.

Get Ready: A Refreshingly Brief Description of HTML

This chapter gives you a basic working knowledge of HTML. We don't burden you with hundreds of pages of HTML tags, tips, and tricks. You can find some of the more technical details and background in the sidebar called "The helter-skelter growth of HTML." (Try it; you'll like it.) After you publish a few Web pages, you can take the time to find out more about HTML. At that point, you may want to buy that 400-page HTML book.

If you like to know everything that's going on before you roll up your sleeves and plunge into things, you may want to start by looking at *HTML For Dummies,* 3rd Edition, a comprehensive guide to HTML by Ed Tittel and Stephen N. James (IDG Books Worldwide, Inc.).

Why bother with HTML basics?

More and more Web authoring tools try to hide HTML from the user; you can use one of these tools to create a Web page without knowing a thing about HTML. But here are several reasons to figure out the basics of HTML:

- **Because everyone else is.** Bad reason. Next!

- **To understand how the Web works.** This understanding is pretty valuable if you're a heavy Web user (or a light one), especially if you plan to publish on the Web. Some of the Web's limitations, such as "what you see is not what you get," are hard to understand if you don't know something about HTML.

- **To use free Web tools.** Many free Web tools enable you to enter HTML tags directly to jazz up your text. Knowing a few tags can go a long way.

- **To work directly in HTML.** Many Web pros tire of managing HTML tags by hand and start using a tool that hides the tags. Others swear by HTML. Everyone swears at HTML, at least some of the time. But the only way to have a choice is to know some HTML.

Working with HTML documents

An HTML document is simply a plain-text document that has HTML tags embedded in it. A *plain-text document* is a document with nothing in it but regular keyboard characters; any formatting codes in a plain-text document are visible to the person creating or editing it. (Unlike a plain-text document, word-processing documents and other kinds of formatted documents have special formatting codes embedded in them that are not readable by other people.) The formatting in an HTML document is embedded in tags, such as the <B> and </B> tags we describe in Chapter 1. You need to know a few basic things to start working with HTML documents.

Viewing HTML documents

You can see HTML anytime you use the Web. Just pull up a Web page and choose View⇨Source, or a similar command, in your browser. The command displays the HTML source code that underlies the Web page. This capability naturally leads to the temptation to borrow attractive documents from the Web, save them to your disk as HTML files, and then use them as templates for your own work — kind of a magpie approach to Web page building.

Borrowing someone else's material is okay for basic HTML formatting, but for more sophisticated formats that are distinctive and embody a great deal of work, get permission before you use them. Simply contact the Webmaster at the site you admire, describe how you want to use the format, and request permission. You may be surprised how many people say yes — without even exacting a promise from you that you hand over your firstborn.

Creating HTML documents

You can create HTML documents in a word processing program, in a text editor, or by using an HTML tool. Each method has its advantages:

- ✔ **Word processing program.** Most newer versions of popular word processing packages include "save as HTML" capability. You can open and edit a document in the word processing program and then save it as HTML-tagged text that makes up a Web page. However, this process works best if you only format your document in the same ways that HTML supports directly, which you find out about in this chapter.

- ✔ **Text editor.** A text editor is a program that edits regular text, such as the dull, boring, plain text that most people send e-mail messages in — no fonts, no bold or italic text, and no styles. When you save a file from a text editor, it saves as plain text, with no added codes for formatting. Although most text editors lack the advanced features found in word processing programs, many HTML experts swear by them. (You can also create a file in a word processing program, then save it as a text file, to achieve the same effect.)

- ✔ **HTML tool.** An HTML tool hides some of the details of HTML from you. But you have to go through a learning curve for any HTML tool, and few tools completely hide HTML. So the basics we present in this chapter will help, even if you plan to use a tool. By knowing the basics, you can make better use of the tool and have some alternatives if the tool doesn't do everything you need it to. (And what tool does?)

After you create an HTML file, save it with the extension .HTM. The extension enables the Web browser to recognize the file and interpret it correctly.

Every computer allows different kinds of filenames. But for your Web pages to work on the widest possible range of systems, you should keep your Web filenames short, and within the 8 x 3 filename limits of DOS. (FILENAME .EXT is an example of an 8 x 3 filename; up to 8 characters before the period, up to 3 characters after.) HTML files should end in the characters .HTM. Also, leave spaces and special characters such as colons or apostrophes out of the name. This way, your filenames are valid regardless of the type of computer that ends up being the Web server for your pages.

Previewing HTML documents

However you create your HTML file, you need to see what it's going to look like on the Web. Some HTML tools offer special preview modes, but you can get the best idea of how your HTML file will look on the Web by using your Web browser.

While working in your text editor or word processing program or using an HTML tool, simply save your file to disk. (Remember to save the file using the .HTM extension.) Then open your Web browser. In Netscape Navigator, choose File⇨Open Page to open the file you just saved; in Internet Explorer, choose File⇨Open and then click the Browse button to find the file, then open it.

The file appears in your browser just as it does on the Web. (Well, except that other people may use different browsers, and they may specify different fonts for displaying Web pages. But at least you get an idea of how the page looks.) If you're connected to the Internet, you can even click links in your document to see the appropriate graphic or Web page.

The helter-skelter growth of HTML

HTML is a markup language that follows rules stipulated in a more complex specification — SGML (Standard Generalized Markup Language). HTML has evolved to Version 4.0, but not all browsers and tools support that version. Many users never upgrade the browser they get with their computers, so old versions of browsers stick around for a long time. And some users access the Web through devices like WebTV, which don't support advanced features such as frames and Dynamic HTML (DHTML). For the widest possible audience, stick with older tags, such as those in the HTML 3.2 specification or earlier.

Navigator bookmarks as a Web page

If you have Netscape Navigator, or another browser that saves its bookmarks file as an HTML file, you can create a Web page in a big hurry. Find your bookmarks file and make a copy of it. (The bookmarks file is called BOOK-MARK.HTM on the PC or BOOKMARKS.HTML on the Macintosh.)

Open Netscape Navigator. Then choose File⇨Open Page to open the file you just copied. Your bookmarks file appears as a Web page! The sidebar figure shows the use of the same

file as both a bookmarks file and a Web page. You can edit the copy of the bookmarks file in a text editor or word processing program and even publish it on the Web. Then you can always get to your bookmarks file, no matter where you're browsing from!

Then again, so can anyone else; but if anyone makes snide remarks about some of your book-marked links, you can always claim that the links are for research purposes.

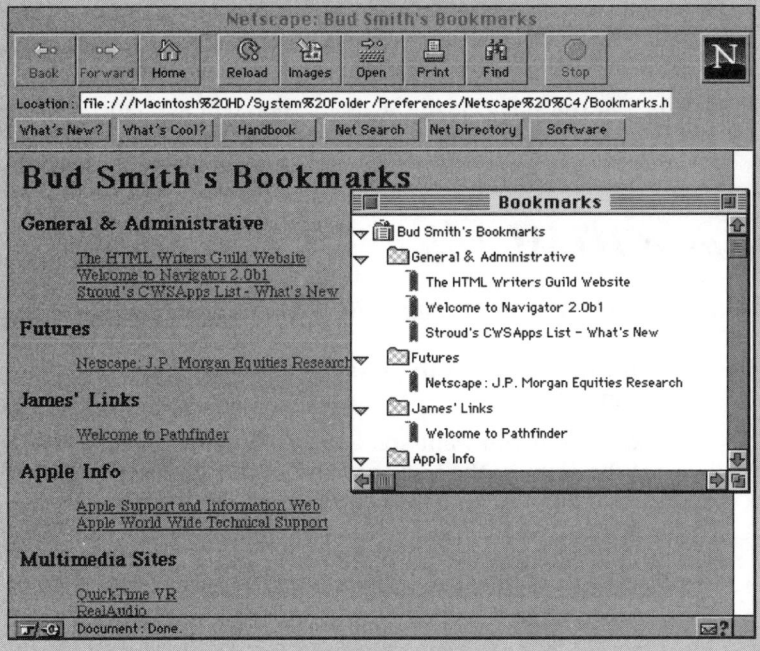

If you can run your editing tool and your browser at the same time, all the better. (In Windows, use the Alt+Tab key combination to shift quickly between applications. On the Mac, use the application pull-down menu in the upper-right corner of the screen.) You can change the document in your editing tool, save the file, and then use the Reload command or similar command in your browser to see the changes. (Kind of like those bumper stickers you may have seen on the freeway that say "Keep Honking, I'm Reloading.") This way, you never need to be surprised by what you see after something you created is published on the Web.

If you're tricky, you can size and arrange the windows on your screen so that you can see both the HTML file you're editing and the browser window that displays the resulting Web page at the same time!

But don't stop there. See what your document looks like on different browsers before you publish on the Web. You can get copies of the top browsers from the Web sites of the browser companies and preview your document in them as well.

Get Set: HTML Horse Sense

People used to refer to common sense as "horse sense." Most things about HTML fall under the realm of horse sense. After you see HTML tags a few times, most of the rules "feel right," and you will have little trouble remembering or using them.

Basic HTML rules

Here are a few basic HTML rules and some "gotchas" to watch out for:

✔ **Most HTML tags work in pairs.** (Does that make these dynamic duos "tag teams"?)

For example, if you want some text to appear in bold, you have to put `<B>` at the front of the text that you want to have appear in bold, and you have to put `</B>` at the end of the text. If you forget the `</B>` at the end, you can easily end up with a document that looks fine at the start but then switches to bold somewhere in the middle — and this bold continues all the way through to the end.

So remember to use paired tags and to check your document for unpaired tags before you publish it. If you still end up seeing bold all over your document, you know what to look for.

✔ **HTML tags are written in ALL CAPS.**

Convention says to put HTML tags in ALL CAPS so that they stand out from the text they're embedded in. But inside an anchor, put the hypertext reference (such as a URL) in the case it would normally have (upper or lower) if you were using it elsewhere. The following example illustrates this use of capitalization:

```
<A HREF="textver.htm">Text version.</A>
```

The parts of the tag that are predefined HTML tags, such as A, /A, and HREF, are in ALL CAPS. The filename is in all lowercase letters, a convention used by *UNIX* (a type of operating system) that may save you some problems if your Web page ends up on a UNIX server. You can capitalize the text between the tags, which appears on the Web page as link text, in whatever way makes sense for your Web page's readers.

UNIX machines are case-sensitive: If you call one file MyFile.txt and another file myfile.txt, they are saved as separate files. The Macintosh and PC are case-insensitive and treat the names MyFile.txt and myfile.txt the same. Because you may end up putting your Web files on a Web server that's a different kind of machine from the one you create them on, you need to pay attention to the use of upper- and lowercase. The easiest rule is the one followed by UNIX users: Always use lowercase letters for filenames.

✔ **HTML ignores paragraph symbols and tabs in your text.**

One of the most confusing things about HTML is that the paragraph markers created in your text when you press Enter are ignored, and so are tabs. When displaying HTML, the browser automatically breaks lines to fit the current window size. And the browser makes a paragraph break only when it sees the paragraph tag, <P>, or some other tag that implies the start of a new line (such as a top-level heading tag, <H1>).

✔ **HTML needs you to put paragraph tags (<P>) between paragraphs.**

No matter how many times you hit Return while typing your text, you won't prevent the text from showing up as a big blob on your Web page unless you put paragraph tags (<P>) between paragraphs.

✔ **Basic HTML looks different on different types of browsers.**

Basic HTML doesn't give you much control over the appearance of your document. (Newer versions of HTML allow more control, but aren't supported by older versions of popular browsers, so we suggest that you avoid the new stuff.) Different browsers handle the same tags differently. For example, a top-level heading (specified by the <H1> and </H1> tags) may look much larger in one browser than in another browser.

✔ **Some tags don't work on some browsers.**

Some browsers (such as Netscape Navigator) support tags that other browsers can't handle. We recommend that you stick with the tags in HTML 3.2 to avoid the chance of giving users nasty surprises when they view your documents. We use only those tags in this book.

✔ **Users configure their browsers differently.**

As if the differences among browsers weren't enough, users can configure their browsers differently. Users who have bigger monitor screens tend to look at documents in a bigger window. But because these users sit farther back from their big screens — remember your mother telling you always to sit at least six feet from the TV? — they may also use larger font sizes to display text. Some users set their browser to display all graphics as the page transmits; others turn off graphics. All these idiosyncrasies can make your document look different to different users. Figures 7-1 and 7-2 show the same Web page from the Fullerton School District in Southern California, but are displayed with different option settings. As you can see, the figures don't look the same. The URL is

```
www.fsd.k12.ca.us/art/local/local.html
```

Ten key HTML tags plus one

The Cheat Sheet at the beginning of this book shows an example of an HTML document, which is just regular text plus tags — those funny things with the angle brackets around them. If you haven't already, tear out the Cheat Sheet so you can look at the sample HTML document while you read this section.

Table 7-1	Key Tags to Use
Tags	*Tag Location*
`<HEAD>`, `</HEAD>`	Put these tags around the `<TITLE>` and `</TITLE>` tags at the start of the document.
`<TITLE>`, `</TITLE>`	Put these tags around a short title that describes the document but doesn't appear on-screen. (For more information about the `<HEAD>`, `</HEAD>`, `<TITLE>`, and `</TITLE>` tags, see the section "Head users your way to win" in this chapter.)
`<BODY>`, `</BODY>`	After you add the `</TITLE>` and `</HEAD>` tags to end the title and header area, you surround everything else in the document with the `<BODY>` and `</BODY>` tags.
`<H1>`, `</H1>`, `<H2>`, `</H2>`,...	Put the initial heading at the top of your document between the `<H1>` and `</H1>` tags. Then use higher-numbered tags for progressively lower heading levels. You can go down six levels (`<H6>`, `</H6>`), which is a lot — this book uses only three heading levels. If a book that weighs in at 350-plus pages needs only three levels, you have to create something pretty detailed before you need five or six.
`<B>`, `</B>`	Surround text you want to display in bold with these tags.

Tags	Tag Location
`<I>`, `</I>`	Surround text you want to display in italics with these tags.
`<P>`, `</P>`	You don't need to place the paragraph-break tag at the end of headings and in some other places, such as within a list, but you do need the tag everywhere else. Besides the anchor tags (`<A></A>`), `<P>` may be the easiest common tag to misuse. The end paragraph tag, `</P>`, is basically optional for beginners.
`<HR>`	The horizontal rule tag displays a horizontal line that is good for separating sections of documents.
`<A>`, `</A>`	The anchor tags define hypertext links and contain hypertext references, somewhat complicated information about where the link goes to. Link text — the text that gets underlined to indicate a hypertext link — goes between the tags. When the user clicks the underlined link text on a Web page, the display changes to show the Web page indicated by the hypertext reference.
`<A HREF="http://www.aSite.edu"> My kid's site. </A>`	The `<A>` and `</A>` tag pair defines an anchor. `HREF` indicates a hypertext reference — in this case, a pointer to a Web site's URL. The link text is `My kid's site`; the user sees this text, underlined, as part of the Web page. See the section on anchors near the end of this chapter for details on these and other kinds of hypertext links.
`<IMG SRC="BudPic.gif">`	The `IMG` tag brings in an image in a format that the browser understands, either GIF or JPEG. The `SRC` part of the tag tells the browser where to find the file. In this example, the filename is `BudPic.gif` and is in the same directory or folder as the HTML file that the `<IMG>` tag is in. (You can tell it's in the same directory because the filename doesn't have any pathname information in front of it, such as `\images\BudPic.gif`.) In addition to this chapter's description of this tag and other "Top Ten" tags, you can find a further description of the `<IMG>` tag in Chapter 7.

For an example that uses these tags, see the Cheat Sheet. For a complete list of tags, see Appendix C.

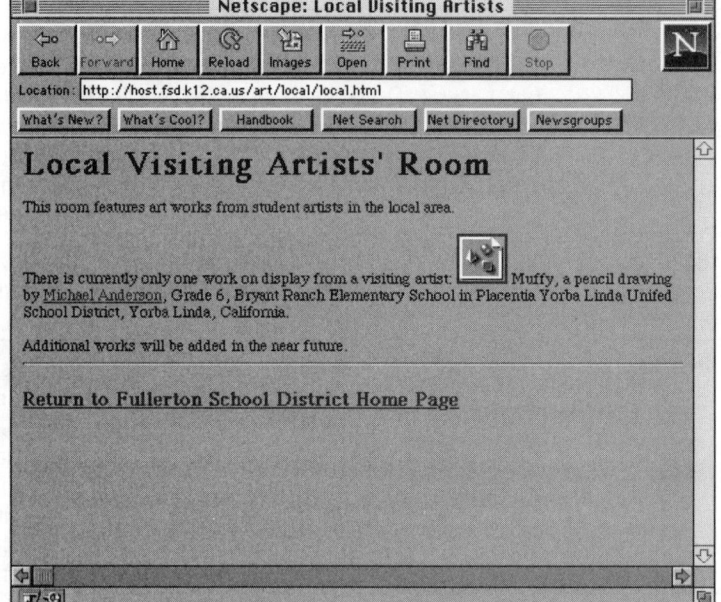

Figure 7-1:
A Web document with default settings, including images, turned off.

Figure 7-2:
The same document shown in Figure 7-1, but with different settings.

Go: Create a Web Page with HTML

Yes, you are just about ready to create a Web page with HTML. However, the whole secret of using HTML is knowing what tags to use and when. So now that you know what a tag is, what more do you need to know? Well, tags can be divided into three kinds:

- ✔ **Tags that contain meta-information about your document.** *Meta-information,* such as the title in the header section of your document, doesn't affect how your document appears on-screen; instead, this information is used by various Web tools, such as search engines, that look at the title to see what your document is about. (And we never "meta" Web tool we didn't like!)

- ✔ **Tags that format characters in your text.** These tags (<B>, </B> and <I>, </I>, for example) do nothing but modify the way your text looks when the browser displays it.

- ✔ **Linking tags.** These tags connect the user to different kinds of information and even to other documents. The section "Look back (and forward) in anchor," in this chapter, explains linking tags in detail.

After you create and save an HTML file with text and these different kinds of tags, pat yourself on the back. You've just created a complete HTML document, and you're well on the way to being a tagger yourself! (Not the kind that puts graffiti on buildings, but the kind that expresses himself or herself electronically on the Web.)

Create a blank file for your HTML

HTML files should include only plain text — no formatting from your word processing program. And the name of the document should always end with .HTM. So start by creating a text-only file to hold your Web page's text and HTML tags.

To create a blank plain-text document that you can insert HTML code into, follow these steps.

1. **Start your text editor or word processing program.**

2. **Open a new document.**

   Some programs automatically open a new document when you start them. In that case, you can skip this step.

3. **Start the process of saving your document so that you can name it.**

   If you use a word processing program, use the Save As or similar command and choose Text as the type of file.

   Don't choose the Text with Line Breaks option; line breaks make the document harder to edit. The good old Text option will do.

4. **Name the document.**

   Put **.HTM** at the end of the name.

5. **Save the document.**

   In most programs, you click a Save button or press Enter.

The steps enable you to create a blank HTML document — which wouldn't be very interesting if you were to put it on the Web! So you want to start filling in your document by adding heading information.

Head users your way to win

First, some bad news: You start your HTML documents with some tags that don't really do anything for you. In fact, the tags add a few more things to worry about. And you thought that you could finally start getting some real work done!

Now, the good news: These tags make the Web a better place. They contain introductory *meta-information* — descriptive information about your document that doesn't affect how the user sees your document. But although the user doesn't see these tags directly, the tags support search tools and other tools that make finding a Web page — hopefully, finding *your* Web page — so quick and easy that users can get to it straight away. (Of course, looking at a lot of other things in between can be half the fun of using the Web.)

- ✔ <HTML>, </HTML>. These tags surround everything in your document and identify the document as being in HTML. As the Web supports more and more different types of files, these tags become increasingly important.

- ✔ <HEAD>, </HEAD>. These tags go around the title of your document and any other information that doesn't appear within the Web page itself. For now, that just means the title.

- ✔ <TITLE>, </TITLE>. These tags go around the title of your document. The title is a short phrase that describes your document and does not appear on your Web page.

- ✔ <BODY>, </BODY>. These tags go around everything in your document that isn't part of the head. The <BODY> tag goes just after the </HEAD> tag, which goes just after the </TITLE> tag.

If you use a tool that creates a Web page for you, such as the free tools in Chapters 3, 5, and 6, you don't need to put these introductory tags in because the tool does it for you. However, you may need to add the <TITLE> and </TITLE> tags, and put the title of your Web page in between them yourself.

Look at this well-mannered, albeit nearly empty, HTML document to see what the top should look like:

```
<HTML>
<HEAD>
<TITLE>A Brief Introduction to Electric Guitars</TITLE>
</HEAD>
<BODY>
Some introductory information about electric guitars.
</BODY>
</HTML>
```

Popular Web tools use these tags. The Advanced Search option of the AltaVista Web-searching service enables users to search specifically by words in the title; just enter the phrase "title:" followed by the text you want to search for in the title. To access the AltaVista search engine, go to

```
www.altavista.com
```

Netscape Navigator and Microsoft Internet Explorer use the title of your document — the phrase between the <TITLE> and </TITLE> tags — as the document description in their Bookmarks menu. (No, we don't keep mentioning these products because we own stock in Microsoft and America Online, the companies that develop those products; this is just one of those cases where the best products and the market leaders are the same.) The title also appears in the title bar of the browser window when the page is displayed.

To give yourself a head start each time you want to begin a new HTML document, create a text-only document in your word processing program or text editor with the head, title, and body tags already in place. When you're ready to begin a new HTML document, start by making a copy of this document.

Follow these steps to create a text-only document that contains the introductory tags:

1. **Open a new document.**

2. **Save your document as a text-only document with the name you want, ending with .HTM.**

3. **On the first line of the document, enter the tag** <HTML>.

4. **On the second line of the document, enter the tag** <HEAD>.

5. **On the third line of the document, enter the tags** `<TITLE>` **and** `</TITLE>`.

   Don't enclose anything within the `<TITLE>` and `</TITLE>` tags for now. After you copy this text-only document to create an HTML document, you can enter the material that you want to use as the "title." When you are deciding what to include between these tags, remember that many Web tools use the information between these tags when searching for documents.

6. **On the fourth line of the document, enter the tag** `</HEAD>`.

7. **On the fifth line of the document, enter the tag** `<BODY>`.

8. **Leave the sixth line of the document blank.**

   The main content of the document goes here.

9. **On the seventh line of the document, enter the tag** `</BODY>`.

10. **On the eighth line of the document, enter the tag** `</HTML>`.

    Whatever else you do in your document, `</HTML>` is always the last tag.

11. **Save the document.**

Get a heading and some body

Underneath the headings, your document needs some content — just plain old words, maybe highlighted with **bold** and *italics* where needed.

Don't overuse the bold and italic tags. Like early desktop publishers, who put *three* different fonts on every **line** of text, HTML novices tend to put **lots of bold** *and italics* in their documents. When you preview your document in your Web browser, look for areas where you overuse bold and italic formatting. And when in doubt, don't use bold and italics. Your readers will thank you.

Here's how to put a top-level heading and some basic text into your Web document:

1. **After the** `<BODY>` **tag, and before the** `</BODY>` **tag, put in your top-level heading. Surround the heading with the** `<H1>` **and** `</H1>` **tags so that the browser knows that the text is a level-1 heading.**

   You may also use your top-level heading between the `<TITLE>` and `</TITLE>` tags, as many Web publishers do.

2. **After the heading, type some text.**

   For optimal use by Web search tools, the first paragraph in your document should be a brief summary of the document's contents.

3. **At the end of each paragraph, put in a** `<P>` **tag.**

No matter how many times you press Enter in your document, your dense browser doesn't get the message. It only understands that you want to end a paragraph and start a new one when it sees the <P> tag.

4. **Surround text with the** <B> **and** </B> **tags to make it bold.**

Don't overdo the use of the <B> and </B> tags! But starting out, use bold once or twice just to get a feel for it.

5. **Surround text with the** <I> **and** </I> **tags to make it italic.**

Don't overdo italicizing, either! But use italics a few times in your first document or two for practice.

6. **Try adding a horizontal rule.**

Add the <HR> tag in one or two places to create horizontal rules. (Not to start an argument with those who think that vertical or diagonal rules.)

As with headings and other elements of your document, put the <HR> tag on a line by itself so that you can find it easily later to move or remove it.

7. **After you're done, check your tags.**

Paragraphs should end with a <P> tag to start the next paragraph. All <B> tags should have a matching </B> tag, and all <I> tags should have a matching </I> tag.

The most effective way for many of us to check tags, believe it or not, is to print out the document and then cross out pairs of tags with a pencil.

8. **Save your document.**

If you use a word processing program rather than a text editor, be sure to save your document as text-only.

The Cheat Sheet at the front of this book shows a simple sample Web page.

Add a little list

One of the best ways to "break up" your Web page is to insert lists. HTML supports bulleted lists, numbered lists, and lists of definitions or descriptions. Although HTML makes creating lists easy, it doesn't give you direct control over how lists turn out. (Repeat after me, "Trust your browser, trust your browser. . . .")

✔ **Unnumbered lists** (often called bulleted lists). Unnumbered lists display as lists with bullets next to them and are "appropriately" indented (the indentation varies with different browsers and browser settings). The list you're reading now is a bulleted list, but it uses check marks in place of the bullets.

✔ **Ordered lists** (often called numbered lists). These lists are similar to bulleted lists, but with — you guessed it — numbers in place of the bullets. You can rearrange the items in the numbered list as much as you like. The browser automatically keeps things in order by putting in the right numbers when it displays the list.

✔ **Definition lists.** These lists usually alternate terms and their — duh — definitions. The term goes where the bullet goes in a bulleted list, and the definition goes next to it or on the line immediately below.

You create all lists in basically the same way: You start the list with a beginning tag, such as ⟨UL⟩ for an unnumbered list. You then tag each item separately to let the browser know that it's a separate item. You use the tag ⟨LI⟩ at the beginning of each item in both unnumbered and numbered lists; you don't use an end tag for individual list items. The list finally ends with a closing tag — ⟨/UL⟩ to end an unnumbered list, for example.

The following instructions describe how to create an unnumbered (bulleted) or ordered (numbered) list:

1. **Put in a tag to start the list:** ⟨UL⟩ **for an unnumbered list,** ⟨OL⟩ **for an ordered list.**

2. **Put in an** ⟨LI⟩ **tag to indicate a list item.**

3. **Starting on the same line, enter the text for the list item.**

   "Red Hot Chili Pepper Potato Chips" is a good way to start.

4. **For the remaining items in the list, enter the** ⟨LI⟩ **tag followed by the item text. Press Enter at the end of each line to visually separate the items on-screen as you edit.**

   You don't need to use an end tag for list items. Also remember that hitting Enter at the end of a line causes the cursor to move to a new line on-screen but doesn't cause line breaks to be put in the HTML-tagged text; the browser starts a new line when it sees a new ⟨LI⟩ tag or a ⟨/UL⟩ tag.

5. **Enter a tag to end the list —** ⟨/UL⟩ **to end an unnumbered list or** ⟨/OL⟩ **to end an ordered list.**

To create a definition list, follow these steps:

1. **Enter the** ⟨DL⟩ **tag to start the definition list.**

2. **Enter the** ⟨DT⟩ **tag to indicate a definition term.**

3. **Enter the text for the definition term.**

4. **Enter the** ⟨DD⟩ **tag to indicate definition data — the description of the definition term.**

5. **Enter the text for the definition data.**

6. **For the remaining items in the list, enter the** ⟨DT⟩ **tag followed by the definition term and then enter the** ⟨DD⟩ **tag followed by the description of the term. Press Enter at the end of each line to visually separate the items on-screen as you edit.**

   As with other list items, you don't need to enter an end tag for definition terms or definition data.

7. **Enter the** ⟨/DL⟩ **tag to end the list.**

Figure 7-3 shows an example that includes the three kinds of lists. Because people use the Web to find out new things and to look things up, lists are some of the most important formatting elements in HTML.

Look back (and forward) in anchor

Remember that HTML stands for HyperText Markup Language? Well, applying all those tags is the markup part. Now hang on to your hat: Here's everything you need to know about the hypertext part. In this section, we demonstrate how to use hypertext to create links between information in your document and information in other documents. This stuff is a bit confusing at first, but after you understand it, you'll think of many exciting ways to use hypertext in your Web pages.

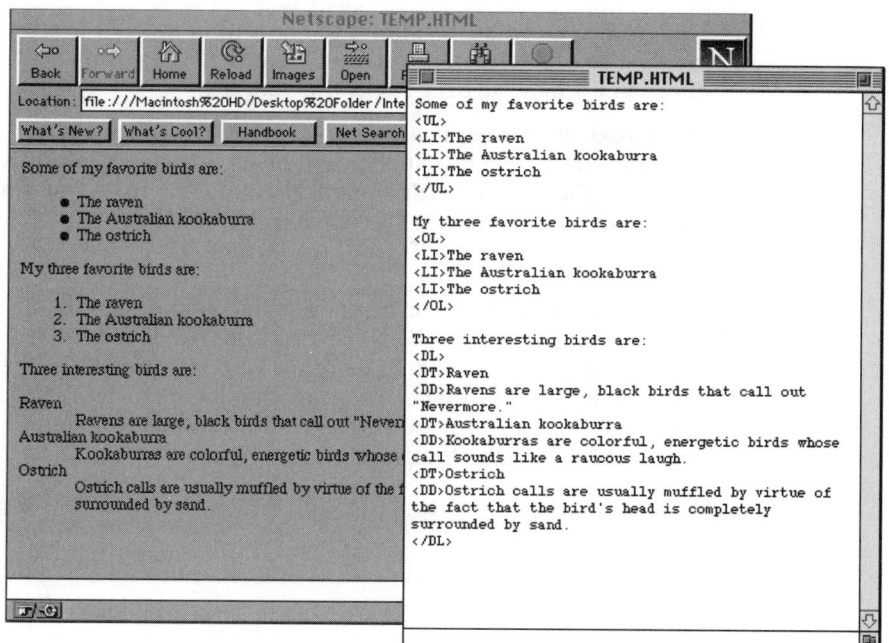

Figure 7-3:
Using lists
in your
Web page.

In HTML, every hypertext link has two ends, which are called *anchors*. (Some people think that putting anchors into a Web page makes them anchorpersons — but sorry, no seven-figure salary.)

When you define an anchor, you use tags to specify two things:

- ✔ The text or image that is highlighted as the place you click to follow the link
- ✔ The other anchor that you want to go to when you click the link

Anchors are among the most complicated tags in basic HTML. But you don't want to say "Anchors away," as the old movie had it. Anchors expand the possibilities of your Web page tremendously. The following is an example of an anchor:

```
<A HREF="http://www.trainingyourdog.com">How to train
    dogs</A>
```

Here are the parts of an anchor:

- ✔ `<A>`, `</A>`. These tags go around text that you want highlighted as a hypertext link (`How to train dogs` in the preceding example). Try to use text that represents the thing that you want to link to, such as "Adobe Corporation" or "my résumé." The better this text describes the thing that you link to, the more helpful the text is to the user.
- ✔ `HREF`. This information follows the `<A` within the `<A>` tag. It tells the browser to link to the information located at the pathname that appears after `HREF` when the user clicks the link text.
- ✔ **Hypertext reference.** These characters follow the equal sign in the `HREF` part of the anchor and should be enclosed in parentheses. They are the pathname of the document that you link to. In the example, the hypertext reference is the name of a Web site: "`http://www .trainingyourdog.com`".

When you post an HTML file on a server, some anchors in the file can point to Web documents on the same Web server as the HTML file, while other anchors point to Web documents on other Web servers. When the document is on another server, the anchor contains the document's full URL, in the same form as you type it in your browser. For example, an anchor pointing to the *For Dummies* Web site looks like this:

```
<A HREF="http://www.dummies.com">"...For Dummies"</A>
```

When the document that's pointed to by the initial anchor is on the same machine, the anchor contains the pathname of the document. The pathname specifies the file's location on the machine.

For simple Web sites that you create, put all the documents in the same directory or folder so that you have simpler anchors. Then you don't have to worry about pathnames!

The pathname looks different depending on where the second document is in relation to the HTML document. If the two documents are in the same directory or folder, the pathname is simply the filename. But if the second document is in a different directory, you can use two methods to specify how to reach it: absolute addressing and relative addressing. In _absolute addressing,_ you use the path from the lowest-level, or _root,_ directory of the server to the second document. In _relative addressing,_ you use the path from the current document to the second document.

To specify an absolute address, start with a forward slash (/) to indicate the root directory of the Web server. Then specify the full pathname from the root directory to the file. The following example shows an absolute address:

```
/photoshp/samples/sunrise.gif
```

To specify a relative address, start with the directory of the HTML document that the anchor is in and then enter the path that leads to the desired file from there. A pair of dots (..) specifies the directory one level above the current one.

For example, if you have an HTML file called sunset.htm in the directory /mysite/html, and you need a GIF graphics file that is in /mysite/html/pix, a subdirectory of the current directory, the relative address is the following:

```
pix/sunset.gif
```

If you also need a file that is in /mysite/trial/pix, you use the .. characters to specify the subdirectory above this one and then go back down the directory tree to the needed file. Put a slash after the dots. In this case, the relative address is as follows:

```
../trial/pix/moonrise.gif
```

Starting at the beginning of the path, ".." means "the directory above the current one." The words separated by slashes, "/trial/pix/," are the names of the directory and subdirectory in which the file is stored. And "moonrise.gif" is the filename.

Usually, you create your Web site on one machine, then publish it by copying the files to another machine, the Web server. It is very easy to forget to copy all the files needed to the Web server. If you keep all the files in one overall folder — that doesn't have any files in it that aren't part of the Web site — you'll have a fighting chance of making the transfer successfully.

Table 7-2 shows examples of anchors.

Table 7-2	Examples of Hypertext Links (Anchors)
Destination	*Sample Anchor*
Document on a different server	`<A HREF="http:// www.mycorp.com/Job Requirements">link text</A>`
Document in same directory	`<A HREF="MyDoc2.html">link text</A>`
Document in different directory; relative addressing	`<A HREF="Personal/Resume">link text</A>`
Document in different directory; absolute addressing	`<A HREF="/Maya/Personal/ Resume">link text</A>`

Link for yourself

Absorbing all this knowledge about hypertext links is pretty useless if you don't actually use the knowledge yourself. Here's a description of how to create a link (note how we cleverly work several different types of links into the instructions):

1. **Open an existing HTML document.**

2. **Move to the place in the document where you want to insert a link.**

3. **Start the link by entering the opening tag, including the hypertext reference that you want the link to lead to.**

   For a link to a file in the same directory, enter the filename in quotation marks, as in `<A HREF="AnotherDoc.HTM"></A>`. ("AnotherDoc.HTM" is the filename.)

   As described previously in this chapter, you can enter a relative or absolute address for a document that's in a different directory within your Web site.

   For a link to a file in the `graphics` subdirectory of the current directory, enter the pathname: `<A HREF="graphics/dancers.gif">Dancers</A>`.

For a document that's on a different server, enter the document's URL (for example, `<A HREF="http://www.ACoolSite.com"></A>`).

If you don't enter a specific filename, the browser looks for the default file: index.htm or index.html.

4. **After the opening tag, enter the link text.**

5. **Don't forget the closing tag!**

   After the opening tag and the link text, enter the closing tag.

Link from within

That's a lot of stuff to absorb! Just one more thing to consider: What if you want to link to a specific spot *within* the same Web page?

To link to a specific spot, you need a pair of anchors. The first is at the spot from which you want to link. This first anchor is just like the external links, but it has one more element — the name of the link that's at the spot to which you want to link. For example, the following anchor links to a spot that's named "Bebak," within the same file as the anchor:

```
<A HREF="#Bebak">Bud's coauthor</A>
```

The pound sign, #, denotes an anchor within a Web page. The second anchor, also called the link, is at the spot to which you want to link. The second anchor exists only to specify that spot and doesn't cause the link text to show up as underlined on the user's screen. Here's the link for the second anchor:

```
<A NAME="Bebak"> </A>Arthur Bebak
```

The link doesn't need a pathname, but the anchor that links to it needs a pathname if the anchor and link are in different files. And you don't need any text between the anchor's beginning and ending.

Try using internal links in an HTML document on your own machine, and test the links in your browser. Experiment with different kinds of relative addresses, or pathnames. Trying different links and pathnames gives you the experience you need to easily use these features in your "real" Web pages.

Linking to specific spots in your own Web page is common. Many Web sites have long Web pages that include clever internal links that move the user around in the page. Linking to specific spots in other people's Web pages is less common. Why? Because it's hard to control where the other page's author chooses to put link anchors — and harder still to make sure that link anchors don't get moved around on you unexpectedly, rendering your anchor invalid. How would you like it if, for example, you defined a link to a serious essay on home wine making and later discovered that the essay had been replaced by a discussion of Greek philosophy? (Though much of the latter may have been inspired by consumption of the results of the former.) Sheesh!

Can your browser handle it?

An anchor can link the current document to another HTML file or to some other type of file, such as a graphic, a sound, a video clip, or almost anything else. Most browsers know how to handle HTML files and GIF or JPEG graphics files automatically. Different browsers may handle other types of files in different ways — automatically, or by the user's specifying a program to handle them. So for these examples, we stick with links to HTML files and GIF and JPEG files because we know that those files work with just about any browser.

Browse your own weblet

Here's the moment you've been waiting for: Whether you've followed all the previous steps, or just some, you now have a ready-to-use little HTML document. To see whether you did it right, all you have to do is try it in your Web browser. That's right — you can view your very own HTML document in your very own browser!

Not only can you view your HTML document from your browser, but you can even follow the links to other HTML documents on your local system and from your system out onto the Web. (We assume that your browser is connected to the Web at the time. If not, following a hypertext link to a Web URL will be a short trip!) Using the Back command in your browser, you can even return to your own document.

There's only one limitation to this testing: Other Web sites can't link to your HTML document because it's only saved on your local machine, not on a Web server. And that's the one thing that's stopping your HTML document from being a Web page: It's not hosted on a Web server. Details, details — we take care of that little omission in Chapter 11.

For now, you need to figure out how to view your HTML document in your browser. This is something you do every time you work on HTML documents. Start a document; view it in your browser. Change the document; view it in your browser. And on and on. . . . (Maybe it's finally time to buy that 20-inch color monitor you've been thinking about so that you can see both documents at once as you switch back and forth.)

To view your HTML document in your browser:

1. **Start your browser.**

2. **Select the Open Page command (for Netscape) or Open File command (for Internet Explorer) under the File menu.**

3. **Find your HTML document on your hard disk and open it.**

4. **View your own HTML document in your own Web browser.**

   You can even follow links by clicking them. Use the Back command in your browser to return to your HTML document.

5. **Look for problems in your HTML document, or things you want to add.**

   So half of your *document is in italics* and <u>the rest is underlined</u> as if it's all part of a link. Who cares?! Go fix it!

6. **Open the HTML document in your text editor or word processing program and fix it.**

   The earlier sections of this chapter may be of some help here.

7. **Save the changed HTML document.**

   If you forget to save the document, your changes don't show up in your browser, and you wonder whether your changes "took" or whether you're losing your sanity.

8. **Use the Reload command or a similar command in your Web browser to reload the fixed HTML document.**

   If you forget to reload the document, your changes don't show up in your browser, and, again, you wonder whether your changes "took" or whether you're losing your sanity.

   If you forget to save the document after you make changes, or forget to reload the document in your browser, the changes you just made don't show up. Anytime you think that this may have happened, just go back to your text editor or word processing program, save the document, return to your Web browser, and reload. The changes appear.

9. **Repeat Steps 5 through 8 until done.**

   (*Done* can mean until the HTML document is done, as in finished, or until the HTML document's author is done, as in toast!)

   Don't forget to use the Reload command when you're done modifying your document and want to look at it again in the browser.

Look to the next HTML steps

The parts of HTML that we cover in this chapter represent just the basics. As you create, test, and deploy your own Web pages, you may want to understand more about HTML.

If you use a tool such as the ones described in Parts I, II, and V, you may be protected from the gory details of HTML. But you never know when you may end up back in "raw" HTML to add a feature or fix a problem. You can find lists of HTML tags on the Web at sources such as `w3.org`. And don't forget, *HTML 4 For Dummies,* 3rd Edition, by Ed Tittel and Stephen N. James (IDG Books Worldwide, Inc.) is an excellent source for more detail on HTML.

Chapter 8

Grappling with Graphics

In This Chapter
▶ Using graphics
▶ Making the most of graphics using HTML
▶ Creating advanced graphics

*L*ong before the Web came into existence, substantial and productive online activity took place using text. E-mail, Usenet news, and discussion forums in online services were the main vehicles for communication and for online publishing. Gopher was a text-only precursor to the Web. But just after 1990, when the first Mosaic browser gave users the capability to seamlessly combine graphics and text, the Web took off. One of the main factors contributing to the Web's success is the blending of graphics and text in Web pages. This blending makes the Web a dish that can be enjoyed by all who try it.

People enjoy color and pictures, so graphics, like seasoning, make the Web attractive to people. You can use graphics to convey a thematic "look and feel," to accent certain portions of a Web page, or even to contain the main content of a Web site. Some use of graphics is necessary for any site except the blandest and most utilitarian.

In this chapter, we look at the nitty-gritty of using graphics and explain how to create the most common graphic "special effects."

 To succeed in the somewhat complex task of adding graphics to your Web pages, you need to know some basics of HTML and of Web pages in general. Create your basic Web page by using the information in Chapters 3, 5, and 6 before trying to add any graphics but the simplest. And if you aren't yet familiar with HTML tags, review Chapter 7 before reading this chapter.

If you plan to use graphics and/or multimedia in your Web site, you should seriously consider investing some time and, for professional-level work, money in a Web authoring tool such as those we describe in Part V. These tools are designed specifically to take the worry out of tedious or complex tasks such as placing and sizing graphics, embedding multimedia, and so on.

Dealing with Graphics

The most difficult aspect of including graphics in your Web pages is resolving all the design issues that accompany the use of graphics. Creating effective graphics and placing them properly in relation to your text is not as easy as boiling water. This book doesn't cover all the complexities of graphic design. However, we can tell you the additional concerns that arise when you use graphics on the Web so that you can effectively apply your own graphics skills, or those of people who work with you, to your Web pages.

Speeding up slow pages

One of the Web's ongoing problems is *download speed* — the amount of time a Web page takes to appear on the user's screen. Download times are especially slow for graphics-rich pages, which, although more interesting to view, can be more frustrating because they appear more slowly. And the trade-off is not simple; lots of variables intervene. For example:

✔ **Access speeds.** Different users access the Web through connections that run at different speeds. And the same server can serve up a Web page at different speeds, depending upon how busy the server is. When you test your brand-new, graphics-rich page on your local machine, everything may run fast. But when you upload that same page to a server and access the page over a 28.8 Kbps (kilobits per second) modem at a time when many people are accessing the same server, the page loads more slowly.

✔ **Good and bad graphics.** If you plan to spend your users' time on downloading big graphics, invest some of your own time and money up-front to make sure that the graphics are as good as possible. People don't mind waiting for a good graphic nearly as much as they do for a bad one. A good graphic may be a clickable image with lots of different embedded options. A bad graphic may be a banner that says "HELLO!" in six Day-Glo colors.

✔ **Frustration levels.** The same users who enjoy watching your page appear in the morning while drinking a cup of coffee may be tempted to scream at their browser when they try to quickly check out your page just before heading home from work, especially if they had a bad hair day, a bad boss day, or even a bad browser day. The better the job you do with your graphics, the more your page pleases people.

What on earth can you do to address all these factors, especially when they combine to make your page slow and your users grumpy? Be clever! Limit the number of colors in your graphics to make the files smaller so that they download more quickly. Get expert advice — from someone you know or a book — or look at cool sites online to help you make the graphics you do use more interesting to look at. You can also lightly sprinkle your page with small graphics, rather than burden it with big ones. We explain these tricks and more in this chapter.

Table 8-1 shows the time necessary to download 100K (kilobytes) of data. A text-only page is usually just 2-3K, but pages with graphics are much larger. A complex, quarter-screen GIF image, for example, may be about 50K. Compare the total size of all the elements in the page you plan to the times shown in Table 8-1 to get an idea of how quickly your page loads for the most speed-deficient user, and then design with that person in mind.

Table 8-1	Slowest Download Times	
Access Speed	*Description*	*Time to Download 100K File*
14.4 Kbps	Low-end Internet modem	60 seconds
28.8 Kbps	Mid-range Internet modem	30 seconds
56 Kbps	Fast Internet modem	15 seconds
ISDN	Special phone line, modem	7 seconds
DSL	Special phone line, modem	2 seconds
Cable modem	Special cable hookup, modem	<1 second
Ethernet	Standard network	<1 second

Using GIF and JPEG graphics formats

Each graphics program saves files in its own *proprietary graphics format* — the specific arrangement of data that the program uses to save its files. For instance, the popular graphics program Photoshop saves files in the .psd format (for Photoshop Document); Paint Shop Pro, another popular graphics program, saves its files as .psp files. (You guess what "psp" stands for!) Web browsers typically don't know how to display files stored in these formats.

Fortunately, for the purposes of using graphics in HTML, you need to concern yourself with only two formats for graphics files, GIF and JPEG — and even then you don't really need to know a lot about the gory details of these formats to use them.

Standards for graphics and multimedia

Any up-to-date Web browser can display three types of data: text with HTML tags, GIF graphics, and JPEG graphics. (Some people pronounce GIF as "jiff," others as "giff" as in "gift." We prefer "giff" as in "gift.") A typical Web browser displays HTML-tagged text appropriately, although not all browsers understand all the same tags. A browser also displays GIF and JPEG graphics inline — that is, embedded within the Web page. A Web page with inline graphics looks like a page in a magazine, with text and images mixed seamlessly together. However, the graphics file is stored separately from the HTML-tagged text that makes up the underlying Web page. This makes the Web work better overall, but contributes to some of the problems — such as the difficulty of keeping all your Web files together for proper display — that we describe later in this chapter.

GIF, or *Graphics Interchange Format,* is the file format used by most people to exchange graphics. Originally made popular on CompuServe, GIF spread to other online services and then to the Internet and the Web. Any browser that supports graphics supports GIF.

GIF images may contain up to 256 colors, so GIF formatting works effectively for images that have anywhere from a few colors to a few hundred colors, which includes most simple images and most images created on a computer. If an image has more than 256 colors, it loses some color information when you convert the image to GIF. You have to look at the image before and after you convert it to GIF to see if the conversion noticeably affects the image's appearance.

JPEG, or *Joint Photographic Experts Group* format, compresses complex images such as photographs. Currently available browsers support JPEG in the same way they do GIF, displaying a JPEG image right in the Web page. JPEG is a necessity for images containing many colors, such as photographs and other natural-looking images. (What makes the image look natural is the way different shades of a color appear as light falls differently on various parts of an object.) These images retain their appearance well when compressed with JPEG.

Controversy abounds about whether using GIF or JPEG is better. (Of course, one of your authors can remember a desktop publishing meeting years ago that spent three hours on the merits of an older format called gray-scale TIFF!)

JPEG efficiently compresses complex images with many color variations. This capability makes JPEG the image format of choice for displaying photographs on your Web page. Figure 8-1 shows a Web page that uses a photo of Marc Andreesen, founder of Netscape, to illustrate graphically the difference in GIF and JPEG photo file sizes. The Web page in this figure shows one complete picture of Marc Andreesen and part of a subsequent picture. On the Web page itself, you find several versions of the same picture saved using different types of compression; go to the Web page to see the comparison. Here's the URL for this Web page:

```
cgi.netscape.com/assist/net_sites/impact_docs/e-jpeg.html
```

Use this GIF/JPEG test page to test the speed of your own Internet connection. The total size of the page with graphics is about 70K.

For images with lots of large blocks of solid color, GIF file sizes tend to be small. Thus, most people prefer GIFs for banners or images with large areas of solid color, such as bar graphs or icons. In other words, the simple drawings that most of us create work best with GIF. Dense artistic graphics and photos work better with JPEG.

GIF files also give you some Web page display options that you don't always get with JPEG files. You can make the colors in GIF images transparent to whatever is in the background of the image, and you can save GIF images in *interlaced* format. Images saved in this way, and then downloaded by a browser, first appear in a very low resolution and then in progressively clearer resolution, until the whole image appears. This feature makes GIF images preferable for quickly displaying a rough-looking graphic that improves with time and for creating fancy special effects. We explain interlaced GIF images in more detail, with pictures, later in this chapter.

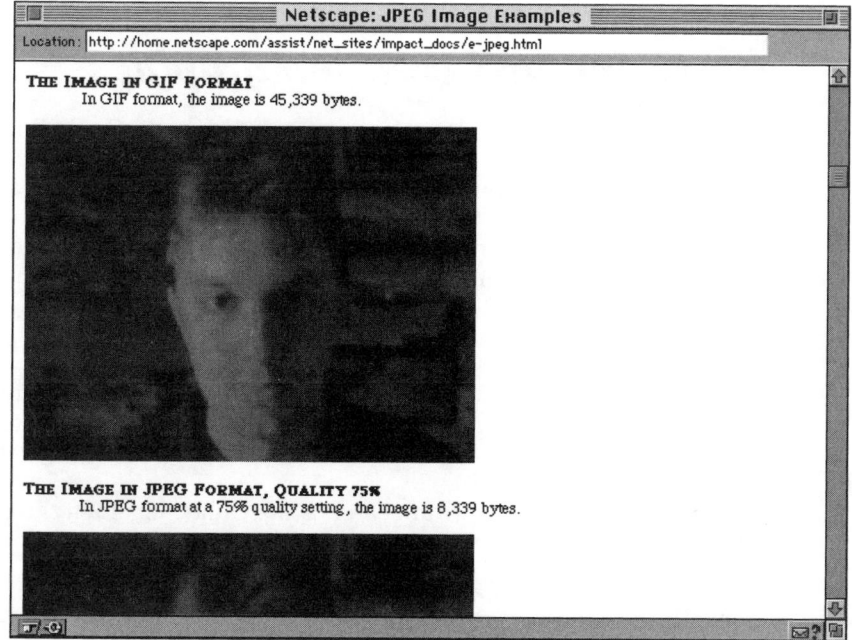

Figure 8-1: Marc Andreesen served up in a GIFfy.

Transparent images have a clear area surrounding the object of interest. For example, in a photo of a watch, you may not want any background color surrounding the watch, just the watch itself sitting directly on the Web page. To achieve this effect, you use a transparent GIF, an image with a clear border area. The background color of the overall Web page shows through the transparent area, and the object of interest appears to "float" over the background. We explain transparent GIF images in more detail, with pictures, along with interlaced images later in this chapter.

In some cases, the advantages of GIF outweigh the smaller file sizes that are more typical of JPEG. Use GIF if you need its special features; use JPEG the rest of the time. When you feel more confident in your design skills, you can play around with both formats and choose the one that's right for each image. Read on to find out how to obtain and create graphics for your Web pages and how to save your graphics in either format.

Newer versions of JPEG that support GIF-like features are now available. However, not as many graphics tools or as many browsers support these new JPEG features as support GIF. Stick with GIF for these features until your expertise grows.

Some colors don't work well on computers that are set up to display only 256 colors. You can use a set of 216 colors that always looks good on any computer or browser. To find a list of the acceptable, "browser-safe" colors, visit

www.bagism.com/colormaker

Obtaining and creating graphics

So you want to put various graphics on your Web page. Great. But how do you create them and get them in the right format (GIF or JPEG)? Fortunately, creating the graphics you want, or finding some to use, is pretty easy.

The easiest way to obtain graphics is to get access to a clip art collection. Computer stores sell many inexpensive collections of business and recreational graphics on CD-ROM. You can also access a number of royalty-free graphics and icon collections online.

You can spend endless hours looking for art online. In fact, just this search alone may make you glad to be creating a Web page. You may not get a lot done for a few hours while you're looking, but you see a lot of neat stuff!

One great site for starting your search is the Online Image Archive, at the following URL:

www.maths.tcd.ie/pub/images/images.html

For backgrounds, visit the following site:

```
www.webreference.com/authoring/graphics/backgrounds.html
```

And for photographs, try a site with preexisting stock photos, a site with all kinds of graphics, and another that converts your photographs into digital form:

```
www.weststock.com
www.eyewire.com
www.filmworks.com
```

Many more sites for images and image conversion exist. Start with the sites that we mention and expand your search until you find what you need.

The Image Search feature on the AltaVista search engine is one of the best ways to look for suitable graphics. Be careful, though: most of the graphics you find are not copyright-free, and you should only use images that are explicitly made freely available. Visit AltaVista at:

```
www.altavista.com
```

In addition to searching online, another way to get graphics is to whip out any paint program and draw the graphics that you want. For example, Windows includes a free graphics program, Windows Paint, that you can use for your initial graphics work. Even inexpensive paint programs today enable you to create some stunning graphics; you're limited mostly by your imagination and artistic ability (which for some of us can be quite limiting!).

For big-bucks commercial work and fine art, people regularly use high-end programs such as Adobe Photoshop and Adobe Illustrator. If you lack talent, you can always ask one of your artistically inclined friends to help you, or you can even recruit a starving art student.

More on graphics

The Graphics File Formats FAQ (Frequently Asked Questions file) can answer almost any conceivable question about graphics. For the latest information, visit the following Web site:

```
www.dcs.ed.ac.uk/~mxr/gfx/
    utils-hi.html
```

Links from this site lead to detailed technical information about GIF, JPEG, and other file formats.

For a detailed description of how to use images well, see the following site:

```
cgi.netscape.com/assist/net_
    sites/impact_docs/index.html
```

Another technique is to use a scanner. You may already have one at home, or have use of a scanner in your office. If not, head to your favorite copy shop and use its scanner. Scanning is a perfect way to put photographs online. Simply scan your graphic or photo, save it in GIF (for graphics) or JPEG (for photographs) format, and slap it on your Web site. Or work with a photo developer, such as a suitably equipped local developer or a bigger operation such as Seattle Filmworks (www.filmworks.com), that can develop your film right to diskette or PhotoCD.

The fourth way is to take photographs with a digital camera. Digital cameras come with cables to connect the camera to your PC to download the photographs onto your computer. They also come with software that enables you to edit the photos on your PC and save them, usually in JPEG format.

But how can you make sure that your graphics are in the proper format? That turns out to be easy, too. Many paint programs and most scanning software let you save a graphic in either GIF or JPEG formats. If your program doesn't save in these formats, it may be for one of two reasons:

- ✔ During installation, you may have chosen not to install converters for GIF and JPEG. Haul out your original install disks and see whether you can reinstall the program with the correct translators.

- ✔ If converters are not the problem, call your program's manufacturer or visit its Web site and see whether it has an update that enables the program to save to GIF and/or JPEG formats. If your software vendor can't sell you a program that handles GIF or JPEG, you can easily find one that does.

No matter what format your graphic came in originally, you can convert it to GIF or JPEG by using software that you can easily obtain from the Web. Mac users can run GIFConverter, and Windows users can run the excellent LView program to convert between multiple formats. Save your graphic as a GIF or JPEG file, and you are ready to incorporate the graphic into your Web page. See Appendix D for more information on how to obtain converters and other programs.

Save your image in the program's normal format as well as GIF or JPEG. When you save to GIF or JPEG, you can lose information from the image. If you reopen the GIF or JPEG image, edit the file, and then save it again, you lose even more information. So save your file in its original format to preserve the data in it for later editing, and save a separate copy in GIF or JPEG to use on the Web.

Avoiding three big mistakes

Don't make these three big mistakes relating to graphics on the Web:

- ✔ **No graphics.** Having no graphics on your Web pages means boring pages. Because you're reading this chapter, we assume that you're trying not to make this mistake.

- ✔ **Too many graphics.** Using too many large, slow-to-download graphics may be the biggest "newbie" Web author mistake. (A lot of old hands make this mistake as well.)

- ✔ **No text alternative.** Some users don't have graphical capability at all, and many others run around the Web with graphics turned off, only turning graphics capability on when absolutely necessary. You need to accommodate these users by creating your page in a way that supports text-only access as well as graphical access.

Try an experiment: Go into your browser, turn off the graphics display, and load your Web page. If you can't tell what is on the page or what links go where, then you need to redesign your page. (Then, just to blow off steam, try the same experiment on some other people's pages and send them a note if you have problems.)

The usual way to redesign your page for text-only access is to include a textual menu linking to the same places as your graphical menu. Some sites provide a whole parallel set of Web pages that are purely textual rather than graphical. Providing parallel, text-only pages lets the user choose whether to go for the attractive, bandwidth-sucking graphical pages or for the very fast text-only pages. However, because the percentage of users who choose text-only access continues to drop, providing a complete set of text-only pages may be overkill.

What about rights?

You can find a number of great graphics in books and magazines and on Web sites. Can you just scan or copy these graphics and use them in your own Web site? Should you?

Yes and no. Yes, you *can,* but no, you *shouldn't.* Publishers either own the images that they use or obtain a license for them. You can't legally use most images without either buying or licensing them.

For many images on the Web, simply sending a note to the publisher gets you a quick okay. But for other Web images and for most images in print, permissions may be very hard to get. Creating a new image that serves the same purpose is often easier than negotiating permissions. And then maybe you can make a little money licensing your own images out to other people!

The <IMG> tag is the HTML tag that causes an image to appear embedded in your Web page. (See Chapter 7 for more on HTML.) Here are the HTML tags for a page that displays the image MANUGRAPHIC.GIF by using the <IMG> tag, and then a text menu as an alternative:

```
<IMG SRC="manugraphic.gif" ALT="Menu Graphic"> [ <A
HREF="about.html">About</A> | <A
HREF="home.html">Home page</A> | <A
HREF="links.html">Fun Links</A> | <A
HREF="map.html">Site Map</A> | <A
HREF="search.html">Search Map</A> ]
```

Figure 8-2 shows an example of image links combined with text links, from the Apple Power Mac G4 page, one of the more interesting technology pages on the Web, at this URL:

```
www.apple.com/powermac
```

Figure 8-2:
Click the images, or the text, or anything you want.

Here are the most important rules for supporting text and graphical access:

- ✔ As you design and create your page, think about how your page will look with all graphic access turned off as well as on.
- ✔ Test your page with graphics turned off.
- ✔ Test your page in different browsers.
- ✔ Include ALT tags in all images so that explanatory text appears whenever a graphic is not displayed (see Chapter 7 and Appendix C for details about HTML tags).
- ✔ Provide text-only menus in addition to icon-based selections and image maps.
- ✔ If you want to make everyone very happy, consider creating a separate, text-only version of your site.

Using Graphics in HTML

It's good to know some HTML even if you are using a Web authoring program that allows you to drag and drop images, specify compression options, and so on. Why? Because you may need to make specific changes in options like the ALT text for the image or the directory that a file lives in. Your Web authoring program, or a text editing program, will allow you to go in and change the HTML directly, quickly, and accurately — if you know a little HTML.

With that in mind, here are three useful graphical effects for your Web pages:

- ✔ **Accents.** Small graphical images that serve as labels or highlights ("New," "Top Ten," and so on).
- ✔ **Icons.** Small graphical images that serve as links to another page. Click the icon, and you move to a different Web page.
- ✔ **Thumbnails.** Small graphical images that serve as previews of a larger image. Click the thumbnail to download the larger image.

Accents use the HTML tag <IMG> (short for "image") to link to a small graphic — an inline graphic that appears as part of the page, unless graphics display is turned off.

Icons and thumbnails combine the <IMG> tag, which makes the icon or thumbnail image appear, with the <A> (or anchor) tag. (Don't start singing "Anchors Aweigh" on this one — you need anchors here!) The anchor tag establishes a link to the Web page or larger graphic that appears when you click the inline graphic.

The steps in the following sections describe how to use the image tag, the anchor tag, and the ALT option separately and together. With these tags, you can combine graphics and navigation to create all kinds of effects.

Review the HTML tag definitions in Appendix C to find out about other options for these tags. You may also want to check out more advanced books, such as *HTML 4 For Dummies,* 2nd Edition, by Ed Tittel and Stephen N. James, and *Creating Cool HTML 4 Web Pages,* 3rd Edition, by Dave Taylor (both from IDG Books Worldwide, Inc.) for more details and how-to information on advanced HTML options.

Use the <IMG> tag for inline graphics

To use the <IMG> tag to link to an inline graphic that appears as part of your Web page, along with the ALT option to specify ALTernate text, follow these steps:

1. **Create or find a graphic that you want to use.**

   Inline graphics that are embedded in the page should be small for fast display — about the size of a business card or smaller. Use the sources we describe in the "Obtaining and creating graphics" section earlier in this chapter to find or create graphics.

2. **In your HTML file, add the <IMG> tag with the SRC, or "source," option to specify the image's pathname.**

   For a graphic that's in the same directory as the HTML file, use the <IMG> tag and SRC option like this:

   ```
   <IMG SRC="new.gif">
   ```

   For a graphic that's at a different Web site, use the <IMG> tag and SRC option like this:

   ```
   <IMG SRC="http://www.grafixsite.com/new.gif">
   ```

3. **Add the ALT option to specify text that appears if the graphic can't be viewed — for example, if the user is running a text-only browser or has graphics turned off.**

   ```
   <IMG SRC="http://www.grafixsite.com/new.gif" ALT="New!">
   ```

Don't depend on someone else's site being up at all times and always staying unchanged. If possible, copy the graphic that you need into your own site's directory and refer to it there.

Add an A-for-anchor to create a graphical link

As we note in the first part of the section on graphics and HTML, one of the best ways to jazz up a Web page "cheaply" — that is, without slowing down the page for everyone — is to use graphical elements as icons that link to outside information, such as a larger image or a different Web page. This technique is a great way to make your page appear graphically rich without burdening your users with long download times.

To add an anchor to create a graphical link, use the <IMG> tag within beginning and ending anchor tags. If you also embed a word or phrase between the beginning and ending anchor tags, you give the user a choice between clicking the image or the phrase. The following steps demonstrate how to create a graphical link:

1. **Within your HTML document, use the <IMG> tag to bring in the inline image that you want to use as a thumbnail image (a small image that represents a larger one) or an icon:**

   ```
   <IMG SRC="minibud.jpg">
   ```

2. **Add an anchor tag to specify the link.**

   To display a larger image when a user clicks the small image, specify an anchor with an HREF, or Hypertext REFerence, that points to an image file:

   ```
   <A HREF="maxibud.jpg"> <IMG SRC="minibud.jpg"> </A>
   ```

   Figure 8-3, from John Forrester, shows a thumbnail graphic and the larger image that appears when the user clicks the thumbnail. John Forrester's travelogue can be found at this URL:

   ```
   www.mediacity.com/~astral/china
   ```

   For a link to another page, specify an anchor with an HREF that points to an HTML document:

   ```
   <A HREF="bebakpg.htm"> <IMG SRC="bebak.jpg"> </A>
   ```

An HTML 3.2/Netscape option not only allows you to resize an image, but also speeds up page displays. Add the HEIGHT= and WIDTH= options within the <IMG> tag to specify, in pixels, the height and width of your image. Browsers use this information to fill in the rest of the page around the image first, allowing the user to scroll up and down in the page and read it before the graphic appears, and then to fill in the image itself.

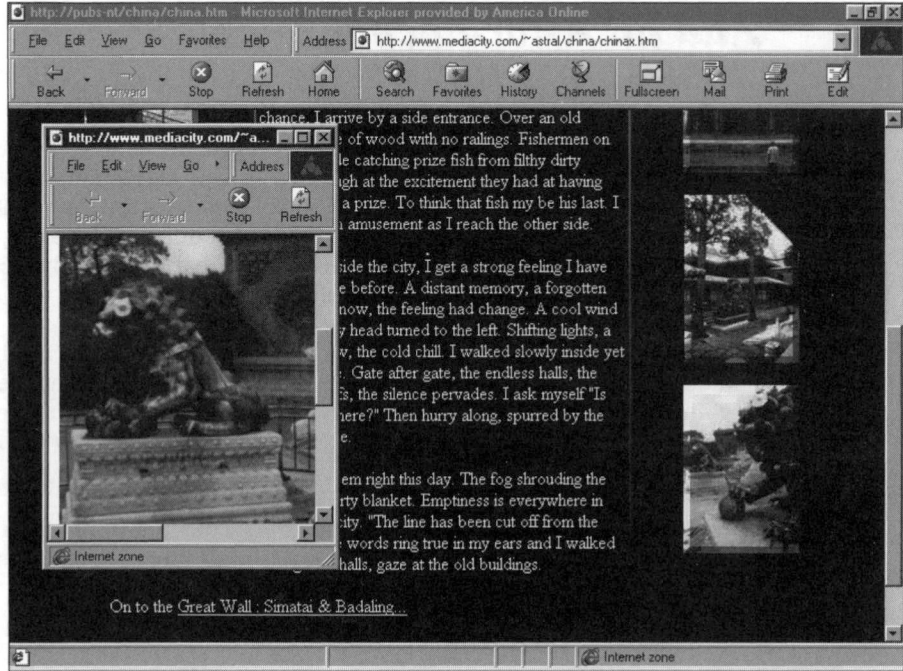

Figure 8-3:
Combining
mini- and
maxi-
graphics.

One of the most important ways for intermediate and advanced Web authors to organize their pages is by using invisible tables to position text and graphics relative to one another. Chapter 10 has a brief description of tables. This method is tricky! For example, a table-structured page that looks great at one monitor size can easily look terrible on a larger or smaller screen. Find some well-laid-out Web pages and view the Web pages' HTML source to see how other Web publishers use invisible tables. To see one expert's work, visit Creating Killer Web sites at

`www.killersites.com/1-design/jpeg.html`

Experimenting with Advanced GIFfery

GIFs are widespread on the Web, and download times are important; therefore, four advanced techniques exist for doing fancy things with GIFs:

✔ **Transparent GIFs.** Everyone needs to know this one. All GIFs are rectangular, but many of them seem to "float" over the background with no obvious border. Why? Because they're cool! (Beavis, shut up!) Actually, some GIFs are "transparent" — the images' backgrounds are invisible —

so they blend seamlessly into the browser's background. Figure 8-4 shows a nontransparent and a transparent GIF from the Web 66 Web site, which is part of a cooperative effort between the University of Minnesota College of Education and Development and Hillside Elementary in Minnesota, with support from 3M.

✔ **Interlaced GIFs.** Not everyone needs to know about this one, but we mention it (again!) because if you use complex graphics, interlaced GIFs are worth knowing about. An interlaced GIF depends on an HTML 3.2 feature that paints every fourth line of an image, then one-fourth of the remaining lines, and so on until the image is complete. The image seems to appear in low resolution and then gradually sharpen until complete.

✔ **Animated GIFs**. To the surprise of many, the basic GIF specification, GIF89a, turns out to support animation as well as static images. All you need to do is create a series of images that, when viewed in sequence, form an animation (like an old-fashioned flip-book). Then you package the images together as a single GIF, using readily available tools, and include the GIF file in your Web page. Voilà! Instant animation.

✔ **Clickable image maps.** Clickable image maps are very common in big-money sites and even in many smaller ones. A clickable image map is a graphic with different *hot spots* that, when clicked, take you to different Web pages or locations within a Web page. This kind of graphic is cool, but it's YABG (Yet Another Big Graphic), and you need design skill to make a good one.

Graphics can be a time sink

We spend a lot of time in this chapter discussing how much time the user can spend downloading graphics. But what about the demand that using graphics places on your time as a Web page developer?

Creating and editing graphics is fun! But creating even a simple business graphic, such as a bar graph, can consume hours of fooling around with fonts, colors, and image sizes. Getting your images Web-ready and testing them takes up even more time. Working with graphics can easily become the most time-consuming part of creating and updating your Web site.

What to do? Use small graphics and use graphics sparingly while you gain experience. After you have experience, or after you hire someone who does, you can develop and deploy those knockout graphics that distinguish the best Web sites.

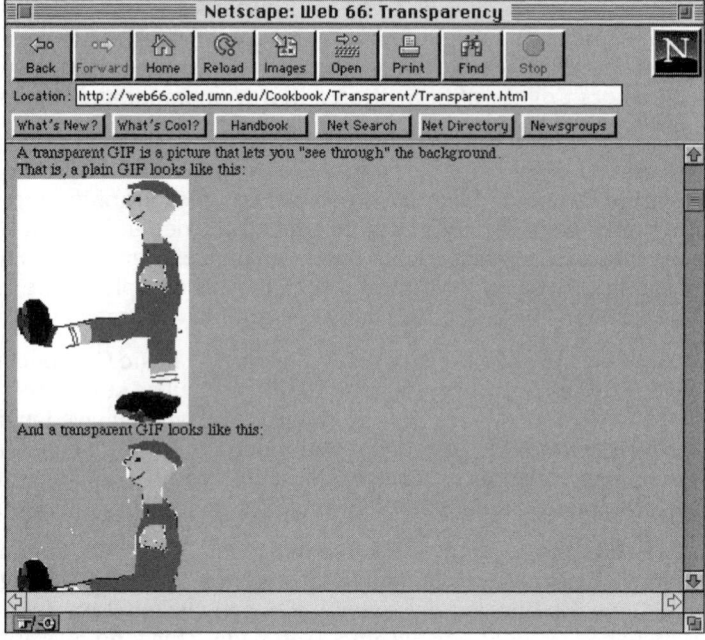

Figure 8-4:
Now you
see it (the
white
rectangle
around the
graphic),
now you
don't.

Here are the steps to create a transparent GIF:

1. **Choose a color in the image's background to make transparent.**

   Every pixel in your image that's of this color becomes transparent. Choose a color that's used only in the area around the image, not in the image itself, since every pixel of the selected color becomes transparent. You may need to edit the image's surrounding area — the area that you want to be transparent — so that it's a different color from the rest of the image. The usual choices for transparency are white or the light gray background color most browsers use.

   For details on the procedure for choosing an area to make transparent, see the Web 66 Web site, shown previously in Figure 8-4:

   ```
   web66.coled.umn.edu/Cookbook/Transparent/Transparent.html
   ```

2. **Use your graphics package or a tool to make the image transparent.**

   For the Macintosh, use Transparency, which you can find on the Web.

   For Windows, use Paint Shop Pro, which you can find on the CD-ROM that comes with this book.

   For any platform, you can use a Web-based package called TransWeb on the Massachusetts Institute of Technology (MIT) site. This package reads the image, converts it, and displays the result. You can then right-click on the image to save it to disk.

To use TransWeb, you have to move your image to a Web server, as we describe in Chapter 11. (You can also do this as part of the process of creating a simple GeoCities Web page, as described in Chapter 3.) Then go to the TransWeb Web page at this URL and follow the instructions:

```
www.mit.edu/tweb/map.html
```

3. **Add the image to your page.**

   Add the image to your page, as we describe earlier in this chapter.

4. **Test to be sure that the image remains transparent with several different backgrounds. Bring up the image in your browser and then change the browser's default background color.**

Animated GIFs are also supported online. You can find out how to use them and start putting them in your Web pages by using info out on the Web. To read the true and fascinating story of how animated GIFs were invented, and to link to many supporting examples and resources, go to these two Web sites:

```
www.webreview.com/96/02/09/tech/edge
builder.cnet.com/Graphics/Webanim/
```

To create a clickable image map, you must first create the graphic. (See the Apple and SGI sites online for examples of attractive, clickable image maps.) Then you have to create a special file that maps regions of the image to specific URLs. A program that you can download from the Web, Mapedit (see Appendix D), maps image regions for either Macintosh or Windows. Just load the image, click and drag over it to define clickable regions, and then enter the URL you want to link to.

The complication arises during the final part of this process. The original form of image maps, called *server-side image maps,* require that the map file be in a special place where the server can find it. Unfortunately, to use this kind of image map, you may need to talk to the server administrator, because no universal standard exists about where this file should be.

Netscape 2.0 and higher, Microsoft Internet Explorer, and all other up-to-date browsers support what are known as *client-side image maps* that don't require server involvement in any processing when the user clicks an image. Browsers are now smart enough to map the image, click to a URL, and fetch the URL directly without going through the server. See the Netscape 2.0 documentation or the Netscape site for more information.

You can find a cool tool on the Web called GIFwizard that can shrink the size of GIF graphics and animations by up to 90 percent. Try it! Go to

```
www.gifwizard.com
```

Chapter 9

Making It Multimedia and More

• •

• •

*T*he Web has the potential to be the ultimate multimedia network. There are just two little problems — the solutions to which will take ten years or more to be realized.

The first problem is bandwidth. The Web seriously needs more bandwidth for multimedia capabilities to grow. It isn't just the thin 56K connection to a typical home PC that's a problem. Corporate networks and the entire global Internet structure are not nearly ready yet for full-scale multimedia.

The second problem is creative capability. It takes scores of people to put on a typical TV show, or run a radio station day and night, from camera people to editors to on-air talent. When you create your own multimedia, you're taking on — or arranging for someone else to perform — many of those jobs yourself.

The opportunity, though, is tremendous. Multimedia — from the simplest animation or sound clip to a full-screen, surround-sound movie — can be much more engaging than static text and graphics. And solutions that allow you to add low-bandwidth multimedia to your Web page are becoming more and more readily available.

So expect to see and hear more and more multimedia on the Web — and start including it, where appropriate, in your own Web pages right away.

How TV beats PC

As an entertainment transmission system, TV beats the PC hands down. The "user experience" of watching *Why Animals Attack Scary Police Videos* far surpasses — from a technical point of view, anyway — the best of Web multimedia.

Why? Just do the math. A typical text-only Web page takes about 2KB (kilobytes, or thousands of bytes) of storage space. Let's say we're willing to make the user wait one second to see a page. So the minimum bandwidth needed for effectively transmitting text Web pages through the Internet — from the server, across the Internet backbone, and all the way down to your PC — is 2KB in a second, which is 16 Kbps (kilobits per second; 8 bits are in a byte). A 56K modem is about three times faster than this, so we're in good shape for text-only Web pages.

Now add graphics. Major Web sites try to keep their total "page weight" under 50KB for fast viewing. 50KB (kilobytes) equals 400Kb (kilobits). So to experience good response times for typical Web pages, we need a 400K connection — about as fast as a DSL connection or a well-managed corporate network. So we're pushing the limits of the technology available to a typical user if we want to see today's typical Web pages at a reasonable speed.

Now let's look at multimedia. A typical TV displays 30 frames per second at roughly 560 x 420-pixel resolution, or over 200,000 pixels. That's 6 megabytes, or 48 Megabits, per second. (Remember, 8 bits in a byte.) Not even a cable modem, on a good day and with none of your neighbors on with you to share the cable line to your home, can hope to deliver this. And that's just the picture — no sound! Displaying multimedia as good as an uncompressed TV broadcast is really beyond the capability of the worldwide Internet or of the connections to your home.

To work around these problems, we need all sorts of tricks. Compression makes sound files and really, really small video clips ready for Internet downloading and use. Streaming technology, running on a server, can dole out multimedia packets at a rate that the user's system can handle. And creative people work hard behind the scenes to try to extract acceptable quality from the highly compressed multimedia files they have to work with.

Do-it-yourself Web authors, though, are generally the kind of people who enjoy a challenge. Multimedia on the Web is in the same early stages that the Web itself was a few years ago, when we wrote the first edition of this book — there are technical difficulties, and both authoring and using multimedia is difficult, but interest and use are exploding. Use the information in this chapter to get started now while it's still early.

Making It Multimedia and Beyond

Getting your page right by using the basic Web ingredients of text and graphics is a real challenge but a lot of fun. Get the Web publishing basics down before you push forward into the realm of multimedia. However, if you're adventurous, you can use the information that follows to add exciting multimedia flavorings to your Web pages.

Sound and video

Five years ago — almost a person's lifespan in Web time — people down-loaded multimedia files from the Web, saved them to disk, then started up a special player to view the files. Now, people embed multimedia files in Web pages, and users are able to view them "in place," with very little waiting, by using multimedia players such as QuickTime and RealPlayer.

Using multimedia causes some of the same problems as using graphics files, only more so. Many users don't have the right players for viewing multimedia and don't know how to get the players and set them up when needed.

Performance is also a problem. Waiting several minutes to download a small-sized, brief video clip is frustrating. Many Web sound files don't sound good. And multimedia files can affect the overall performance of the Internet itself. A few hundred people listening to live audio at once may be enough to com-pletely tie up an Internet service provider, limiting access by others as well as causing poor performance for the listeners.

However, when you get multimedia working right, it spices up a Web site like nothing else. Just look at the tremendous popularity of the MP3 format for transmitting music over the Web. Operating at nearly the level of quality of FM radio, MP3 files have spawned a whole culture of music trading and shar-ing on the Net. (Unfortunately, at this point much of the sharing is of MP3 files of songs that have copyright protection and therefore shouldn't be pub-lished for free on the Net.)

The secret to MP3 is the widespread use of compression technology that makes relatively small files with quality near what people are used to (FM radio). It will take a new generation of compression technology to create movies anywhere near as good as TV. At that point, expect an explosion of movies and TV shows on the Net that will rival the MP3 phenomenon in importance. The most important players for Web multimedia are

- ✔ **RealPlayer.** RealPlayer is a plug-in for real-time playback of audio and video files that works pretty darn well. The user of a RealAudio-enhanced Web site typically clicks a link to get an audio or a video clip. A reasonably brief pause ensues, while an initial part of the file down-loads, and then sound starts playing. The sound is *streamed* in real time, meaning that no big file is stored on the user's hard disk. (Streaming also means that a faster Internet connection produces better sound quality.)

- ✔ **RealJukebox.** RealJukebox is a specialized, audio-only player from Real Networks player for MP3 and other audio file types such as RealAudio and WAVE files. You can also use it to manage files to use in portable MP3 players such as Diamond Multimedia's Rio device. Other programs such as WinAmp are also very popular for playing back MP3 files.

✔ **QuickTime.** QuickTime is Apple's multimedia technology that has become the industry standard for video editing and playback on computers. QuickTime VR is an offshoot of QuickTime that creates high-resolution virtual reality panoramas and objects. The QuickTime player is bundled with Netscape Navigator and supports all kinds of multimedia formats including animation, sound, QuickTime VR, and QuickTime video clips. A large percentage of the movie files on the Web are QuickTime files. QuickTime is easy to use in your Web page, and no licensing or server fees are involved. Newer versions of QuickTime support streaming, so expect to see more streamed QuickTime content soon.

✔ **ShockWave/Flash.** The ShockWave plug-in allows presentations and experiences created in Macromedia Director to be played back over the Web. Figuring out Director is no mean feat, but ShockWave is a powerful tool for delivering multimedia experiences over the Web. Flash is a simple format for delivering animations in your Web page and is rapidly becoming popular. If you are a Director user, or want to become one, or if you're interested in Flash, run, don't walk, to the Macromedia Web site to get more info about ShockWave and Flash.

To find out more about how to use multimedia on the Web, start by checking out the following URLs:

```
www.apple.com/quicktime
www.realaudio.com
www.macromedia.com
```

QuickTime video files

Many different multimedia formats exist, each with its own strengths and weaknesses. But no other multimedia format is as widely accepted, capable, or supported by so many different multimedia and Web page creation tools as QuickTime. Adding multimedia to your Web page is easy with QuickTime, and using QuickTime-based multimedia is likely to be easy for your users as well. Here are the necessary elements for a successful QuickTime Web publishing experience:

✔ **Multimedia content.** You need a QuickTime multimedia file to put in your page. Dozens of multimedia tools create QuickTime multimedia; for starters, use one someone else has created.

✔ **HTML commands.** A few Web tools, notably PageMill, support embedding of QuickTime content directly. But unless you have such a tool, you need to write HTML commands to embed QuickTime content. Luckily, the commands are simple; an example follows shortly.

✓ **QuickTime and the QuickTime plug-in.** You and your users need the latest version of QuickTime and the QuickTime player. (New versions of QuickTime include QuickTime VR support as well, adding virtual reality to what you can do with QuickTime.) Many of your users may have the latest version of QuickTime, but many may not; to help your users get updated, provide a link to the QuickTime Web page at

```
www.apple.com/quicktime
```

QuickTime is big! Users who don't already have QuickTime on their machines have to download it from the Web, and several megabytes is a lot to ask your users to download. However, doing so gives them a lot of capability. Just be aware that you may get some questions and complaints about the download hassle.

You don't have to pay fees or sign special licenses before using QuickTime, as you do with competing technologies. From a business point of view, using QuickTime is as easy as putting a GIF or JPEG image in your Web page. Figure 9-1 shows an example of QuickTime content in a Web page. The URL for this page is

```
www.apple.com/trailers/newline/lord_of-the-rings/
               fullscreen_preview.htmlhtml
```

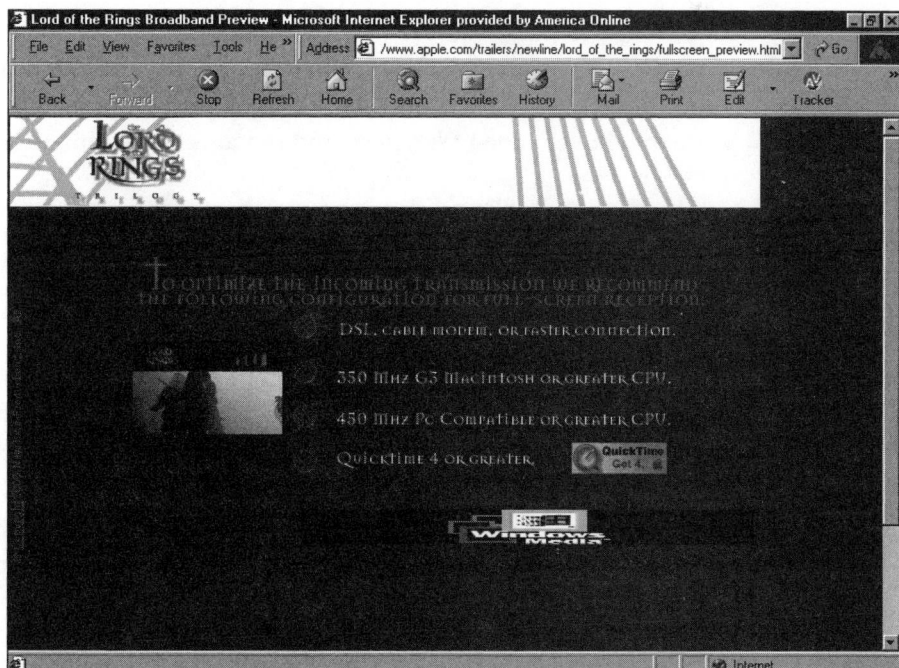

Figure 9-1: A little QuickTime can have a lot of impact.

For more information, visit the QuickTime VR home page and the Berkeley Macintosh User's group QuickTime authoring site at the following Web URLs:

```
www.apple.com/quicktime
www.bmug.org/quicktime
```

Here are the steps to add a QuickTime movie to your Web page:

1. **Install QuickTime and the QuickTime plug-in on your own machine.**

   To download these files, go to the QuickTime software page at

   ```
   www.apple.com/quicktime
   ```

2. **Get a QuickTime movie — animation, sound, video, or VR.**

3. **Embed the movie in your Web page.**

   Use the EMBED HTML command. In its basic form, for a file in the same folder as the Web page, it's very simple:

   ```
   <EMBED SRC="file.mov">
   ```

   You have additional options when you use the EMBED command with the QuickTime plug-in; for details, see the QuickTime Web page. But try the simple command shown above first to make sure that you don't accidentally introduce a problem when you try to add options.

4. **Test it on your own machine.**

   Test the Web page by opening it in Netscape Navigator and seeing if the movie acts properly. Then test in Internet Explorer.

5. **Upload the changed Web page and the multimedia file to the Web and test.**

   Congratulations — you're a multimedia Web publisher!

MP3 Audio Files

MP3 audio files bring about many questions. The quality of the audio is just okay, and many of the files are illegal copies. They are, however, extremely popular, and a whole industry of sites — even new playback devices — has sprung up around MP3.

Creating MP3 files is a lot of work, and you need to search the Web for the right tools and resources to do it. But once you have an MP3 file — and even fully legal ones are easy to find — it's easy to put one on your Web page. Just follow these instructions:

1. **Get an MP3 file.**

   Just search the Web using any search engine, it won't take long.

2. **Link to the file from your Web page.**

   Use the A (for anchor) HTML command. In its basic form, for a file on another Web server, it's as simple as for any Web page:

   ```
   <A
   HREF="www.christcore.com/audio/feeltheburn.mp3"
   >A Christian MP3 file</A>.
   ```

   The file given is just one example, many thousands more are out on the Web.

3. **Test it on your own machine.**

   Test the MP3 file by opening it from the Web page and playing it back.

Page description languages

HTML is not a page description language — that is, a specification for exactly how your text and graphics should look when they're displayed or printed. But Adobe Acrobat *is* a page description language, and so are Envoy from Novell, Inc., and the MiniViewer that's part of Common Ground from Hummingbird Communications, Ltd. (**Note:** Even though you may overhear at the supermarket: "Give me a pound of premium Java and half a pound of that common ground," Common Ground is not a cheap version of Java, the programming language we describe later in this chapter.) Adobe Acrobat is the only page description language that has gained widespread acceptance on the Web.

So if you want to put up a formatted page that keeps its look, feel, fonts, and more, use Acrobat. You can put the page up on the Web so that it looks exactly like a printed version. The problem: Users have to download a special viewer for your information, which they're unlikely to bother with unless you have something they really, really want to see. (And expect a few technical support calls from users who can't figure out what to do.) *The New York Times* is the biggest "name" to adopt Acrobat so far, and many organizations use PDF files internally.

To bypass this viewing problem, Acrobat is now supported by a plug-in for Microsoft Internet Explorer and Netscape Navigator. For more information and for a look at *The New York Times* daily online edition that uses Acrobat, see the following URLs:

```
www.adobe.com/prodindex/acrobat
nytimesfax.com/sample/sample.pdf
```

Programming Your Pages

You can do an awful lot on the Web with only text and graphics, and adding multimedia extends your powers even further. However, to really "do business on the Web" and support interactivity, you need to consider doing some programming.

Web programming is a complicated topic that is beyond the scope of this book. However, after you get your text and graphics right and then spice up your pages with some multimedia, you may be able to extend your site further by doing some Web programming. JavaScript, for example, is a scripting language that gives you increased control over your Web pages without true programming. To go further requires more books, more training, and more work. Want to read *JavaScript For Dummies,* 2nd Edition, by Emily A. Vander Veer (IDG Books Worldwide, Inc.), anyone? Check out Web sites that you like to see how they achieve certain effects, and then search your bookstore and the Web to see the different techniques that are available.

For a long time, a big advantage of living in certain areas was the improved access some places have to large and specialty bookstores. For example, both authors of this book live in Silicon Valley, home of the excellent Computer Literacy bookstores, which used to give the authors a leg up over people living elsewhere. Now, through the Web, most people can find whatever books they need. You can start by looking at the following URLs:

```
www.amazon.com
www.barnesandnoble.com
www.fatbrain.com
```

Figure 9-2 shows the home page for Fatbrain, the Web representation of the Computer Literacy chain of bookstores.

Forms and CGIs

Forms are text boxes and pull-down menus that allow users to enter information that you request. Forms are actually pretty easy to create. As part of HTML 2.0, they've been around for years, and most HTML books describe them. Getting data from users via forms is pretty easy. What's more complicated is figuring out what to do with the information after you have it.

Processing the data from a form requires a CGI script and an application. A *CGI script,* sometimes simply called "a CGI," is a Common Gateway Interface script — a program that sends the data to an application that you create. The CGI script runs on the server that hosts your Web page. CGI scripts are different on NT, UNIX, and the Macintosh. Many CGI scripts are written in C language or PERL, a cross-platform scripting language.

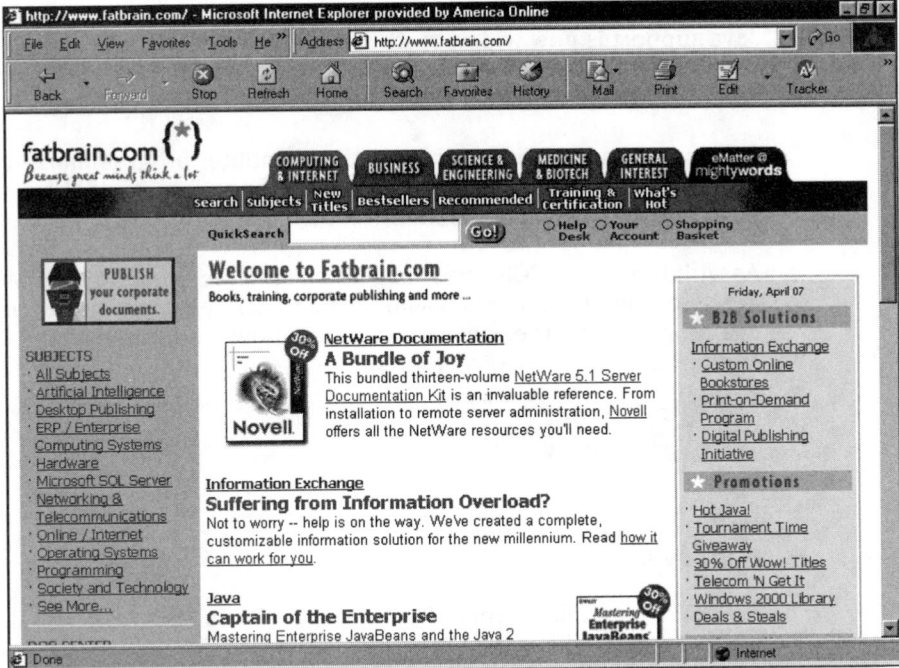

Figure 9-2:
Fatbrain
exists
"because
great minds
think a lot."

To run a CGI script, you need the permission of the *sysop* (system operator) responsible for the server that hosts your Web page. Sysops are paid to protect their systems from harm, so getting your sysop to run an unknown program on his or her precious server may take some doing. Many hosts have prepackaged forms or CGI packages that handle common tasks such as counting visitors, allowing users to register, and more. Finding and using one of these prewritten packages is a good intermediate step toward creating your own CGI scripts and applications.

For more information about CGI scripting, see this Web site:

```
www.comvista.com/lessons/CGI.html
```

Java

Java is the Sun Microsystems programming language that makes the creation of interactive Internet applications easier and more flexible. Java promises much more spectacular Web pages, incorporating animation, smart updating, and collaboration applications. Downloading Java programs, called *applets,* to your computer allows for fast execution and interactivity but also raises concerns about security. Java is implementing different models that allow robust interactivity while protecting against virus-type activity. Although Java support is now widespread, some users turn off Java support in their browsers to avoid problems, so not all people with the latest browsers are ready to run Java applications.

Java is a variant of the overly complex computer programming language C++ and so requires considerable experience and skill to use. (At least, that's what our well-paid programmer friends tell us.)

As with forms and CGIs, most beginning and intermediate Web page creators are better off plugging in Java applets written by others than doing the requisite programming themselves. For more about Java, see the Sun Java Web site and the Gamelan Java directory site:

```
java.sun.com
www.gamelan.com
```

ActiveX

ActiveX is technology from Microsoft that allows Microsoft Visual Basic programs to work with the Web. The good news is that ActiveX enables you to do some pretty amazing things. The bad news is that it has had serious security problems, doesn't work well on the Macintosh, and doesn't work at all on 16-bit Windows (Windows 3.1 and before) or on UNIX. However, if you are willing to do Windows-only Web work and want more information on ActiveX, you can start at Microsoft's Distributed interNet Applications Architecture site:

```
www.microsoft.com/dna/default.asp
```

Also, see Appendix D and the *resource.htm* file on the CD-ROM that comes with this book for more information and pointers.

Going beyond HTML

While the simplicity and flexibility of HTML has been key to the success of the Web, HTML does, of course, have limitations. Two major languages, Dynamic HTML and XML (eXtensible Markup Language), address many of the limitations.

Although you should be aware of upcoming technologies, you're better off waiting to implement them in your own Web pages until most users have browsers that support the new capabilities. In the case of Dynamic HTML and XML, even an optimist would agree that it will be a couple of years before most users are equipped with browsers that support either of them.

HTML gets Dynamic

Dynamic HTML is an extension of HTML that allows multiple layers of information to be sent to the user during a server connection. The user only sees part of the information at first. Additional information can be unveiled as time passes or as the user undertakes different actions, all without having to reconnect to the server.

At this writing, Netscape and Microsoft offer somewhat different implementations of Dynamic HTML. Netscape uses its own LAYER tag to allow some layering to be defined fairly simply. Both browsers support Style Sheets, a more complex and more capable way of supporting Dynamic HTML being defined through the official Web standards process. But Microsoft, which always followed Netscape's lead on new tags in the past, refuses to support the LAYER tag.

Only the 4.0 and later versions of Netscape Navigator and Microsoft Internet Explorer support any of these Dynamic HTML features, which leaves out users of other browsers. If Netscape and Microsoft can agree, and if the majority of users upgrade their browsers to gain access to Dynamic HTML extensions, many Web authors may take the time and trouble to support these new features in their Web pages.

XML x-es out HTML

XML, or *eXtensible Markup Language,* is a superset of HTML, and a subset of the overall *SGML (Standard Generalized Markup Language)* standard upon which HTML is based. XML allows complex data structures to be built into a Web page. With XML, authors can create database applications and deliver them across the Web. Our guess is that XML will be deployed on intranets first because companies will want to develop such applications for internal use and will be able to ensure that all Web authors and users in the company use the same version of XML. If you're responsible for intranet-related activity, keep an eye on this one.

The Web enters the twenty-first century

Because of its flexible nature, the Web has the theoretical capability to support almost anything that can be done or imagined on a computer. As the connection speed accessible to the average user improves, as more technology is used in advanced Web pages, and as users move up to more capable browsers, more and more will be possible. The trick is not to chase down any of the new pathways before they settle into widely used standards. Develop your skills in the key areas that make the Web useful and productive today. Using the capabilities of today's mainstream Web is the best way to prepare yourself to take advantage of the advanced Web that will be here the day after tomorrow.

Part IV
Sites for Sore Eyes

In this part . . .

Now that you know quite a bit about Web publishing, you're ready to make your Web page into a Web site — even a business site that can help you market and make money online. Then you need to know how to publish your Web site to a "real" Web server that you set up or pay a fee for. This part helps you get up to speed at this higher level.

Chapter 10

From Web Page to Web Site

In This Chapter

▶ Setting goals for your site

▶ Adding Web pages to your site

▶ Improving your pages

▶ Setting up a basic business site

*I*f after following some of the instructions in previous chapters, you are now a published author of a page on the World Wide Web, congratulations! If not, go back and use the instructions in Chapter 3, Chapter 5, or Chapter 6 to put up a Web page on GeoCities, America Online, or CompuServe. Creating a Web page is really easy and makes the rest of this book "real" to you in a way that nothing else can.

After you complete a basic Web page, the next steps are to improve the original home page and to build it into an interesting, multipage site. This chapter describes just how to do that. We show you how to do things by using HTML directly, which all the easy-to-use Web publishing tools and services we describe in earlier chapters allow you to do on your Web pages.

However, at this point you also have the option of using one of the Web publishing tools we describe in Part V, or something similar. A Web publishing tool either handles the management of the HTML tags for you or hides them completely, which makes carrying out the steps in this chapter that much easier. If you use HTML directly, as this chapter describes, you find out more about how Web pages work and gain more control. If you switch to a tool, your work probably becomes easier, but you should read this chapter anyway as background. Whether you work directly in HTML or use a Web publishing tool, this chapter helps you move up to the next stage of Web publishing.

Getting a Target in Your Site

As you get beyond your single Web page into a multipage Web site — which may include interactivity, graphics, and multimedia — the amount of time you spend on your site increases dramatically. To get the most value out of your time and create the best site you can with the resources you have available, you should set some goals for your site. Personal sites, topical sites, business sites, and entertainment sites each have different purposes and needs, so you want to set different kinds of goals for each. See Chapter 2 for more information on these four types of sites and the different considerations for each.

Personal sites

For a personal site, your overall goal is likely to be to have fun, both in creating Web pages and in letting the world see them. However, creating Web pages, linking them together, adding graphics and multimedia, and so on can become very time-consuming. The more you work on your Web pages and the more feedback you get, the more you want to create. Yet no matter how much you like working on your personal Web presence, at some point, the rest of your life — job, spouse, kids, bills — is likely to intrude. So setting some simple goals is a good idea.

One way to set your goals is inner-directed. What do you want from your site:

✔ To show the world something about your life and interests?

✔ To make yourself more employable?

✔ To promote some interest or group?

First, figure out what your goal is for the next stage of construction of your Web site, based on what you want from your site. Then, depending on your goal, you can decide how much time and energy to put into your Web site, how many pages to create for your site initially, and whether you then want to put the site in maintenance mode or just keep developing it. Keep the answers to these questions in mind as you work on your site.

The other way to set your goals is outer-directed: Find sites that are already out on the Web that have the kind of content and links that you want in your site. Finding existing Web sites that have one or more similarities to what you want to accomplish is both fun and educational. You can see how other people handle (or avoid) the concerns that you face in making your site work well. And you can save dozens of hours by avoiding approaches that don't work and by borrowing ideas from the best of what does work.

Personal sites that just show the world something about your life and interests, without going too far into any one special topic, become part of what makes the World Wide Web so full of surprises. The Web page creation services that we mention in earlier chapters — GeoCities, America Online, CompuServe, and others — are home to thousands of such pages. Find several sites that resemble what you want your site to look like.

Topical sites

Many personal sites, including some of the best ones, aren't just personal. They include topical interests, business interests, or both. Kevin Werbach's home page is a good example. It links to *The Bare Bones Guide to HTML* (see Appendix C), for which Kevin is justly famous, and also to other pages with information about himself and his interests. Figure 10-1 shows the home page for Kevin's personal site, illustrating his wide range of interests while still highlighting *The Bare Bones Guide to HTML.* You can find it at

```
www.werbach.com/home.html
```

Topical sites often grow out of personal sites, as one of a person's many interests crowds out the others and dominates the personal site. Eventually, the topical info may even become its own, separate site. Or the personal side of the site may dwindle or disappear, leaving a purely topical site behind. Other sites continue as interesting mixes of personal and topical.

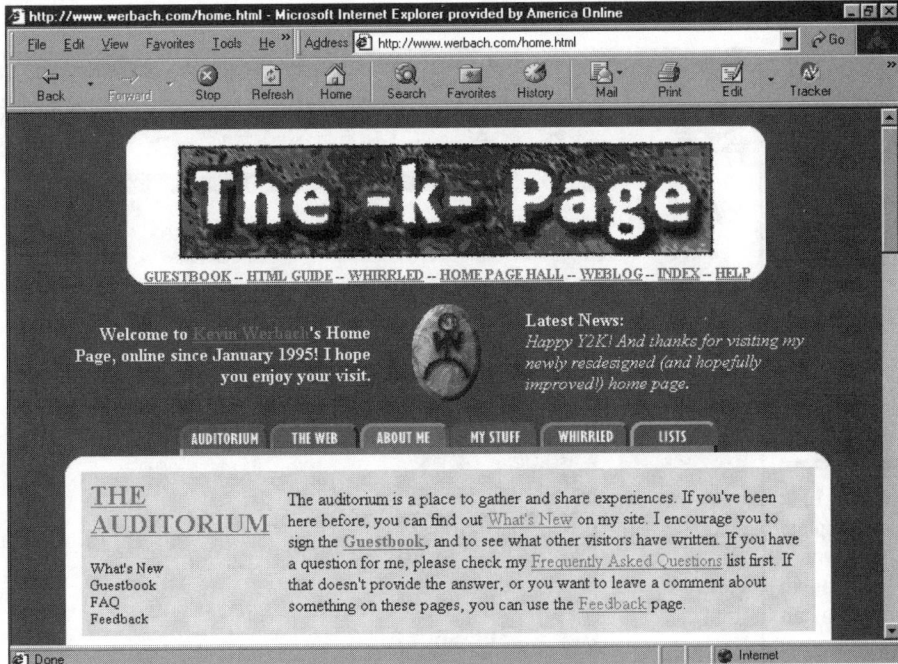

Figure 10-1: A personal page with a link (HTML Guide) to topical info.

Topical sites, just like personal sites, need goals. If one topical part of your site grows, or if you know that you want to create a topical site, consider splitting off the topical part from your personal info. Do people who want to know the latest in underwater botany really care about your kids' braces coming off? And vice versa, of course. Then follow the same steps as for a personal site: Decide how much time and energy you can put in; set achievable intermediate goals and then implement them; and continuously look for examples of what works and doesn't work among sites similar to yours.

Eventually, a topical site may grow in content and complexity to become something resembling a business site in terms of organizational concerns caused by the sheer number of pages and the range of subtopics involved. If you find yourself adding things to your site based on other people's requests, rather than strictly your own interests, you're probably well on the road to a business-type site. In this case, you need to look at the concerns for business sites and keep those concerns, as well as purely topical concerns, in mind as you develop your site. You might even think about selling advertising or products on your site to bring in some money!

One cool topical site is shown in Figure 10-2, an Internet culture magazine with contributions from people on the Web. As you can see, Internet sites are always subject to change. You can find many more interesting topical sites as you surf the Web. This topical page's address is

```
www.infoculture.cbc.ca
```

Figure 10-2:
A topical site where Canadian culture can grow on you.

Using Web page creation tools

One of the biggest questions you face in creating Web pages is whether to work directly in HTML or use a Web page creation tool such as those we describe in this book. The answer may surprise you.

If you're relatively inexperienced and working on a single Web page or a small set of pages, consider working directly in HTML. Why? Because HTML is easy to figure out and widely understood. (If you use a tool, you have to select, buy, and learn the tool, which may take longer than figuring out a little bit of HTML.) You can always see the HTML underlying any Web page and use it as a model for creating similar effects yourself. And you discover a lot about the Web as you work. These reasons are why this book includes a moderate amount of HTML.

If you already understand the basics of HTML and are responsible for building or maintaining more than a couple of Web pages, consider getting a Web page creation tool to help. Why?

Because doing a lot of work in HTML is boring and repetitive, which makes mistakes more likely. If you do a moderate amount of Web page creation work, a tool saves you time and energy, easily paying off the up-front costs of buying and figuring out the tool. These reasons are why this book includes info on several easy-to-use, inexpensive Web page creation tools.

If you're creating advanced Web pages or building or maintaining a lot of pages, use HTML and Web page creation tools — as many as you need. Why? HTML gives you ultimate flexibility and control. Web page creation tools give you speed and ease of use, and they enable you to hand off less demanding tasks to others who can accomplish the tasks by using a tool. Combining tools and direct work in HTML can help you create a large, high-tech, interactive Web site — which is the topic of other, more advanced books.

 To view the HTML code behind any Web page, use the View⇨Page Source command in Netscape Navigator, or similar commands in other browsers. Alternatively, use your browser's Save command and save the Web page as "source" into a file on your hard disk. Then open the file in any word processing program or text editor to view the HTML source code.

Business sites

Business sites are becoming the main reason most people surf the Web. And big money is involved: Web commerce is now a multibillion-dollar industry and is more than doubling each year. (Dell Computer alone did several billion dollars' worth of business on the Web in 1999.) It's getting to where any business worth its salt must have some kind of Web presence in order to remain competitive.

The best way to get started on a business site is to shoot for exactly that: a Web presence. You can add and alter all kinds of things later, time and money permitting, but people expect a few basic Web-related things of most businesses today:

✔ A URL that reflects the name of the business

✔ A home page

✔ Additional pages with basic info about the business itself

✔ Additional pages with basic info about products and services

A business site with just this info is called a *Web presence* site. Getting a Web presence site up and running enables you to say, without embarrassment, that your business is on the Web. Your Web presence reduces nuisance phone calls and mail to your business by making some basic information easy for people with Web access to find. Your Web presence also increases useful phone calls and mail to your business by letting potential customers know how to reach you. A Web presence site doesn't cost too much to create or maintain. And yet, despite its low cost and modest goals, it sets the stage for future growth in your business's use of the Web and the Internet.

You can have a lot of different goals for a business site, but this chapter and the information in the rest of this book are suitable for creating a basic Web presence site, with goals such as those in the preceding paragraph. If you want to go further — by adding more information, more complex navigation, and interactive features such as online ordering — you need more advanced information and probably some consulting help as well. (Unless your business goal is to become a Web consultant yourself!) Even if you have bigger goals that require more information than what's in this book, or more time and expertise than you can invest yourself, consider creating a basic personal or business site yourself first; your ability to get where you're going efficiently increases immeasurably if you have a little hands-on experience.

Far more than for personal or topical sites, you should create a business site with an eye on existing sites that attempt to meet similar goals. Figure 10-3 shows a Web presence site with a pointer to needed information about an upcoming trade show right on the home page. The eMotion Web site is at

`www.eMotion.com`

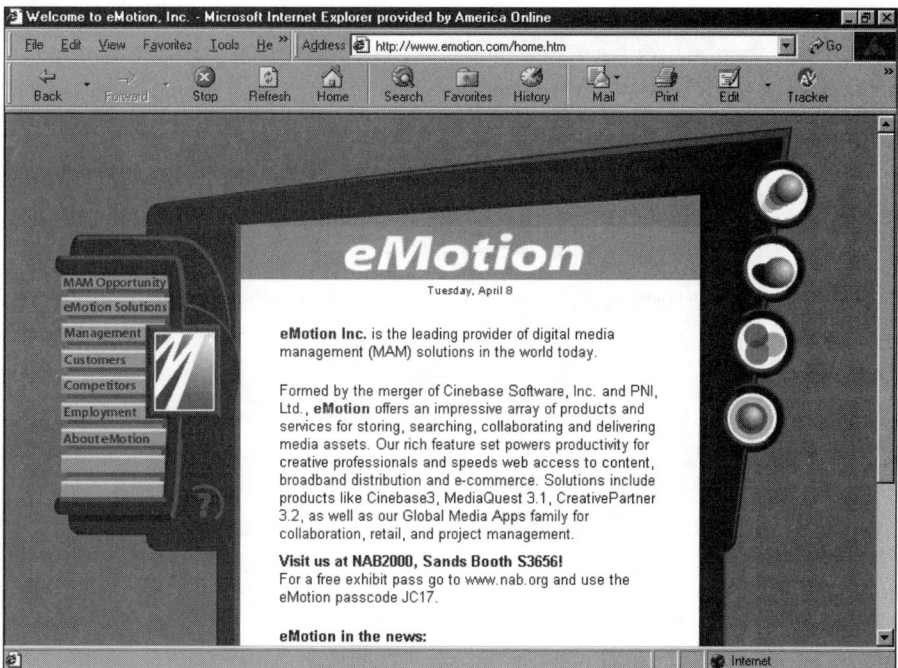

Figure 10-3:
A model of a Web presence site.

Use this and other sites as a model for your own similar site.

Figure 10-4 shows, for contrast, the Dell site, one of the leading sites for Web commerce. Note that it has many of the same elements and even similar icons to the eMotion site, yet also includes online ordering. If you visit both sites, you will also see that the Dell site is much larger. A full-scale e-commerce site like Dell's requires an experienced team of in-house Web professionals, plus outside consultants, and active management input on a daily basis. A smaller site like the eMotion site is in the range of many small businesses.

Later in this chapter, we show exactly how to create a Web presence site for a small business. Many businesses, from small storefronts and consultancies right up to major corporations, have only this kind of site. (The major corporation sites may be fancier and have more pages, but when you look closely, you see that many of them just provide the basic information of a Web presence site, with more pages to reflect their larger number of divisions, products, and services.) This kind of site suits the purposes of many businesses. Creating a Web presence site is all you need to do to turn the Web from being a hole in your business strategy to being an asset to your business.

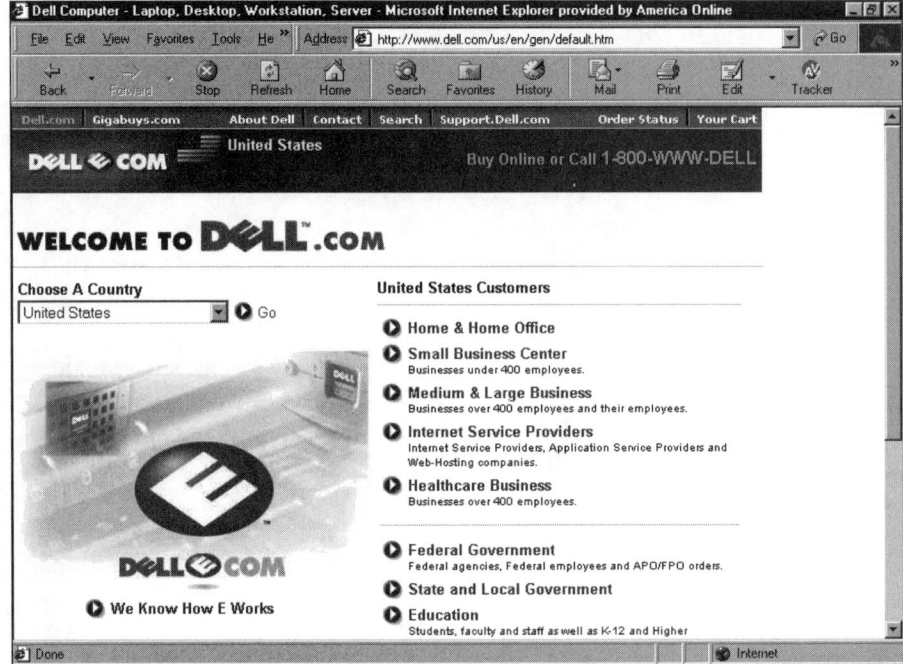

Figure 10-4:
A model of
an online
commerce
site.

Improving Your Site

No, "improving your site" is not an ad for an eyeglass company. (Though if you spend enough time on the Web, you may need the help of one!) It means "here are some things you can do to turn your simple, solitary Web page into a robust Web site."

The sections that follow talk about ways to improve the design, layout, and structure of your site. Site-improving techniques include using links, tables, frames, and more, but do not include graphics and multimedia; Chapters 8 and 9 cover those topics, respectively.

Adding more pages to your site

The easy-to-use Web page creation tools hosted on the Web, which we describe in earlier chapters, all make it easy to add pages to your Web site. But how do you link one page to another? Luckily, linking is pretty easy; just remember a few HTML tags, and you've got it. Here's how to make different kinds of links.

What's your job?

Getting into Web page creation can be challenging, but getting out can be much harder!

HTML and Web tools are so easy to figure out that most people can create a basic site themselves. But developing and maintaining that site is another matter. You can easily become an "accidental expert" as you try to keep up with the seemingly insatiable demands of a Web site.

So decide up-front how far you want to go in becoming a Web page creation expert. And when the job starts to get too big, be quick to call in a consultant or hire an employee whose sole job is Web site creation and maintenance.

Links to other pages in the site

If you want to link between pages within a site, you need to provide the user some link text to click in one page, and tell the Web browser where to find the other page. You do this with the <A>, or *anchor*, HTML tag.

To create links between pages, first create the two pages. Then add an anchor in one page that points to the other. Here's a typical link between pages within a Web site:

```
If you want to give me a job, check out my <A HREF=
  "myresume.htm"> resume </A>.
```

On the screen, the text appears like this:

```
If you want to give me a job, check out my resume.
```

Here's what each part of the HTML code does:

`<A>`	Tells the browser that an anchor follows and to display the anchor text as underlined.
`HREF= "myresume.htm"`	Tells the browser, when the user clicks the underlined text, to get the file myresume.htm, which is the link destination, and display it. Most up-to-date browsers display the link destination URL in the bottom of the browser window when the user moves the mouse pointer over the underlined text.

`resume`	The text surrounded by the `<A>` and `</A>` tags is link text. The browser displays the link text underlined and in a different color (usually blue) to let the user know the text is a link. When clicked, it causes the current Web page to be replaced by the page at the link destination.
`</A>`	Tells the browser where the anchor ends and that, from this point on, the browser should no longer display text as part of a link (underlined and in a different color).

You can also link to page files that are stored in a different subfolder, but doing so is complicated and the source of many, many problems in transferring files and in maintaining links. For sites with relatively few files, keep them all in one folder.

Figure 10-5 shows a variety of links, including links to other pages within a Web site, as they appear both in HTML code and on the screen in a Web browser.

You can try out all this linking without even firing up a connection to the Internet. Just create a couple of text-only documents with the appropriate HTML tags inside. Use your Web browser to open one of the files. You should be able to click on the link in one file to open the other file!

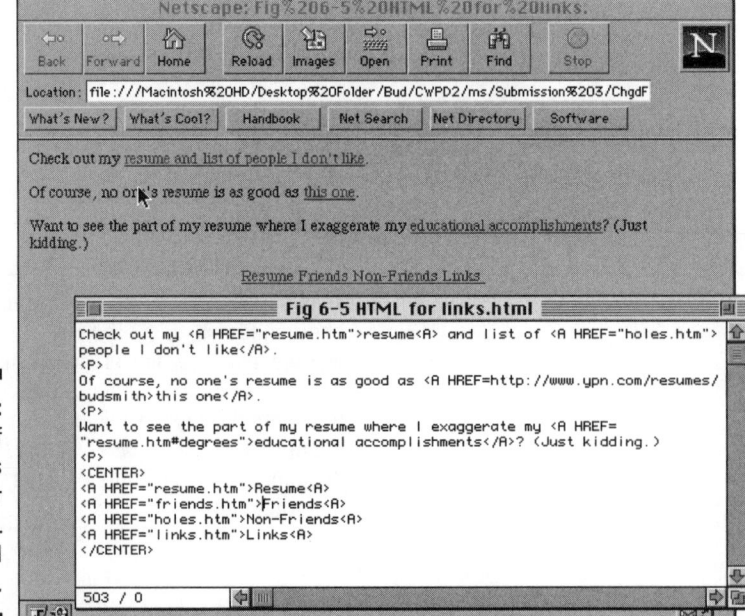

Figure 10-5:
Examples of linking as they appear in HTML code and on-screen.

Links within a page

The anchors we describe in the previous section automatically point to the top of a Web page. You can also create a link to a spot within a page.

To enable users to link to a spot within a page, also known as an anchor, you have to give the spot a name. Here's an example of the HTML code for that:

```
<A NAME="education"></A>
```

Here's what each part of the HTML code does:

`<A>, </A>`	Begins and ends the anchor.
`NAME="linktarget"`	Indicates the name of the target. In the example, the target name is *education*.

To link to the anchor, just add the anchor name to the link tag. If the anchor is in the same page as the link, just give the anchor name:

```
If you want to see my college degrees, check out the
<A HREF="#education">appropriate spot</A> in my resume.
```

Here's what each part of the HTML code does:

`<A>, </A>`	Begins and ends the anchor.
`HREF="#education"`	Indicates the name of the target.

On the screen, the link looks like this:

```
If you want to see my college degrees, check out the
appropriate spot in my resume.
```

If the anchor is in a different page than the link, give the page name first, then the anchor name:

```
If you want to see my college degrees, check out the
<A HREF="myresume.htm#education">appropriate spot</A>
in my resume.
```

For large documents that you publish on the Web, such as a résumé, provide lots of anchors in the document and put a list of anchors at the top. But if you're creating Web pages from scratch, you should avoid creating long pages that need anchors for navigation. The user sees your Web pages only one screenful at a time, so try to avoid making the user scroll down through long pages. If you want to begin a new topic, start a new page and create a link to it.

Navigating intrasite

After you have more than four or five Web pages on your site, you should really think hard about navigation within your site. Don't just toss intrasite links into body text, mixed in with links to other sites, graphics, and who knows what else. Provide centralized areas that help the user move around within your site.

A simple solution to the intrasite navigation problem is always to provide a list of all your major site areas at the bottom of each page. (For small sites, each "major area" of your site is a single page; for larger sites, you have major areas, subareas within major areas, and more.)

Early in the development of your Web site, create a graphic that provides links to the major areas of your site. Use the graphic at the bottom of each page. Keep the graphic simple, but do provide one; it really upgrades the appearance and usability of your site.

Adding external links to your site

The easiest way to extend the impact of your site is to add links to external sites. However, you should be a little careful when adding external links. After all, you don't want people surfing away immediately; you want them to experience what you worked so hard to create! Yet a site with no external links often comes across as boring and "dead."

So think before you link. Make your site a useful set of Web pages with links among them; then decide how and where to use external links. Link to the Web sites of specific companies and products that may interest your site's visitors. Create tables of links on topics that you know something about. But don't toss in "big-name" links such as *Wired* magazine just to show that you too are, well, wired: Don't randomly drop in links that don't have a clear purpose. (Useless links are tired, not wired!)

Adding an external link to your site is easy, just like adding a link within your site, but the destination is a Web URL. All the easy-to-use Web tools we describe in Chapters 3, 5, and 6 make including at least some external links easy; but to have full control over them, you need to know in detail how to create and edit them yourself.

To create an external link, include the prefix `http://` in the destination URL to make clear that the link is an external link. Refer to Figure 10-5 to see the link text as it appears in HTML code and on the screen in a Web browser. Here's an example of a typical link to another Web site:

```
If you want to give me a job, check out my <A HREF="http:/
www.geocities.com/SiliconValley5325/resume_pjh.html">
resume</A>, hosted on the GeoCities personal Web page
service.
```

On the screen, this text appears like this:

```
If you want to give me a job, check out my resume, hosted on
the GeoCities personal Web page service.
```

Here's what each part of the HTML code does:

`<A>`	Tells the browser that an anchor follows and to display the anchor text as underlined.
`HREF="http://www. geocities. com/ SiliconValley5325/ resume_pjh.html"`	Tells the browser, when the user clicks on the underlined text, to go get the file `resume_pjh.html`, in the directory `SiliconValley5325`, on the Web server `www.geocities.com`.
`resume`	As with other links, the text surrounded by the `<A>` and `</A>` tags is link text. The browser displays the text underlined and in a different color (usually blue) to let the user know that the text is a link. When clicked, it causes the current Web page to be replaced by the page at the link destination.
`</A>`	Tells the browser where the anchor ends, and that, from this point on, the browser should no longer display text as part of a link (underlined and in a different color).

Note that the example doesn't link to the GeoCities home page but instead goes directly to the résumé itself. Why? First, linking only to the résumé keeps the number of links down. Second, a link to the GeoCities home page is already provided by GeoCities at the bottom of each GeoCities home page. Third, any Web surfer worth his or her salt knows to try to open `www.geocities.com` if he or she wants more information about a company called GeoCities. If something is important to your Web surfers, make it very easy to get to. If it's of only peripheral interest, don't clutter up your site by trying too hard to provide easy access.

Setting a table in your site

You can use an HTML table in two very different ways: One way is to create a basic table. That's what we show you in this chapter. The other way is to create a sophisticated page layout. The user doesn't really see that it's a table, just that the page is laid out in an attractive and unusual way. We cover that in Chapter 7.

A simple table is fairly easy to create by using HTML. However, as you begin to create more complex tables or to use tables to control your overall page layout, the HTML quickly becomes complicated and tedious to create and maintain.

Tables are a big reason why the easy-to-use tools that we profile in Part V are so popular. These tools make managing tables much easier. So if you start to work much with tables, consider using one of these tools.

How do you create a simple table with, say, headers, two rows, and two columns? Here's an example of how to create such a table in HTML:

```
<TABLE>
<TABLE BORDER=2>
<TH><TD>Production (tons)</TD><TD>% of goal</TD></TH>
<TR><TD>North 40</TD><TD>87</TD><TD>102%</TD></TR>
<TR><TD>South 40</TD><TD>93</TD><TD>110%</TD></TR>
</TABLE>
```

Just add this HTML code to your Web page, and you have a simple table. Figure 10-6 shows how this simple table looks in HTML when viewed in Netscape Navigator.

Here's what each part of the HTML code does:

`<TABLE>, </TABLE>`	Begins and ends the table.
`<TABLE BORDER=2>`	Creates a 2-pixel-wide border around the table. Don't forget to include a border, so other text and graphics in your Web page don't crowd too close to the table.
`<TH>, </TH>`	Begins and ends the table header. (Automatically leaves first entry blank so rows can contain a column name.)
`<TR>, </TR>`	Begins and ends the table row.

<TD>, </TD>	Begins and ends the table data item.

So creating a table in HTML is fairly simple but also fairly tedious. You just create the rows and data items; if you get the data items right, the columns take care of themselves.

Getting the data items right can be a problem, though. To make your table look just right, you have to use a number of alignment and formatting options. Making mistakes becomes very easy, and updating the table's appearance becomes very hard. That's why so many people use HTML tools to create and manage tables — and then, in some cases, do final tweaking in HTML to get them just right.

Tables weren't part of the original HTML standard; they were introduced in Netscape Navigator Version 1.1. As a result, some much older browsers don't support tables at all. (Tables are the main reason why some Web pages still say "Best viewed with Netscape Navigator" — for a while it was the only browser with table support.) Also, the official HTML standard and Navigator 1.1 used different versions of the same tags. Luckily, most browsers available today support both versions.

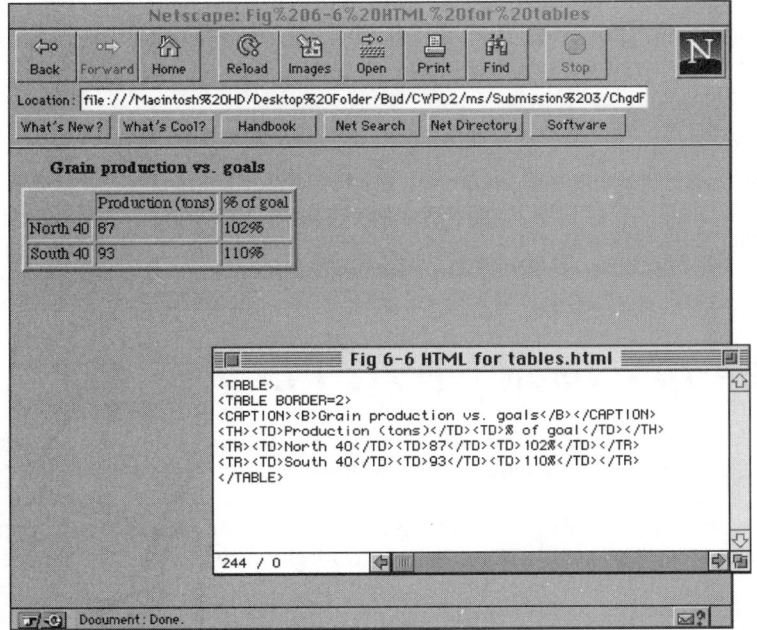

Figure 10-6:
All gather 'round the table....

Friends don't let friends do frames

Frames, like tables, are a Netscape innovation. Frames separate a Web page into separate areas that can be updated individually. For example, you can click a link in a frame in the bottom half of a Web page and update it with new content while the other frame stays the same. This seems like a powerful capability. However, frames have proved to be less popular than tables.

Why are frames not as popular as tables? Well, frames are hard to create and manage, just like tables. But advanced Web authors are willing to do just about anything to make their Web pages more attractive and more useful, and tables help them do so. With frames, the trouble comes with the "useful" part; users have a hard time with framed Web pages.

When using a framed page, users have difficulty finding where the cursor is. So if they scroll, which frame scrolls? Also, going forward and backward in a frame is different from going forward and backward in the overall Web page, so users may easily get lost. Finally, frames create a functional problem or two. When users resize a browser window, framed pages don't always resize correctly. And designing a framed page to work well for various monitor sizes is significantly harder than designing regular pages.

All that aside, framed pages can be very useful to show complex sets of data and to support navigation. Figure 10-7 shows an example of frames used for an online chat session hosted at

```
www.fcg.net/chat/chat.html
```

Because creating and managing the HTML for frames is even harder than for tables, we don't describe that process here; use one of the HTML tools in Part V if you want to use frames in your pages. (Or look up the appropriate HTML tags in Appendix C and start experimenting!)

Getting good form(s) in your site

Forms are one of the best things in HTML; unlike tables and frames, they're right there in the original HTML definition. That's the good news.

The bad news is that after you put a form in your site, the user is probably going to enter data in it. So far, so good; but where does the data go? That's the problem: Handling the data from the form requires something called a *CGI (Common Gateway Interface)* script. (No, this is not something a certain South Dakota company uses to sell computers!)

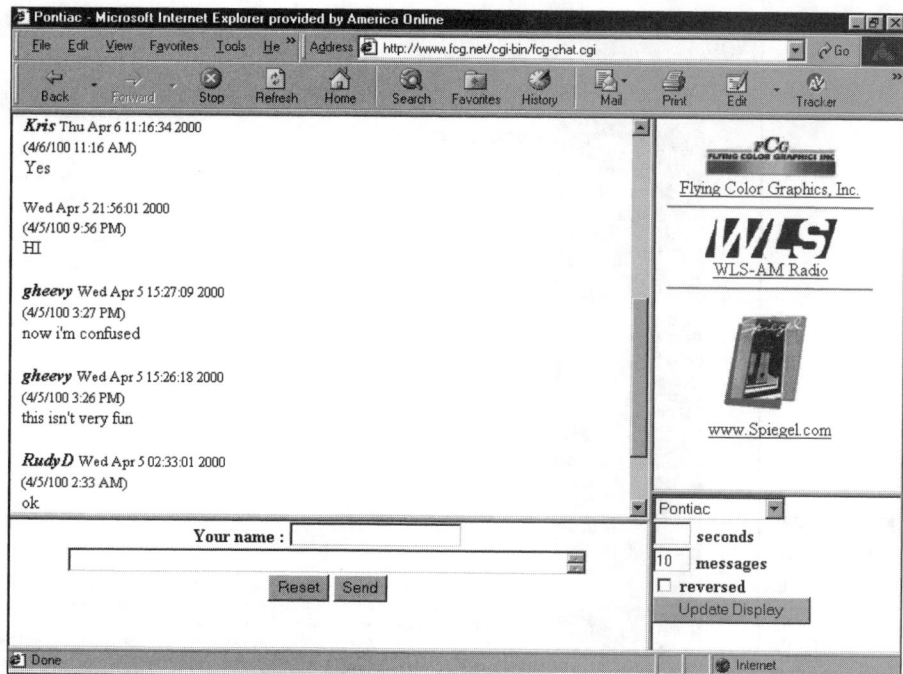

Figure 10-7:
I've been
framed.

Even worse, figuring out how to write CGIs, as CGI scripts are called, is not enough. You have to get special permission from the Webmaster of your site to run them, or ask the Webmaster to create the script for you. Why? A bad CGI can bring down the entire server. Webmasters can't afford the risk of allowing CGIs to run without their being notified of the script first.

So if you need to use forms, check with the Webmaster of the site your page is on to see what the policies are for CGI support of forms on the server. If necessary, you may even have to move to a different site that offers the CGI support you need. Figure 10-8 shows a forms example from a forms tutorial at the following URL:

```
www.webcom.com/webcom/html/tutor/forms/radio.shtml
```

See Chapter 7 for more information about forms.

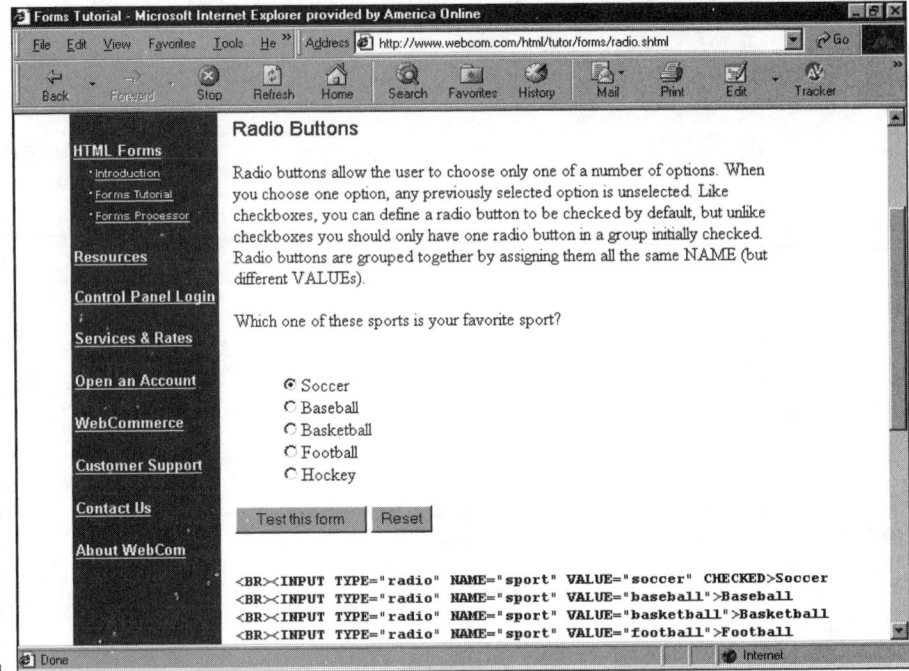

Figure 10-8:
Forms line
up to the
rear.

Making sure your site counts

Counters are one of the best things to have in a Web site. In fact, any serious Web site should have a counter on each page, to make knowing what users visit and what they don't easier. The counter doesn't have to display its count to the user, but it should make the count available to you. (You can also see count information on the logs produced by the Web server software, but the logs can be hard to read, and you probably don't have access to them unless you run your own Web server. Counters are a nice shortcut.)

However, counters, like forms, require CGI support. Most Webmasters provide counter support. Check with the Web site that your Web page is on to see how to put counters in your Web pages.

Creating a Basic Business Site

Even the smallest businesses can benefit from being on the Web, and any business larger than the smallest *needs* at least a basic Web presence to be taken seriously. But how do you get a basic Web presence without getting in over your head with expensive consultants and Internet service providers who may gouge you?

Never fear, *Creating Web Pages For Dummies* is here! In this section, we describe the skeleton of a basic business site. You can use this site as a model for your own business Web site and publish it with any Internet service provider. Literally thousands of service providers are ready and willing to help you.

Some of the Web authoring tools covered in Part V include templates for sites of different kinds, including business sites. Different Internet service providers and many Web sites also provide this kind of information, and you can find thousands of books and magazine articles on the topic. Combine ideas from as many resources as you can get your hands on to create a site that suits your needs.

A sample business site

The sample business site we describe here is not fancy. Its goal is to provide a basic skeleton that you can add your own information to and then put up on the Web, probably with just a few hours' work.

In addition to its simplicity, the site's structure also helps you see *why* each Web page in the site exists and how each works with the others. When you start adding to the site, using either your specific business information or resources from other places, keep in mind what you want to accomplish and what each addition can do to help.

The home page in the sample site is designed as a *panel* — it fills a regular-size screen without requiring the user to scroll down to see if there's anything more to look at! When you have pages in your site that exist mostly to provide navigational information, strongly consider designing them as panels, or at least putting the key and most-used information into the top-most area of the page.

Home page

The home page of the Silicon Valley Publishing Group site, shown in Figure 10-9, is a brief description of the business and has a set of pointers to other parts of the site. The home page serves a few purposes:

- ✔ To let the Web surfer who doesn't need the information in the site know to "surf on"

- ✔ To let the Web surfer who does need the information know that he's found the kind of site he's looking for

- ✔ To provide a positive initial impression of the business

- ✔ To help each user easily get to the specific information in the site that he or she needs or explore the whole site in a systematic way

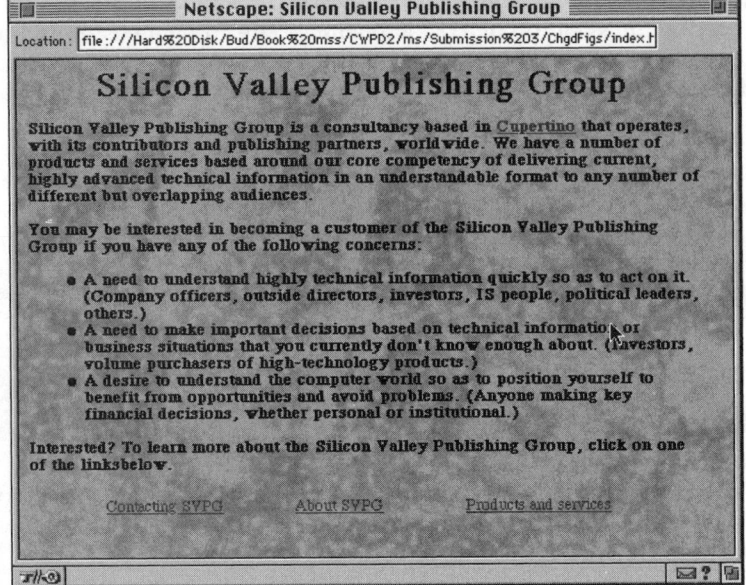

Figure 10-9:
Home page
of the
Silicon
Valley
Publishing
Group.

Contact info

The easiest thing to find in the entire site should be contact info for the business. Remember, people around the world don't have your local phone book! They may only know the name of your business, a product name, or the name of an employee. With the Web, they can guess your business's URL or use a search engine to find your site in several different ways. After users reach your site, they need to know other ways to contact you. Always make contact information very easy to find in any Web site you create.

Business info

People need to know what you do and why. What are the main impressions you try to leave in the minds of people who do business with you? Your business Web site is the place to reinforce those impressions. Why do your customers work with you instead of someone else? Use those strengths to communicate a positive and accurate image of your business. In addition to self-description, you can use your business site to provide information about, and links to, key partners, customers, and suppliers. Each such connection provides another way to make a potential customer feel comfortable about working with you.

Product/service info

Here's where you list the products and services that your business provides. This information alone, backed up by suitable descriptions and photos, is worth its weight in gold to potential customers. (Of course, information doesn't weigh anything, but why let mere facts undermine the point we're trying to make?) Provide a simple, clean list of your products and services and offer brief descriptions, illustrations, and photographs to make key points. Then provide a way for the Web surfer to get more information, such as a brochure, the name of a dealer, or a person within your business to talk to.

Beyond the basics

As a first step, create, test, and publish a simple business site like the one we describe in the preceding sections. (For details on how to publish your Web site, see Chapter 11.) Then get ready to develop it.

To figure out the next steps, look both inside your business and outside it. Within your business, look for resources such as white papers that explain areas of your business or your product line, brochures, advertisements, presentations, even "canned" sales pitches. Figure out how you can get this info onto the Web. In doing so, you save time and money, and you end up with more effective content than you are likely to create otherwise.

After you figure out basic content, add more sophisticated graphics and even a bit of multimedia. (See Chapters 8 and 9 for more information.) Don't try to "wow" the world at first. Just create a simple, clean look for your Web site. Use photographs of products, your facilities, and so on to add interest. Add a few multimedia highlights such as a spoken welcome message from the head of the company, or a video clip of a presentation or advertisement.

Also look outside your business. First, look at the Web sites of competitors, partners, and customers. What elements do their Web sites include? Which of these elements does your Web site need most? Then extend your Web site in the directions indicated.

Finally, look at your overall advertising and marketing budget, and then compare it to the budgets of competitors and other companies like yours. How many of your customers and potential customers are on the Web? What place should the Web play in your plans? Where do you most want your business to distinguish itself: on the Web, in print, in broadcast, or in person? The answers to these questions help you determine whether your Web presence should be just enough to cover your rear end, or something more ambitious. For a great deal more information on using your Web site and other online tools to extend your business's marketing presence into cyberspace, see *Internet Marketing For Dummies,* by Frank Catalano and Bud Smith (IDG Books Worldwide, Inc.).

As your site becomes more complex, consider hiring out some or all of the work. The knowledge you gain in creating and publishing your own initial Web site makes you a sharp and savvy shopper when looking to hire someone to take over some of the work.

Get help with this bigstep

That's not a typo; while it's a "big step" to get a site up on the Web, bigstep.com is the name of a Web business that is designed to help you publish a business Web site for free. Visit www.bigstep.com to learn whether you qualify to create a free business Web site there. (It's also a great place to go to get ideas for your own simple business Web site.)

Chapter 11

Publishing Your Web Pages

* *

* *

*P*ublishing is the most exciting stage of creating your Web home page or Web site. After all the fooling around with tools, HTML, GIFs, and other kinds of files, and after figuring out what you want to say and how you want to say it, you can finally "go live" and let the world see your creation.

Publishing on the Web can be straightforward if you're putting up a personal or topical home page that a few friends and/or coworkers see. But if you're creating a site for a business, or just need room to grow, publishing involves several steps.

The first step is to get Web server space. You have a lot of options here. Can you get free space or must you pay for it? Do you want your own domain name, so that your site has a simple URL, or are you willing to let your site be a subdirectory in someone else's domain? You need to choose a server space provider that gives you reasonable pricing and support now and room to grow later. Then you need to transfer your files to the site and confirm that you're really online.

But you're not done yet. The whole purpose of getting your Web site online is for people to see it. With all the sites out there, you have to cut through the noise and get people to visit your site. After they see your site, you need to know that they were there. You also need to receive and respond to feedback. Kind of reminds us of those U.S. Army ads — "It's not just a job, it's an adventure."

After your site is up and publicized, you may expect to get a chance to relax. But then, while you cruise the Web, you see something neat that you want to put into your own site. Or looking back at your own pages, you suddenly see a problem in how you describe yourself, your company, or your interests. Or maybe you get a blizzard of e-mails asking a question that you thought you already answered on the site — or, worse, you get no feedback at all. Maybe it's time to fire up that HTML editor again. . . .

Sorry to plug a book cowritten by one of the authors, but if you're in a hurry to create a Web site for a business, you may want to consult *Internet Marketing For Dummies,* by Frank Catalano and Bud Smith (IDG Books Worldwide, Inc.). *Internet Marketing For Dummies* goes into more depth about business-related issues, such as how to register the right domain name, how to present your business online, and how to use other Internet services besides the Web as part of your marketing effort.

Getting Web Server Space

A *Web server* is a computer that's connected to the World Wide Web and runs special software that enables the computer to provide information to Web users. Hundreds of thousands of such servers are connected to the Web. Only by creating your own Web server with your site's files on it, or by placing your Web site's files on someone else's server, can your site really become part of the Web.

You can easily get space on a Web server. For example, the free Web-based publishing services we describe in Chapter 3 and the easy-to-use online service Web publishing tools we describe in Chapters 5 and 6 all include free Web server space. You may have a friend or an affiliation with an organization that can lend you Web server space. These are all good options for a single Web home page or a small site.

If real money is involved, though, things get tricky. When you create a site for a business or another kind of organization, most of the services we mention in the preceding paragraph don't give you free space. So if you're going to start paying for server space, you want to do some comparison shopping. And to do comparison shopping, you have to know what to compare.

America Online is the one service that continues to allow free Web server space for businesses as well as individuals. See Chapter 5 for details.

Web hosting service features

A number of businesses and organizations offer Web hosting service — that is, space on their Web server for your Web site. Most of these organizations charge for this service, and fees vary. You should look at a number of concerns when choosing a Web hosting provider for your Web pages. Figure 11-1 shows an introduction to the Web hosting services offered by UUNet, the first company to offer such services. For more information, visit UUNet at

```
www.uu.net/lang.en/products
```

Focusing only on price when you compare Web hosting service providers is understandable. But you should look at many other factors that may actually be more important than the immediate cost:

- **Pricing structure.** Instead of focusing only on the charges for your initial, bare-bones site, consider also what providers charge you when your site grows larger and attracts a moderate number of visitors, say a few hundred or a few thousand a month. Some hosting providers charge a very low rate for your initial site but sock it to you when your needs grow.

- **Support.** We all need support of one kind or another, but technical support for your Web publishing effort is one of the hardest — and most important — kinds of support. You need support for putting your pages onto the server, for answering questions about your site, and for solving problems about speedy access, uptime (how long the service is on the air trouble-free), and so on. Find out what support providers offer for each type of Web hosting option that interests you. Ask other users of each service if they're able to get support fast when a problem comes up.

- **Web-related consulting services.** Some Web hosting providers, even those that offer some services for free, also offer other Web-related services that they charge for, such as hosting business sites. (See the section on GeoCities in Chapter 3 for an example.) What do the providers charge for these services? How well do they work? Most Web-related services are billed by the hour, but some service providers get things done better and faster than others. So a less expensive hourly rate may not mean a lower total bill at the end.

Figure 11-1: They get you-you on the Net-Net.

✔ **Site services.** Some Web hosting providers offer helpful services, such as counting the number of users who visit your site. Other providers, at least, allow *you* to create and run Common Gateway Interface (CGI) scripts that perform sophisticated functions. Other Web hosting providers neither provide site services nor allow you to run CGIs. Look for a provider that does the simple stuff for you and supports you in doing the more complex functions yourself.

✔ **Domain name.** The *domain name* is the name of the server where your site resides, but clever providers can put multiple domain names on a single computer. So you can have your own domain name, even for a small site, but your Web hosting provider must register the name. Registering your name costs your provider $70 initially, plus a $35 per year maintenance charge. Expect your provider to pass this charge on to you, but don't let the provider charge you a great deal more. Having your own domain name is very desirable because it helps users find your site easily and gives the impression that you're serious about your Web site.

What's in a (domain) name?

If you do get your own domain name, your URL is whatever you want, within the rules of how URLs are created, such as

```
www.mysite.com
```

If you can't get your own domain name, your URL includes the computer's domain name, plus your site's name — something like this:

```
members.compuserve.com/mysite
```

After you announce your site and its URL, people may put your site in their Web bookmarks list, and you can put your site's name in press releases, marketing materials, and so on. If that URL includes someone else's business name, you're just providing free publicity for them, rather than for yourself. If you want to switch to your own URL later, you have to try to update your materials as well as everyone else's address book. This process is like changing your business address or phone number — not something anyone does easily or quickly.

Consider getting your own URL right up front. If not, limit the degree to which you publicize your Web site and its URL until you do get your own.

Some Web hosting providers offer to register a domain name for you but then retain ownership of the domain name themselves. This situation reminds us of those Peanuts cartoons in which Lucy sets up the football and then pulls it away when Charlie Brown runs up to kick it. Not owning your domain name free and clear can severely hamper your ability to move your site later.

Find out whether the Web hosting provider allows you to get your own domain name, either immediately or later. And if the provider does, ask for a clear, written statement that you own the domain name and can take your Web site to another host if you want to.

When you consider a Web hosting provider, consider in your evaluation the following factors:

- ✔ **Speed.** How fast can users access your Web site? How fast can users download files hosted on the site? You can ask, but you should also test. Try accessing some Web sites hosted by any service that you're considering and see how fast they are, especially at busy times of the day. Compare what you find to other Web sites.

- ✔ **Uptime.** Is the Web hosting service that you're considering ever "off the air"? You may think that downtime is rare but, actually, even entire online services such as America Online have downtimes. Find out the track record for uptime of the Web hosting service that you're considering and compare that service's record with your needs.

- ✔ **Switchability.** Having the ability to switch Web hosting providers is crucial. With the right to switch, you can resolve any other problems. Without the right to switch, you may be unhappy with some key element of your Web site for a long time. Two things can keep you "locked in" to a provider: Contractual provisions and control of your domain name. Don't sign a contract that locks you in for more than a few months, and don't let the Web hosting provider register your domain name for you unless the provider states, in writing, that you control your domain name and can take it elsewhere with you.

- ✔ **Price.** If all other things are equal, price is the determining factor. But all other things are rarely equal. Consider other factors first, but don't let yourself get ripped off on the price you pay.

  Another potential "gotcha" is *data transfer fees*. When users look at a page on your site, all the data on that page is transferred to their machines. If users download files, more data is transferred. Many Web hosting services offer some free data transfer, but your costs can rise sharply if traffic at your site increases and data transfer rises above a minimal amount. Compare data-transfer pricing carefully.

TECHNICAL STUFF

What makes a Web server fast?

A Web server is usually rated by the number of *connections* — brief communication sessions between two machines — that it can handle in a given period of time. The number of connections that the server handles depends on how quickly the server establishes a connection, deciphers the request, sends the requested file, and terminates the connection. Most people assume that the most time-consuming step in this process is the speed with which files are transmitted. Surprise! When small files are transmitted, the bottleneck is usually not how fast the files are transmitted, but how quickly the server's hardware and software establish connections for each of the file transfers and terminate them.

Here's a really technical tip: Engineers and hangers-on, such as people who write computer-related books, like to call the cause of a bottleneck a *gating factor*. For example, the gating factor for completing this book on schedule is the speed at which the authors write. The gating factor in serving simple Web pages is the speed with which the server can connect and disconnect, not the speed with which data can be sent over the wire.

In addition to the speed of connecting and disconnecting to other machines, the speed of the server's connection to the Internet makes a big difference, especially for larger files such as big graphics. If you have a direct connection to the Internet (as you find at most large companies and most universities), your client-side connection may be even faster than the server's connection: Lots of personal and small business home pages are sitting on Web servers with nothing but a 56 Kbps modem connecting them to the Internet. So don't start cussing at your own modem when that full-color JPEG photograph of the winning Weimaraner takes forever to download; the problem may be at the other end.

The key factors in choosing a Web hosting provider are the freedom to switch when you need to and having control of your domain name.

Options for Web server space

Now that you know what to look for in a host server, where can you find Web server space? Finding the right place for your Web site to be hosted is not an easy task. Major Web hosting options include sites that offer free server space, online service Web hosting options, Web hosting services, and a Web server of your own creation. No matter what choice you make initially, be sure to keep your options open, because your needs may change rapidly as new Web hosting providers arise, as your own knowledge grows, and as the Web's role in business and in daily life increases.

Using free server space

You can get free server space for relatively small Web sites from several places (see Chapters 3, 5, and 6 for details). These sites are great places to create small, initial Web sites to find out about Web page design and construction. However, businesses generally can't use free server space for straightforward business promotion. (But you do see lots of not-so-straight-forward promotions there!) Also, to get your own domain name, you either have to move to paid server space or create your own Web server.

If you have access to free server space through a friend or work, that's also a good place to get started. Be careful, though, that you don't violate any expectations that the host has about the content of your Web site.

As we mentioned in the previous chapter, bigstep.com, a Web business, will help you create a starter business Web site for free. Visit them at www.bigstep.com.

Using online-service server space

The major online services — America Online, CompuServe, and The Microsoft Network — continue to develop their business-oriented Web services. (Well, not Microsoft, but maybe they will get it going.) Use the free Web services we describe in Chapters 3, 5, and 6 to get started with a personal home page, and then check the features and services of each of the online services against your needs. Don't rush in too fast, though. The online services get a lot of Web-related business simply because of their established name, and they may charge more or have more restrictive policies than other hosting services.

Using Internet service providers

Internet service providers (ISPs) may be best known for offering Web access, but they also offer a wide range of Web services, from consulting to hosting to programming and more. In fact, as larger players, such as AT&T, continue to establish their Web access business, the smaller ISPs that prosper will be those that move "upstream" into consulting and specialized hosting services.

Some ISPs offer free server space to customers, just like the major online services. They also offer varying levels of paid-for service. Compare major ISPs, such as NetCom, MindSpring, TheOnRamp, and UUNet, to see what they offer. If you already have Web access, don't stop checking. Most ISPs offer their add-on services even to those who get their access elsewhere, and some ISPs may offer attractive bundles for access plus other services. You still have to be a customer to get that free server space deal, though.

Using paid-for server space

Thousands of Web hosting services exist. The providers vary tremendously in service, price, and competency. Some offer hosting only and charge you per stored or transferred megabyte. Others offer additional services, which may be billed separately or bundled with the "pure" hosting services in an overall fee. This business is changing and growing so rapidly that you need to exercise great care in the selection process to protect yourself. The largest service, Verio, which recently acquired Best Internet, is also considered among the best (no pun intended); you may want to start your search by checking on them at

```
www.verio.com
```

As the Romans figured out, just a few years before the Internet caught on, *caveat emptor* — let the buyer beware!

Creating your own Web server

Deciding whether to create your own Web server depends, as do many other choices about the Web, on what you want to accomplish and how much experience you have. If you've set up a Web server before or have a lot of computer and communications experience, setting up your own Web server may work out very well for you. If not, setting up a Web server may turn out to be an expensive nightmare — and slow to boot! (That's "slow as well," not slow to start when you hit the On switch!)

Many proponents of doing business on the Web are quick to suggest that you set up your own Web server, but we don't share that view. Unless you're an expert, we recommend that you start with a Web hosting provider of some kind. Then consider setting up your own server after you gain some experience and get to know some people who can help if problems arise. If you want details, refer to *Setting Up An Internet Site For Dummies,* 3rd Edition, by Jason Coombs, Ted Coombs, David Crowder, and Rhonda Crowder (IDG Books Worldwide, Inc.).

Two things to remember: If you set up your own server for any but the most casual purposes, use a dedicated machine that isn't doing any other work. (If you follow this very good advice, you must spend $2,000 or so before you store or serve a megabyte!) And be ready to devote time and energy to find out about the computer, communications link, and associated Web technologies so that you can set up your own server to meet your needs as effectively as a Web hosting service.

Web hosting providers

The growing number of people and organizations that want to get on the Web increases the demand for the services of experienced people, bringing about an influx of new providers driven, at least in part, by a gold-rush mentality. This scenario means that finding someone who can really help may be difficult and finding someone who wants to learn at your expense is easy. To find a good Web hosting provider — someone who can provide the Web hosting services we describe in the previous section — we recommend the following steps:

✔ **Start small.** Asking the right questions to help you find a Web hosting provider is difficult if you have no Web publishing experience of your own. Start by creating a home page and then a small, special-purpose site of some kind before doing anything more robust. The experience will be valuable even in finding a good hosting provider.

✔ **Figure out what services you need.** Are you going to create a simple site or a complex one? Do you want to create the site yourself and buy hosting services only, or do you want to contract out most of the work? List your needs, and then find someone who's well-suited to fill them.

✔ **Investigate sites like your own.** Find Web sites that look like the kind you want to create. Ask the Webmasters how they got their sites up and running and what Web hosting providers they use. Ask others in your area about their Web sites and whether they're happy with the services they receive. When you consider a specific provider, check into a few of the sites that the provider hosts and ask customers whether they're happy.

✔ **Go local.** You may want to meet occasionally, or even regularly, with your Web hosting provider, which means choosing a provider with a local presence. (Even with all our technological aids, looking someone in the eye can contribute to better and deeper understanding, unless you find that you really dislike the person!) Although going local greatly restricts your choices, it may significantly improve your working relationship.

✔ **Be involved.** No consultant or service provider can do everything. The person or organization that pays for the site must provide content and guidance throughout the process. You need to be very much involved in the process, so plan to devote many hours to working with your consultant or service provider.

Is your site too cool?

What if your site is *too* successful? Believe it or not, the success of your site *can* be a problem. Many sites become overloaded when they "catch on," are chosen as the Yahoo! Cool Site of the Day, get a Point Top 5% award, get a link in a prominent spot on a major portal site, or receive other similar recognition. Be ready to upgrade your Web hosting provisions if your site suddenly gets popular. In particular, if you pay extra for transferred megabytes, make sure that you have a cap on how much you must pay if usage suddenly shoots up. If you don't, set up some method to to track usage frequently or to receive an alert if usage shoots up. That way, you avoid a potentially nasty surprise on your bill.

Get it all in a cybermall

A *cybermall* is a Web site that hosts a variety of businesses and handles a variety of chores for a moderate price. A cybermall operator may provide any or all of the following:

- ✔ Initial goal-setting for your Web site

- ✔ Creation of the Web page itself (expect to provide raw materials such as product or service descriptions, photographs, and price lists)

- ✔ Advertising and publicity

- ✔ Support for online sales

Yahoo! and Amazon.com have cybermall-type arrangements that you can use to get publicity for your online selling. Using the right cybermall can be a good way to get started on the Web, especially if you want to go from zero (no Web presence or expertise) to sixty (a robust Web presence with online transaction capabilities) in a few months. Expect to pay several thousand dollars up front and several hundred dollars in monthly fees. Working with the mall operator also gives you a chance to develop Web expertise, so that you can eventually do more of the work yourself. (Make sure that your contract allows you to leave the cybermall quickly if you want to take over the whole job on your own.) For a popular online cybermall, see the following site:

```
www.netplaza.com
```

Transferring Your Files

One of the really cool things about Web publishing is the capacity to set up, test, and modify your Web site on your own machine. The problem is that, at some point, you have to transfer your files to the Web server. Until you become proficient at transferring files, you may have some anxious file-transferring moments. In this section, we try to eliminate some of the worry in getting your site online.

Arranging your files before transfer

Some of the most difficult things about creating, testing, and transferring your Web pages relate to directory structures. The problem is that a link from, say, your HTML-tagged text to a graphic has to specify what sub-folder the graphics file is in. When you transfer your files to a different machine, the subfolders change, which breaks the link from your Web page to the graphics file. You can take steps, however, to keep your links from breaking when you transfer your Web files from your development machine to the Web server.

For sites with a dozen files or fewer, a simple solution exists: Just put all your files in the same subfolder. That way, your links are simple — you only need to specify the filename, not the directory name — and when you transfer files, you don't need to match up subfolder structures between machines.

For sites with many files, use the simplest directory structure you can — only one level deep, if possible. Also, create your links by using relative addressing (see Chapter 10 for details). Relative addressing doesn't specify the entire pathname from the root directory downward, just the relative path from the file with the link embedded in it to the file with the link target. Relative addressing enables you to move files from one machine to another without having to change all the links between files.

Some people prefer to use a compression program, such as PKZIP, to package files before sending them. Before you compress files, make sure that the recipient wants zipped files and that he or she can unzip them. Also realize that the largest files in a Web site are usually GIF or JPEG graphics files. Because these files are compressed already, the compression programs don't compact them much further. But the compression program does help get all the files into a single package, with relative folder locations preserved.

As you can see, the underlying theme for anyone starting out is to "keep it simple." After you have some initial successes under your belt, you can begin taking steps to organize your site better and to make it more convenient to manage and update.

Transferring your files with FTP

File Transfer Protocol (FTP) is an Internet service for transferring files between different machines. FTP helped make the Internet popular even before the World Wide Web caught on. FTP is a relatively easy way to move files from one machine to another. Most Internet users rely on FTP to download files from an FTP host to the users' own machine; however, the user often starts the file transfer from a Web page, bypassing the details of FTP. To publish your Web pages, you may be asked to send files from your own machine to a host using FTP. (You will probably be asked to "FTP the files to us.") Using FTP is a new operation for most people, but it is not all that complex.

Dozens of FTP programs exist for Macintosh, Windows, and UNIX, each with pluses and minuses. (The major online services also have facilities for uploading files, which we describe in the "Connect to an FTP site" section that follows.) You can find many free FTP clients on the Web. The steps we provide work with most popular FTP programs. However, to upload files you need a "real" FTP program. Many programs with FTP capability can download files from FTP sites but not upload files to an FTP site. So make sure that your FTP program can put (write) as well as get (read) files.

Connect to an FTP site

The following steps specifically work with Fetch, the most popular Macintosh FTP program, shown in Figure 11-2. (Notice the little dog, probably a Scottie, running to fetch the file!) But the same steps generally apply to other FTP programs as well.

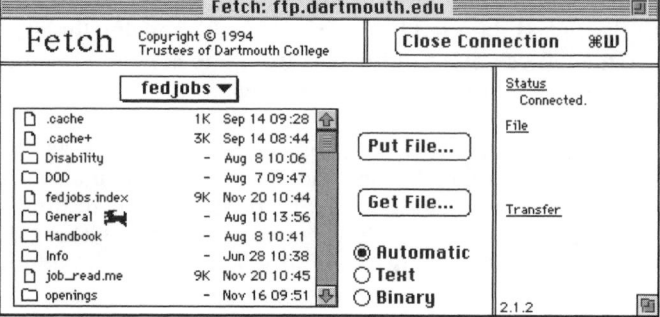

Figure 11-2:
A fetching
Mac FTP
client.

Use these steps to transfer files to a Web site:

1. **Connect to the Internet.**

2. **Start your FTP program.**

3. **Enter the host name.**

For a Web site, the FTP host name is often the same as the host name in the Web site's URL but with ftp in place of www; for example, if the Web site's URL is www.mysite.com, the host name is likely to be ftp.mysite.com.

4. **Enter the user name.**

Many sites allow you to enter anonymous as the user name and avoid having to enter a specific user name. Other sites give you a user name and password to use when uploading your Web files.

5. **Enter the password.**

If you entered anonymous as the user name, enter nothing or your e-mail address as your password.

6. **Enter the directory that you want to put files in (that is, to write to).**

You can also go to the correct directory after you connect, but the process is more convenient and less error-prone if you enter the correct directory first.

7. **Click OK to connect to the FTP site.**

   If you do everything right and the site is up, you connect. Refer to Figure 11-2 for the Fetch FTP dialog box that appears after you connect. Dartmouth College owns Fetch.

Upload your file (s) and disconnect

Getting connected is half the battle. Writing your files is usually pretty easy.

1. **Click the appropriate option for the file(s) that you want to write: Automatic, Text, or Binary.**

   For HTML files, use Text. For graphics and multimedia files, use Binary. For a combination of both types, either upload the types one at a time with the proper designation, or upload them together and choose Automatic; the server tries to figure out which is which. Until you have experience with a specific server, transfer files one at a time and specify the correct file type before each transfer.

2. **Click Put to write your file.**

   This option may be named "Send," "Upload," or something else on some clients; to initiate the process, you may have to select the option from a menu rather than click a button.

3. **In the dialog box that appears, click the name of the file that you want to write and then click OK.**

   The file transfers. Repeat Steps 1 through 3 for each additional file that you need to transfer.

4. **Choose Quit (or Exit) from the File menu.**

Using online service file transfer

In Chapters 5 and 6, we describe how to use the Web publishing programs on the major online services to create and publish a home page. However, the online services' Web facilities are flexible. You can create HTML-tagged text and graphics files with any tools and then upload the files to a server. The online service file transfer tools resemble FTP. Figure 11-3 shows the America Online file transfer program. Other file transfer programs are similar.

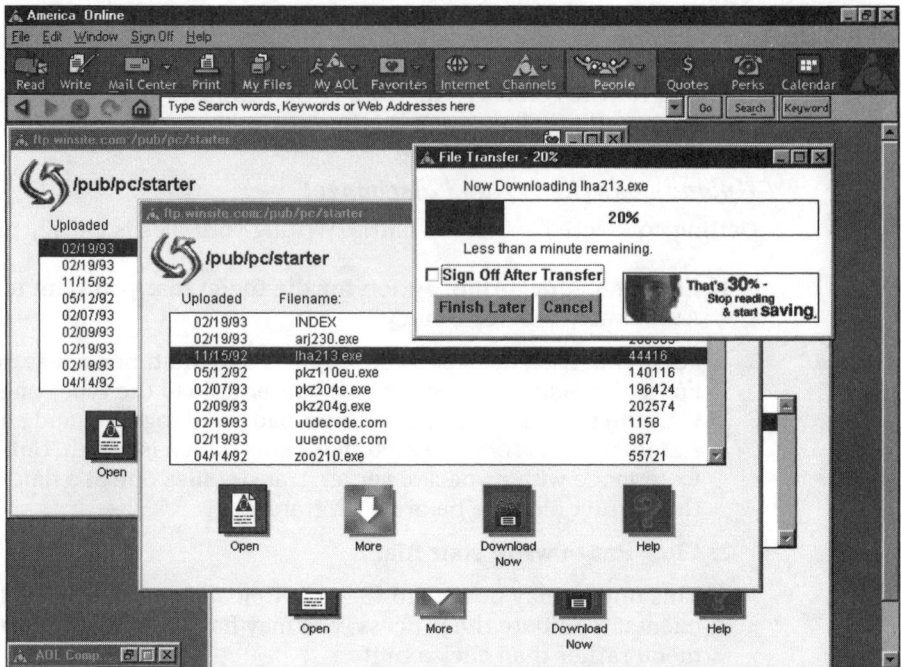

Figure 11-3:
File transfer
that's
not too
AOL-ful.

Putting Your Site to Work

After you put your site up on the Web, you're probably too relieved and happy to worry about the site for a while. But "going live" isn't an ending; it's really just the beginning of a whole new process. The following sections describe some initial steps to make your newly published site really stand out and accomplish your goals.

Test your site

As soon as you get your site up, log on to it as a normal user. See if the site works. Test all links to make sure that they go where they should. Make sure that you can easily move between pages. Try accessing your site from a computer with a slow modem connection to see how usable the site is at slow speeds.

Also note how you would react if you were a new user. What does the site look like it's for? Do you experience any difficulties or confusion in using it? This open-minded approach to your own site can help you quickly fix subtle problems that otherwise are hard to identify.

Testing your site is a bit frustrating because you find all sorts of things to fix, but if you follow through, you end up with a much better site. Be ready to take notes on your reactions from the moment you first log on to your site until the end of your visit — remembering first impressions later is difficult.

Use your browser's Print capability to print out the pages in the Web site, and then put your notes right on the printout. A printout enables you to easily keep track of your ideas as you go along and to make the right changes the first time.

Get feedback on your site

Ask for feedback! You can put the request for feedback right in your Web site. You can also ask friends and colleagues to try the site and give you their honest opinions. Ask them some leading questions, such as "What do you think the site is for? How does it compare to other sites you've seen? What's the one thing you'd change about the site if you could?"

Publicize your site

After your site is up and tested, publicize it. The amount and type of publicity you need depends upon your goals for the site. If you are trying to impress press and analysts, issue a press release. If you are publicizing a personal site, you may find that telling friends and family about it is sufficient. If you are trying to give customers another avenue for communicating with you, put your URL on stationery, business cards, and advertisements. If you are trying to sell on the Web, put ads on other Web sites that attract your prospective customers. Tailor your publicity strategy to your goals.

The first and most important place to publicize your site is on the Web itself. Your basic goal is to get as many links as possible to your site from What's New lists, What's Cool lists, and especially directories or pages that are specific to the interests your site addresses. Find pages with a similar purpose and trade pointers from their site to yours and from your site to theirs.

The Web publicity picture changes all the time, so the best place to go for information is any of several Web sites with publicity info and pointers:

```
webmagnet.com/howtodoit.html
www.cyberwave.com/ppoint2.html
www.submitit.com
```

These sites give you information on how to get your pages publicized on popular sites such as the Yahoo! What's New page. (See Figure 11-4 for an example.) You can find this page at

```
www.yahoo.com/new
```

You can also use non-Web means of publicizing your site. Put out a press release — but be sure to wait until your site's really ready, not full of Under Construction signs. Many companies proudly include their Web site URLs on business cards, stationery, print ads, and even television ads. You've invested a lot in your Web site — now's the time to benefit from your efforts.

Count and keep users

For Web pages in general, and for business Web pages in particular, knowing how many users visit your site is important. For a business site you need to establish goals for the number of users who visit your site and for the number who take specified actions, such as downloading software, visiting certain parts of the site, or buying products. Set goals and then measure against them. Microsoft's Bcentral site at `www.bcentral.com` includes many useful tools for Web traffic measurement.

Figure 11-4:
Yahoo! for
new stuff.

Among the things you can track are the number of e-mails you receive from users and the number of people who register on your site (if you support that option). But the most widely accepted measurement of success is *hits,* or accesses to files on your site. (Each displayed Web page or graphic counts as a separate hit.) Not a great measurement, but it's a start. Obtain the server log for your site from your Internet service provider and then consider more sophisticated ways to track usage, such as various Web server log analysis tools that give you *pageviews,* a more sophisticated measurement. Such tools look at logs generated by Web servers and give you statistics on the number of hits on your pages, the number of pageviews, and the number of separate visitors. Many Web hosting providers give you a monthly report, or at least let you access the log files from your site for your own review and analysis.

Part V
Web Publishing Tools

The 5th Wave — By Rich Tennant

"What do you mean you're updating our Web home page?"

In this part . . .

Web publishing tools are programs that help you create Web pages and manage a Web site. Some help by making it easier for you to remember and manage HTML tags; some tools hide the tags from you by using a graphical interface that is much like a word processing program. Other tools work within your existing word processing program or convert files from a word processing format to HTML-tagged text. Many very good tools are free; others cost under $100. Free tools are also available to help you make your site look good on WebTV, and WebTV users can publish on the Web for free. This part introduces you to many of the best Web publishing tools and tells you how to use them to create your own Web pages.

Chapter 12

Be True to Your Web Authoring Tools

In This Chapter

▶ Understanding Web authoring tools

▶ Evaluating tools

▶ Finding tools

▶ Using cross-platform tools

▶ Using PC-only tools

▶ Using Mac-only tools

Literally dozens of Web authoring tools appeared quickly in the early stages of the Web's growth. These tools continue to attract users; some are *shareware* — copyrighted computer programs available on a trial basis, with payment expected after some period of use — and others are *freeware* — copyrighted programs available without any charge. Two of the leading freeware tools for Web authoring are Microsoft's FrontPage Express, which we describe in Chapter 13, and Netscape Composer, which we cover in Chapter 14.

However, *retail software products* — boxed products with documentation and technical support, sold in retail channels such as computer superstores, printed catalogs, and online catalogs — are now the major players in Web publishing.

Another option for Web publishing is the "save as HTML" capability that's part of many word processing programs. This feature allows you to create and edit a document by using the normal word processing commands that you're already familiar with and then to save the document in a ready-to-publish HTML form. If you have a program with this capability, try it out — that way, you don't have to fiddle with figuring out all that HTML or an unfamiliar program. However, you may find frustrating the fact that not all your word processing program's capabilities translate to your Web pages when you use the "save as HTML" feature. For example, text that wraps around graphics or many font and font size formatting options may not transfer perfectly (or at all) from your word processing program. Also, you may find yourself plunging into the HTML file created by the "save as HTML" function in order to fix problems. We discuss the "save as HTML" capability in this chapter.

Not all the top Web authoring tools are full-fledged authoring packages, such as those we cover in detail in Chapters 13 through 16. Many standard office applications now support Web publishing to some degree; and on the Web and elsewhere, you can find word processing program add-ons, file converters, simple packages to create an initial Web page, and more. We gather many of the best into this chapter and onto the CD-ROM that comes with this book.

The Web is a fast-changing place, and new tools appear all the time. We think that the full-fledged authoring packages we cover in later chapters and the additional tools we cover here are the best, but you may disagree. Better tools and upgrades to currently available tools are on the way. So use this book and the CD-ROM as starting points, and then check the Web for new tools, new versions, and new ideas.

The *Creating Web Pages For Dummies* CD-ROM has, we think, the best collection of Web authoring tools yet committed to optical media. In this chapter, we describe the different characteristics that you may want in a Web authoring tool and how the tools on the CD-ROM and elsewhere fit those characteristics.

We also tell you how to find out what others say about Web authoring tools and how to track down tools that aren't on the CD-ROM. All this information may help guide you to the right tool for your needs. But if you're more of a hands-on person than a planner, go right ahead — try all the tools on the CD-ROM until you find the one that meets your needs. Then come back, read this chapter, and send us an e-mail about what we got right and what we got wrong. The e-mail address to use is

```
bud_smith@compuserve.com
```

What to Know about Web Authoring Tools

A Web authoring tool helps you create and edit the *HTML-tagged text file*s that, when viewed from a Web browser, appear as Web pages. (If the phrase *HTML-tagged text file* means nothing to you, please read Chapter 7.) If you sort of understand HTML's purpose but want to refresh yourself on what specific tags do, see the Cheat Sheet.

Use these five factors to determine the best Web authoring tool for you:

- ✔ **Effort.** How much effort does figuring out the tool require? How much effort does using it require? (The answers to these two questions can be quite different: For example, figuring out how to use the "save as HTML" capability in your word processing program is very easy, but using the capability to do advanced work — such as complex Web text and graphics layouts — can be hard.)

- ✔ **Platform.** Does the tool run on your system — Windows 3.*x*; Windows 95, 98, and Windows 2000/NT; the Mac; or your version of UNIX?

- ✔ **Add-on versus stand-alone.** Does the tool run on top of or within some other program, or is the tool a stand-alone application? We prefer stand-alone tools.

- ✔ **HTML focus versus WYSIWYG focus.** Does the tool help you work directly with HTML tags in text? Or does the tool hide HTML tags and present you with a more intuitive *WYSIWYG* (What-You-See-Is-What-You-Get) interface so that you can see what the page looks like, as in a word processing program?

- ✔ **Free versus paid for.** Does the program cost money? If so, does the program's owner let you try before you buy?

You are going to find a rough correlation among increasing effort to figure out a tool, increasing capabilities of the tool, and increasing purchase price of the tool. Free tools, such as FrontPage Express, Netscape Composer, and the "save as HTML" capability of your word processing program, are easy to figure out but not fully capable.

Mid-priced tools costing less than $100, such as PageMill, are a little harder to figure out but more capable. And more expensive tools costing over $100, such as Microsoft FrontPage 2000 and NetObjects Fusion, are noticeably harder to figure out but significantly more capable; for example, these tools can manage a large Web site as well as create individual Web pages. Figure 12-1 summarizes the tools that we cover in Part V in terms of the preceding criteria.

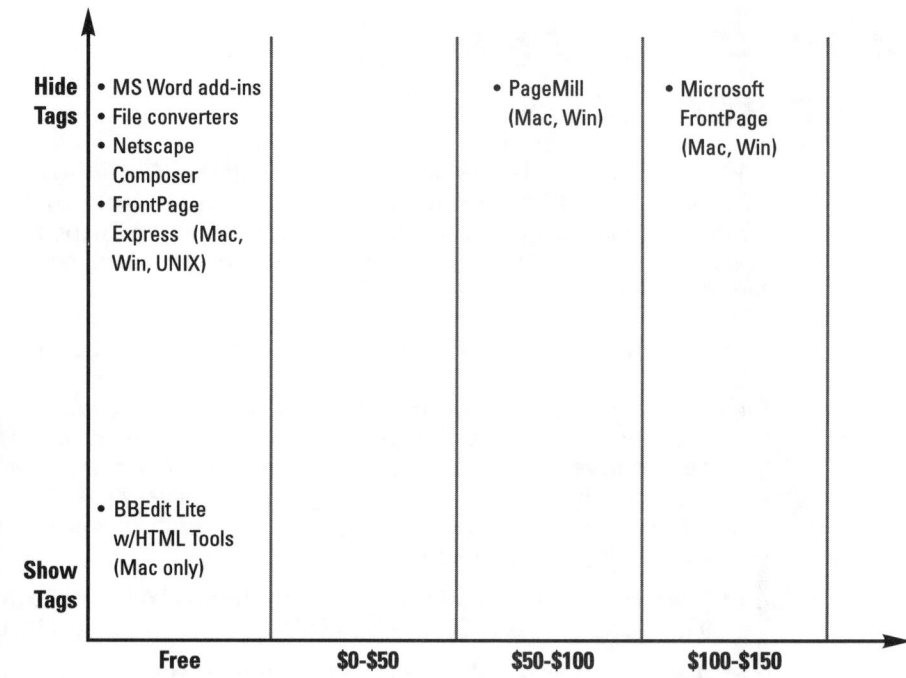

Figure 12-1:
Comparison
of some
popular
Web author-
ing tools.

How to Evaluate Tools

Use the following techniques to evaluate HTML tools. Each technique is valuable, and by combining them, you can get a pretty good idea of which tool is
right for you:

✔ **Read this book.** Just reading the tool descriptions and "how-to" information in the next few chapters, plus looking at the pretty pictures, gives
you a good idea of which tool may be right for you. As Obi-Wan Kenobi
says in *Star Wars,* "Trust your feelings."

✔ **Try the tools.** The CD-ROM that comes with this book has trial versions
of many of the HTML authoring tools discussed in this book. These versions are often time-limited or save-disabled, but they're fine for trying
the program to get a feel for it. You can quickly install them and do your
own "taste test." Then check to see whether any similar tools are also
worth a try.

✔ **Think about where you're going.** Decide whether you want a tool that
enables you to get started easily or one that can do a lot. If the most you
can see yourself doing in the near future is creating and editing a small
personal Web site, go for ease of use and a low or no price. If you want
to build a big, frequently updated site, or if you seek to make Web
authoring a saleable skill in your personal toolkit, look for a more powerful tool, or work in several tools.

✔ **Ask friends and colleagues.** Word of mouth is often the best source of information about products, especially if the people you ask have interests, backgrounds, and needs similar to yours. But be careful about following the advice of others. People tend to commit early, so the tool that your friend raves about may now be outdated or just no longer the best of its type. And people vary widely in their tolerance for working with straight HTML — the same tool that you like because it puts the HTML tags right up front may drive another person crazy.

✔ **Check newsgroups and online sources.** Use the Web to check online sources for specific tools and for comments about tools. You can choose from many online sources — we mention some of them in the next section, "Where to Find Online Information about Tools."

Don't get too caught up in the process of choosing the right tool, though. As Yoda says in *Star Wars,* "There is no try, only do." Your goal is to create Web pages, not to become an expert in the tools that create Web pages. So spend a little time researching, and then plunge in. With all the free Web authoring software demos on the CD-ROM that comes with this book, you can create a few Web pages in one tool and then try another one if necessary until you find the tool that suits you best.

Where to Find Online Information about Tools

We recommend several sites as excellent sources for information on Web authoring tools. Unfortunately, more complete review information exists for Windows tools than for Macintosh. But Macintosh users, don't despair — good tools are out there. (And you got PageMill before the PC users did.) Also, no matter which platform you use, look at information on all tools. The best and most popular of the tools that are single-platform today may be available for other platforms tomorrow.

Check out these sites for information and reviews of Web tools:

✔ **Stroud's Consummate Winsock Apps list.** This excellent list by Carl Stroud (see Figure 12-2) is one of the best online sources for Windows HTML Web authoring applications, including quick ratings and full reviews of all these tools. The list moves around the Net as the list and demands for it grow. You can find the site at the following URL:

```
cws.internet.com
```

✔ **TUCOWS, The Ultimate Collection of Winsock Software.** This is another great list and also a great Web site (see Figure 12-3). Each tool gets a rating in number of cows.

To find it, go to

```
www.tucows.com
```

✔ **Carl Davis' HTML Editor Reviews.** This site was once very popular and is still valuable. You can find it at several places on the Web, including Carl Davis' personal site:

```
www.webcommando.com
```

The Davis site has a big table that compares the basics of each package — perfect for matching your specific needs with the current state-of-the-art editing packages.

If you compare the information in Stroud's list, TUCOWS, the Davis list, and this book, you can get a really good idea of which key applications may meet your needs.

✔ **Deja Research Service.** This site combines user reviews and a search engine for searching Usenet newsgroups, in which people comment on almost anything, including HTML authoring tools. Start your search at

```
www.deja.com
```

When you search the Deja site, just use the name of the application that you're interested in. You can see lots of comments that may alert you to features and benefits, as well as problems, that you may not know about otherwise. Searching by name is the best way to find out the "dirt" on the latest version of a great tool that you may have heard about — which may turn out to be not so great after all.

✔ **AltaVista.** One of the authors works at a well-regarded search engine, AltaVista. You can use AltaVista for simple searches, power searches, and integrated features such as RealNames support or typing your search in the form of a question, supported by Ask Jeeves. Check out AltaVista at

```
www.altavista.com
```

Just search for the tool by name, and you're sure to find where to download the tool and Web pages developed with it.

✔ **Newsgroups.** The main newsgroup for Web authoring is

```
comp.infosystems.www.authoring.html
```

Join this newsgroup to keep up with ongoing comments and to contribute your own insights. But before you ask a question, check the Frequently Asked Questions (FAQ) list. If your question is not there, ask away.

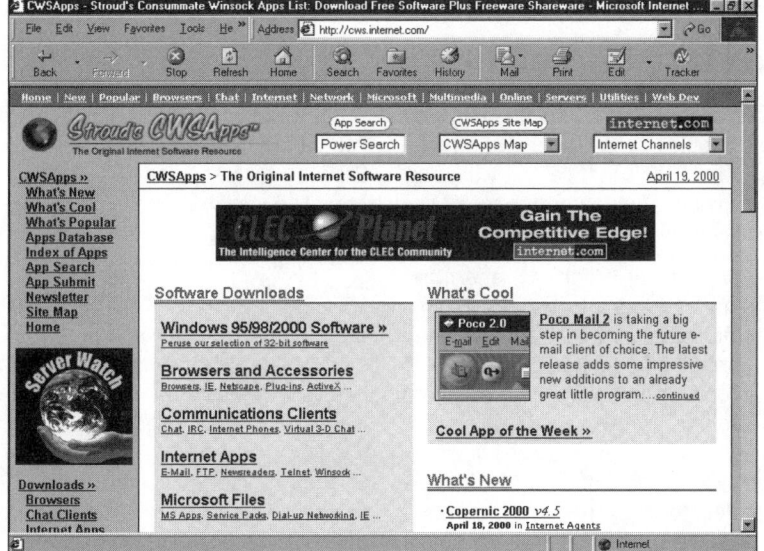

Figure 12-2:
Stroud
should be
proud of
his list.

Figure 12-3:
TUCOWS
for the price
of one.

Converters and so on versus Web authoring tools

As an aspiring Web author, you're going to face the question: Should I try to create my first Web page using "office" tools that I already have, or should I use specific Web authoring tools? We lean toward using specific Web authoring tools.

Many word processing programs, and other office programs such as spreadsheets, have "save as HTML" capability that allows you to save your normal office files in Web-ready format. And converters exist that translate almost any file into Web-ready HTML format. The trouble is, the result rarely comes out looking exactly the way you expect it to. This formatting problem occurs because standard office programs were not originally built for the Web, so they allow you to think that you have much more control over the look of your page than the Web allows. When you convert files from your office program to the Web, most of the formatting is thrown away in the conversion to the much simpler Web formatting. Also, the resulting Web page may have formatting errors or may work well on some browsers but not others.

When you see problems in your converted Web page, your natural reaction may be to go in and fix them — but to do so requires detailed knowledge of HTML and lots of time, neither of which

you are likely to have. (If you knew HTML well, you would have just written the Web page in HTML in the first place!) The better course is to create your Web pages by using one of the full-featured, Web-specific tools we describe in this Part, which only let you create formatting that works well on the Web.

So why bother with built-in "save as HTML" capabilities or conversion tools at all? Some people love their word processing programs so much that they would rather use them than anything else, which is fine. But the major purpose of such tools is to convert large numbers of existing "legacy" documents to the Web. (For our purposes here, legacy documents are earlier documents saved in a format not commonly used on the Web.) Another purpose is to create a large number of least-common-denominator documents that don't look great in print or on the Web, but don't look bad on either. To perform either of these functions, you need to become somewhat an expert in using your word processing program and somewhat an expert in HTML. If you need to convert or create large numbers of Web-ready documents, use this chapter to get started; then use your word processing program's documentation and the HTML information in Chapter 7 to understand enough HTML to get good at converting files.

Cross-Platform Authoring Tools

As Web page creation tools become more powerful and more popular, the importance of their being cross-platform increases as well. Being cross-platform helps the product gain market share and enables large, multi-platform shops — for example, a company with Windows, Mac, and UNIX machines — to standardize on one tool.

Increasingly, the computer world may seem to be Windows 95, 98, or NT–centric. However, this impression is less true of the Web than elsewhere. The Macintosh has a significant share of the Web page creation market and of the market for lower-volume Web servers; and UNIX is widely used for Web servers. Even Windows 3.1 is well represented on the Web. So no computer platform can be ignored in the quest for the best tools.

The ultimate cross-platform tool is HTML itself. Editable from any text editor or word processing program, HTML-tagged text is extremely portable. A basic knowledge of HTML serves you well no matter which kind of computer you use.

Right behind HTML is Netscape Composer, which we describe in detail in Chapter 14. Netscape Composer runs on 32-bit Windows, 16-bit Windows, the Macintosh, and ten different kinds of UNIX. Netscape Composer is also very easy to use, if a little behind in the features race.

Multi-platform shops do well to standardize on Netscape Composer and then let experts use other tools as well.

Other cross-platform tools run on Windows and Macintosh only, and even that can be sliced more thinly: some tools don't run on Windows 3.1, others don't run on 680 x 0–based Macintoshes (that is, most Macs sold before 1996). Add-ons that work with a specific word processing program may run only on the most recent versions of the program. So check the system requirements carefully before you buy a tool, or you may end up having to return it and try again.

High-end authoring tools

This book is written for users who are just getting into Web authoring, so the book includes tools that meet the needs of beginning and intermediate users. Because of this focus, we don't spend as much time on tools that are best suited for higher-end users, such as tools that include built-in site management features and that, not coincidentally, tend to have a street price of more than $100. Two excellent tools that fit this description — and deserve a brief description from us — are Microsoft FrontPage and NetObjects Fusion.

Microsoft FrontPage

Microsoft FrontPage is a very powerful Web authoring and site-management tool that retails for about $140. It supports drag-and-drop Web site management as well as drag-and-drop Web authoring. FrontPage is available as FrontPage 2000 for Windows and as FrontPage 1.0 for the Macintosh. It's the "big brother" of FrontPage Express, the free Web authoring tool we describe at length in Chapter 13.

Among its many very powerful features, FrontPage has an outstanding image editor for creating Web-based graphics. FrontPage also leads in support for ActiveX, which we describe in Chapter 9. (Netscape Navigator, still one of the leading browsers, doesn't support ActiveX.) FrontPage also includes other features that Web server packages, except those from Microsoft, don't support. So if you use FrontPage, you may have to put your site on a Microsoft-powered server and get all your site's users to move to Internet Explorer to take advantage of ActiveX. However, FrontPage is the most popular Web authoring tool and one of the most powerful.

If you are a heavy user of Microsoft Office, or just need a full-featured Web authoring and site management tool at a reasonable price, consider Microsoft FrontPage.

NetObjects Fusion 5.0

NetObjects Fusion is a site-oriented tool for Web page creation and site management, available for both Windows and Macintosh, and retails for about $300. Two outstanding features of this tool are use of a site view as the starting point for your Web work and support for precision layout of Web pages — something normally not possible in HTML.

Fusion also has outstanding support for Java-based interactivity. As is the case with ActiveX, not all Web browsers support Java, or support it the same way. However, Java seems to be the wave of the future, and its capabilities make using it worth serious consideration.

NetObjects Fusion 2.0 was called "the king of Web authoring tools" by no less an authority than C I NET, the online computing resource, and the power and breakthrough features of Version 5.0 support that description as well. However, like other kings, the program may seem somewhat unapproachable at first. But if you want to jump into the deep end of the pool, or shoot for the stars, consider NetObjects Fusion 4.0.

Dreamweaver 3

The full version of Dreamweaver 3 is a bit high-end for our purposes, at $299, but *PC Magazine* calls it "the leading Web authoring program," so we can hardly ignore it. Dreamweaver 3 is also available as a free 30-day demo, so you can get off to a running start before you buy it.

Dreamweaver 3 is notable for its support for numerous high-end elements: Flash and Shockwave, which (like Dreamweaver) are from Macromedia, as well as Java, ActiveX, and much more. But Dreamweaver's real claim to fame is that it never tampers with your HTML code. You can work in a graphical editor, then dive into HTML and make changes, and Dreamweaver won't change your code on you when you return to the graphical editor. This is a huge win versus other programs such as FrontPage. If you're serious, you need to shell out $299 and get a full copy of Dreamweaver.

Windows-Only Authoring Tools

You can find more full HTML authoring tools — as well as other types of tools — for Windows than we are able to cover in this book, although we think we have the best of them:

- **Full-authoring tools.** Numerous full-authoring tools exist in addition to the cross-platform Netscape Composer and Adobe PageMill, the Windows-only FrontPage Express and HotDog Pro, and the Windows-compatible full-authoring tools that we cover in upcoming chapters. One good tool is InContext Spider, which we cover later in this chapter.

- **Application extensions and add-ins.** Most major word processing and desktop publishing programs now have updated versions or add-ins that provide varying levels of HTML authoring capability. Check Deja News, which we describe earlier in this chapter, or check with the manufacturer of your favorite word processing or desktop publishing package to see what's available for your application. In this chapter, Ant Tools is an example of an application add-in.

- **Limited-function authoring tools.** A number of authoring tools have limited functionality because their design makes them easy to use for a specific purpose. One such tool that has received lots of applause is WEB Wizard, a tool for creating an initial Web page.

- **Other tools.** Dozens of PC tools are available for other Internet functions such as Web graphics, Common Gateway Interface (CGI) scripting, Web site management, and many, many other purposes. Another book would be required to even begin to cover all these tools. After you master the basics of HTML authoring, use the sites listed earlier in this chapter to investigate these additional kinds of tools.

InContext Spider

InContext Spider is a full-fledged HTML authoring tool from InContext. It hasn't been maintained or improved over time, like other HTML tools, but may be worth a look for its unique approach to looking at your overall site. The Logical Editor is a special feature that provides a tree-like view of your document. But it is part of an interface that is confusing to novices, in some ways because of the program's power.

What it's like

The demo version of InContext Spider is certainly among the more robust demos that you're likely to see. The file that we downloaded for testing was 9MB, and the installation took several minutes. The demo version's time limit runs out quickly — 30 days after you install it. Clearly, with such a short time limit, InContext intends for anyone who uses the program to buy it.

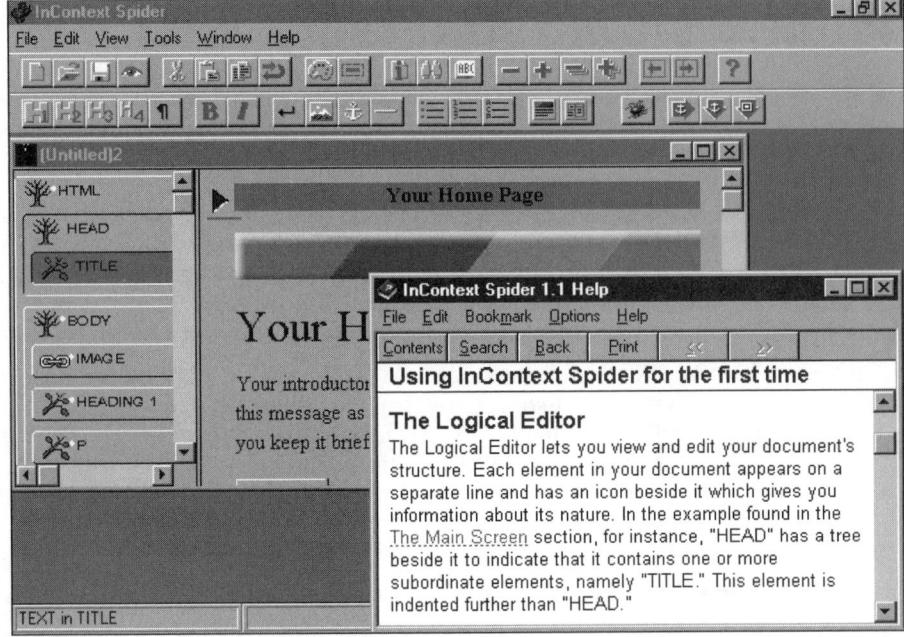

Figure 12-4:
Spin a
Web with
InContext
Spider.

When you start InContext Spider, you get a choice of templates to use. After you choose a template (and you should preview them all at some point to see what's available), the program really begins. The editing window is split between a tree-and-leaf representation of your document and a more typical editing window (see Figure 12-4). You have to figure out the tree-and-leaf thing to feel comfortable working, and that requires a look at the documentation that comes with the demo. The documentation is in Microsoft Help File format and is easy to access through the program's Help menu, but expect to click around and read for a while.

After you make the initial effort to figure out Spider, you discover that it is a powerful tool for use with larger Web sites. The Logical Editor works as an outliner that can enable you to quickly move through your document.

Where to get it

To check for the latest version of the demo, buy the product, or get more information, go to the InContext Web site at

www.incontext.com

The InContext Web site also has information on other InContext tools, including authoring tools for SGML. Many large shops use SGML as a standard way of saving and exchanging documents.

When to use it

If you're using SGML or working in an environment that does, take a close look at Spider and other tools from InContext. And if you really like using an outlining program or the outlining features of your word processing or spreadsheet program, you may feel very comfortable with InContext Spider. Otherwise, take a look at the program and its documentation and see whether the look and feel of the program appeal to you. If so, consider plunging ahead and using Spider as your main Web authoring tool.

What's the buzz?

The main newsgroup comments about InContext are how hot its stock was just after the company went public several years ago, not the merits of Spider or other InContext products. Oh well.

Online reviews have been mixed. People aren't sure how to use Spider, and they think that the product takes too long to figure out compared to most other Web authoring tools. True enough. But Spider is a deeper program than most, and it rewards the serious efforts of those who master it.

InContext added to Spider some specific Internet Explorer and Netscape Navigator extension support. This extension support helps you create Explorer-specific or Navigator-specific Web pages, but may not be that helpful if you want your pages to be readable by users of all browsers.

The bottom line

InContext Spider is probably a bit much if you're a novice, unless you really like outlining tools, and it's falling out of date. But keep this program in mind for more advanced work.

WEB Wizard

WEB Wizard is a very easy-to-use tool with a specific purpose: to create an initial, uncomplicated Web page. In its purpose and workings, WEB Wizard is not unlike the Web-based Web page creation tools we describe in Chapter 3 and the online-service Web page creation tools we describe in Chapters 4, 5, and 6. However, WEB Wizard is just as easy — or maybe even easier — to use. And when you finish, you have the HTML file right there on your hard disk, in case you need to do more editing. The bad news is that you have the HTML file right there on your hard disk, not on a Web server (yet). You need to find space on a Web server and upload the HTML file to it when you're ready.

Where to get it

You can find the Windows version of WEB Wizard at

```
www.arta.com/halcyon/webwizard/
```

Be forewarned that if you search the Web for WEB Wizard information, you may get lots of hits because so many people describe themselves as Web wizards!

What it's like

It's, as we keep saying, easy. WEB Wizard puts up eight screens covering the following topics:

- ✔ Title
- ✔ Background color
- ✔ Image
- ✔ Text
- ✔ List
- ✔ Links
- ✔ E-mail address
- ✔ Filename

Simply provide the information requested in each screen. Figure 12-5 shows a sample screen from WEB Wizard. To go into more detail here would probably take more of your time than if you just try WEB Wizard for yourself.

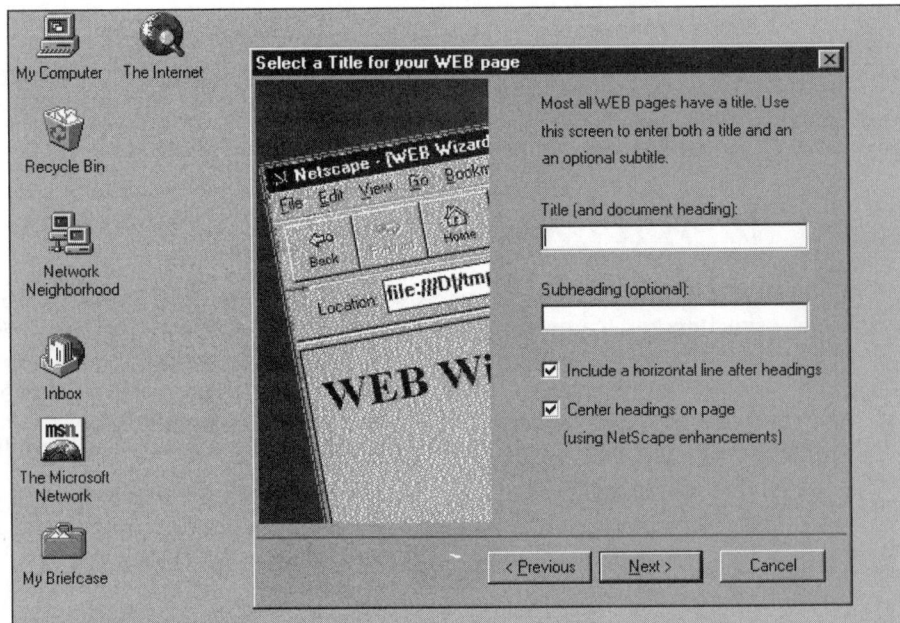

Figure 12-5:
Whiz onto
the Web
with WEB
Wizard.

When to use it

Use WEB Wizard for two purposes:

- ✔ To create your own first Web page
- ✔ To give to your friends who bug you about how to create a Web page

What's the buzz?

The good news: ARTA Media says that a Mac version of WEB Wizard is coming soon.

The bad news: They've been saying that since late 1995, and we still haven't seen it yet.

More good news: The tool does what it says it's going to do — and does so very well. (And no bad news with this one!)

You don't need WEB Wizard much after you master some HTML or figure out another Web authoring tool. But you still have WEB Wizard for fending off your friends who are home-page-deprived.

The bottom line

Try this tool just for fun and spread it around — it's a good one.

Macintosh-Only Authoring Tools

You can find fewer full HTML authoring tools for the Macintosh than for the PC, and we cover the best of the easy-to-use offerings thoroughly in this book. But look for upcoming developments and check out some of the other HTML-related tools.

- ✔ **Full-authoring tools.** The most popular Macintosh Web authoring tools include: Netscape Composer (also a Windows and UNIX tool — see Chapter 14), Adobe PageMill (also a Windows tool), and BBEdit with HTML tools (see the following section). Also worth knowing about are NetObjects Fusion 5.0 and Microsoft FrontPage 1.0, which is available on Macintosh. (Later versions of FrontPage, such as FrontPage 98, are not available for Macintosh.)

- ✔ **Application extensions and add-ins.** As for the PC, most major word processing and desktop publishing programs for the Mac now have updated versions or add-ins that provide varying levels of HTML authoring capability. Check Deja.com, which we describe earlier in this chapter, or check with the manufacturer of your favorite word processing or desktop publishing package to see what's available for your application.

✔ **Limited-function authoring tools.** A number of authoring tools have limited functionality because their design makes them easy to use for a specific purpose. Such tools include several easy-to-use HyperCard stacks for Web authoring. For information on limited-function tools, check the Macintosh-related areas of the Web information sources that we describe in the "Where to Find Online Information about Tools" section earlier in this chapter.

✔ **Other tools.** Dozens of Macintosh tools exist for other Internet functions such as Web graphics, Common Gateway Interface (CGI) scripting, Web site management, and many, many other purposes. After you master the basics of HTML authoring, use the sites listed in the "Where to Find Online Information about Tools" section earlier in this chapter to investigate these additional kinds of tools.

BBEdit and HTML Tools

BBEdit is a very popular shareware text editor for the Macintosh, and the popularity has greatly increased because of the availability of two excellent sets of BBEdit extensions for Web authoring: Lindsay Davies' BBEdit HTML Tools, and Carle Bellver's HTML Extensions. Lindsay Davies' BBEdit HTML Tools are now included as part of BBEdit, so they're the ones you're more likely to end up using.

BBEdit is very popular and has won awards for its capabilities as a Web authoring tool. If you begin to use BBEdit for HTML authoring, you join a distinguished group of Web authors who work on the Macintosh and do much of their work directly with HTML.

Figuring out BBEdit and the BBEdit HTML tools takes some doing. You work directly with text and HTML tags; no built-in preview mode is available, although you can always look at the HTML-tagged text in a browser to see how the Web page is coming along. Many people use other programs to create their initial Web pages and then use BBEdit to fine-tune the HTML tags directly.

If you are a Macintosh user and need easy-to-master tools for editing HTML text, BBEdit with HTML Extensions is the tool of choice.

BBEdit Lite, a freeware version of BBEdit, and Lindsay Davies' BBEdit HTML Tools are on the CD-ROM that comes with this book. For an updated version and further information about the program, go to

www.barebones.com

TextToHTML

TextToHTML converts text and RTF (Rich Text Format) documents to HTML format. Any word processing program or text editor can save its documents to text or RTF, which makes TextToHTML a flexible tool indeed.

To set up TextToHTML, run the Setup TextToHTML application. Then create or locate a text or RTF document that you want to convert. (To preserve as much formatting as possible, save your word processing documents in RTF format.) Now for the fun part. Just drag your text or RTF document over the TextToHTML icon, and the document automatically converts to HTML.

TextToHTML is flexible and really easy to use. However, it's very much freeware — if the program doesn't work, don't expect any recourse or fixes.

For the latest version and more info, go to

```
www.rorohiko.com/texttohtml.html
```

This URL takes you to an archive file that decompresses automatically to a readme file, which explains more about the program and how to use it.

HTML TableTool

HTML TableTool, shown in Figure 12-6, is a small, special-purpose HyperCard stack that has a valuable role: creating HTML tables. To get the tool, go to this URL and look for HTML TableTool:

```
www.ncl.ac.uk/wwwtools/htmltoolseditorsfilter_479.html
```

The archive file you find at this URL decompresses automatically to a readme file that explains more about the program and how to use it.

To use HTML TableTool, follow this process:

1. **Create your table in a spreadsheet or database.**

2. **Save the table as a tab-delimited text file.**

3. **Double-click on TableTool to open it.**

4. **Click the Open button to open the text file.**

   The text file automatically converts to a table and appears in a scrollable, editable window inside the program.

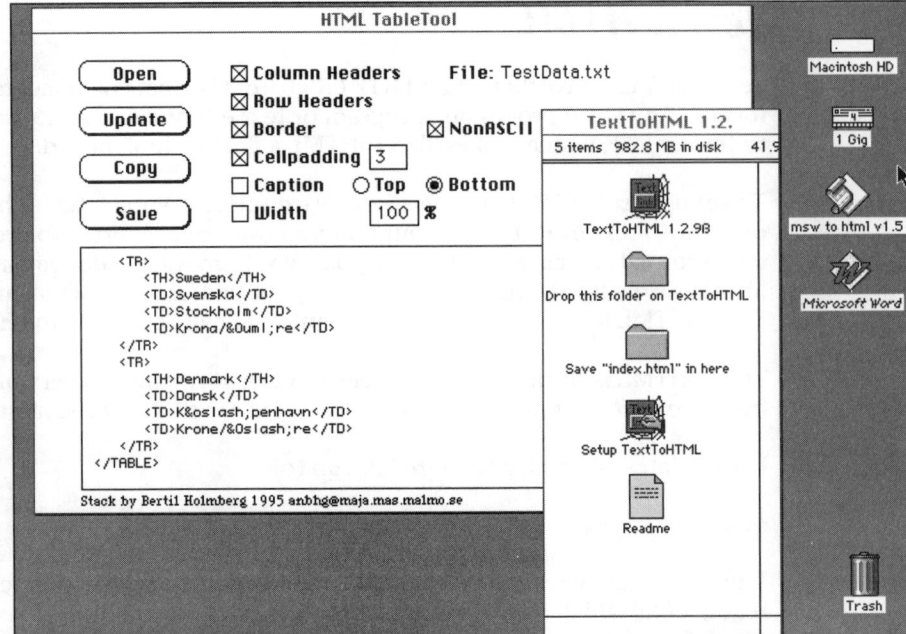

Figure 12-6:
HTML
TableTool
and icons
for others.

The bottom line

These tools are just a few of the best of the hundreds of Windows, Macintosh, and UNIX shareware and freeware utilities available on the World Wide Web. Try these tools and search for additional tools that meet your needs by using the resources in the "Where to Find Online Information about Tools" section in this chapter.

Chapter 13

Tool Along with FrontPage Express

• •

In This Chapter

▶ Understanding the basics

▶ Getting FrontPage Express

▶ Using FrontPage Express

▶ Going beyond FrontPage Express

• •

Microsoft, the acknowledged leader of the personal computer industry, is rapidly moving into a position of Internet leadership as well. Although Microsoft's sales of over $20 billion a year are less than the sales of some other computer companies — such as Compaq, IBM, and Intel — its profits outdistance any other computer company.

More importantly, Microsoft software runs on about 90 percent of all computers, and the company sets technical standards that affect how the PCs of today and tomorrow work. Microsoft also has a large and growing share of the browser market (Internet Explorer), the best selling Web authoring tool (Microsoft FrontPage 2000), and two Top Ten Web sites (`www.microsoft.com` and `www.msn.com`). Microsoft has acquired WebTV (see Chapter 15) and many other exciting Internet-related companies. And Microsoft plays a leading role in the Internet standards-setting process, having recently developed strong alliances in areas such as push technology and new versions of HTML.

Microsoft supports the efforts of Web page creators with its Developer Network. As the name suggests, the Developer Network is for professionals who develop complete Web sites, rather than those who simply create individual Web pages, which we describe in this book. However, the Developer Network is worth visiting, if only to whet your appetite for moving further into Web publishing. You can visit the Developer Network at

```
msdn.microsoft.com
```

From this site, you can access information about and download the latest versions of Internet Explorer and FrontPage Express, a stripped-down version of Microsoft's excellent FrontPage Web authoring product.

Discovering FrontPage Express

Though much less functional than FrontPage 98 or its successor, FrontPage 2000, FrontPage Express has drag-and-drop WYSIWYG (What-You-See-Is-What-You-Get) Web page authoring and even advanced features, such as support for Java, ActiveX, and Dynamic HTML — all advanced programming and page-design standards that even some commercial programs don't support.

FrontPage Express currently runs only on Windows 95, Windows 98, Windows NT, and Windows 2000. Unfortunately, if you use Windows 3.1, the Macintosh, or UNIX, you can't run FrontPage Express. However, you have an excellent alternative in Netscape Composer, which does run on all these computing platforms — see Chapter 14 for details.

If you do become a FrontPage Express user and your Web authoring needs grow, you can buy a copy of FrontPage 2000 and move smoothly to its very similar interface and more powerful capabilities. FrontPage 2000 enables you to manage entire Web sites as well as create stand-alone Web pages. It includes the ability to automatically verify HTML links, supports finding and replacing text across multiple pages, supports HTML frames, and has a set of design capabilities called Themes, which you can program as well as modify.

If you do move to FrontPage 2000, be aware that some of its capabilities don't work correctly when you put your page on the Web unless you have your Web page published on a site running Microsoft server software that supports special capabilities called *FrontPage extensions*. FrontPage Express doesn't have this problem.

FrontPage 2000, the next version of FrontPage, will be bundled as a no-cost add-on to Microsoft Office 2000.

FrontPage Express hides HTML formatting tags, but easily enables you to view them at any time during the editing process. This option enables you to have the direct control that you sometimes need to fix problems or add features. For an introduction to HTML, see Chapter 7.

FrontPage Express or Netscape Composer?

As an aspiring Web publisher, you have a choice between two excellent free programs, Microsoft FrontPage Express and Netscape Composer, which come from the companies that make the two leading browsers. In this sidebar, we discuss the best features of FrontPage Express over Netscape Communicator; in a similar sidebar in Chapter 14 we discuss the best features of Netscape Composer over FrontPage Express. May the best free Web authoring tool win! Superior features of FrontPage Express include:

✔ **Truly free.** FrontPage Express is truly free. The Netscape Communicator suite with Netscape Composer is truly free, as well. (Netscape used to ask users to pay for the Netscape Communicator suite within 90 days, but now makes it available for free.) But you may find FrontPage Express has another advantage for you: it now comes pre-installed on many computers along with Internet Explorer, so you may not even need to download or install it.

✔ **Upgrade path.** If you outgrow FrontPage Express, you can smoothly move up to its big brother, the powerful, popular, and not-free FrontPage 2000, and you'll already know how to use FrontPage 2000's basic functions. Netscape Composer has no such upgrade path.

✔ **Programming controls.** You can insert Java applets or ActiveX controls — Web-friendly computer programs — in a FrontPage Express Web page. If you don't write code yourself, you can get these programs from others and then integrate them into your Web page.

✔ **IE-style Dynamic HTML.** A new version of the HTML language that underlies the Web, called Dynamic HTML, works differently in Microsoft's Internet Explorer 5.0 browser and Netscape's Navigator 4.5 browser. If you use Dynamic HTML, FrontPage Express gets you the Microsoft-supported style until the two companies agree on a unified format.

Both FrontPage Express and Netscape Composer are good products, but if you are a Windows 95, Windows 98, or Windows NT/2000 user and want a Web authoring tool that's capable, free, and has an upgrade path to a powerful Web page creation and Web site management tool (FrontPage 2000), then FrontPage Express is the way to go.

Understanding the basics

Feel free to use the version of FrontPage Express bundled with Internet Explorer 5.0 on the CD-ROM that accompanies this book, or you may want to download it from the Microsoft Web site as part of the Internet Explorer 5.0 browser suite (www.microsoft.com/ie). The best thing about FrontPage Express is that you don't have to pay for it!

The system requirements for FrontPage Express are the same as those for the overall Internet Explorer 5.0 browser suite: a PC-compatible computer running Windows 95, Windows 98, or Windows NT 4.0 or higher, 16MB RAM, and at least 50MB of available hard-disk space. If, while running FrontPage Express, you want to browse the Web to find links, to look at HTML authoring information, or for other reasons, you need more RAM (we recommend 32MB) and more free hard-disk space (about 80MB free should suffice).

For a free tool, FrontPage Express has all the important basic features that you need to build basic Web pages. Using these features, you can

- Create and edit Web pages without seeing HTML tags.
- Drag and drop links to other Web locations without typing the URL or pathname.
- Cut and paste graphics into your Web page, resize graphics, and add alternate text.
- Create and edit tables.
- Create and edit *forms* — interactive data entry fields commonly found on Web pages.

You can also insert multimedia files and computer programs into your Web page. However, not all users can play back those files or run those programs because the users may not have the appropriate browser or the right plug-ins installed. If you add advanced elements, such as multimedia files or computer programs, into your Web page, be prepared to test your pages with several different browsers and to tell your Web visitors what to expect.

FrontPage Express supports forms, but it can't give you the *CGI scripts,* also known as *CGIs* — short for Common Gateway Interface scripts — that are needed to make the forms work. These CGI scripts process the data that the user enters into a form; if you can create CGI scripts, you're probably ready for a more advanced tool than FrontPage Express. However, if you don't want to mess with creating these scripts, you can get CGIs that you can use in your Web pages from others on the Web.

FrontPage Express doesn't support *frames* — advanced HTML elements that split up a Web page into separate, scrollable pieces. Designing Web pages that work well with frames isn't easy, so it makes some sense that FrontPage Express, a free tool, doesn't support frames.

Though FrontPage Express doesn't support frames, it does enable you to add directly into your Web page any HTML tags that you want. However, the whole point of using a tool is to reduce the amount of HTML coding that you have to do; if you find yourself coding directly in HTML to avoid the limitations of FrontPage Express, consider buying a more capable tool, such as FrontPage 2000 or Adobe PageMill.

Going to the bottom line

Like Netscape Composer, which we describe in Chapter 14, FrontPage Express is a very good tool for getting started with Web page authoring. If you use Windows 95, Windows 98, or Windows NT/2000, and use the Internet Explorer browser, FrontPage Express is probably the best choice for you. (If you use a different computing platform or use Netscape Navigator, try Netscape Composer first.) Getting started with FrontPage Express is easy and fun: The program is very simple, yet surprisingly powerful, considering its support for multimedia and computer programs. And it has a more capable big brother, FrontPage 2000, for you to buy when you need more power.

Getting FrontPage Express

You can copy FrontPage Express and the Internet Explorer 5.0 browser for Windows 95, Windows 98, and Windows NT/2000 from the CD-ROM that comes with this book. You can also check for newer versions at the Microsoft Web site and download them (as we describe later in the chapter). To buy the full version of FrontPage 2000 on CD-ROM, see the up-to-date instructions on the Microsoft Web site.

If you already have Internet Explorer installed, you may already have FrontPage Express on your computer. Check Start⇨Programs⇨Accessories⇨Internet Tools to see if FrontPage Express is already there. If so, you don't need to download or install it, you can just use the version that's already there.

If you already have Internet Explorer installed, and just need FrontPage Express, follow the steps in the next section to download the online version. The Internet Explorer Setup program detects your existing files and only installs updated Internet Explorer files plus FrontPage Express, if FrontPage is the only additional software that you request.

Downloading the online version

To make sure that you have the most up-to-date version, you may want to download FrontPage Express and Internet Explorer 5.0 from the Web, instead of using the CD-ROM version. (Microsoft considers FrontPage Express an accessory to Internet Explorer 5.0, so it doesn't give you any way to download FrontPage Express separately.) Follow these steps to download FrontPage Express and Internet Explorer from the Web:

1. **Go to the Internet Explorer home page on the Microsoft Web site:**

   `www.microsoft.com/windows/ie`

   The Internet Explorer home page appears, as shown in Figure 13-1.

2. **Click the link, Download Now.**

   A File Download dialog box appears.

3. **Choose the option, Run this program from its current location, and click OK.**

   The initial part of the setup program will download. The file is about 500K in size and takes about ten minutes to download over a 33.6 Kbps modem. This part of the program will determine which of the needed files you already have and which you need to download. (If you already have Internet Explorer 5.0, only updated files and FrontPage Express will be downloaded.)

   After the initial file downloads, a license agreement appears.

4. **Click I accept the agreement and then click Next.**

   The setup program initializes.

   You are given a choice to Install Now - Typical..., Install Minimal, or customize.

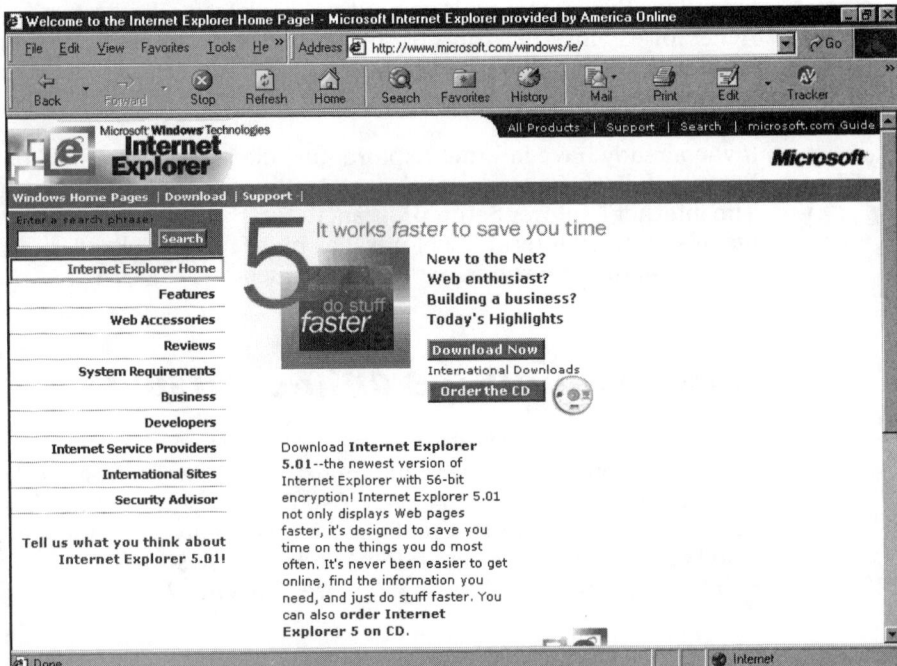

Figure 13-1:
Don't think about it, just download it!

5. **Choose the option, Install Minimal, or customize your browser. Click Next.**

   You must choose this option, or FrontPage Express will not be included in the download.

   The Component Options panel appears.

6. **Choose the location to download to and the components to install. Be sure to check the box for FrontPage Express, under Web Authoring Components. (You may also want to include the Web Publishing Wizard just beneath it to simplify transferring your pages to a server.) Click Next.**

   You are given a choice of regions and download sites.

7. **Choose the appropriate region and a download site, then click Next.**

   The download proceeds. Note that it may proceed very quickly if you already have many or most of the needed files installed. Otherwise, it may take an hour or more.

   After the download completes, the software installs itself. Then a dialog box appears telling you that you should restart your computer.

8. **Click Finish to restart your computer.**

   Restarting your computer allows it to recognize the location of all necessary components and to start with any new files that are needed in the startup process.

Using FrontPage Express

Creating an initial Web page with FrontPage Express is fun because you can easily do most of the things that you may want to do with a Web page, though FrontPage Express doesn't let you do much extra. As you experiment with FrontPage Express, you find that you can re-create many features you have seen on existing Web pages, such as headers, links, and embedded GIF and JPEG graphics. You can discover a great deal about the program (and about the choices available in Web authoring) just by fooling around with menu choices and clicking buttons; you can learn more by creating your own initial Web page.

You can use FrontPage Express to accomplish the following simple Web authoring tasks and create an initial Web page:

  ✔ Create a title for your page.

  ✔ Enter some text and format it.

  ✔ Add a link.

✔ Add an image.

✔ Look at the underlying HTML-tagged text.

✔ Publish the Web page.

The rest of this chapter shows you how to accomplish these tasks with FrontPage Express; in Chapters 14 and 15, we talk about how to accomplish the same tasks with other Web authoring tools. These chapters give you the opportunity to compare tools just by reading the descriptions, and to find out much more about the tools by actually trying the same steps with each program.

Granting yourself a title

Users don't see the title of your Web page in the Web page — instead, they see the title in the title bar of the browser window that displays the Web page. The title is also important because search engines use it to help people find your Web page. You can make the title the same as the document name or the same as the first visible heading in your document, or the title can be different. Take these steps to open a document, save the document, and give it a title:

1. **Choose Start⇨Programs⇨Accessories⇨Internet Tools⇨ FrontPage Express.**

   The program starts, and the Untitled Normal Page window appears.

   Tour the program by trying several options. Rest the cursor over different buttons to see the Tool Tips that show what the buttons do. Pull down all the menus to see what options appear.

2. **Choose File⇨Save.**

   The Save As dialog box appears, as shown in Figure 13-2.

3. **In the Page Title text box in the Save As dialog box, enter the title of your document.**

   In the document we created for this chapter, we entered *Sierra Soccer Club California U.S.A.*

4. **Click the button, As File.**

   The Save As File dialog box appears.

5. **Save your Web page into a folder on your hard disk.**

   FrontPage Express saves the Web page in a folder of its own. You can also save the Web page's graphics, any additional Web pages, and other files that become part of a larger Web site in this folder.

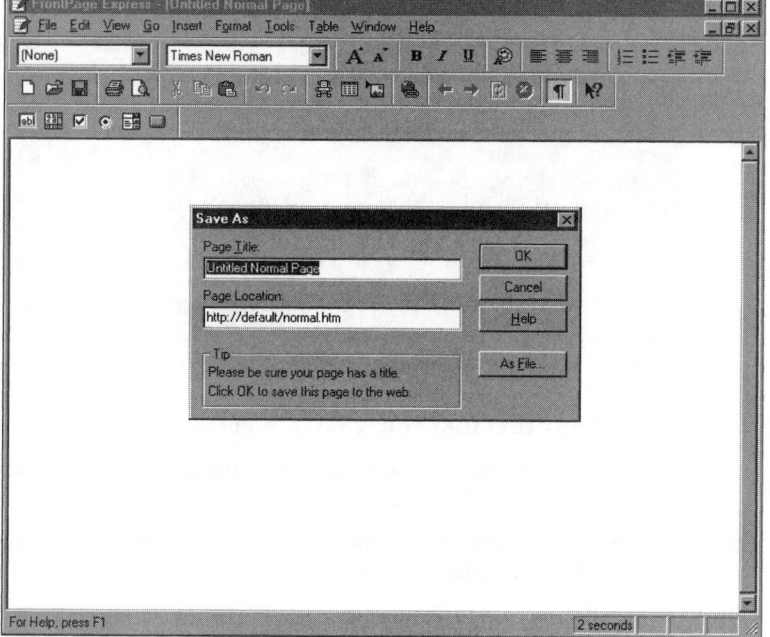

Figure 13-2:
The
FrontPage
Express
main
program
window
with the
Save As
dialog box.

Entering and formatting text

Editing text for Web pages by using FrontPage Express is easy and fun because you can use the formatting options that are allowed on Web pages — and only those options. Follow these steps to type and format some text.

1. **Type in the heading that you want at the top of your Web page.**

   In the document we created for this chapter, we entered *Sierra Soccer Club.*

2. **Move the cursor to the same line as the heading text.**

3. **From the far left pull-down menu, choose Heading 1.**

   The heading text reformats into Heading 1 style.

   Any HTML *styles* — paragraph-level formatting commands — that you choose affect the entire paragraph of text in which the cursor rests.

4. **Move the cursor to a new line.**

5. **Type some text introducing your Web page.**

   When someone searches for your Web page by using a search engine, the search engine may display the Web page title and the first few words that appear in the document. So make the first few sentences of text that follow the title an introduction to the entire page or Web site.

In the document we created for this chapter, we typed:

```
Sierra Soccer Club is a boys' soccer club that practices
and plays at the highest altitude of any in the United
States. If you meet the following qualifications, you
may be eligible to become a member of Sierra Soccer Club:
Born in 1988 or 1989. Sierra Soccer Club has played
together since its founding members were 5 and 6 years
old, and will stick together as they grow up. All our
club members must be born in 1988 and 1989. Some soccer
experience. If you have played in organized leagues
before, or if you're a skilled recreational player, we
may be able to help take your game to new levels. Good
academic record. We are proud that our club members
maintain good standing in school as well as in soccer.
```

6. Highlight any text that you want to format.

In our document, we highlighted the words *Sierra Soccer Club* at the beginning of the first sentence.

7. Click the button for the formatting style that you want: the B button for Bold, the *I* button for Italic, or the U button for Underline.

The highlighted text takes on the formatting you choose.

Formatting items into a list works in much the same way as applying paragraph formats, such as Heading 1. Just select the lines of text and then pick the effect that you want:

1. Highlight the lines that you want to make into a list.

In our document, we highlighted the lines that begin:

Born in 1988 or 1989

Some soccer experience

Good academic record

2. From the pull-down menu, choose the list style that you want: Bulleted List or Numbered List.

The text instantly reformats into the list style that you choose, as shown in Figure 13-3.

If you already know some HTML, terms such as *bulleted list* and *numbered list* should make sense to you. If not, you may want to experiment or read the sections on HTML in Chapter 7 to find out what the choices mean and how best to use them.

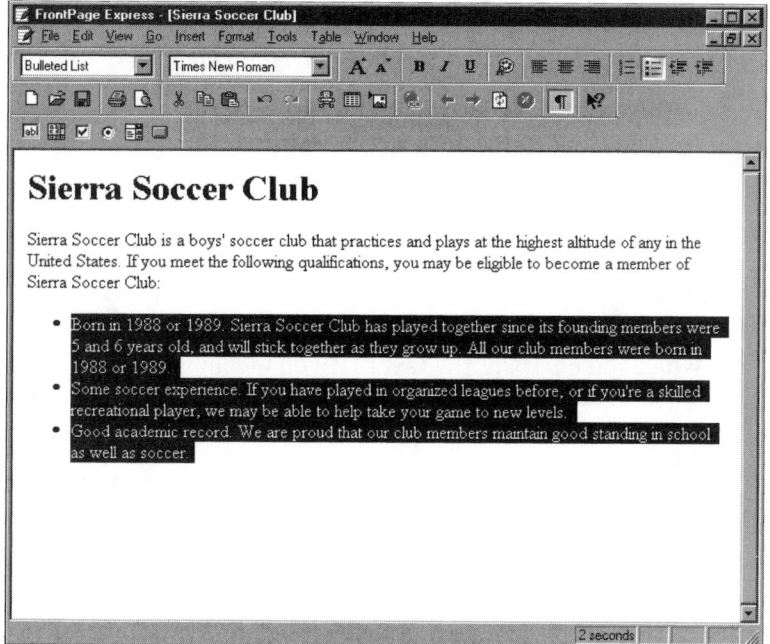

Figure 13-3:
A FrontPage
Express
front page.

Adding a link

Creating and maintaining links is hard work and one area where FrontPage
Express can only help to a certain extent. No matter what tool you use, you
have to understand the different types of links and then carefully maintain
them as you make changes to your Web site. (More advanced tools like
FrontPage 2000 and NetObjects Fusion can help you maintain links across a
site, but that capability isn't available in the free or inexpensive tools we
describe in this book.) See Chapter 7 for much more information on the different kinds of links that are available in HTML. Here's how to use FrontPage
Express to add a link from your Web page to a Web URL.

1. **Insert some text that you intend to add a link to.**

   For our example, we added the following text:

   ```
   This page was created with FrontPage Express. For infor-
   mation about FrontPage Express and FrontPage 2000, see
   the FrontPage Frequently Asked Questions document.
   ```

2. **Highlight the text that you want to serve as a link.**

   In our example, we highlighted the words *Frequently Asked Questions*.

3. **Choose Edit⇨Hyperlink (Ctrl+K).**

   The Create Hyperlink dialog box appears.

4. **Select the Hyperlink Type (http: for a Web page) and enter the URL of the Web page. Click OK.**

   For our example, we chose http: as the Hyperlink Type and entered the URL www.microsoft.com/frontpage/productinfo/faqs .htm#express.

   When you click OK, the text that you highlighted turns into a link and appears in blue with an underline. Figure 13-4 shows how the link looks on-screen with the Edit Hyperlink dialog box open.

If you open a Web page in Internet Explorer before you start this linking process, the URL of the open Web page automatically appears as the URL in the Edit Hyperlink dialog box. This feature can save you time typing the URL and also help you avoid spelling errors. (You can edit or type over the URL if it's not what you want.)

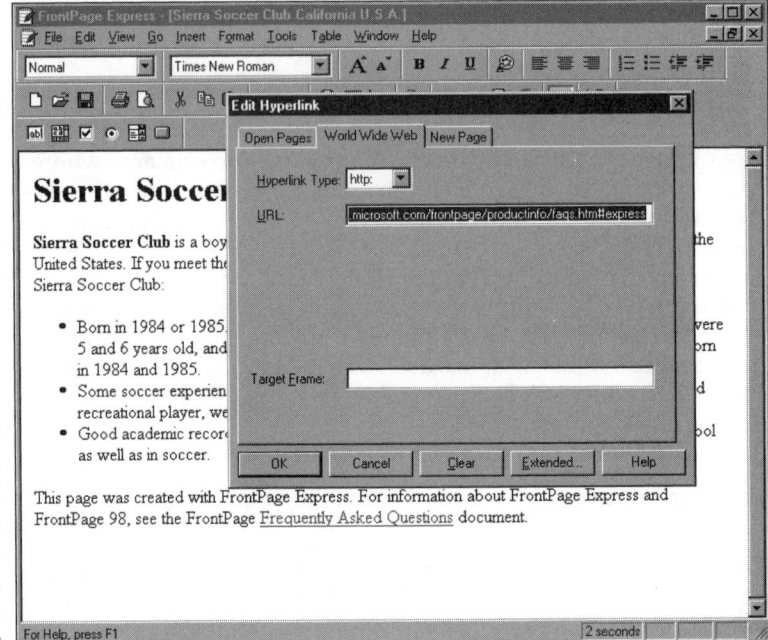

Figure 13-4:
A link that gets people just the FAQs, ma'am.

Adding an image

In FrontPage Express, you can easily add an image to your Web page and, optionally, use that image as an icon to load other documents. Inserting an image in FrontPage Express is a lot like adding a link — as we detail in the following steps:

1. **Create or obtain an image to include in your document.**

   The image should be in GIF or JPEG format. The Web contains a number of sources for free clip art. See Chapter 8 for more information. In this example, we use a JPEG file.

   FrontPage Express doesn't include a preview mode for graphics. Use a program that can view graphics, such as the Windows Paint program that comes with Windows, to search through free clip art resources or files you have available on your hard disk and find the image that you need. Note the filename and pathname of the image so that you can quickly find it to put into your Web page.

2. **Open a Web page in FrontPage Express and position the cursor where you want to place the image.**

3. **Choose Insert⇨Image.**

   The Image dialog box appears with the Other Location tab chosen.

4. **Click the Browse button.**

   The Image File Open dialog box appears.

   The Image File Open dialog box shows you only Web-ready GIF and JPEG graphics files, but you can import other graphics files, including Windows bitmap images, TIFF images, and PostScript images. FrontPage Express converts a file from any of these formats to GIF or JPEG. To see all the file types FrontPage Express handles, pull down the scrolling list, Files of type, in the Image dialog box. Choose the file type that you want to search for on your hard disk.

5. **Browse your hard disk to find the image file that you want to include in your document. Double-click on the image file that you want to use.**

   For our example, we chose the SOCCERP.JPG file from the Sierra folder.

   The image appears on the Web page.

6. **To set graphics options, double-click on the graphic.**

   The Image Properties dialog box appears, as shown in Figure 13-5.

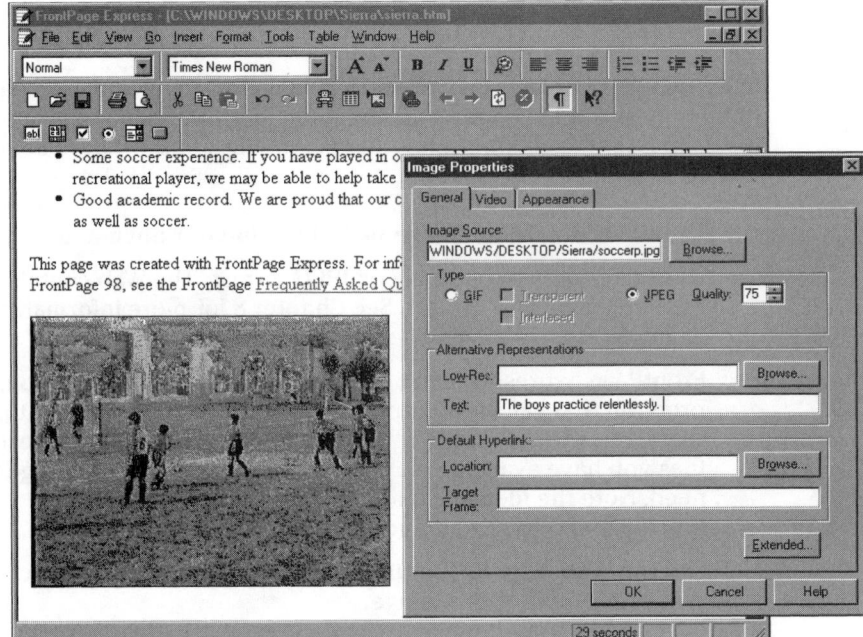

Figure 13-5:
Use Image
Properties
to get your
graphics
right.

7. **In the Image Properties dialog box, set options for the graphic, including**

• **Alternate text:** To display alternative text when the graphic doesn't display, enter text in the Text prompt in the Alternative Representations area of the General tab. (Recommended!)

For our example, we chose the alternative text *The boys practice relentlessly* (see Figure 13-5).

• **Graphical link:** To make the graphic a clickable hyperlink, select or type in a location next to the Location prompt in the Default Hyperlink area.

• **Display options:** To set display options, click the Appearance tab, then enter alignment, spacing around the graphic or a border, and size parameters. If you want to display a text message in browsers that don't display graphics or that have graphics turned off, enter the message next to the Alt prompt.

8. **After you specify options in the Image Properties dialog box, click OK.**

The image updates with the new properties that you entered.

Looking at the HTML

When working in a WYSIWYG (What-You-See-Is-What-You-Get) tool such as FrontPage Express, which shows you what the Web page is going to look like, you often want to look at the underlying HTML code. Doing so enables you to find out how HTML works and gives you the chance to make adjustments in the HTML tags that affect the way your page looks and works on the Web. Here's how to check out your page's HTML code in FrontPage Express:

1. **Choose View⇨HTML.**

   The View or Edit HTML dialog box appears.

2. **Make any changes that you want in the HTML.**

3. **Click the Close box in the upper-right corner of the window to close the dialog box.**

   Any changes you made in the HTML code that cause visible differences in your Web page are displayed in the FrontPage Express window.

Publishing your Web page

Like most other HTML editing tools, FrontPage Express creates HTML-tagged text files that you can publish on any Web server. FrontPage Express offers a special Web publishing service for transferring your site to an FTP site or the Web — you simply choose File⇨Save As, click OK to save the page to the Web, and follow the on-screen instructions. However, the Web saving capability doesn't come with detailed instructions, and FrontPage Express doesn't come with technical support, so you may have trouble figuring out what to do — we did. You can try these built-in Web publishing capabilities if you want to, but we suggest that you use FTP to transfer your files instead, as we describe in Chapter 11. Your ISP or other service that's hosting your Web site can probably give you more detailed information on how to use FTP than on how to use the built-in Web publishing capabilities of FrontPage Express.

Going beyond FrontPage Express

To go beyond an initial Web page and create a full Web site, you need to create a series of linked Web pages that work together. After your Web site grows beyond five or ten linked files, you may find that managing the Web pages as they change becomes difficult — especially maintaining and updating links between files as you add and remove material. You may need to consider a more powerful tool than FrontPage Express to manage your site.

If you like the approach taken by FrontPage Express, you may love the full program, FrontPage 2000. To get it, go to just about any software retailer, including online sources such as PC Connection at www.pcconnection.com, or the Microsoft FrontPage Web site at www.microsoft.com/frontpage. Many reviews describe FrontPage 2000 as the highest-rated and most popular full-featured Web authoring program available today.

Chapter 14

Make Your Web Pages Sing with Netscape Composer

*N*etscape is the company that ignited the spread of the World Wide Web. Started by Jim Clark, founder of Silicon Graphics, and Marc Andreesen, with some fellow refugees from the University of Illinois, the company was begun as Mosaic Communications and then renamed Netscape Communications. Netscape became a classic Silicon Valley success story. The Netscape Navigator browser was *the* ground-breaking application of 1995 and 1996 and made surfing the Web easy, fun, and cool. Despite some loss of momentum in recent years, and in spite of being acquired by America Online a couple of years ago, Netscape is still a leader on the Web.

From its start in ground-breaking, trend-setting browser software, Netscape has expanded into other areas, especially server software. Netscape now calls itself an intranet company and focuses on helping create Internet, intranet, and extranet sites that solve problems within and between businesses. That's understandable; when someone once asked famous criminal Willie Sutton why he robbed banks, he said, "Because that's where the money is." The same is true for intranets and extranets — that's where much of the money is. (Though in the long run, the Internet will probably catch up in terms of financial rewards.)

To fill a gap between its Web browsers and its Web server products, Netscape introduced the Web authoring product Netscape Navigator Gold in 1996. When Netscape introduced its Communicator suite of office products in 1997, it upgraded Netscape Navigator Gold to Netscape Composer. Netscape Composer has much of the appeal of the Netscape Navigator browsers but adds power to facilitate Web authoring as well as Web surfing.

Netscape Composer or FrontPage Express?

The companies that make the leading Web browsers offer beginning Web publishers a choice between two excellent free Web authoring programs, Netscape Composer and Microsoft FrontPage Express. This sidebar describes the best features of Netscape Composer over Microsoft FrontPage Express; in a similar sidebar in Chapter 13, we discuss the best features of FrontPage Express over Netscape Composer. Both tools are excellent — you can try both and choose the one that works best for you! Outstanding features of Netscape Composer include:

✔ **Truly free.** Anyone can now download and use the Netscape Communicator suite, including Composer, for free. (Netscape used to charge a fee for its browser and associated programs, such as Composer, after 90 days of use, but now offers them for free.)

✔ **Support for more computer platforms.** Composer supports all the platforms that the Communicator suite supports, including Windows 3.1, the Macintosh, and many flavors of UNIX — all of which lack support from FrontPage Express.

✔ **Well-integrated with Communicator.** Composer is well-integrated with Netscape Navigator, Netscape e-mail and groupware software, and other parts of the Netscape Communicator suite. Using Composer to send HTML e-mail with all the graphics and formatting options of a Web page, for example, is easy. FrontPage Express doesn't work nearly as well with the Communicator suite.

✔ **Free Design Assistant and templates.** Netscape Composer comes with free plugins that provide additional features such as image maps, file conversion, and special character support for creating your Web page. These plug-ins are available at developer.netscape.com/docs/examples/plugins/compuser. Without the plugins, Composer has fewer features than Frontpage Express, but these additions make Netscape Composer more complete than FrontPage Express and competitive with more expensive, stand-alone packages such as Adobe PageMill.

✔ **More capable than FrontPage Express.** Netscape Composer is a somewhat better tool than FrontPage Express. Composer includes a spellchecker and access to the add-on software of the preceding point in this list. Computer magazine reviews rate Composer as more capable and better integrated. Also, some people consider FrontPage Express simply an introduction to FrontPage 2000, whereas Netscape Composer is Netscape's only Web authoring tool. Netscape puts more energy into expanding and supporting Composer than Microsoft puts into FrontPage Express.

Although Netscape Composer and FrontPage Express are both amazingly good products for the price (free, that is), many people don't have a choice: Composer is the only game in town if you run Windows 3.1, Macintosh, or UNIX. Even if you use Windows 95, Windows 98, or Windows NT 4.0, the only platforms that FrontPage Express runs on, Composer is probably still a better bet if you use the Netscape Navigator browser. Only if you're a Windows 95, Windows 98, or Windows NT user who runs the Internet Explorer browser do you really need to consider FrontPage Express; if that describes you, read about both programs in Chapter 13 and this chapter, and choose the one that seems to better fit your needs.

Netscape has a large site devoted to Web authoring that is definitely worth some serious surfing time. See Figure 14-1 or visit the site at

```
home.netscape.com/computing/webbuilding
```

Figure 14-1: The Netscape Navigator Web authoring site.

From this Web site, you can link to the Netscape Composer download site, a very useful demo, general information about Web authoring, and more.

Discovering Netscape Composer

Netscape Composer is tightly integrated with Netscape Navigator but, unlike previous Web authoring tools from Netscape, is a significantly different-looking program. Figuring out Composer requires a little more time than figuring out previous Netscape Web authoring tools.

Like the Netscape Navigator browser, Netscape Composer is amazing in the breadth of platforms and languages it supports. For those accustomed to waiting many months for each new *port* — the translation of a software product to a new computer system or a new language — Netscape's ability to hit so many targets at once is breathtaking. Like the overall Netscape Communicator suite that it's a part of, Netscape Composer runs on 32-bit Windows, Windows 3.1, Macintosh, and ten versions of UNIX. Composer is available in Brazilian Portuguese, Danish, Dutch, English, French, German, Italian, Japanese, Korean, Spanish, and Swedish.

Netscape Composer is a great starting point for Navigator users who want to get started in Web authoring. You can easily drag and drop hypertext links and graphics from the Navigator browser window to the Composer window. And Composer hides HTML formatting tags but provides a way for you to get at them if you need to.

Although Netscape Composer hides HTML formatting tags, you can be a much better Web author if you have a basic understanding of HTML before beginning. For a solid and well-written introduction to HTML — if you'll excuse our bragging — see Chapter 7.

Understanding the basics

You can download the Netscape Communicator suite, including Composer, for free, just as you can Microsoft's Internet Explorer, including FrontPage Express. Netscape doesn't really specify the system requirements for Composer anywhere that we can find, but you should have a reasonably powerful machine with lots of RAM in order to run Composer. For Windows, a 486 or better with 16MB of RAM should suffice; for the Macintosh, a 68040 or PowerPC-based machine with 24MB of RAM is necessary. You may want 8MB more RAM than the requirements to accommodate simultaneously running the Netscape Navigator 4.72 browser, which uses several megabytes of memory as well. For UNIX, almost any reasonably current machine should work because most UNIX workstations are set up to do heavier work than mere Web authoring.

Netscape Composer is reasonably full-featured, considering that it's free. Using Composer's key features, you can

- ✔ Create and edit Web pages without seeing HTML tags.
- ✔ Create links to other pages on your Web site without typing the URL or pathname.
- ✔ Insert images by dragging and dropping them into your Web page.
- ✔ Resize graphics.
- ✔ Create and edit tables with a very flexible table editor.

Netscape Composer lacks some features that other tools have and some that you expect a tool from Netscape to support:

✔ Composer doesn't allow direct editing of HTML source code; you have to link to an external program to view and edit source code. (This program can be a simple text editor such as SimpleText on the Macintosh or Notepad on Windows, or a more powerful tool such as PageMill for Macintosh or Windows or BBEdit on the Mac.)

✔ Composer doesn't support frames, a controversial but powerful Web innovation pioneered by Netscape; including frames support would make the product significantly more complicated. Nor does Composer support forms, a basic HTML capability supported by all other serious tools, but one not needed by most Web pages.

Netscape Composer creates Netscape-specific pages, using HTML tags created by Netscape, rather than more-standard HTML versions. However, 90 percent of users have either Navigator or Microsoft Internet Explorer, which supports both Netscape and standard HTML tags, so the Netscape-specific nature of Composer shouldn't be a big problem for you or for your pages' users.

Going to the bottom line

Netscape Composer is a great way to get started with Web page authoring. Composer requires little time for most people to figure out because it is so Navigator-like and because it presents the authoring-specific functions in a straightforward way. The fact that the program is missing a few features, such as frames support, actually helps users become familiar with it quickly, because having fewer features contributes to the program's initial simplicity.

If you get more serious about Web authoring, you may need another, more powerful program. But Netscape Composer is a great way to get started with Web authoring.

Getting Netscape Composer

Netscape Composer is on the *Creating Web Pages For Dummies* CD-ROM, or you can get the very latest version, or tell your friends where to get it, from the Netscape Web site:

```
www.netscape.com
```

You say Communicator, I say Composer

Remembering all the names associated with Netscape's products can be hard, especially because the name of the authoring program, Composer, and the name of the overall browser suite that includes the authoring program, Communicator, are so similar. Here's a quick guide to naming the parts:

✔ **Netscape.** Many people say "I use Netscape" when referring to the Netscape Navigator browser, which is understandable, because the company is best-known for the browser. But now that Netscape offers many other products, people need to start saying "Netscape" for the company and the right product name for each product.

✔ **Communicator.** Communicator is the name for the suite of products that you can get with Navigator, including e-mail, collaboration tools, and Web authoring software.

✔ **Navigator.** Navigator is the name of the widely used Netscape browser software. You can download Navigator as part of the Communicator suite or by itself. (But if you download the browser software by itself, you don't get any Web authoring software.)

✔ **Composer.** Composer is the free Web authoring program from Netscape that we describe extensively in this chapter. You can only get Composer by downloading the Communicator suite.

Follow these steps to download Netscape Composer from the Web:

1. **Go to the Netscape Web site at this URL:**

   ```
   www.netscape.com
   ```

   Figure 14-2 shows the Netscape home page.

2. **Click the link, Download.**

   The Netscape Download Web page appears.

3. **Click the link that corresponds to your operating system. For example, if you have Windows 95, click the link, Windows 95/98/NT.**

   The SmartDownload Communicator Web page appears.

4. **Select a Download Location from the pull-down menu, then click the Download button.**

   A Save As dialog box appears.

5. **Specify a save location, then click Save.**

   We recommend you save to your desktop, so you don't have trouble finding the installation file later.

   The first part of the SmartUpdate program downloads. It's about 100KB in size and takes about one minute to download over a 28.8 Kbps modem.

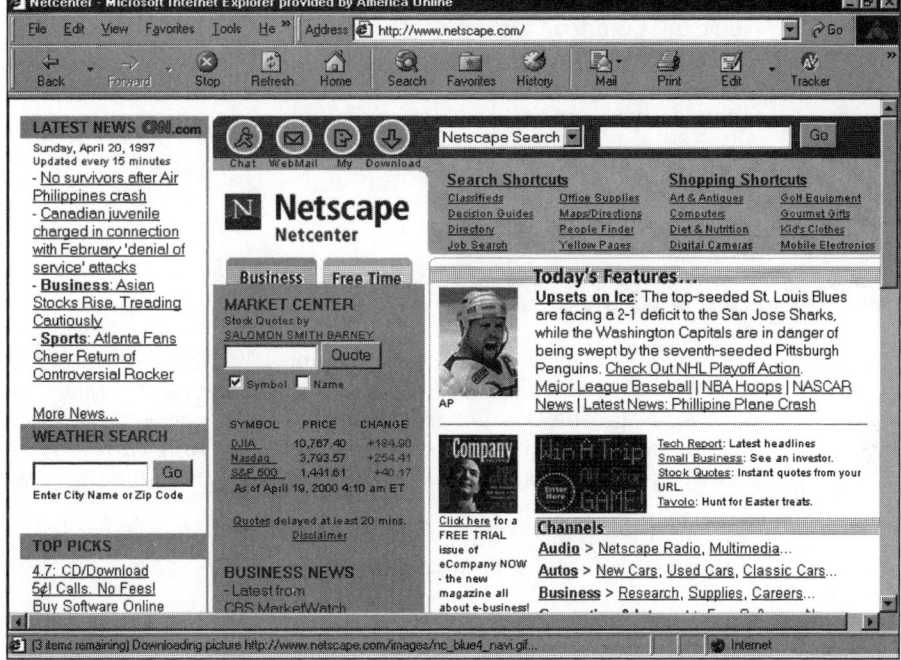

Figure 14-2:
Download
Netscape
products,
including
Netscape
Composer.

The installer for the software downloads. It's about 10MB in size and takes about three hours to download over a 28.8 Kbps modem.

6. Find and double-click the SmartUpdate program.

The version we downloaded was called `sd_cc32e472en.exe`. Follow the instructions on-screen to install the Netscape Communicator suite, including Composer. (You can turn off most options in the installation to save disk space; Composer is one of the core elements that you can't avoid installing.)

The download process can be a bit confusing. Since America Online acquired Netscape in 1998, it has added its somewhat aggressive approach to advertising to the operations of Netscape, and this shows up during the download process. For instance, a window called the InfoBrowser shows ads during the download. (The only "info" that isn't advertising in the window is a link to the SmartDownload FAQ.) You can't turn this window off until the download is over. It's up to you to decide whether you'd rather support this kind of thing by using Netscape's browser and Web creation tools, or other options instead.

You can buy a boxed version of the Netscape Communicator suite, including Netscape Composer, from many computer software sales outlets. You can get a version that includes Internet access software and other extras. For both Macintosh and Windows versions of the software, try the PC Connection Online SuperStore at

```
www.pcconnection.com
```

Using Netscape Composer

Creating a Web page with Netscape Composer is a pleasant surprise because you're looking at a Web surfing-type tool while actually creating a Web page. Because Netscape Composer combines word processing-like features with a Web surfing environment, you aren't limited by your knowledge (or lack of knowledge) of HTML. Just keep experimenting until something works.

You can use Netscape Composer to accomplish the following simple Web authoring tasks and create an initial Web page:

- ✔ Put a title on the page.
- ✔ Enter and format text.
- ✔ Add a link.
- ✔ Add an image.
- ✔ Look at the underlying HTML-tagged text.
- ✔ Publish the Web page.

We cover these steps for each of the Web authoring tools in this part of the book so that you can compare the tools. Using any of the tools, rather than using HTML directly, makes these steps much easier.

Granting yourself a title

Begin by starting a new Netscape Composer document and titling the document.

1. **Choose Start➪Programs➪Netscape Communicator➪Netscape Composer.**

   Netscape Composer starts, and a window called Untitled appears. Then the editing screen appears, as shown in Figure 14-3. You can turn off toolbars later to save screen space and access the same functions by using the program's menus.

For Composer buttons that don't already have a label, rest the cursor on each button; a brief description of its function appears. Buttons that aren't available at any given point are grayed out and don't respond when you click them. For example, the Copy button is grayed out until you select some text or a graphic to copy.

2. **Choose Format➪Page Colors and Properties.**

   The Page Properties dialog box appears.

3. **Next to the Title prompt, type your document's title.**

   In the document we created as an example, shown in Figure 14-3, we typed *My new portable computer* as our title.

4. **Next to the Keywords prompt, type keywords for your document.**

   In our document we typed *Pentium, laptop, Windows 95*.

   Search engines use both the page title and keywords to help people find your Web page. To make your page easy to find by search engine users, give it a descriptive title and relevant keywords.

5. **Click OK.**

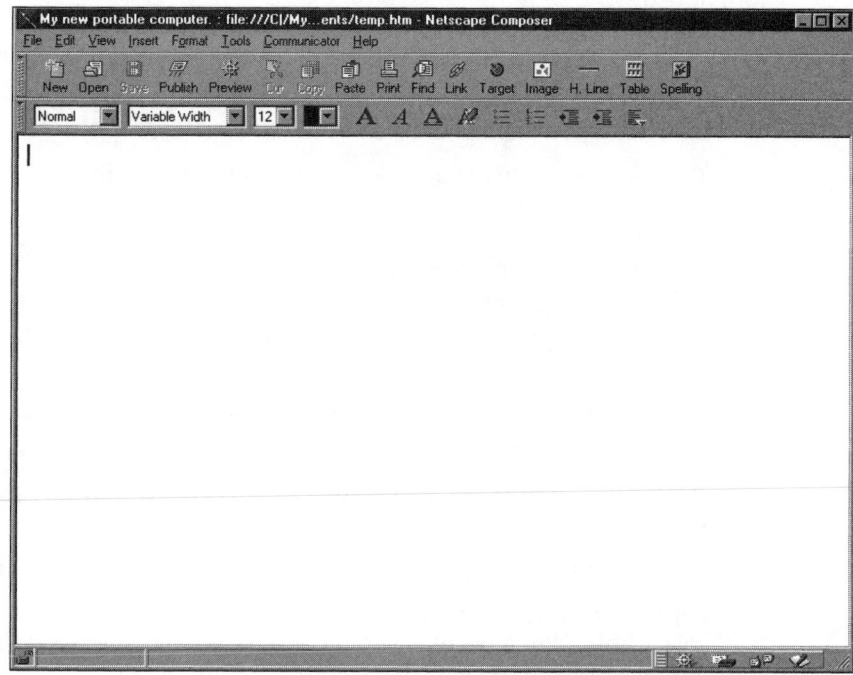

Figure 14-3:
The Netscape Composer editing window.

The title appears in the title bar of the editing window. Composer saves the document title and keywords as a property of the document, but they don't appear on-screen.

In the General tab of the Page Properties dialog box, you can also enter other descriptive information about the document, such as the author's name (that would be you!) and a document description. You can use the Colors and Background tab to set options such as page background, text color, and link color.

Don't worry about required HTML tag pairs such as <HTML></HTML>, <HEAD></HEAD>, and <BODY></BODY>; Netscape Composer automatically embeds them in your document.

Entering and formatting some text

You may have your most fun with Netscape Composer when you apply formatting to your document, as in a word processing program, and see your document instantly reflect the changes — no worrying about remembering to put a slash in the end HTML tag. In this part of the example, you type and format text.

1. **From the File menu, choose Save. Save the document to your hard disk.**

2. **In the Netscape Composer document window, type some text, including a list (you format the text in the following steps).**

   The example in this chapter's figures includes the following text:

   ```
   I just got a new portable computer. I'm extremely happy
           with it. My favorite things about it are:
   133 MHz Pentium MMX processor
   2GB hard disk
   16MB of RAM (I wish it had 32MB though)
   It's much faster than my old portable computer.
   ```

3. **Highlight the text that you want to format.**

   In the sample text, we highlighted *extremely* in the phrase *extremely happy*.

4. **Click the button that corresponds to the text formatting effect that you want.**

   The text immediately appears with the formatting you choose.

   For the example, we clicked the toolbar button with a bold **A** on it to select Bold. When we released the mouse button, the word "extremely" automatically appeared as **extremely**.

If your text has an unwanted style, such as bolding, first highlight the text. Then click the Remove All Styles button in the middle of the Character Formatting toolbar (the one with all the A's in it). The text reverts to normal style.

5. **Highlight the lines that you want to make into a list.**

   In the sample text, highlight the lines about processor, disk, and RAM.

6. **Click the Bullet List or Numbered List button to create the list.**

   The text immediately appears as a list.

   See Figure 14-4 to see how the screen appears at this point in the example.

   If you already know some HTML, you are aware of the types of lists supported by it. For example, in Figure 14-4, we chose a numbered list. (The actual numbers don't appear until a Web browser displays the page.) If you're not familiar with HTML lists, then experiment, or figure out some more HTML, or read Chapter 7 or the Netscape Composer Help files to understand what the choices mean and how to use them.

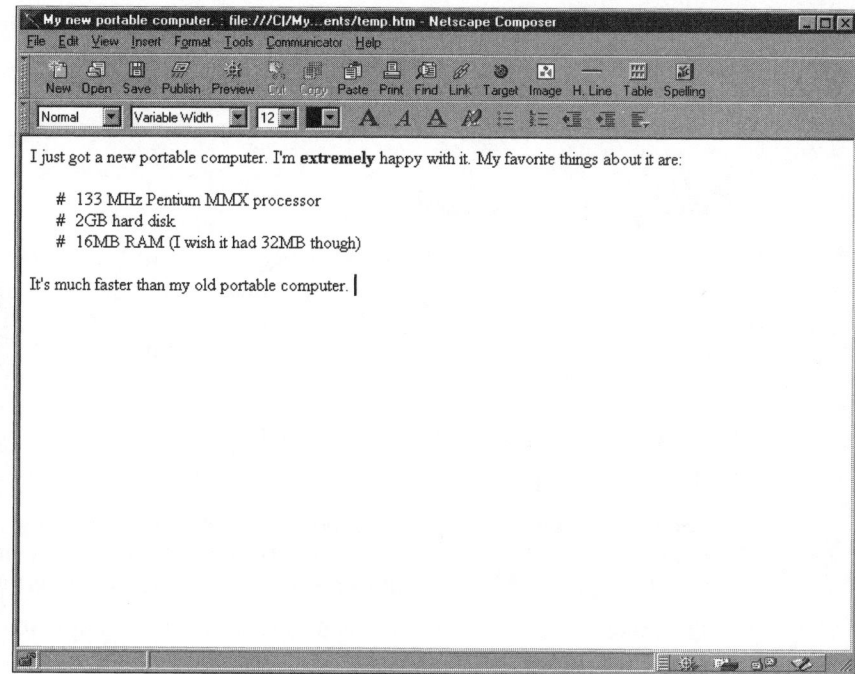

Figure 14-4:
In the Netscape Composer editing window, you see the beginnings of a beautiful Web page.

Adding a link

One of the biggest problems in creating Web pages is accurately creating links. Netscape Composer eases this task considerably. This example shows how to add a link to a Web page:

1. **Highlight the text that you want to serve as a link.**

   In the example, we highlighted the words *Pentium MMX*.

   If your text comes out with an unwanted paragraph format, such as being part of a bulleted list, highlight the text and then choose the Normal paragraph format from the pull-down menu in the Paragraph Format toolbar. The text reverts to normal paragraph format.

2. **Click the Link button (the button that looks like a chain link, located near the middle of the Composition toolbar).**

   The Character Properties dialog box appears with the Link tab front-most.

3. **Enter the URL of the address you want to link to under the prompt, Link to a Page Location or Local File.**

   In the sample Web page, we entered `www.intel.com/mmx/index.htm`.

   You can copy and paste a link or URL from Netscape Navigator into the text entry area for the link.

4. **Click OK to complete the link.**

Adding an image

To add an image in Netscape Navigator, you can either drag and drop from a Navigator browser window or open a file. The file must be in GIF, JPEG, or Windows BMP format. You can get free graphics from the Web and use them in your documents. Follow these steps to put a graphic stored on your hard disk into your Web page:

1. **Create or obtain an image to include in your document.**

   Use a GIF or JPEG image.

2. **Position the cursor in your document at the point where you want to put the image. Then click the Image button (the button with the geometric objects on it, located in the middle of the Composition toolbar).**

   The Image Properties dialog box appears with the Image tab up front.

3. **Click the Choose File button.**

   The Choose Image File dialog box appears.

4. **Select the image file you want. Click Open.**

   The pathname of the file appears in the Image Properties dialog box.

5. **Click the button, Alt.Text/Lo<u>w</u>Res.**

   The Alternate Image Properties dialog box appears.

6. Under the prompt Alternate Text, enter text describing the image.

For our example we entered *Netscape Composer window*.

7. Click OK.

The Image Properties dialog box appears again.

8. Click OK.

- If the image is not a GIF or JPEG image, but is in one of the formats that Netscape Composer can convert into GIF, the Image Conversion dialog box appears. If the dialog box appears, click OK to convert the image.

- If the image is in JPEG format, the JPEG Image Quality dialog box appears. If so, choose a quality setting (we recommend Medium for most images) and then click OK.

The image appears in your Web page.

9. Resize or reposition the image, if needed.

To resize the image, double-click on it. The Image Properties dialog box appears again. In the Image Properties dialog box, you can change the size of the image, create a border around it, and set other options. For the Web page shown in Figure 14-5, we made the image smaller and then used the Alignment button on the Composer toolbar to center it.

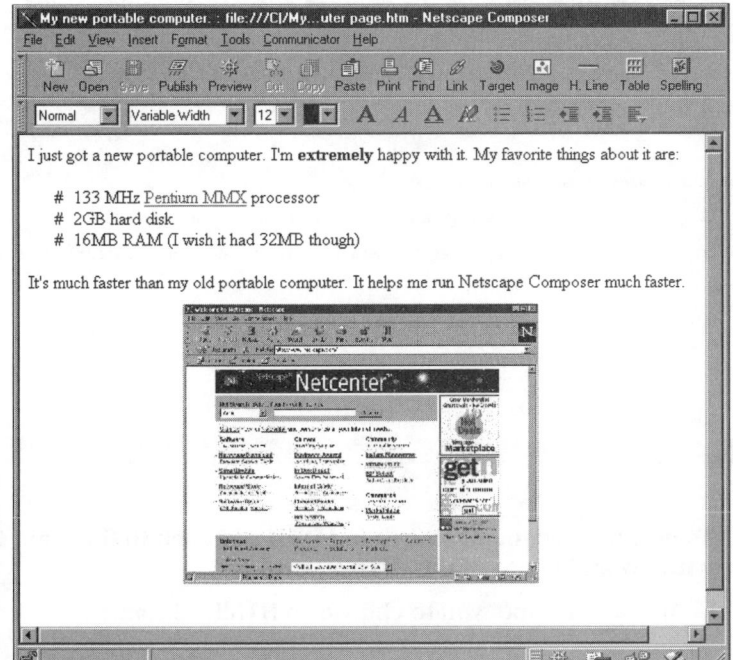

Figure 14-5:
The completed first Web page.

Don't publish a Web page with a "borrowed" graphic in it without first getting permission from the image's owner.

Looking at the HTML

To view the HTML source of a document in Composer, use the same menu command as in Netscape Navigator:

1. **Choose View⇨Page Source.**

   The HTML-tagged text underlying the Web page appears. You cannot edit the document in this window.

   Figure 14-6 shows the HTML-tagged text for the Web page shown in the preceding figure.

```
Netscape

<HTML>
<HEAD>
    <META HTTP-EQUIV="Content-Type" CONTENT="text/html; charset=iso-8859-1">
    <META NAME="Author" CONTENT="Bud Smith">
    <META NAME="GENERATOR" CONTENT="Mozilla/4.02 [en] (Win95; I) [Netscape]">
    <META NAME="KeyWords" CONTENT="Pentium, laptop, Window 95">
    <TITLE>My new portable computer.</TITLE>
</HEAD>
<BODY>
I just got a new portable computer. I'm <B>extremely</B>
happy with it. My favorite things about it are:
<OL>
<LI>
133 MHz <A HREF="http://www.intel.com/mmx/index.htm">Pentium MMX</A> processor</LI>

<LI>
2GB hard disk</LI>

<LI>
16MB RAM (I wish it had 32MB though)</LI>
</OL>
It's much faster than my old portable computer. It helps me run Netscape
Composer much faster.
<CENTER><IMG SRC="../WINDOWS/DESKTOP/Online Services/CWP new figures/CW1102.JPG" ALT="Netsc

</BODY>
</HTML>
```

Figure 14-6: HTML-tagged text for the Web page shown in Figure 14-5.

2. **To edit the document source in HTML, go back to the main Composer window and choose Edit⇨HTML Source.**

   Composer prompts you to choose an HTML editor.

3. **Choose an editor to use for the HTML-tagged text.**

   You can use a text editor such as Windows NotePad, a word processing program, or an HTML editor such as BBEdit (see Chapter 12) or the HTML editing capability in PageMill (see Chapter 16). If you use a word processing program, be sure to always save your HTML files in plain text format. If you don't, the word processor adds formatting commands to the document that Netscape Composer doesn't understand.

4. **Edit the document's HTML-tagged text.**

5. **Save the document and exit the editing program.**

   You return to Netscape Composer.

6. **Click Yes when the Reload File dialog box appears and asks if you want to reload the page to see the changes.**

   Netscape Composer displays the modified page.

Publishing your Web page

Netscape Composer creates HTML-tagged text files that you can publish on any Web server. However, Netscape Composer doesn't offer any special services for Web publishing. As with most other Web authoring tools, you are on your own when it comes to getting an account on a Web server, transferring your Web files to the server, and testing the site after it becomes available on the Web. See Chapter 11 for information on how to publish your Web page.

To publish a Web page or Web site in Netscape Composer, use the program's built-in Publish function.

1. **Click the Publish button.**

   The Publish Files dialog box appears.

2. **Enter the FTP site or http (Web) site to which you want to upload the files.**

   If you don't already know this information, obtain it from the Internet service provider or other party that hosts your site.

3. **Enter your user name and password, if any.**

4. **Click OK.**

   The program transfers the files to the FTP site or Web server. Go surf them!

Going Beyond Netscape Composer

Netscape Composer is free, as is the Netscape Communicator suite that Composer comes in. However, if you need a somewhat more capable product with printed documentation, technical support, and added features such as templates and clip art, you may want to consider moving up to Adobe PageMill (see Chapter 16), a $99 program that has features such as more graphics conversions, drag-and-drop QuickTime multimedia support, and support for both forms and frames. PageMill also includes a "bigger brother," SiteMill, which gives you site management capabilities as well.

Netscape Composer is a great choice for getting started with Web page authoring and for use on UNIX, which has few other easy-to-use Web page creation tools. Look at the other tools that we cover throughout Part V of this book if you want to go further.

Chapter 15

Weaving Web Pages for WebTV

*1*n the fall of 1996, at the crest of one of the waves of Internet euphoria that have repeatedly rolled through the computer industry and the press, a new kind of Web access device was announced. WebTV was, and still is, a wonder. WebTV is a small "set-top box" that connects to your television and for the first time makes possible the display of reasonable amounts of text — a few hundred words, instead of a few dozen — on a television screen. Advanced circuitry in the WebTV box reduces flicker, and the equally advanced WebTV network adjusts Web pages in transit to make them work better on television.

At a cost of about $100 for the most basic WebTV device, or as a built-in feature for some satellite TV controller boxes, WebTV gives you access to e-mail, newsgroups, and the Web — the "killer apps" of the Internet. Early buyers of WebTV found themselves buying additional WebTV units for their parents, other relatives, and friends in order to connect by e-mail. People who had been among the least computer-savvy suddenly found themselves able to put up their own home pages on the Web. Even after its acquisition by Microsoft in 1997, WebTV has continued its life as an innovative company.

You may want to know how your Web pages look when viewed on WebTV, or you may be a WebTV owner and want to know whether you can publish a Web page of your own. Never fear, *...For Dummies* is here! One of the authors has held a privileged position inside WebTV, working for the company on its developer Web site — a resource for those who want to develop Web pages that work on WebTV — at `developer.webtv.net`. He watched the number of subscribers double — from 250,000 to 500,000 — in less than a year. He also discovered some of the problems that WebTV has in Web page browsing and in Web page publishing, as well as how to get around these problems. We now pass that knowledge on to you.

Discovering WebTV

Don't tell anyone, but WebTV is a low-cost computer that uses a television as a display device, as did the very early personal computers first sold in the late '70s, such as the TRS-80 and the first Apple computers. The main differences between then and now are the utter simplicity of using WebTV and the emergence of a new use for a low-cost personal computer (PC): accessing the Internet.

Although the Web has the sizzle, and surfing the Web is indeed a popular use of WebTV, e-mail is the steak for both the Internet and for WebTV. Keeping people connected always has been big business, from the telegraph to the telephone and now through e-mail over the Internet. With the Web adding appeal, and with the low cost and simplicity of getting started with WebTV, the future of WebTV looks bright.

Several kinds of WebTV boxes exist: the early Classic, the newer Plus, and new units integrated into satellite dish systems. These systems come with remote controls and, usually, with an optional keyboard. The WebTV Plus has more memory and a hard disk and has almost completely replaced the Classic in stores. A WebTV Plus currently costs less than $200 plus a monthly fee for Internet access. For information about buying a WebTV unit, or about WebTV in general, visit www.webtv.net.

Note that the URLs for WebTV that we provide in this chapter end with .net, not the more common .com. The .net suffix indicates that WebTV is an Internet service provider.

The best thing about WebTV may well be its utter simplicity. Though the innards of a WebTV box are basically a computer, the user's job is much simpler. As a WebTV user, you don't need to install software or figure out complicated commands. A simple system of menus enables you to access e-mail, the Web, and advanced television functions. For an experienced computer user, using WebTV is fun but limiting; for people who have avoided the Internet because of the complexity of personal computers, WebTV may seem like a near-miracle.

Several competing systems have come and — for the most part — gone, but WebTV continues to grow slowly but steadily. Although Microsoft purchased the company in 1997, it continues to operate as a relatively independent subsidiary, reaching 500,000 subscribers in late 1998. (In a possible sign of slowing growth, the company has since stopped publicizing the size of its subscriber base.)

You should consider WebTV in your Web publishing plans for several reasons:

- ✔ **Steady growth.** WebTV is growing steadily, with growth into Japan and other countries in the offing.

- ✔ **Over one million users.** System sales only tell half the story, because each WebTV system averages about two users. (Any one system can support up to five separate e-mail accounts, although many are used by just one individual.) The WebTV installed base of over 500,000 systems translates into over a million WebTV users already.

- ✔ **Active users.** According to usage measurements from WebTV Networks, Inc., WebTV users are very active users, putting in much more time online than typical, PC-based Internet users.

- ✔ **More on the way.** Other lower-resolution devices are coming. From Palm Pilot to handheld PCs to TV-based WebTV competitors, expect to see more and more users with lower-resolution screens accessing the Web.

- ✔ **WebTV for you?** You may be a die-hard computer user yourself but expect to see WebTV-like systems in classrooms, hotels, and other locations in the future. Also, you may want an affordable Internet access device for your spouse, kids, parents, or friends. In some circumstances, you may need a personal computer to do whatever job you have in mind; but in others, the affordability and simplicity of WebTV-type devices is just the ticket.

Creating Web Pages for WebTV

That WebTV does a very good job of displaying Web pages on a television set — something many people said couldn't be done — bears repeating. Figure 15-1 shows a typical Web page on WebTV, as captured by the WebTV Viewer. (See the sidebar for a description of the WebTV Viewer.)

Although the way WebTV displays Web pages is a real accomplishment, some big differences exist between the way Web pages look and work on WebTV versus on a personal computer. Here are the four main differences to keep in mind as a Web publisher whose pages may well be accessed by WebTV users:

Figure 15-1:
A typical
Web page
as seen on
the WebTV
viewer.

✔ **Brighter colors.** Colors look much different on a television set than on a personal computer monitor.

✔ **Bigger text.** Text looks much different on a television set than on a personal computer monitor.

✔ **Different layout.** An overall Web page "look" that is attractive on a personal computer may be squeezed out of shape on the lower-resolution TV monitor.

✔ **Fewer multimedia technologies.** Some multimedia technologies commonly supported on the Web are not supported on WebTV.

At this point, you may be saying, "What? I've only just now figured out enough about HTML tags to get by, and now you tell me things that make publishing on the Web even more complicated?" But the interesting thing about Web pages that look good on WebTV is that they follow most of the principles in this book — relatively clean, simple pages without gratuitous multimedia. The HTML jockeys trying to do fancy multicolumn table layouts are the ones who are more likely to have problems.

Still, you need to be aware of the issues we discuss in this section. Just remember that for the most part, Web pages that look good on WebTV are also the Web pages that have fewer problems on personal computers. We tackle the concerns one at a time.

Color and WebTV

Some colors that look great on a personal computer monitor look terrible when viewed on television. For example, viewed on a television set, strong reds actually "bleed" into surrounding areas, strong whites seem to glow, and some color combinations cause the screen image to warp. Because reds and whites are commonly used in Web pages, some Web pages that use these colors look bad when viewed on television. (Yes, we've seen Web pages with red text on a white background: They look great on a PC monitor, but look terrible on a television screen.)

We can't really show you what this color problem looks like because even a color picture doesn't convey the full effect — you really have to see the real thing to get a feel for it. You never see these sorts of problems on a regular TV show either. The entire television production process is designed to remove extra-bright colors and patterns such as thin lines and checks that cause weird effects on TV. (If you can catch an old rerun of *The Tonight Show* with Johnny Carson and Ed McMahon, some of Ed's sports coats might cause a bit of visual weirdness on your TV!)

To prevent these problems, avoid using bright colors on your Web page, especially bright red and bright white. WebTV users will thank you. (If you are a WebTV user, you'll thank yourself!)

For more information, you can look at the WebTV developer's Web site at `developer.webtv.net.` One of the authors of this book has written an article describing how to use color in a way that works well on both personal computers and WebTV. Check it out.

Bigger text and WebTV

A television set has a lower resolution than a computer screen. The lowest-end computer screen acceptable for Windows 95 and above is 800 pixels wide and 600 pixels tall. But a television set can only be counted on to display an area about 560 x 420 pixels. The display area of a television screen is only about half the display area of a low-end Windows 95 screen.

Also, the default text size for a personal computer Web browser is typically about 12 points in height; WebTV automatically displays text at a size equivalent to about 18 points. This font sizing is needed to make the text easily readable on TV, but the larger font size also means that you can fit less text on-screen with a TV than with a PC monitor.

Figure 15-2 shows the developer.webtv Web page on a computer screen. Compare Figure 15-2 to Figure 15-1, the same screen shown in the WebTV viewer, to see how much more text and graphics can fit on a PC monitor than on the WebTV screen.

What does this difference mean to you as you create Web pages? We mention earlier in the book that you should consider fitting your message into one or two screens of text, so the user doesn't have to scroll down much. You have to cut your word count even more to accomplish this goal for users viewing your page on WebTV. You may want to design your page with these users in mind, though; "short but sweet" is a good way to communicate in any medium.

You can get a very good idea of how your Web page's text looks on WebTV by viewing the Web page in the WebTV Viewer, a tool available from the `developer.webtv.net` site. See the sidebar "The developer site" for more about this robust site.

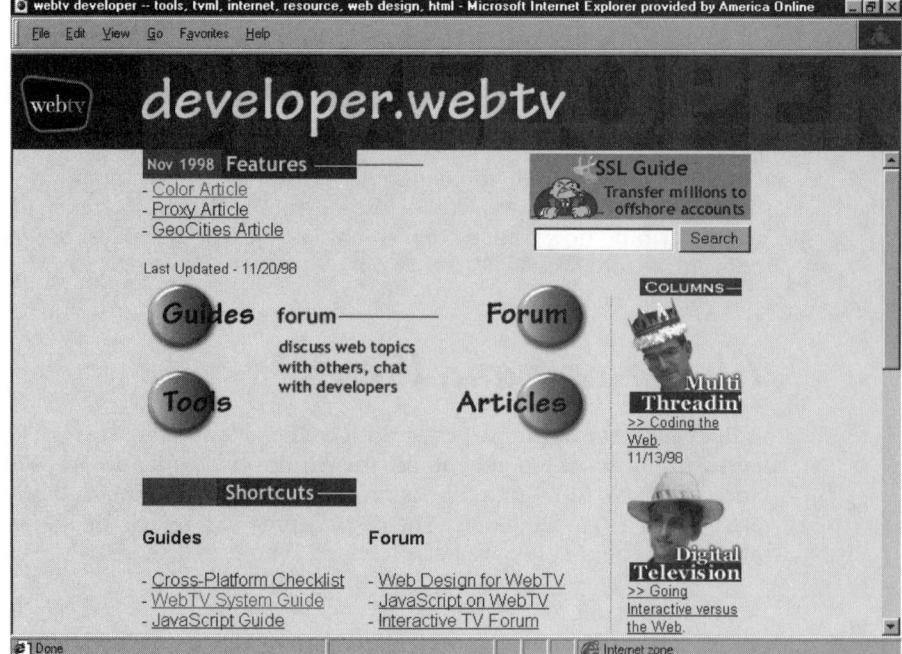

Figure 15-2:
More verbiage fits on a computer monitor than on a TV screen.

You may be thinking, "Why doesn't someone just replace all those crummy television sets?" Well, that is exactly what will happen eventually. High Definition Television (HDTV), a high-resolution television standard, is starting to be deployed in the United States and elsewhere in the world. An HDTV set, equipped with some future version of a WebTV-like device, will be able to display Web pages with as much resolution as your current personal computer monitor, and at a much larger size.

Different layout

Many Web sites favor complex or dense layouts, such as the three-column layouts so popular on many sites. These sites tend to have problems on television, and they challenge the minds and eyeballs of personal computer users as well. Usually, the narrowest column in a three-column layout can't hold enough text to make sense when displayed on television; the text displays in an extra-long column with just a word or two on each line.

With or without WebTV, two-column layouts are easier on users' eyes and also easier to design and maintain. Stay away from complex and dense layouts in all your Web pages, and your pages will look better when viewed on a TV screen.

The developer site

WebTV has a Web site for Web developers — Oh, the repetition! Oh, the repetition! — at developer.webtv.net. Put together at considerable expense and effort by a team that includes one of the authors of this book, developer.webtv, as the Web site is called, provides a great deal of information about a variety of WebTV-related development topics. The major focus of the site is cross-platform Web page development: creating Web pages that look good on WebTV as well as on personal computer browsers.

One of the coolest things about developer.webtv is that the site includes several tools for testing planned or existing Web pages. The Color Picker lets you generate color combinations for testing on both personal computers and WebTV. And the WebTV Viewer is a free computer program that you can download (in a Windows or a Mac version) and use to preview your Web pages in a WebTV-like window.

The best thing of all about developer.webtv is that you can find out a great deal about Web development in general, not just for WebTV. Reading the articles, columns, and guides gives you an additional perspective on many of the issues we discuss in this book. And a fresh perspective may be just what you need in climbing toward the pinnacle of usefulness and fun with your own Web site.

You may want to be really tricky and create special versions of your Web pages to display only to WebTV users, while other users see your "regular" Web pages. The way to do this is to use a CGI or JavaScript script called a *browser sniffer* to identify WebTV users and show them different versions of your Web page. For detailed information about using a browser sniffer, see:

developer.webtv.net/design/sniffer

Fewer multimedia technologies

WebTV actually does a good job of supporting multimedia overall; support for a long list of standards is built into the box or provided by the WebTV Network's ever-active servers. But a few multimedia technologies that are commonly supported by PC Web browsers are not supported by WebTV, including (at this writing) RealAudio 5.0 and QuickTime movies. If you follow the advice in this book, you keep the use of multimedia in your Web pages low anyway, in order to avoid problems. By using multimedia wisely, you also don't run into many problems when WebTV users access your Web pages.

Creating Web Pages with WebTV

WebTV users are enthusiastic users of the Internet and also avid consumers of any information they can get about WebTV. If you are a WebTV user, you probably have read the above with interest and visited both the WebTV corporate Web site and the developer site mentioned in the sidebar. In the following sections, we discuss creating Web pages with WebTV. For more information, see *WebTV For Dummies,* 2nd Edition, by Brad Hill (IDG Books Worldwide, Inc.).

Creating a Web page with GeoCities

Web publishing is a very popular activity for WebTV users. Many WebTV users have become very savvy Web publishers, in some cases largely through trial and error.

To see Web sites created by WebTV users or that relate to WebTV, visit the *Web ring* for WebTV-authored Web pages. (A Web ring is a set of linked Web sites on a specific topic.) The URL for the "Authored with WebTV" Web ring is

```
www.webring.org/cgi-bin/webring?ring=webtv3;list
```

If you want to create your own Web pages on WebTV, we have some good news. The instructions for using the GeoCities Web site, which we describe in Chapter 3, will work for you just fine. GeoCities is a Web site that gives users free space to create their own Web pages. GeoCities is an extremely popular Web site among WebTV users, many of whom have published home pages on GeoCities. The GeoCities site even has specific instructions for WebTV users, as shown in Figure 15-3. Just type in **webtv** and click Search from to the GeoCities Help page at

```
help.yahoo.com/help/us/geo
```

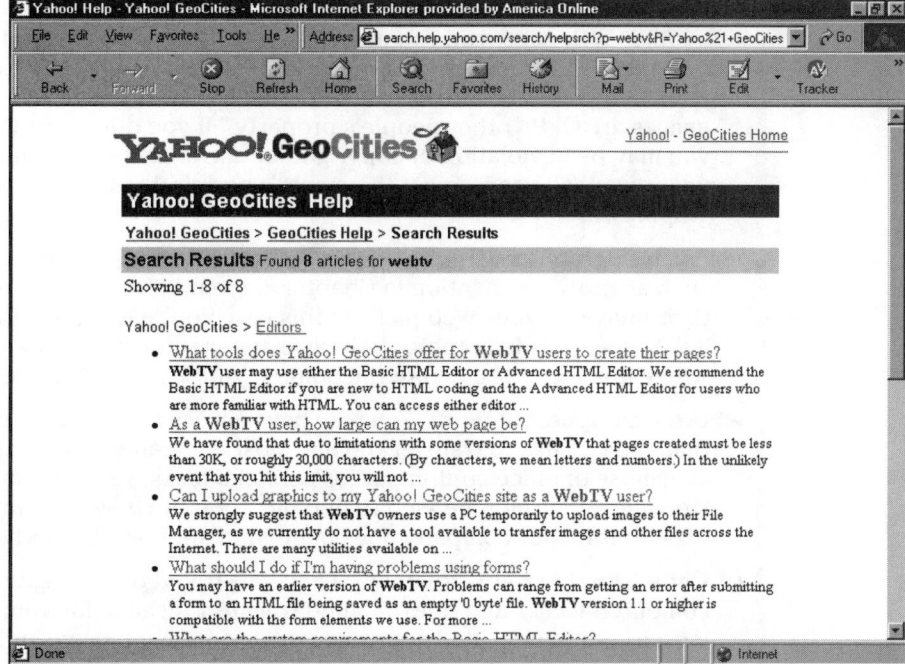

Figure 15-3:
GeoCities
has specific
WebTV
information.

Getting graphics onto the Web

The big problem that you run into in creating Web pages on GeoCities, or using any other technique as a WebTV user, is file transfer. As a WebTV user, you don't have any easy way to save and manage files on your hard disk. (Many WebTV units do have an internal hard disk, but you can't access it directly as a user.) Without access to your hard disk, you can't really use FTP (File Transfer Protocol), the most common technique for transferring files on the Web. As you may know, many PC users have a hard time with FTP as well — that's why GeoCities and other free Web hosting services allow you to enter your basic Web page information without using FTP. The ability to avoid FTP is a real plus for WebTV users.

However, at the point where a PC user saves a file to his computer's hard disk, then uses FTP to transfer the file to a Web hosting service, a WebTV user is pretty well stuck. To get graphics on your Web site, as a WebTV user, you have several alternatives:

✔ **Point to graphics already on the Web.** By linking to a graphic on another Web page, you can make the graphic function as part of your own page. Linking to an existing graphic is a common practice in Web publishing among PC users as well as WebTV users. However, these images are OPP, "other people's property." If you don't own the image, you may be in violation of copyright laws if you make it appear as part of your own Web page, so get the owner's permission before using existing graphics.

✔ **Use free graphics already on the Web.** Some free graphics services, such as those we mention in Chapter 8, intend for you to incorporate their image on your Web page. In this case you're free (pun intended) to link to the outside graphic. As long as the graphic remains located where it is when you create the pointer, you're in good shape.

✔ **Use a computer at work.** You may have access to a computer at work that you can use to transfer the file. Most companies don't mind occasional use of office equipment for personal tasks, such as transferring Web files or surfing the Web to find out about the newest film or music CD — but if your company does mind, find another alternative.

✔ **Get a friend to help.** You may well have a friend or colleague who has computer access and doesn't mind transferring a file for you. In choosing a friend to help, find someone who is computer-savvy and has used FTP before or is willing to help you experiment.

✔ **Get thee to Kinko's.** Kinko's and other copier and computer service stores have scanners, various graphics programs, Web access, and even people who can help. (Warning: Skill levels of support personnel vary widely.) As long as you can afford to pay the per-hour cost of computer use, plus the price of scanning and other services, such stores are a great place to augment your capabilities.

You may also need to pay attention to color combinations that look great on WebTV but are hard to look at for long, or even impossible to read, on some personal computers. After you get your Web page up, look at it on a PC, or ask a real-world or online friend to do so and let you know how your Web page looks to non-WebTV users.

Going beyond WebTV

You can expect WebTV and other lower-resolution Web access devices to grow in popularity, further increasing the audience for everyone's Web publishing efforts but also complicating the world of the Web. However, more advanced Web publishers — who tend to use complex layouts and various multimedia technologies — are the ones who are most likely to run into trouble with devices other than personal computers. If you design your Web pages conservatively, as we recommend throughout this book, WebTV and other new devices can open up a whole new world of users for your Web pages.

Chapter 16

Grinding Out Pages with PageMill

● ●

In This Chapter

▶ Understanding the basics

▶ Getting PageMill

▶ Using PageMill

▶ Going beyond PageMill

● ●

*P*ossibly the most exciting breakthrough ever in Web authoring occurred in late 1995 with the initial demonstrations of PageMill. PageMill was the first drag-and-drop, graphical, easy-to-use Web authoring program. Like many graphical programs of the time, PageMill was Macintosh-based, created by a small start-up company called Ceneca. PageMill was a big hit at that fall's Seybold graphics show and rapidly became one of the leading tools for creating Web pages.

In the following years, PageMill became available for Windows, and Adobe continued to upgrade the product on both platforms. However, the current excitement around PageMill centers once again on the Macintosh. Although PageMill for Windows is a solid seller, PageMill for the Macintosh is the leading Macintosh Web authoring tool. And in late 1998, Adobe and Apple announced a deal to bundle PageMill on the iMac, Apple's exciting consumer system. This bundling on the iMac gave hundreds of thousands of users access to PageMill as a standard part of their computer systems.

For more information about PageMill and other Adobe products on the Web, go to

www.adobe.com

Discovering PageMill

Though no tool can meet the needs of everyone, PageMill is especially well-suited to those starting out in Web authoring because it has the same "look and feel" as a word processing program and because it successfully hides HTML formatting tags from the user. As of Version 2.0, PageMill also allows access to the HTML source code, so you can work in either HTML or a Web-page preview. And the latest version, 3.0, integrates site management into the product, so you can easily manage all the Web pages in a multipage site.

PageMill enables you to quickly create robust Web pages and swiftly experiment with different formatting and content options. Novice Web authors who have posted comments on the Internet say that PageMill made possible for them the creation of attractive Web pages without the effort of figuring out HTML. Experienced Web authors, though, now work mostly in more advanced programs such as Microsoft FrontPage or Dreamweaver, which are more powerful.

Though PageMill, like other advanced Web authoring tools, hides the HTML formatting tags, you still need a basic understanding of HTML to use PageMill most effectively. If you aren't familiar with HTML, see the overview in Chapter 7 before proceeding.

Understanding the basics

Adobe PageMill 3.0 is available for Macintosh and 32-bit Windows for about $79. PageMill can run on a very low-end machine. To run on the Macintosh, PageMill 3.0 requires a PowerPC-based Macintosh with 8MB of available RAM, 23MB of available hard disk space, and a CD-ROM drive. For Windows 95, Windows 98, or Windows NT, Adobe recommends a Pentium machine with 16MB of RAM, 20MB of hard disk space, and a CD-ROM drive. Considering that you may well want to run a graphics program and a Web browser while running PageMill, the more RAM, the better. Having a 32MB system for running several applications at once on either Macintosh or Windows is great. The program also requires at least a 256-color monitor. To find out more about Adobe PageMill, go to the following site:

```
www.adobe.com/products/pagemill/main.html
```

PageMill is reasonably full-featured for an introductory Web authoring package. Using the program's key features, you can

- ✔ Create and edit Web pages without seeing HTML tags.
- ✔ Work directly in HTML if you want to.
- ✔ Create links to other pages on your Web site without typing the URL or pathname.

✔ Insert images by dragging and dropping them into your Web page.

✔ Manage your site by dragging and dropping Web page icons around within a graphical representation of your site's layout.

✔ Use built-in capabilities to handle conversion and resizing of graphics files.

✔ Use Adobe Photoshop LE (included) and free graphics files, animations, templates, Java applets, and other free content included with the PageMill program.

PageMill is one of the few Web editing tools that we can fairly describe as *fast*. PageMill is also one of the few that we can describe as *fun*. PageMill's word processor-like display, with the same kind of familiar pull-down menus and commands as other programs, is what makes PageMill so much fun. You can easily experiment with a variety of "looks" for your Web page without having to think about the underlying HTML.

And what about PageMill support for various HTML versions? PageMill supports HTML tags, including tables and frames, through HTML Version 4.0. (For an explanation of HTML tags and tag levels, see Chapter 7 and Appendix C.)

PageMill's graphics capabilities are excellent. PageMill allows you to drag in images from the desktop, drop them into your Web page, and then resize them. The program directly supports the display of both GIF and JPEG graphics files and automatically converts images in Macintosh PICT format or Windows BMP format to Web-ready GIF format. PageMill also supports the conversion of GIFs to transparent or interlaced format, or both. And PageMill includes tools for creating clickable image maps. (For more information on GIFs, JPEGs, and clickable image maps, see Chapter 8.)

Going to the bottom line

The cost of PageMill may be a concern, considering that you can get FrontPage Express (Chapter 13) or Netscape Composer (Chapter 14) for free. If you're just creating a few pages and are willing to work with HTML even a little bit, you can get by without PageMill. However, if you are creating more than a couple of Web pages, are averse to HTML, or simply value your time, PageMill is a good answer to your problems.

From a beginner's point of view, PageMill is nearly perfect. Its use of a word processing interface makes Web page authoring possible for people who otherwise may not try it. Advanced users are happy with features such as drag-and-drop QuickTime multimedia support and Java applet support.

PageMill formerly lacked any site management features. However, site management is now part of PageMill 3.0, all within the same easy-to-use interface that PageMill has made famous.

Adobe ownership of the program means that PageMill is linked to the Adobe graphics creation tools such as Photoshop and Illustrator — among the best anywhere — and that many talented people are available to improve and support PageMill. PageMill already achieved strong sales as the number one Web authoring program for the Macintosh, and now PageMill is bundled with the iMac. On Windows, PageMill hasn't yet become a big winner against Microsoft FrontPage and Macromedia Dreamweaver, which are the leading Web authoring products on the Windows platform. The odds are that PageMill will continue as a leader in to-die-for ease of use and continue to improve gradually for both the Macintosh and Windows platforms.

If you are a beginning Web page author and don't anticipate the short-term need to manage a large site, PageMill is worth the (relatively low) initial purchase price and the (very brief) time to figure it out.

Cheap versus free

When it first appeared, Adobe PageMill was the only tool that allowed you to create a Web page easily, without HTML coding or complicated site management concerns. Now, however, PageMill is challenged by Microsoft FrontPage Express (Chapter 13) and Netscape Composer (Chapter 14), both free. In fact, these programs are to some extent PageMill clones, with a similar mix of features and capabilities. So why pay for PageMill when you can get these similar programs for free? For both Macintosh and Windows, PageMill is simply a better program than either of the two free tools — though both of the free tools are amazingly good for the price. PageMill supports drag-and-drop insertion of links and comes with a great deal of bonus content such as Web page templates, clip art, animations, and multimedia.

For beginning Web authors on Macintosh or Windows, PageMill 3.0 is an excellent choice. It includes the SiteMill site management program,

so if your needs grow beyond authoring a few Web pages to managing a multipage Web site, you don't have to buy another program.

PageMill shines in the ease-of-use category, and the free trial version of PageMill 3.0 allows you to save files and do anything else the program can do for up to 15 days (Windows) or 30 days (Macintosh). The trial version gives you a chance to create your initial Web page or Web pages for free and then decide whether you need the program in the long run.

If you're only creating a few Web pages and want to keep a close eye on your pocketbook, either FrontPage Express or Netscape Composer, which we describe in Chapters 13 and 14, can do the job. But you can do more, and have more fun doing it, with Adobe PageMill 3.0.

Getting PageMill

If you have an Apple iMac, you have Adobe PageMill on your hard disk for free! If not, a demo version is easy to get. Demo versions of PageMill for both Macintosh and Windows are available on the famous Download.com site. You can get the program, or tell your friends where to get it, at

```
www.download.com
```

The demo versions available on the Download.com Web site have all the Web page creation and editing features of the full version, except that you can only use the program for a limited time (15 days for Windows, 30 days for Macintosh). After you use the demo version for the trial period, you can't run another demo version but instead have to buy the full program.

You can buy Adobe PageMill from most computer software sales outlets or online. To buy the complete version of Adobe PageMill, do either of the following:

✔ Buy PageMill over the Web from Adobe, or find a store that sells PageMill. To order online or to locate a store near you that sells PageMill, go to the Adobe Web page at

```
www.adobe.com/prodindex/pagemill/prodinfo.html
```

✔ Call Adobe at 800-411-8657 (United States) or 206-628-2749 (other countries) and order by phone.

A cheerful Adobe representative takes your order and sends you the software.

Using PageMill

Creating an initial page with PageMill is easy and fun. Because you work in a word processor-like environment, you aren't limited by your knowledge of HTML. Just try different options and keep using the ones that do what you need.

We show you how to use PageMill to accomplish the following Web authoring tasks and create an initial Web page:

✔ Put a title on the page.

✔ Enter and format some text.

✔ Add a link.

> ✔ Add an image.
>
> ✔ See the underlying HTML-tagged text.
>
> ✔ Publish the Web page.

We describe these same steps for each of the Web authoring tools we cover in this part of the book so that you can easily compare the tools. Using any of these tools, rather than using HTML directly, makes most of these steps much easier.

Although we use Windows screen shots and steps in most of this book, the steps and screen shots in this chapter are for the Macintosh version of PageMill. We focus on the Mac in this chapter to reflect PageMill's popularity among Macintosh users and its bundling with the iMac. However, the steps and screen shots are very similar to those in Windows, so you should be able to use them with no problem on either platform.

PageMill includes a tutorial that demonstrates some of the preceding steps, as well as steps for intermediate and advanced tasks. Because the tutorial is business-oriented, we wrote the following example to focus on creating a personal Web page. Use the steps shown here to get started and then use PageMill itself to do more with your Web page.

The following steps work equally well with the online PageMill demo or the full version that you can purchase from Adobe. However, you have a limited time to continue to use the demo version.

Granting yourself a title

Begin by starting a new PageMill document and giving it a title. Remember, you don't see the title on-screen, but Web browsers use it when searching for pages.

1. **Start Adobe PageMill by choosing Start➪Programs➪Adobe➪ PageMill 3.0 Tryout.**

   The PageMill document window, untitled1.html, appears. See Figure 16-1. The inside of the window resembles the inside of a browser window.

   To see what each PageMill icon does, rest the mouse pointer on the icon. A brief description of the icon's function appears just below the mouse pointer.

   The PageMill display is intended to resemble that of Netscape Navigator; test your PageMill documents in other browsers such as Internet Explorer before putting them on the Web.

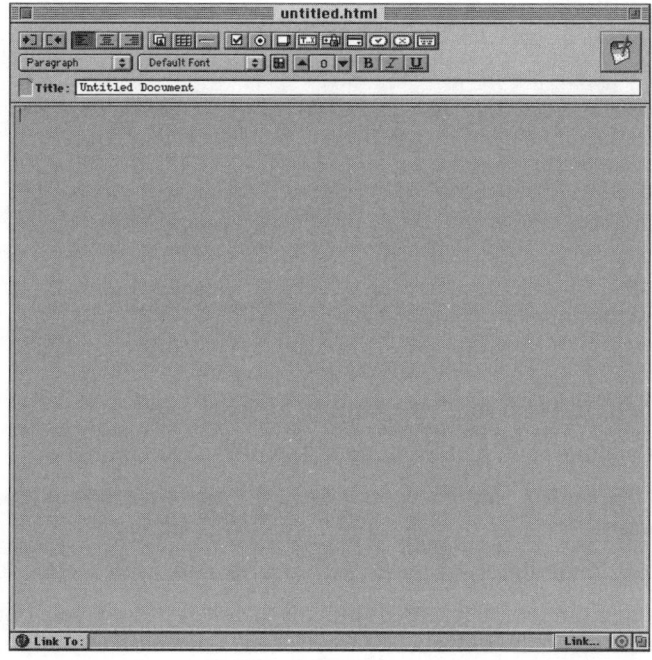

Figure 16-1:
The
PageMill
document
window.

2. **Type a title for your document next to the Title prompt that's just beneath the line of icons. Press Return.**

   For this example, type **My first Web page** as your title.

   When you save your document, PageMill saves it as text with HTML tags. For example, PageMill automatically stores the document title between the `<TITLE>` and `</TITLE>` tags in the HTML-tagged text file.

   Don't worry about required HTML tag pairs such as `<HTML></HTML>`, `<HEAD></HEAD>`, and `<BODY></BODY>`; PageMill automatically embeds them in your document.

Entering and formatting text

Using PageMill is a lot of fun — from quickly formatting text into Web-ready form to dragging and dropping graphics and even multimedia files into your Web page. In this part of the example, we type and format text.

1. **In the PageMill document window, type some text, including a list.**

The example includes the following text:

```
This is my first Web page. It will contain my hopes,
dreams, and fantasies. Plus a few GIFs and a JPEG or two.
I want to begin with a request for some information. In
my many (too many) hours of searching the Web,
there are a few important topics that I haven't
been able to learn much about in my Web searches
so far. If you can help me find Web sites or
newsgroups that have information about these
topics, please send me e-mail.
Waterskiing.
Dachshunds.
Waterskiing dachshunds.
```

2. **Highlight the text that you want to format.**

   In the sample text, highlight *too* in the phrase *too many*.

3. **Click the button that corresponds to the text-formatting effect that you want.**

   The text immediately appears with the formatting you choose.

   In the sample text, click the B button to select Bold. When you release the mouse button, the word "too" automatically appears formatted as **too**.

4. **Highlight the lines that you want to make into a list.**

   In the sample text, highlight these lines:

   > *waterskiing.*
   >
   > *dachshunds.*
   >
   > *waterskiing dachshunds.*

5. **Select the Change Format pull-down menu — the one that says Paragraph initially — to see the choices.**

   The Change Format pull-down menu appears, which includes the list choices Bullet List, Directory List, Menu List, Numbered List, Definition List, and Term List.

   If you already know some HTML, these terms should make sense to you. If not, you must experiment. Read Chapter 7, Appendix C, or the PageMill documentation to find out more about the different types of lists and how to use them.

6. **Choose the type of list that you want.**

   For a simple list, the best choices are Bullet List and Numbered List.

   For the sample list, choose Bullet List. The sample text looks like the text in Figure 16-2.

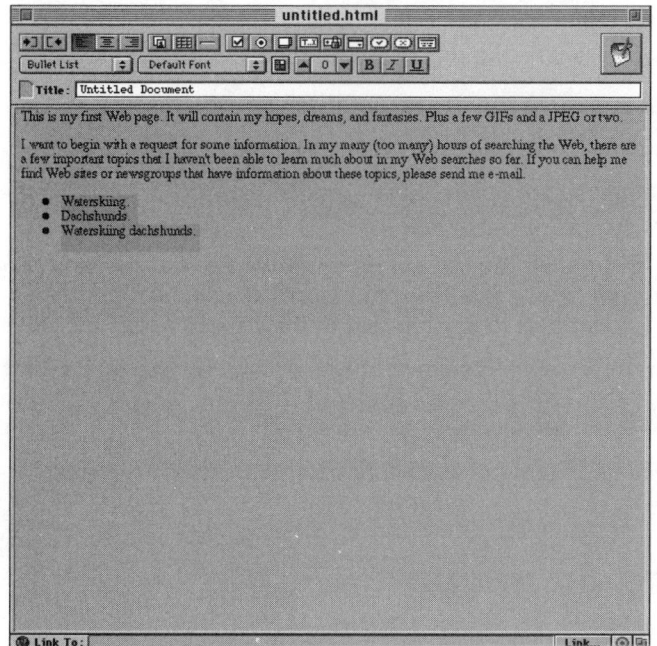

Figure 16-2:
A beginning
PageMill
Web page.

Adding a link

One of the biggest problems in creating Web pages is accurately creating and maintaining links. PageMill eases this task considerably. The following example shows how to add a link to a local document on your own hard disk. Later, to publish your Web page, you upload the document that you've linked to, as well as the HTML document that you're editing, to a Web server. Follow these steps to create the link:

1. **Insert some text to which you intend to add a link.**

   As an example, add the following text:

   ```
   For more information about PageMill 3.0, see the
            Resource file.
   ```

   If your text comes out with an unwanted paragraph format, such as being part of a bulleted list, just place the insertion point in the text and then choose Paragraph from the Change Format menu. The text reverts to normal paragraph format — no bullets, numbers, or anything else.

2. **Highlight the text that you want to serve as a link.**

   In the example, highlight the word *Resource*.

3. **Choose Open from the File menu.**

   The Open File dialog box appears.

4. **Select and open the document that you want to link to.**

   Usually, you open another HTML document at this point.

   For the example, open the resource file, Resource.htm, on the CD-ROM that comes with this book.

5. **Drag and resize the document windows so that the spot in your main document where you want to insert the link and the upper-left corner of the document that you want to link to are both visible.**

6. **From the upper-left corner of the document that you want to link to, next to the Title prompt, drag and drop the page icon (which looks like a turned-down page) to the selected text in your main document.**

   The selected text becomes a link to the other document.

Adding an image

Adding an image in PageMill couldn't be easier — just drag and drop.

1. **Create or obtain an image to include in your document.**

   The image should be in Macintosh PICT, Windows BMP, GIF, or JPEG format.

   On the Macintosh, you can quickly create a PICT file by "capturing" your screen: Hold down ⌘+Shift and then press 3. An image of your screen is saved in a file with the name Picture 1 on your start-up hard disk.

2. **Arrange your desktop so that the image file you want is visible next to the PageMill window.**

   For this example, make the icon for any GIF or JPEG graphics file visible on-screen beside the main PageMill window. (Sample graphics files come with your version of PageMill.)

3. **Click the open PageMill document window to return to PageMill.**

4. **Drag and drop the image's icon to the location where you want it to be in your document.**

   The image appears in your document. If the image is a Macintosh PICT file or Windows BMP file, it automatically converts to a GIF file.

5. **Resize or reposition the image if needed.**

   For this example, center the image by clicking the Center button on the button bar and dragging the image's handles to make it larger. The result is shown in Figure 16-3.

Figure 16-3:
The
completed
first Web
page.

Don't publish a Web page with a "borrowed" graphic in it without first getting permission from the image's owner.

Looking at the HTML

You can look at the HTML-tagged text for your Web page by doing the following:

1. **From the View menu, choose Source Mode.**

   The HTML-tagged text underlying the Web page appears. You can edit the document in this window as well.

   Figure 16-4 shows the HTML-tagged text for the Web page shown in the preceding figure.

2. **Save the document and exit PageMill.**

Publishing your Web page

PageMill creates HTML-tagged text files that you can publish on any Web server. However, PageMill does not offer any special services for Web publishing. As with many other Web authoring tools, you are on your own when

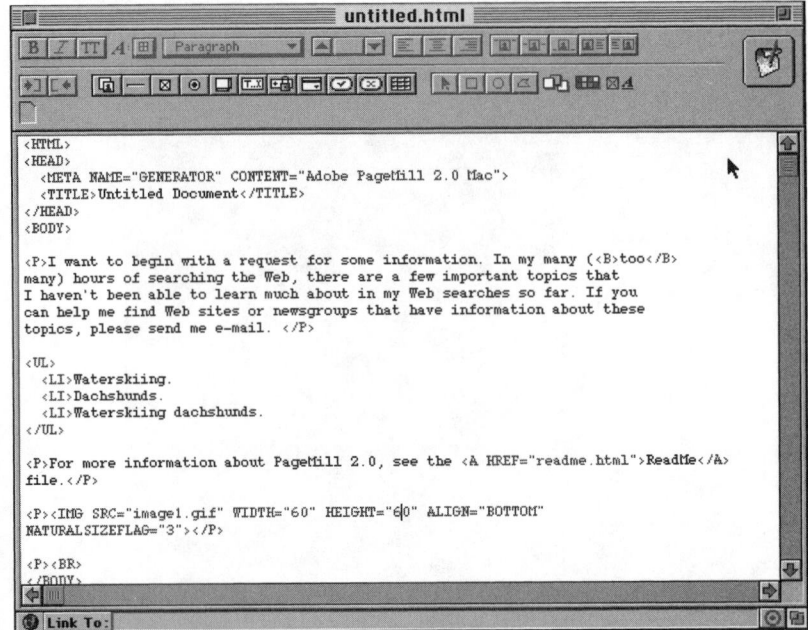

Figure 16-4:
HTML-
tagged text
for the Web
page shown
in Figure
16-3.

it comes to getting an account on a Web server, transferring your Web files to the server, and testing the site after it becomes available on the Web. See Chapter 11 for information on how to publish your Web page.

Going Beyond PageMill

To use PageMill for any kind of actual work, you need to move up to the full, paid-for version. The $79 investment for PageMill should be all you need to spend to generate a lot of Web pages. PageMill includes a lot of great extras such as site management features, Adobe Photoshop LE, templates, clip art, and animations as part of the package, so the full version really is worth the price if you're doing any serious amount of Web page creation.

PageMill, with its complete feature set, should save you both time and money. You don't need separate tools to convert Macintosh PICT or Windows BMP files to GIF or to create transparent or interlaced GIFs. And you can be very ambitious with graphics and even multimedia. We look forward to seeing your PageMill-created sites on the Web!

Part VI
The Part of Tens

The 5th Wave   By Rich Tennant

Andy soon began to think he shouldn't have opted for the cut-rate Web hookup after all.

In this part . . .

Our Top Tens tell you the DO's and DON'Ts of creating Web pages so you can look like a pro your first time out on the Web.

Chapter 17

Ten Web Publishing DO's

Anyone else remember Mr. Do-Bee from the *Romper Room* TV show of the 1960s? He was famous for words of wisdom that always began, "Mr. Do-Bee says. . . ." Well, if Mr. Do-Bee were a Web author, here are ten things he would definitely do.

DO Think About Your Target Audience

Who is your Web site targeting? A little thought along these lines can make your pages much more appealing to your visitors. Before you begin creating your Web site, choose the right look and feel and a style of presentation that is appropriate for your audience. Include links that your visitors find interesting, not just the ones that you find interesting — unless that's the point of your page, of course. In addition to using good sites as models (see the next "DO"), research other media, such as newspapers and magazines — the articles and the ads — that have an audience similar to yours, to find good and bad examples.

DO Use Good Sites as Models

Many good sites are out there. Ignoring those good examples when designing your own site is not the best idea. Take a look around and find the designs that work. (Many top-rated sites have settled on relatively simple designs.) Think about why each design you like works well for you. Is it the use of color and the layout of the Web page? The fact that the site loads quickly? Well-organized content? Note what works and why, and then strive to duplicate that effect in your own Web pages. Look for conventions in presenting information that Web users have grown accustomed to, neat design ideas, and various types of content. You'll be surprised by how many ideas you get from this huge reservoir of Web expertise.

DO Get Permissions for Content

You can easily peek at the HTML source of any Web page, and that's a good way to figure out new design techniques. But you can also easily grab any content that exists on the Web, even privately owned content that belongs to others. However, the fact that you can easily grab others' content does not make doing so right or legal. It's also not necessary.

A great deal of public domain content is out there, and getting permission to use some private content is not all that hard. If a Web page does not explicitly say that its content can be freely borrowed, assume that it's copyrighted or otherwise protected — which means you should ask before borrowing any of it. Many people are happy to let you use their content in order to gain exposure on your pages, as long as you provide proper attribution and reciprocal links. In the process, you may just gain new friends or business contacts, as well as avoid legal problems down the road. (And in case you get tempted to borrow quietly, keep in mind that word of unethical practices gets around quickly on this amazing global network.)

DO Use Links to Outside Sites

No matter how great your content is, you are wasting the most important feature of the Web if you don't include links to sites outside your own. No matter what your topic, you can find complementary sites out there on the Web. Giving your visitors links to those sites is only courteous. If you research your links carefully and organize them well, your links can be a valuable resource to others. In your own Web surfing, you've probably found that one of the best experiences on the Web is the serendipity of stumbling upon some cool link that you had no idea existed. Give your visitors that same experience. Point them to the outside world. That's why it's the Web and not the Dead End.

DO Use Graphics and Multimedia

A prime attraction of the Web is that it is designed to present graphical information, yet there are still many beginning Web authors who are intimidated by graphics and shy away from using them. Include pictures, icons, bars, and graphical menus in your Web page. Go ahead, try out transparent and interlaced GIFs. Multimedia is a great addition, too; one or two sound files, a QuickTime movie, even a simple animated GIF can really liven up a site. The bottom line is that sites that carefully use graphics and multimedia are much more interesting than purely text-oriented ones. Give it a go. (But be prudent; see Chapter 18 for a matching DON'T.)

DO Think Before You Create

A surprising number of people just jump in and start throwing around text and HTML tags with no clue about where they're going or what they want to accomplish. That approach is fine if you just want to play around — in fact, that approach can be a lot of fun. But if you want to make a good impression on the Web, sitting down and thinking about a few things ahead of time really pays off. Sketch your ideas on paper. Then describe them to someone else and ask for feedback. This prep work forces you to consider things that you may not think about otherwise: Ppage layout, graphic design, relationship between pages, target audience, content structure, link grouping, and other issues that, when properly integrated, can make your site a first-class Net surfing experience.

DO Ask for Feedback

You'll be amazed by what people say about your pages. (Some of the comments may even be complimentary!) Put your e-mail address on your home page and ask for comments. People who have never before seen your site can offer a good, fresh perspective and give you feedback on things that you may not have thought about. Everyone can benefit from outside input. Criticism by your prospective audience is not only useful, it's also educational. You can learn a lot about what people expect and want. Criticism can't hurt anything but your pride and almost always improves your site.

DO Test Your Pages

Testing your pages is easy. You probably don't write a memo without spell-checking it. Similarly, you should not put up your Web pages without testing them. That means looking at your pages on your own machine before testing them on the Web — follow links, see how graphics and text fit together, and so on. Also, looking at your pages in different browsers doesn't hurt. If you can't do it, ask a friend or even a stranger to help. Oh, again, don't forget to spellcheck your pages.

DO Publicize Your Site

Nothing is more frustrating than putting up a site that no one visits. Fortunately, publicizing your site is not hard. Add your site to the popular indexes, for example, through the excellent Submit-It site:

```
www.submit-it.com
```

You can also post to appropriate Usenet newsgroups, put out a press release, send e-mail to friends and business contacts, or shout from the rooftops. Just building a site doesn't necessarily mean people will come to it. You still have to get the word out.

DO Update Your Site

A static site is a boring site. True, it works for some purposes, but in general, if you want people to continually revisit your site, you must keep it updated. The best sites are those that continually provide new and interesting content. Include pointers to information that's frequently updated, like "Thought for the day" or "Links to new, cool sites." Let users know how often to expect updates and be sure to showcase new content. A "New" icon next to recently added or updated content can work wonders.

Chapter 18

Ten Web Publishing DON'Ts

So, does Mr. Do-Bee, the character we mention in Chapter 17, have an evil twin, Mr. Don't-Be? Well, don't be repeating others' mistakes: avoid these Web publishing don'ts.

Don't Inadvertently Limit Your Audience

Be careful when designing your pages not to inadvertently limit your audience by using some oddball feature that can't be read by large numbers of people who use different Web browsers. Stick to basic HTML through HTML Version 3.2. Think twice before using HTML frames, Java programs, or ActiveX programs — some people won't be able to access Web pages with these features. Warn people if you use nonstandard features. Often, providing alternative pages, such as text-only versions of your pages, is worthwhile. And including links to the software that works with your pages often pays off — a link to Netscape if you use Navigator-specific tags or a link to the RealAudio site if you include RealAudio sound are two good examples.

Don't Abuse Netiquette

Abusing the etiquette of the Internet is easy to do and can bring you a lot of negative attention. If you make any serious offenses, your Web service provider's server may remove your pages. And you can even get into legal problems. Avoid dubious practices such as *spamming,* sending unwanted e-mail to publicize your site; *flaming,* being fervently disparaging of other people or other Web pages; or putting up offensive material without some kind of warning label. Netiquette is an amorphous and evolving area of online behavior, so you may want to join a Web-oriented newsgroup where you can ask questions before publishing. Also, check out this site for more info:

```
www.fau.edu/rinaldi/netiquette.html
```

Don't "Borrow" Content Without Asking

Make sure that content you get from the Web to use on your own Web page is labeled as being freely available for reuse, or else get permission to reuse it. Many people are quite happy to help if you ask nicely and credit their work. The best part is that you make some good contacts with other interesting people. You also keep the law on your side.

Don't Abuse Graphics and Multimedia

The biggest mistake that beginning Web authors — and some experts — make is overusing graphics on a page. Keep in mind that not everyone has a cable modem or DSL connection wired directly to his or her home PC; the majority of folks receive your Web pages via a more limited 56K or slower modem. Keep your page size, including both text and graphics, under 100K. Here are ways that you can keep down your page size without sacrificing design flexibility:

- Convert photos to JPEG format.
- Use simple icons and banners — images without very many colors or complex textures — in GIF format.
- Lay out your site to limit the amount of graphics on any one page, adding pages if you need to display more graphics.
- Use thumbnail icons to give access to larger images.

All these strategies make your pages smaller and faster for others to download. Your Net surfers will thank you.

Don't Forget ALT Tags and Text-equivalent Menus

Another basic mistake is not using text-equivalent menus — forgetting that some people turn off graphics when surfing the Net. Who would turn off graphics, you ask?

Many home users turn off graphics to speed things along, downloading only the graphics that they really need. Some people pay a high hourly rate for their Internet access, especially in much of the non-Western world, and turn off graphics to save money on their connection time. Others may be looking at your Web page through a palmtop computer or Web-enabled cell phone with no graphics capability. And some people who are visually impaired use the Web with software that translates text — but not graphics — into spoken words. Always use the ALT tag to provide text equivalents to your graphics, as we describe in Chapter 8. Using the ALT tag is easy to do and makes it easier for all these people to access your content.

Don't Forget the Basics

Your site may be the greatest thing since sliced bread, but if you forget to include contact information for yourself in the site, how will you find out that you misspelled "bureaucracy" all over the place? Similarly, you won't get many orders for your spiffy new widget if you put the ordering information five levels down in a Web page called "Fruitbat guano statistics - 1876." More basics:

✔ Include your e-mail address on your Web page.

✔ Include a copyright notice.

✔ Add a site map.

✔ Give credit where credit is due.

✔ Make the important info prominent.

✔ Be ready to revise, based on user feedback.

Don't Start by Setting Up Your Own Web Server

Several "easy-to-use" Web server packages exist on the market, and Web server capability is even being built into Macs and PCs. But even with these efforts, buying, setting up, and maintaining a Web server can become the most expensive, most complicated, and most frustrating part of Web publishing. Luckily, you can use the free services we describe in this book, or inexpensive paid services, to put your content on someone else's Web server while you figure out the other tricks of the trade. Then, as your knowledge and experience grow, consider setting up your own Web server.

Don't Make Your Site Hard to Navigate

Beginners often organize their pages so that their sites are hard to navigate. If your site has more than two levels, you should give some thought as to how your visitors navigate it. Nobody likes wandering from link to link with no idea what is where or having to follow ten links to find one piece of information. Keep the relationship between your pages simple. Make clear which links are internal to your own site and which go out to other sites. Provide a site map or a common menu. And make navigation work consistently throughout the site.

Don't Forget the "World" in World Wide Web

Remember that your Web pages are available and accessible to the whole world. Think a bit about the foreign audience. Is including some foreign language content worthwhile? Do you use colloquialisms that may not be understood by your foreign Net surfers? How do your pages look to your overseas colleagues who view them through the slow transoceanic Net link? Will your humorous or risqué content offend someone in another country or culture?

When you become a Web publisher, you also become a global citizen, and your Web pages play on a global stage. Think through the meaning of your pages in advance.

Don't Be Afraid to Find Out More

Web publishing is not rocket science. It is computer science, but it's relatively easy computer science. You're not trying to land the space shuttle here — and chances are, lives are not at stake. After you have your site working the way you want it to using the basics that we describe in this book, experiment. Try weird things. Ask for feedback. Never be afraid to figure out complex and hard stuff. (It's only complex and hard because you don't understand it yet!)

Neat stuff is out there that can make your Web publishing even more exciting — Java, JavaScript, new browsers and publishing tools, groupware, Net-based games, and online business infrastructure. All this new stuff is understandable and usable by normal folks like you. Don't be intimidated. You can use all of it. (If you've come this far, you've got what it takes!)

Part VII
Appendixes

The 5th Wave   By Rich Tennant

"HONEY! OUR WEB BROWSER GOT OUT LAST NIGHT AND DUMPED THE TRASH ALL OVER MR. BELCHER'S HOME PAGE!"

In this part . . .

This part includes appendixes that are a bridge to a wide range of different kinds of resources, including Web publishing definitions, Internet service providers, HTML tag definitions, and developer resources that are online.

Appendix A

Web Words Worth Knowing

● ●

*T*his glossary defines important terms used in this book. To see where a term is used in the book, check the index.

56K. The name of a faster standard for Internet access that is now used by most new modems. 56K is nearly twice as fast as the previous standards, 28.8 Kbps and 33.6 Kbps. However, online access speeds are actually limited by U.S. government regulation to a top speed of about 53 Kbps, and your 56K modem may not even achieve that speed reliably, depending on the quality of the connection you get when you dial in.

absolute address. A description of a file's location that starts with the machine name or disk name on which the file is located. See also *pathname* and *relative address*.

anchor. One end of a link between two files. When you look at a Web page, the underlined, colored text that you see is an anchor at one end of a hypertext link. Clicking the text brings up another Web page, which is the anchor at the other end of the link.

animated GIF. A GIF graphic that includes several slightly different images in sequence. Up-to-date browsers that support animated GIFs display the graphics one at a time to create an animation.

attribute. In HTML, an attribute is a set of characters after the first set within an HTML tag. The attribute modifies the tag's purpose. Example: In the tag `<IMG SRC="budpic.jpg">`, the attribute is `SRC`. See also *tag*.

broadband. A newly popular term for any kind of fast Internet access, whether by cable modem, DSL, or other connection significantly faster than the 56K top speed of a modem.

browser. A program used to look at World Wide Web documents. Mosaic was the first popular browser, and Netscape Navigator and Microsoft Internet Explorer are the current market leaders.

bulleted list. See *unordered list*.

cable modem. A form of fast access to the Internet through a cable TV connection. If the local cable company that serves your house offers this service, it's worth a look.

clickable image map. A graphic that includes areas called "hot spots," which, when clicked, take you to different Web pages or locations within a Web page. Many large Web sites use clickable image maps on their home pages to entice the user to move farther into the site.

Common Gateway Interface script (CGI script). A program used to transfer data from an HTML form to an application. The CGI script runs on the server that hosts the Web page that has the form. See also *form.*

definition list. A type of HTML list in which terms occupy a column on the left side of the screen and definitions occupy a wider column on the right side.

domain name. A domain name represents a Web site to the outside world. In the United States, the domain name can end in `.com` (for businesses), `.edu` (for educational institutions), `.org` (for nonprofit organizations), or the prestigious `.net` (for organizations that are part of the structure of the Web itself). Other countries can use different suffixes. Additionally, a country code such as `.uk`, for United Kingdom, can be added to represent a country or region. The part before the suffix, such as `stanford` in `stanford.edu`, is either the name of the group that puts up the Web site, or something that attracts people to the site. Domain names can start with `www` if desired, but it's not necessary.

downloadable image. An image that's associated with a Web page but not displayed unless the user clicks a graphic to display it.

DSL. Digital Subscriber Line, a form of fast Internet access through a phone line. Only available in limited areas, but worth serious consideration if it's available to you.

electronic mail (e-mail). A message sent over a network from one computer user to another computer user. The most popular service on the Internet. Used as a noun ("I just got an e-mail.") and a verb ("E-mail me on that, will you?"). Also used as singular ("I just deleted an e-mail.") and plural ("I just deleted all my e-mail.").

element. In HTML, an element is the first character or set of characters within a tag that specifies the tag's purpose. Example: In the tag `<IMG SRC="budpic.jpg">`, the element is `IMG`.

File Transfer Protocol (FTP). An Internet service for transferring files between different machines, including those that run different operating systems.

firewall. Hardware, software, or a combination that protects a network from unauthorized access while allowing authorized access.

form. An HTML-defined way to specify text boxes and pull-down menus to enable users of a Web page to enter data. The data from the form must be processed on the Web server by a CGI script.

freeware. Software that can be used for free, without payment, though often with a license that contains some restrictions on its use. See also *shareware*.

Graphic Interchange Format (GIF). Can be pronounced "jiff" or "giff." A format for encoding images, including computer-generated art and photographs, for transfer among machines. GIF format is the most popular means for storing images for transfer over the Internet and is supported by all graphical Web browsers. An image stored in GIF format is often referred to as "a GIF." See also *interlaced GIF* and *transparent GIF*.

Graphical User Interface (GUI). Software that enables you to interact with a computer by using a mouse and keyboard to manipulate images and menus on the computer's screen. The Windows and Macintosh user interfaces are both examples of GUIs.

helper application. An application used to view data associated with a Web page but not supported directly by the browser. Originally, a helper application was needed to view any data not in HTML or GIF format, but browsers are expanding to handle different types of data directly. Users specify which helper applications to use for different data types in the user preferences options of their Web browser.

hexadecimal. What the witch did to her accountant so that her tax bill would be more favorable. More commonly, a way of counting that uses 16 "digits," 0–9 plus A–F, instead of the 10 digits that common decimal numbering uses. Hexadecimal numbers are often used to describe values stored inside a computer.

In hexadecimal numbering, 0–9 have their normal values, but A represents 10, B represents 11, and so on through F, which represents 15. Place values are also different; each successive place represents the next greater power of 16. Example: 2F in hexadecimal translates to 47 in decimal; the 2 represents two 16s, and the F represents fifteen 1s.

hit. This is what you hope your Web site will become. Also: A successful connection, file transfer, and disconnection between a Web client and a Web server. Accessing a single, text-only page generates one hit; accessing a single page with three graphics on it generates four hits. Hits can be counted fairly easily and are a crude measure of the popularity of a Web site. When you see a site that advertises "a million hits a week," remember that the number of hits may be ten times or more greater than the number of different people who visited. See also *Web client* and *Web server*.

home page. A Web page that you intend users to come to directly. If a Web site has multiple pages, the home page usually serves as a guide to all the pages.

HTML 3.2. Currently the most broadly used version of HyperText Markup Language. All browsers available today support this version of HTML, though different browsers may interpret some tags differently.

HTML 4.0. The newest version of HyperText Markup Language at the time of this writing.

HyperText Markup Language (HTML). The language used to "mark up" text documents so that they can be formatted appropriately and linked to other documents for use on the World Wide Web.

HyperText Transfer Protocol (HTTP). The agreed-upon format for exchanging messages among World Wide Web servers and between Web servers and clients.

image map. See *clickable image map.*

inline image (also spelled in-line image). An image displayed as part of a Web page.

Integrated Services Digital Network (ISDN). A special type of phone line available to many businesses and homes. ISDN supports faster transmission of data than standard phone lines.

interlaced GIF. A GIF graphic displayed gradually by showing every fourth line, then showing the next one-fourth of the lines, and so on, until the entire image is displayed. This process quickly displays a blurry version of the graphic that sharpens as time passes and the missing lines are filled in. Interlaced GIFs save users time by allowing them to quickly see the initial, blurry version and, if desired, move on before the image is entirely displayed.

Internet. The hardware and software that together support the interconnection of most existing computer networks, allowing a computer anywhere in the world to communicate with any other computer that's also connected to the Internet. The Internet supports a variety of services including the World Wide Web.

Internet Protocol (IP). The networking specification that underlies the Internet. IP's most important feature is its support for routing of the packets — small chunks of information that make up a communication — across multiple connections to the final destination.

Internet service provider (ISP). An Internet service provider offers connections to the Internet and support for Internet services such as the World Wide Web.

intranet. An internal network used for distributing information broadly within an organization but not to the general public. Many intranets work just like the Internet and World Wide Web, only on a smaller scale.

Java. A programming language that supports the creation of distributed programs, called *applets,* whose functionality can be easily and flexibly split between a client computer and the server that it's connected to. Java provides a way for the Web to support easy sharing of programs as well as data.

Joint Photographic Experts Group (JPEG). A format for storing compressed images. JPEG images were once supported by helper applications but are now directly supported by nearly all browsers. JPEG is the best format for most photographs.

link. A connection between two documents on the Web, usually specified by an anchor in an HTML document.

mirroring. Keeping a copy of data on additional servers to make data available more quickly and to a greater number of simultaneous users.

multimedia. Literally means "many media," and in this sense, a Web page with graphics is multimedia. However, multimedia is usually understood to mean either more than two types of media or, alternatively, time-based media such as animation, sound, or video and space-based media such as 3-D and virtual reality. On the Web, multimedia is also used to mean any extension of the Web beyond the basics of text, hyperlinks, GIF graphics, and JPEG graphics.

newsgroup. An ongoing exchange of electronic messages about a specific topic, such as pets, restaurants, or Web authoring. To access newsgroups, use news reader software, which you can find on the Web or included as a feature of current browsers.

numbered list. See *ordered list.*

online service. Also referred to as a "traditional" or "proprietary" online service to differentiate from the Internet, which is seen as an "open" online service. Traditional online services, such as America Online, CompuServe, and The Microsoft Network, package access and content into a single branded product. The Internet and the Web are eroding the boundaries between online services by allowing cross-service functionality, such as e-mail between subscribers of different online services. The online service providers are further eroding these boundaries by offering Internet access, Web access, and Web authoring support.

ordered list. A type of HTML list in which each item is given a number, in sequence, when the list displays. The author of the list can rearrange the items as needed, and the numbers adjust accordingly because the numbers are assigned only when the list appears on-screen.

page description language. A defined format for specifying the appearance of a document when displayed or printed. Adobe's PostScript, used by many programs and in many laser printers, is a page description language, not a structural markup language such as HTML or SGML.

pathname. A description of the location of a file. Pathnames can be specified by absolute addressing or relative addressing.

plug-in. A small program that works with a Web browser to allow multimedia files to be displayed in a Web page, or that otherwise extends the capabilities of the browser.

protocol. A format for exchanging data.

QuickTime. A multiplatform standard from Apple Computer, Inc., for multimedia. See also *multimedia, QuickTime plug-in,* and *QuickTime VR.*

QuickTime plug-in. A plug-in for Netscape Navigator and Microsoft Internet Explorer that supports user interaction with QuickTime and QuickTime VR content embedded in a Web page. See also *QuickTime* and *QuickTime VR.*

QuickTime VR. A multiplatform standard for image-based virtual reality. See also *QuickTime* and *QuickTime plug-in.*

relative address. The path from a base document, such as an HTML document, to another document on the same computer, such as another Web page on the same site. See also *pathname* and *absolute address.*

service. In general, a service is a method for providing people with the use of something. Specifically, an online service is a method for providing computer users with the ability to exchange information and computer programs via a computer modem; a Web-based service is a method for providing Web users with the ability to exchange information and computer programs via the Web.

shareware. Software that can be used for free for a limited period of time, after which the user is requested (though usually not forced) to pay a fee for continued use. See *freeware.*

shrink-wrapped software. No, this is not software developed and packaged by psychiatrists. Actually, shrink-wrapped software is just software that is sold as a product, with the user paying up-front before taking possession of the software. See also *freeware* and *shareware.*

site management. Capabilities in a Web authoring package that help authors work on characteristics of an entire Web site, instead of just one page at a time. Site management capabilities include the ability to easily manage links between Web pages, the capacity to spell-check and search and replace across an entire site, and notification when links are no longer functional.

standard. An agreed-upon way to do something, such as building a computer system (for example, the IBM-compatible standard) or exchanging data (for example, the ASCII standard). Many different standards exist, ranging from those created by a single manufacturer for its own purposes (the DOS standard) to those created by internationally recognized standards bodies such as ISO (the International Standards Organization). In other words, in computing, the definition of standard is not very standard.

Standard Generalized Markup Language (SGML). A full-featured specification for describing the content and structure of documents but not their exact appearance when displayed. HTML is a subset of SGML.

syntax. A fee paid for moral or legal violations — no, wait, that's a "sin tax." A syntax is the ordering of the elements in a language or protocol.

system operator (sysop). A person responsible for some part of the operations of a computer system, including online services. A sysop's responsibilities can vary from the technical, such as backing up a computer hard drive, to the non-technical, such as monitoring a newsgroup for inappropriate or irrelevant content and removing it if found.

tag. An HTML element that contains information besides the actual document content, such as formatting information or an anchor. Example: The `<B>` tag starts bolding the characters that follow it, and the `</B>` tag ends bolding. So to make a word or phrase bold, surround it with the `<B>` and `</B>` tags.

text editor. A program that allows text to be entered and edited but not formatted for display. Text editors save their files without proprietary formatting information, so the files are portable across different application programs and different computer systems. Examples are Notepad (Windows), BBEdit (Macintosh), and vi (UNIX).

thumbnail. A small graphical image that serves as a preview of a larger image.

Transmission Control Protocol/Internet Protocol (TCP/IP). A communications protocol developed under contract from the U.S. Department of Defense in the 1970s to connect different systems and different networks. TCP/IP is the protocol on which the Internet is based.

transparent GIF. A file stored in Graphic Interchange Format and modified so that the area around the objects of interest is assigned the color "transparent." This capability makes the rectangular frame around the objects seem to disappear so that the graphic appears to "float" over the page on which it appears.

Uniform Resource Locator (URL). A specification for identifying any file on the Internet. The URL is made up of the name of the protocol by which the file should be accessed, the name of the server that the file is stored on, and the pathname of the file on the server. Here is a sample URL for an HTML file named `MyCruise`, to be accessed by using the Web protocol `http`, which is stored on a server called `www.bigweb.com` in the `Travel` subdirectory:

```
http://www.bigweb.com/Travel/MyCruise.html
```

If no filename is given at the end of the path, a default file, typically index.html for Web servers, is returned.

unordered list. A type of HTML list in which each item is displayed next to a symbol such as a bullet.

Virtual Reality Modeling Language (VRML). A set of standards for displaying 3-D data on the Web.

Web authoring. Creating documents for use on the World Wide Web. Web authoring includes creating text documents with HTML tags, as well as creating or obtaining suitable graphics and, in many cases, multimedia files.

Web-based service. See *service.*

Web browser. See *browser.*

Web client. A computer that connects to the World Wide Web and downloads Web pages and other data from it.

Web page. A text document with HTML tags to specify formatting and links from the document to other documents and to graphics and multimedia files.

Web publishing. The entire process of creating and maintaining a Web site, from creating text documents with HTML tags and graphics, to putting the documents on a server, to revising the documents over time.

Web server. A computer that connects to the World Wide Web and hosts HTML-tagged text documents, graphics, and multimedia files to be downloaded by Web clients.

Web site. One or more linked Web pages accessed through a home page. The URL of the home page is made available to users on the Web, and often through other advertising and marketing means as well.

word processor. A program for creating and editing text files with formatting. Files created by a word processor contain formatting codes and cannot be used on the Web unless specifically saved in "text-only" or "plain-text" format, without the proprietary codes that word processors embed in the file to indicate formatting.

World Wide Web (also known as the Web or W3). An Internet service that provides files linked by HyperText Transfer Protocol. The Web specification allows formatted text and graphics to be viewed directly by a Web browser and allows other kinds of files to be opened separately by helper applications specified in the Web browser's setup. The Web is the most popular Internet service, partly because it can also be used to access other Internet services, such as newsgroups and FTP.

Appendix B

Internet Service Providers

● ●

*O*ne of the best resources for Internet service providers is on the Web itself at

```
www.boardwatch.com
```

You can log on to Boardwatch to get a directory of local Internet service providers (ISPs) in any part of the United States or Canada. Local providers sometimes offer the best access, but, of course, the level of service you get varies from one provider to another. Boardwatch also offers a list of national service providers.

Another great source for Internet access providers is Yahoo!; check out

```
www.yahoo.com/Business_and_Economy/Companies/
          Internet_Services/Access_Providers
```

Typing out the long URL is worth it; Yahoo! provides links to regional, national, and international ISPs, as well as links to other ISP directories online.

For your browsing pleasure — in the old-fashioned, analog sense of the word "browsing" — here's a brief list of some of the top national Web service providers. This list is U.S.-centric; if you live elsewhere or travel, check online sources, or check with the providers listed in this appendix to see which can meet your needs.

AltaVista

Palo Alto, CA
877-584-5551

```
www.altavista.com
```

America Online

Tyson's Corner, VA
800-827-6364

```
www.aol.com
```

AT&T
Basking Ridge, NJ
800-309-3349

```
www.att.com
```

CompuServe
Columbus, OH
800-848-8990

```
www.compuserve.com
```

MindSpring
Atlanta, GA
800-719-4664

```
www.mindspring.net
```

The Microsoft Network
Redmond, WA
800-373-3676

```
www.msn.com
```

Prodigy
White Plains, NY
800-776-3449

```
www.prodigy.com
```

UUNet Technologies
Fairfax, VA
800-488-6383

```
www.uu.net
```

WebTV Networks
Mountain View, CA
800-984-9449

```
www.webtv.net
```

Appendix C

A Quick Guide to HTML Tags

. . . .

*O*ne of the best resources on the Web is *The Bare Bones Guide to HTML.* At this writing, this excellent reference lists nearly all the tags in the most widely supported version of HTML, Version 4.0, plus Netscape extensions. Unless otherwise noted, HTML tags are compatible with later HTML versions. This site was developed and is maintained by Kevin Werbach, a Harvard Law graduate and former FCC attorney in Washington who has invested a lot of time and thought into Web authoring. You can find out an awful lot about Web authoring from the thoughts, resources, and examples on Kevin's home page at

`www.werbach.com`

The Bare Bones Guide lists tags from the different versions of HTML with notes describing which version of HTML a given tag supports. We thought splitting out the HTML tags into separate tables by the version of HTML they support would help you.

In the version of *The Bare Bones Guide* in this book, we include only HTML tags from HTML versions up through Version 4.0. For frames only, we use HTML 4.0 tags; see Table C-26 at the end of this chapter. We do this because these tags are the most commonly used by the broad range of Web pages and Web browsers out there. The online version of *The Bare Bones Guide to HTML* lists tags up to the current version of the HTML standard at the time that you access the site.

The original *The Bare Bones Guide to HTML,* from which we adapted this version, is copyrighted (©1995-2000) to Kevin Werbach. You can reproduce the original, as long as you include this statement:

Copyright ©1995-2000 Kevin Werbach. Distribution is permitted, so long as there is no charge and this document is included without alteration in its entirety. This Guide is not a product of Bare Bones Software. More information is available at `http://werbach.com/barebones`.

Note: *The Bare Bones Guide to HTML* is not affiliated with Bare Bones Software, makers of the BBEdit text editor for the Macintosh (`www.barebones.com`).

Twenty-two world languages in *The Bare Bones Guide*

Online, you find versions of *The Bare Bones Guide* in English in plain text, formatted text, and table versions, as well as translations into 21 additional languages: Chinese, Danish, Dutch, Estonian, Finnish, French, German, Hebrew, Icelandic, Indonesian, Italian, Japanese, Korean, Norwegian, Portuguese, Romanian, Russian, Slovenian, Spanish, Swedish, and Turkish.

Versions of HTML

The tags in this table are part of the HTML 4.0 standard and are supported by all up-to-date browsers. So if you aren't worried about ancient history — in Web terms, that's anything that happened more than a year ago — and aren't worried about the stubborn few users of your Web pages who may still have old browsers, you can ignore this section and go straight to the tables. But if you really want to know the details, read on.

The versions of HTML we describe in this appendix are

- **HTML 2.0.** All browsers available today support this basic version of HTML. However, some tags are interpreted differently by different browsers. For example, a top-level heading, marked by an <H1> tag, may appear very differently in different browsers.

- **Netscape Navigator 1.0, 1.1.** These early versions of Netscape Navigator fueled the first huge surge in the growth of the Web. These were the first browsers to provide support for centered text, floating graphics, and colored text and backgrounds by using new "extensions" to HTML 2.0. Other browsers and HTML 3.2 have adopted many of the features and new tags introduced by Netscape in Netscape Navigator 1.0 and 1.1.

- **HTML 3.2.** This is a widely supported version of the HTML standard. Many of the ideas originally included in the HTML 3.0 proposal, such as tables and paragraph alignment, were first supported by Netscape Navigator 1.0 and 1.1.

- **Netscape Navigator 2.0.** This widely used version of Netscape Navigator implements a few minor features, plus a major one: frames, which are specific areas within the browser window that contain different content and can be updated separately.

✔ **HTML 4.0 and later browser versions.** HTML 4.0 is the latest standardized version of HTML. It includes some features that were introduced by Microsoft and Netscape in their own browsers. However, HTML 4.0 includes some complex features that are not consistently implemented in current browser versions.

Over time, browsers are updated and improved to support a wider range of tags. However, some users still have the old version of their browser. So don't assume that just because a new version of a browser supports specific tags, all users of that browser will upgrade and gain the ability to view those tags correctly.

How to Use This Appendix

To use this appendix when creating your own pages, start with the first table, a basic list of HTML 2.0– and HTML 3.2–compliant tags that work with almost any browser. If you use only the tags in this list, your pages will be as widely usable as possible. Then you can selectively spice up your pages by using tags from the different sets of HTML extensions listed in the later tables. You can also use this list to create separate versions of your pages: one version for all browsers and another for browsers that support the specific extensions that you use.

This appendix includes HTML tags that we did not discuss in the text of this book. To find out more about a specific tag, experiment with it in your Web text and your browser. If you need more information than you can get by experimenting, buy a more advanced book on HTML, *HTML 4 For Dummies*, 2nd Edition, by Ed Tittel and Natanya Pitts (IDG Books Worldwide, Inc.).

Reading the Tables

Within the tables you may see some tags that are not preceded by a dash, followed by tags preceded by a dash, such as

Tag Name	*Tag*	*Notes*
Preformatted	`<PRE></PRE>`	Display text spacing as-is
- Width	`<PRE WIDTH=?></PRE>`	Width in characters

The tags with descriptions that start with a dash are actually options within other tags. These optional tags modify the effect of the tag that they appear with. You will always see the option listed with the tag that it modifies, so that you can see how to use it in your own HTML-tagged text.

The use of the dash symbol to indicate optional tags and other symbols in the tables are described in Table C-1.

Note: In order to align columns correctly, some tags are broken. At the points that these tags break, we placed a downward, left-curving arrow ⤶ to indicate the break.

Table C-1	Symbols Used in the Tables
Symbol	*Meaning*
URL	URL of an external file (or just filename if in the same directory)
?	Arbitrary number (for example, `<H?>` means `<H1>`, `<H2>`, `<H3>`, and so on)
%	Arbitrary percentage (for example, `<HR WIDTH=%>` means `<HR WIDTH=50%>`, and so on)
***	Arbitrary text (for example, `ALT="***"` means fill in with text)
$$$$$$	Arbitrary hexadecimal number* (for example, `BGCOLOR="#$$$$$$"` means `BGCOLOR="#00FF1C"`, and so on)
|	Alternatives (for example, `ALIGN=LEFT|RIGHT|CENTER` means pick one of these)
- *Option*	An option within a tag

For an explanation of hexadecimal numbering, see Appendix A.

HTML 2.0– and 3.2–Compliant Tags

The following tags are in the HTML 2.0 or 3.2 specification and should work in all browsers.

Table C-2	Generally All HTML Documents Should Have These Tags	
Tag Name	*Tag*	*Notes*
Document Type	`<HTML></HTML>`	Beginning and end of file
Title	`<TITLE></TITLE>`	Must be in header

Tag Name	Tag	Notes
Header	`<HEAD></HEAD>`	Descriptive info, such as title
Body	`<BODY></BODY>`	Bulk of the page

Table C-3 **Structural Definition: Appearance Controlled by the Browser's Preferences**

Tag Name	Tag	Notes
Heading	`<H?></H?>`	The HTML 2.0 specification defines six levels
Block Quote	`<BLOCKQUOTE>`	Usually indented `</BLOCKQUOTE>`
Emphasis	`<EM></EM>`	Usually displayed as italic
Strong Emphasis	`<STRONG></STRONG>`	Usually displayed as bold
Citation	`<CITE></CITE>`	Usually italics
Code	`<CODE></CODE>`	For source code listings
Sample Output	`<SAMP></SAMP>`	
Keyboard Input	`<KBD></KBD>`	
Variable	`<VAR></VAR>`	
Author's Address	`<ADDRESS></ADDRESS>`	

Table C-4 **Presentation Formatting: Author Specifies Text Appearance**

Tag Name	Tag	Notes
Bold	`<B></B>`	
Italic	`<I></I>`	
Typewriter	`<TT></TT>`	Displayed in a monospaced font
Preformatted	`<PRE></PRE>`	Displays text spacing as-is
- Width	`<PRE WIDTH=?>↵ /PRE>`	Width in characters

Table C-5	Links and Graphics	
Tag Name	*Tag*	*Notes*
Link	`<A HREF="URL"></A>`	
Link to Target	`<A HREF="URL#***"></A>`	If in another document
	`<A HREF="#***"></A>`	If in current document
Define Target	`<A NAME="***"></A>`	
Display Image	`<IMG SRC="URL">`	
- Alignment	`<IMG SRC="URL" ALIGN ↻ =TOP|BOTTOM|MIDDLE| RIGHT|LEFT>`	HTML 3.2 only
- Alternate	`<IMG SRC="URL" ALT="***">`	
- Imagemap	`<IMG SRC="URL" ISMAP>`	Requires a script

Table C-6	Dividers	
Tag Name	*Tag*	*Notes*
Paragraph	`<P>`	See Table C-14 for more info
Line Break	` `	A single carriage return
Horizontal Rule	`<HR>`	HTML 3.2 only

Table C-7	Lists: Can Be Nested	
Tag Name	*Tag*	*Notes*
Unordered List	`<UL><LI></UL>`	`<LI>` before each list item
Ordered List	`<OL><LI></OL>`	`<LI>` before each list item
Definition List	`<DL><DT><DD></DL>`	`<DT>` = term, `<DD>` = definition

Table C-8	Special Characters: Must All Be Lowercase	
Tag Name	**Tag**	**Notes**
Special Character	&#?;	Where ? is the ISO 8859-1 code for the character
<	&lt;	
>	&gt;	
&	&amp;	
"	&quot;	
Registered TM	&reg;	
Copyright	&copy;	

See a complete list of special characters at

`www.bbsinc.com/symbol.html`

Table C-9	Forms: Generally Require a CGI Script on Your Server	
Tag Name	**Tag**	**Notes**
Define Form	`<FORM ACTION=` `"URL" METHOD=GET|` `POST></FORM>`	
Input Field	`<INPUT TYPE="TEXT|` `PASSWORD|CHECKBOX|` `RADIO|IMAGE|HIDDEN|` `SUBMIT|RESET">`	
- Field Name	`<INPUT NAME="***">`	
- Field Value	`<INPUT VALUE="***">`	
- Checked?	`<INPUT CHECKED>`	Check boxes and radio buttons
- Field Size	`<INPUT SIZE=?>`	In characters
- Max Length	`<INPUT MAXLENGTH=?>`	In characters
Selection List	`<SELECT></SELECT>`	
- Name of List	`<SELECT NAME="***">` `</SELECT>`	

(continued)

Table C-9 *(continued)*

Tag Name	Tag	Notes
- # of Options	`<SELECT SIZE=?>`↵ `</SELECT>`	
- Multiple Choice	`<SELECT MULTIPLE>`	Can select more than one
Option	`<OPTION>`	Items that can be selected
- Default Option	`<OPTION SELECTED>`	
Input Box Size	`<TEXTAREA ROWS=? COLS=?>`↵ `</TEXTAREA>`	
- Name of Box	`<TEXTAREA NAME="***">` `ccc </TEXTAREA>`	

Table C-10   **Miscellaneous**

Tag Name	Tag	Notes
Comment	`<!-- *** -->`	Not displayed by the browser
Prologue	`<!DOCTYPE HTML`↵ `PUBLIC " -//IETF//`↵ `DTD HTML 2.0//EN">`	
URL of This File	`<BASE HREF="URL">`	Must be in header
Relationship	`<LINK REV="***"`↵ `REL= "***" HREF="URL">`	In Header
Meta Information	`<META>`	Must be in header

Other Widely Used Tags

These tags work with nearly all the browsers currently in use. For a frequently updated list of widely used tags, see *The Bare Bones Guide to HTML* at the URL listed at the beginning of this chapter.

Table C-11	Structural Definition: Appearance Controlled by the Browser's Preferences	
Tag Name	*Tag*	*Notes*
- Align Heading	`<H? ALIGN=LEFT|` `CENTER| RIGHT></H?>`	HTML 3.2 Option within the HTML 2.0–compliant Heading tag
Division	`<DIV></DIV>`	HTML 3.2
- Align Division	`<DIV ALIGN=LEFT|` `RIGHT| CENTER|` `JUSTIFY></DIV>`	HTML 3.2
Large Font Size	`<BIG></BIG>`	HTML 3.2
Small Font Size	`<SMALL></SMALL>`	HTML 3.2

Table C-12	Presentation Formatting: Author Specifies Text Appearance	
Tag Name	*Tag*	*Notes*
Subscript	`<SUB></SUB>`	HTML 2.0
Superscript	`<SUP></SUP>`	HTML 2.0
Center	`<CENTER></CENTER>`	Netscape 1.0. widely implemented; for both text and images

Table C-13	Links and Graphics	
Tag Name	*Tag*	*Notes*
Dimensions	`<IMG SRC="URL"` `WIDTH= "?" HEIGHT=` `"?">`	HTML 3.2. Image width and height in pixels

Table C-14	Dividers	
Tag Name	*Tag*	*Notes*
Paragraph	`<P></P>`	HTML 3.2. Paragraph tag, `<P>`, redefined as a container tag, `</P>` is optional
- Align Text	`<P ALIGN=LEFT|`↵`CENTER|RIGHT|`↵`JUSTIFY></P>`	HTML 3.2
- No Line Breaks	`<P NOWRAP></P>`	Internet Explorer only

Table C-15	Backgrounds and Colors	
Tag Name	*Tag*	*Notes*
Tiled Background	`<BODY BACKGROUND=`↵`"URL">`	HTML 3.2
Background Color	`<BODY BGCOLOR=`↵`"#$$$$$$">`	HTML 3.2. Color order, red/green/blue
Text Color	`<BODY TEXT=`↵`"#$$$$$$">`	HTML 3.2. Color order, red/green/blue
Link Color	`<BODY LINK=`↵`"#$$$$$$">`	HTML 3.2. Color order, red/green/blue
Active Link	`<BODY ALINK=`↵`"#$$$$$$">`	HTML 3.2. Color order, red/green/blue
Visited Link	`<BODY VLINK=`↵`"#$$$$$$">`	HTML 3.2. Color order, red/green/blue

You can find more info at

`www.werbach.com/web/wwwhelp.html`

Table C-16	Tables	
Tag Name	*Tag*	*Notes*
Define Table	`<TABLE></TABLE>`	HTML 3.2
- Table Border	`<TABLE BORDER>`↵`</TABLE>`	HTML 3.2. Either on or off

Tag Name	Tag	Notes
- Table Border	`<TABLE BORDER=?>` `</TABLE>`	HTML 3.2. Can set the border width in pixels
- Cell Spacing	`<TABLE CELLSPACING=?>`	HTML 3.2
- Cell Padding	`<TABLE CELLPADDING=?>`	HTML 3.2
- Desired Width	`<TABLE WIDTH=?>`	HTML 3.2. In pixels
- Width Percent	`<TABLE WIDTH=%>`	HTML 3.2 Percentage of page
Table Row	`<TR></TR>`	HTML 3.2
- Alignment	`<TR ALIGN=LEFT|RIGHT| CENTER|JUSTIFY VALIGN=TOP| MIDDLE|BOTTOM>`	HTML 3.2
Table Cell	`<TD></TD>`	HTML 3.2. Must appear within table rows
- Alignment	`<TD ALIGN=LEFT| RIGHT| CENTER VALIGN=TOP|MIDDLE| BOTTOM>`	HTML 3.2
- No Line Breaks	`<TD NOWRAP>`	HTML 3.2
- Columns to Span	`<TD COLSPAN=?>`	HTML 3.2
- Rows to Span	`<TD ROWSPAN=?>`	HTML 3.2
- Desired Width	`<TD WIDTH=?>`	HTML 3.2. In pixels
- Width Percent	`<TD WIDTH=%>`	HTML 3.2 Percentage of table
- Desired Height	`<TD HEIGHT=?>`	HTML 3.2. In pixels
- Height Percent	`<TD HEIGHT=%>`	HTML 3.2 Percentage of page
Table Header	`<TH></TH>`	HTML 3.2. Same as data, except bold centered

(continued)

Table C-16 *(continued)*

Tag Name	Tag	Notes
- Alignment	`<TH ALIGN=LEFT|RIGHT|↵ CENTER|JUSTIFY|CHAR. VALIGN=TOP|↵ MIDDLE|BOTTOM>`	HTML 3.2
- No Line Breaks	`<TH NOWRAP>`	HTML 3.2
- Columns to Span	`<TH COLSPAN=?>`	HTML 3.2
- Rows to Span	`<TH ROWSPAN=?>`	HTML 3.2
- Desired Width	`<TH WIDTH=?>`	HTML 3.2. In pixels
- Width Percent	`<TH WIDTH=%>`	HTML 3.2. Percentage of table
- Desired Height	`<TH HEIGHT=?>`	HTML 3.2. In pixels
- Height Percent	`<TH HEIGHT=%>`	HTML 3.2. Percentage of page
Table Caption	`<CAPTION></CAPTION>`	HTML 3.2
- Alignment	`<CAPTION ALIGN=TOP|↵ BOTTOM>`	HTML 3.2. Above/below table

Table C-17   **Miscellaneous**

Tag Name	Tag	Notes
Script	`<SCRIPT></SCRIPT>`	
Location	`<SCRIPT SRC="URL"> </SCRIPT>`	
Type	`<SCRIPT TYPE="***"> </SCRIPT>`	
Language	`<SCRIPT LANGUAGE="***"> </SCRIPT>`	
Java Applet	`<APPLET>`	HTML 3.2
- Applet Name	`<APPLET NAME="***">`	HTML 3.2

Tag Name	Tag	Notes
- Alternate Text	`<APPLET ALT="***">`	HTML 3.2
- Applet Code Location	`<APPLET CODE="URL">`	HTML 3.2
- Code Base Directory	`<APPLET CODEBASE="URL">`	HTML 3.2
- Applet Window Height	`<APPLET HEIGHT=?>`	HTML 3.2. In pixels
- Width	`<APPLET WIDTH=?>`	HTML 3.2. In pixels
- Horizontal Offset	`<APPLET HSPACE=?>`	HTML 3.2. In pixels
- Vertical Offset	`<APPLET VSPACE=?>`	HTML 3.2. In pixels
- Alignment	`<APPLET ALIGN=[left| right|top| middle|bottom]>`	HTML 3.2
Applet Parameter	`<PARAM>`	HTML 3.2
Parameter Name, Value	`<PARAM NAME="applet name", VALUE=" parameter value">`	HTML 3.2
3.2 Prologue	`<!DOCTYPE HTML PUBLIC"- //W3C//DTD HTML3.2 FINAL//EN">`	HTML 3.2

Less Frequently Used Tags

Some Netscape Navigator-only tags were slow to be adopted by non-Netscape browsers. However, most of these tags can be used with up-to-date browsers. HTML 4.0-specific tags are only supported by recent browsers.

Table C-18	Structural Definition: Appearance Controlled by the Browser's Preferences	
Tag Name	**Tag**	**Notes**
Defined Content	`<SPAN></SPAN>`	HTML 4.0
Quote	`<Q></Q>`	HTML 4.0. For short quotations

(continued)

Table C-18 *(continued)*

Tag Name	Tag	Notes
- Citation	`<Q CITE="URL"></Q>`	HTML 4.0
Insert	`<INS></INS>`	HTML 4.0. Marks additions in a new version
- Time of Change	`<INS DATETIME=":::"></INS>`	HTML 4.0
- Comments	`<INS CITE="URL"></INS>`	HTML 4.0
Delete	`<DEL></DEL>`	HTML 4.0. Marks deletions in a new version
- Time of Change	`<DEL DATETIME=":::"></DEL>`	HTML 4.0
- Comments	`<DEL CITE="URL"></DEL>`	HTML 4.0
Acronym	`<ACRONYM></ACRONYM>`	HTML 4.0
Abbreviation	`<ABBR></ABBR>`	HTML 4.0

Table C-19	Presentation Formatting: Author Specifies Text Appearance	
Tag Name	**Tag**	**Notes**
Blinking	`<BLINK></BLINK>`	Navigator 1.0. Most derided tag ever
Font Size	`<FONT SIZE=?></FONT>`	HTML 3.2. Ranges from 1-7
Change Font Size	`<FONT SIZE=+|-?></FONT>`	HTML 3.2
Base Font Size	`<BASEFONT SIZE=?>`	HTML 3.2. From 1-7; default is 3
Font Color	`<FONT COLOR="#$$$$$$"></FONT>`	HTML 3.2
Underline	`<U></U>`	HTML 2.0
Strikeout	`<S></S>`	HTML 2.0
Select Font	`<FONT FACE="***"></FONT>`	HTML 4.0

Table C-20	Links, Graphics, and Sounds	
Tag Name	*Tag*	*Notes*
- Target Window	`<A HREF="URL"⤶` `TARGET="***"></A>`	HTML 4.0
Action on Click	`<A HREF="URL"⤶` `ONCLICK="***"></A>`	HTML 4.0
Mouseover Action	`<A HREF="URL"⤶` `ONMOUSEOVER="***"></A>`	HTML 4.0
Mouseover Action	`<A HREF="URL"⤶` `ONMOUSEOUT="***"></A>`	HTML 4.0

- Alignment	`<IMG SRC="URL"⤶`
	`ALIGN= LEFT|RIGHT|⤶`
	`TEXTTOP|ABSMIDDLE|⤶`
	`BASELINE|`
	`ABSBOTTOM>`
		Navigator 1.0. Option within the HTML 2.0-compliant Display Image tag

- Image Map	`<IMG SRC="URL"⤶` `USEMAP="URL">`	HTML 3.2. Option within the HTML 2.0–compliant Display Image tag
- Map	`<MAP NAME="***">⤶` `</MAP>`	HTML 3.2. Describes the map. Option within the HTML 2.0–compliant Display Image tag

- Section	`<AREA SHAPE="RECT"⤶`
	`COORDS="#,#,#,"HREF=⤶`
	`"URL"|NOHREF>`
		HTML 3.2. Option within the HTML 2.0–compliant Display Image tag

- Border	`<IMG SRC="URL"⤶` `BORDER=?>`	HTML 3.2
Runaround Space	`<IMG SRC="URL"⤶` `HSPACE= ? VSPACE=?>`	HTML 3.2. In pixels
Low-Res Proxy	`<IMG SRC="URL"⤶` `LOWSRC= "URL">`	

(continued)

Table C-20 *(continued)*

Tag Name	Tag	Notes

N1.1 Client Pull	`<META HTTP-EQUIV=↵`
	`"Refresh" CONTENT=↵`
	`"?; URL=URL">`
		HTML 2.0

Embed Object	`<EMBED SRC="URL">`	Navigator 2.0. Insert object into page

- Object Size	`<EMBED SRC="URL"↵`
	`WIDTH ="?" HEIGHT=↵`
	`"?">`
		Navigator 2.0, Internet Explorer

Object	`<OBJECT></OBJECT>`	Navigator 4.0
Parameters	`<PARAM>`	Navigator 4.0

Table C-21   Dividers

Tag Name	Tag	Notes
- Clear Text Wrap	`<BR CLEAR=LEFT|↵` `RIGHT|ALL>`	HTML 3.2. Option within the HTML 2.0–compliant Line Break tag
- Alignment	`<HR ALIGN=LEFT|↵` `RIGHT|CENTER>`	HTML 3.2. Option within the HTML 2.0–compliant Horizontal Rule tag
- Thickness	`<HR SIZE=?>`	HTML 3.2. In pixels. Option within the HTML 2.0–compliant Horizontal Rule tag
- Width	`<HR WIDTH=?%>`	HTML 3.2. In pixels. Option within the HTML 2.0–compliant Horizontal Rule tag
- Width Percent	`<HR WIDTH=?%>`	HTML 3.2. As a percentage of page width. Option within the HTML 2.0–compliant Horizontal Rule tag
- Solid Line	`<HR NOSHADE>`	HTML 3.2. Without the 3-D cutout look. Option within the HTML 2.0–compliant Horizontal Rule tag

Tag Name	Tag	Notes
No Break	`<NOBR></NOBR>`	Navigator 1.0. Prevents line breaks
Word Break	`<WBR>`	Navigator 1.0. Where to break a line if needed

Table C-22	Lists: Can Be Nested	
Tag Name	**Tag**	**Notes**
- Bullet Type	`<UL TYPE=DISC|⤸` `CIRCLE| SQUARE>`	HTML 3.2. For the whole list. Option within the HTML 2.0–compliant Unordered List tag
	`<LI TYPE=DISC|⤸` `CIRCLE| SQUARE>`	HTML 3.2. This and subsequent list items. Option within the HTML 2.0–compliant Unordered List tag
- Numbering Type	`<OL TYPE=A|a|I|i|1>`	HTML 3.2. This and subsequent list items. Option within the HTML 2.0–compliant Ordered List tag
	`<LI TYPE=A|a|I|i|1>`	HTML 3.2. This and subsequent list items. Option within the HTML 2.0–compliant Ordered List tag
- Starting Number	`<OL START=?>`	HTML 3.2
- Count	`<OL VALUE=?>`	HTML 3.2 For the whole list. Option within the HTML 2.0–compliant Ordered List tag

Table C-23	Backgrounds and Colors	
Tag Name	**Tag**	**Notes**
N1.1 Active Link	`<BODY ALINK=⤸` `"#$$$$$$">`	HTML 3.2

You can find more info at

werbach.com/web/wwwhelp.html#color

Table C-24 Forms: Generally Require a CGI Script on Your Server

Tag Name	Tag	Notes
- File Upload	`<FORM ENCTYPE=⤵ "multi part/form-data"></FORM>`	HTML 4.0
- Wrap Text	`<TEXTAREA WRAP=OFF| VIRTUAL|PHYSICAL>⤵ </TEXTAREA>`	HTML 2.0
Button	`<BUTTON></BUTTON>`	HTML 4.0
- Button Name	`<BUTTON NAME="****"> </BUTTON>`	HTML 4.0
- Button Type	`<BUTTON TYPE="SUBMIT| RESET|BUTTON"> </BUTTON>`	HTML 4.0
- Default Value	`<BUTTON VALUE="****"> </BUTTON>`	HTML 4.0
Label	`<LABEL></LABEL>`	HTML 4.0
- Item Labelled	`<LABEL FOR="****"> </LABEL>`	HTML 4.0
Option Group	`<OPTGROUP LABEL="****"> </OPTGROUP>`	HTML 4.0
Group Elements	`<FIELDSET></FIELDSET>`	HTML 4.0
Legend	`<LEGEND></LEGEND>`	HTML 4.0. Caption for fieldsets
- Alignment	`<LEGEND ALIGN="TOP| BOTTOM|LEFT| RIGHT"></LEGEND>`	HTML 4.0

Table C-25	Tables	
Tag Name	**Tag**	**Notes**
- Table Alignment	`<TABLE ALIGN=LEFT |RIGHT|CENTER>`↵	HTML 4.0
- Table Color	`<TABLE BGCOLOR="$$$$$$">` `</TABLE>`	HTML 4.0
- Table Frame	`<TABLE FRAME=VOID| ABOVE|BELOW|HSIDES| LHS|RHS|VSIDES|BOX| BORDER></TABLE>`	HTML 4.0
- Table Rules	`<TABLE RULES=NONE|GROUPS| ROWS|COLS|ALL></TABLE>`	HTML 4.0
- Desired Width	`<TD WIDTH=?>`	HTML 4.0. In pixels
- Cell Color	`<TD BGCOLOR="#$$$$$$">`	HTML 4.0
- Desired Width	`<TH WIDTH=?>`	HTML 4.0. In pixels
- Cell Color	`<TH BGCOLOR="#$$$$$$">`	HTML 4.0
Table Body	`<TBODY>`	HTML 4.0
Table Footer	`<TFOOT></TFOOT>`	HTML 4.0. Must come before `<THEAD>`
Table Header	`<THEAD></THEAD>`	HTML 4.0
Column	`<COL></COL>`	HTML 4.0. Groups column attributes
- Columns Spanned	`<COL SPAN=?></COL>`	HTML 4.0
- Column Width	`<COL WIDTH=?></COL>`	HTML 4.0
- Width Percent	`<COL WIDTH="%"></COL>`	HTML 4.0
Group columns	`<COLGROUP></COLGROUP>`	HTML 4.0. Groups column structure
- Columns Spanned	`<COLGROUP SPAN=?> </COLGROUP>`	HTML 4.0

(continued)

Table C-25 *(continued)*

Tag Name	Tag	Notes
- Group Width	`<COLGROUP WIDTH=?>` `</COLGROUP>`	HTML 4.0
- Width Percent	`<COLGROUP WIDTH="%">` `</COLGROUP>`	HTML 4.0

Table C-26	Frames: Define and Manipulate Specific Regions of the Screen	
Tag Name	**Tag**	**Notes**
Frame Document	`<FRAMESET></FRAMESET>`	HTML 4.0. Instead of `<BODY>`
- Row Heights	`<FRAMESET ROWS=`↩ `#,#,#,> </FRAMESET>`	HTML 4.0. Pixels or percent
- Row Heights	`<FRAMESET ROWS=*>`↩ `</FRAMESET>`	HTML 4.0. * = relative size
- Column Widths	`<FRAMESET COLS=`↩ `#,#,#,> </FRAMESET>`	HTML 4.0. Pixels or percent
- Column Widths	`<FRAMESET COLS=*>`↩ `</FRAMESET>`	HTML 4.0. * = relative size

- Borders	`<FRAMESET FRAMEBORDER`
	`="yes|no"`↩
	`</FRAMESET>`
		HTML 4.0

- Border Width	`<FRAMESET BORDER=?`↩ `</FRAMESET>`	HTML 4.0

- Border Color	`<FRAMESET BORDERCOLOR`
	`="******"`↩
	`</FRAMESET>`
		HTML 4.0

Define Frame	`<FRAME>`	HTML 4.0. Contents of an individual frame
- Display Document	`<FRAME SRC="URL">`	HTML 4.0
- Frame Name	`<FRAME NAME="***"|`↩ `_blank |_self|`↩ `_parent|_top>`	HTML 4.0

Tag Name	Tag	Notes
- Margin Width	`<FRAME MARGINWIDTH=?>`	HTML 4.0. Left and right margins
- Margin Height	`<FRAME MARGINHEIGHT=?>`	HTML 4.0. Top and bottom margins
- Scroll bar?	`<FRAME SCROLLING= "YES |NO|AUTO">`	HTML 4.0
- Not Resizable	`<FRAME NORESIZE>`	HTML 4.0
Borders	`<FRAME FRAMEBORDER ="yes|no">`	HTML 4.0
Border Color	`<FRAME BORDERCOLOR ="#$$$$$$">`	HTML 4.0
Inline Frame	`<IFRAME></IFRAME>`	HTML 4.0. Takes same attributes as FRAME
Dimensions	`<IFRAME WIDTH=? HEIGHT=?> </IFRAME>`	HTML 4.0
Dimensions	`<IFRAME WIDTH="%" HEIGHT ="%"></IFRAME>`	HTML 4.0
Unframed Content	`<NOFRAMES></NOFRAMES>`	HTML 4.0 For non-frames browsers

Note: Frame tags introduced prior to HTML 4.0 are not supported by all browsers.

Table C-27	Miscellaneous	
Tag Name	**Tag**	**Notes**
- Prompt	`<ISINDEX PROMPT= "***">`	HTML 2.0. Text to prompt input
Base Window Name	`<BASE TARGET="***">`	HTML 2.0. Must be in header
Other Content	`<NOSCRIPT></NOSCRIPT>`	HTML 4.0. If scripts not supported
Base Window Name	`<BASE TARGET="***">`	HTML 4.0. Must be in header
Bidirect Off	`<BDO DIR=LTR|RTL></BDO>`	HTML 4.0. For certain character sets

Appendix D

Using Resource.htm

A great many resources are available online for Web developers of all skill levels. On the CD-ROM enclosed with this book, you will find a file called *resource.htm*. To use this file, start your browser and then use the Open command from the File menu to open the *resource.htm* Web page.

In *resource.htm*, you will find links to numerous sources of Web authoring information and links to sites that support some of the more popular Web software packages. The CD-ROM includes some of those packages, but it is always good to check the support sites for the latest upgrades and bug reports. The following is a short description of the key sites and software packages that you can access via this resource page. Note that some of the resources will lead you to more advanced Web page creation topics not covered in this book, such as XML, Java, and VRML.

General Web Developer Resources

Probably the most useful sources of Web information are the excellent World Wide Web FAQ files by Thomas Boutell. The files are brimming with answers to many questions about the Web and contain numerous links to a variety of sites that provide further information or support for Web and Internet-related software. We're giving you the URLs for both his new and old FAQ documents, since both are still wonderfully useful. These files are an excellent starting point for any would-be Web author and netsurfer.

✔ World Wide Web FAQs

```
http://www.boutell.com/faq/oldfaq/index.html
http://www.boutell.com/faq/
```

The indispensable Yahoo! index has a superb collection of links to just about every Web- and Internet-related topic under the sun. We saved you the trouble of searching and provide a link to the Yahoo! World Wide Web section directly. The topic selection is vast and comprehensive.

✔ Yahoo! World Wide Web Resources

```
http://dir.yahoo.com/Computers_and_Internet/Internet
        /World_Wide_Web/
```

For more advanced topics and resources specifically related to Web authoring, check out the following sites:

✔ ZDNet Devhead

```
http://www.zdnet.com/devhead/
```

✔ The Web Developer's Virtual Library

```
http://www.wdvl.com/
```

✔ Internet.com's Web Developer Channel

```
http://www.internet.com/sections/webdev.html
```

Four special topic resources are always in high demand. A great basic HTML tutorial can be found at the NCSA Beginner's Guide to HTML site. The WWW Security FAQ covers various aspects of maintaining secure Web sites and writing secure Web scripts. Finally, the GIF-related sites teach you all you need to know about creating transparent, interlaced, and animated GIFs.

✔ NCSA Beginner's Guide to HTML

```
http://www.ncsa.uiuc.edu/General/Internet/WWW/
```

✔ The World Wide Web Security FAQ

```
http://www.w3.org/Security/Faq/
```

✔ The Transparent/Interlaced GIF Resource Page

```
http://www.best.com/~adamb/GIFpage.html
```

✔ CNet Feature on GIF89a Animation

```
http://coverage.cnet.com/Content/Features/Techno/Gif89/
```

Microsoft Windows Web Resources

In this section, you find a number of sites that deal specifically with Microsoft Windows Internet and Web software. You will find everything from browsers to file viewers to FTP and Telnet clients to helper applications, and even various system administration utilities. If you're looking for just the right Windows netsurfing tool, these sites are the place to start:

✔ Tucows: The Ultimate Collection of Winsock Software

```
http://www.tucows.com/
```

✔ Stroud's Consummate Winsock Applications

```
http://cws.internet.com/
```

✔ ZDNet Software Library

```
http://www.zdnet.com/downloads/
```

✔ Stardust Technologies' WinSock Software Directory

```
http://www.stardust.com/wsdir/
```

Microsoft Windows Software

The *resource.htm* Web page on your CD-ROM contains links to support sites for a variety of software programs that make life easier for the Web developer. You can find some of these programs on the enclosed CD-ROM. Others are freely available online either as shareware, freeware, or demo versions.

Your *resource.htm* Web page offers links to no less than two browsers (Netscape Communicator and Microsoft Explorer) and six HTML editors (Macromedia Dreamweaver, Adobe PageMill, InContext Spider, SoftQuad HotMetal, HomeSite, and HotDog). Other goodies include Mapedit, the elegant image map editor, a couple of spiffy graphics programs (Paint Shop Pro, and LView Pro), a program to generate background patterns (Reptile), a GIF animator (Ulead), a site which will let you choose your Web page colors (ColorCenter), as well as several other generally useful Web page utilities (CSE HTML Validator, Weblater, and Wusage). One other site provides a great source for filter programs that convert just about any word processing or database format to HTML.

Macintosh Web Resources

This section contains Macintosh-oriented sites. For general Web authoring resources, nothing beats the ULTIMATE Macintosh Web site. MacUpdate and the Info-Mac HyperArchive are large repositories of Mac software. StarNine has an excellent site devoted to tools that work with their very popular WebSTAR Macintosh Web server. NCSA, the birthplace of the Web, has many useful utilities, while MacTech magazine is a great resource for Web developers.

✔ ULTIMATE Macintosh

```
http://www.ultimatemac.com/
```

✔ MacUpdate

```
http://www.macupdate.com/
```

✔ Info-Mac HyperArchive

```
http://hyperarchive.lcs.mit.edu/HyperArchive.html
```

✔ StarNine Development Services Resource Page

```
http://dev.starnine.com/index.html
```

✔ NCSA Mac Helpers FTP directory

```
ftp://ftp.ncsa.uiuc.edu/Mosaic/Mac/Helpers/
```

✔ MacTech

```
http://www.mactech.com/
```

Macintosh Web Software

We include links to both Netscape Communicator and Microsoft Explorer, as well as several Mac HTML editors (Macromedia Dreamweaver, Adobe PageMill, BBEdit, SoftQuad HotMetal, and HTMLPro). SiteCheck will make sure you don't have any broken links, while GIFConverter, GraphicConverter, and JPEGView can meet your graphics display and conversion needs. The image-map editing program, Mapedit will let you create images with clickable hot spots. The Web Page Starter kit has all sorts of graphics and page templates you can use to start your Web pages. Finally, the Web standards organization W3.ORG has numerous filters for translating files to and from HTML format.

Perl

Perl is an immensely powerful and flexible scripting language that has become insanely popular with system administrators and Web developers. If you want to delve into the creation of more sophisticated Web-based applications, you can take advantage of a huge base of existing programs and tools written in Perl. The key sites for Perl include the commercial ezine Perl.com, and the Perl Mongers users group Web site. The Comprehensive Perl Archive Network lets you tap the power of a worldwide Perl developer community through thousands of pre-built applications and modules. Essential magazines include the Perl Journal and the ZDNet Devhead Perl section. Finally, the Macintosh user can obtain a first-class Macintosh Perl FAQ.

✔ Perl.com

```
http://www.perl.com/
```

✔ Perl Mongers

```
http://www.perl.org/
```

✔ CPAN — Comprehensive Perl Archive Network

```
http://www.cpan.org/
```

✔ The Perl Journal

```
http://www.tpj.com/
```

✔ ZDNet Devhead CGI Perl and TCL pages

```
http://www.zdnet.com/devhead/filters/cgiperltcl/
```

✔ Macintosh Perl FAQ

```
http://www.perl.com/CPAN local/doc/FAQs/mac/
        MacPerlFAQ.html
```

Java

Java is the language of choice in creating interactive Web applications. These sites contain a plethora of information about Java, with both developer resources and numerous sample applications.

✔ The official Sun Java Site

```
http://java.sun.com/
```

- Gamelan; A Directory and Registry of Java Resources

  `http://www.gamelan.com/`

- Yahoo! Java Resources

  `http://dir.yahoo.com/Computers_and_Internet`
  `        /Programming_Languages/Java/`

- Java FAQ Archives

  `http://www-net.com/java/faq/`

JavaScript

JavaScript (no relation to Java, despite the similar name) is a scripting language built into Web browsers. It lets Web page authors create more dynamic Web pages by using the built-in browser features running on the netsurfer's computer. If you look at the Yahoo! JavaScript resources you'll see how widely used it is. JavaScript FAQ's at IRT.ORG and Internet Design Magazine (IDM) will answer all your questions, while the ZDNet Devhead Javascript Library will give you plenty of examples to work with.

- Yahoo! JavaScript Resources

  `http://dir.yahoo.com/Computers_and_Internet`
  `        /Programming_Languages/JavaScript/`

- JavaScript FAQ's at IRT.ORG

  `http://developer.irt.org/script/script.htm`

- JavaScript FAQ at Internet Design Magazine (IDM)

  `http://idm.internet.com/faq/js-faq.shtml`

- ZDNet Devhead Javascript Library

  `http://www.zdnet.com/devhead/resources/`
  `        scriptlibrary/javascript/`

XML

XML is a method of marking up content using tags that look very similar to HTML tags about which you've been learning in this book. What's nice about XML is that anybody can define a standard set of XML tags in a very structured way so that others can use them. This allows content to be easily interchanged and displayed on all sorts of devices. The official keeper of the XML standard is World Wide Web Consortium (W3C). Numerous commercial Web sites cover the rapidly developing XML technology beat, the best of which we list here.

- ✔ W3C XML Specification

  ```
  http://www.w3.org/TR/REC-xml
  ```

- ✔ XML.ORG: The XML Industry Portal

  ```
  http://xml.org/
  ```

- ✔ XML.com

  ```
  http://www.xml.com/
  ```

- ✔ The XML Cover Pages

  ```
  http://www.oasis-open.org/cover/
  ```

- ✔ IBM XML Zone

  ```
  http://www.ibm.com/developer/xml/
  ```

ActiveX

ActiveX is Microsoft's answer to Java for Web interactivity, although Microsoft is hedging its bets; the company is very active in the Java world as well. ActiveX enables programmers to extend the Web to do a great deal more, with many different kinds of data, than plain old HTML. Even so, not many developers work with ActiveX these days, despite Microsoft's strong efforts to make it popular.

- ✔ Microsoft's ActiveX site

  ```
  http://www.microsoft.com/com/tech/activex.asp
  ```

- ✔ C|NET Download.com ActiveX site

  ```
  http://www.activex.com/
  ```

- ✔ Yahoo! ActiveX Resources

  ```
  http://dir.yahoo.com/Computers_and_Internet/Software/
      Operating_Systems/Windows/Windows_95/Information_
      and_Documentation/ActiveX/
  ```

VRML

VRML is a language designed explicitly for the description of three-dimensional virtual reality on the Internet. While the excitement over the technology has waned, it is still a useful tool for the advanced Web designer. These sites cover the VRML language and provide links to numerous virtual worlds that already exist in cyberspace.

- ✔ The VRML Repository

  ```
  http://www.web3d.org/vrml/vrml.htm
  ```

- ✔ The Web3D Consortium

  ```
  http://www.vrml.org/
  ```

- ✔ VRMLWorks: comp.lang.vrml FAQ

  ```
  http://home.hiwaay.net/~crispen/vrmlworks/faq/index.html
  ```

- ✔ Yahoo! VRML Resources

  ```
  http://dir.yahoo.com/Computers_and_Internet
     /Internet/World_Wide_Web/
     Virtual_Reality_Modeling_Language__VRML_/
  ```

USENET Newsgroups

Whatever your Internet- or Web-related passion, you are sure to find others with the same interests on Usenet. In the *resource.htm* file on the accompanying CD-ROM we include an extensive selection of newsgroups dealing with various aspects of Web page creation. Here you can ask and answer questions, debate, and participate in standard-setting projects.

Appendix E

About the CD

*H*ere are some of the useful things you will find on the *Creating Web Pages For Dummies,* 5th Edition, CD-ROM:

- ✔ A Web page with links to numerous useful online Web page creation sites
- ✔ Signup software for MindSpring, a popular Internet service provider
- ✔ Microsoft Internet Explorer Web browser
- ✔ Netscape Communicator Web browser
- ✔ FrontPage Express, an easy-to-use Web page editor from Microsoft
- ✔ Dreamweaver HTML Page Editor, a trial version of a full-featured professional HTML editor
- ✔ HotDog HTML Editor, a demo of the popular text editor for Windows computers useful for HTML editing
- ✔ Mapedit, a fully functional 30-day trial, which lets you easily create image maps for your Web pages
- ✔ Paint Shop Pro evaluation version, a great graphics program for Windows
- ✔ BBEdit, a full featured demo version and a freeware "Lite" version, text editor for Mac OS computers useful for HTML editing
- ✔ Numerous miscellaneous utilities useful for the beginning Web page creator
- ✔ Astro3D arcade game, for when you want to take a break from creating Web pages

System Requirements

Make sure that your computer meets the minimum system requirements listed below. If your computer doesn't match up to most of these requirements, you may have problems using the contents of the CD.

- A PC with a Pentium 133 or faster processor, or a Mac OS computer with a PowerPC processor.
- Microsoft Windows 95 or later, Windows NT 4 or later, or Mac OS system software 7.5.5 or later.
- At least 16MB of total RAM installed on your computer. For best performance, we recommend at least 32MB of RAM installed.
- At least 280MB of hard drive space available to install all the software from this CD. (You need less space if you don't install every program.)
- A CD-ROM drive — double-speed (2x) or faster.
- A sound card for PCs. (Mac OS computers have built-in sound support.)
- A monitor capable of displaying at least 256 colors at 800 x 600 resolution.
- A modem with a speed of at least 56 Kbps.

If you need more information on the basics, check out *PCs For Dummies,* 7th Edition, by Dan Gookin; *Macs For Dummies,* 6th Edition, by David Pogue; *iMac For Dummies,* by David Pogue; *Windows 98 For Dummies, or Windows 95 For Dummies,* 2nd Edition, by Andy Rathbone (all published by IDG Books Worldwide, Inc.).

Using the CD with Microsoft Windows

To install the items from the CD to your hard drive, follow these steps:

1. **Insert the CD into your computer's CD-ROM drive.**

2. **Choose Start⇨Run.**

3. **In the dialog box that appears, type** D:\IDG.EXE.

   Replace *D* with the proper drive letter if your CD-ROM drive uses a different letter. (If you don't know the letter, see how your CD-ROM drive is listed under My Computer.)

4. **Click OK.**

   A license agreement window appears.

5. **Read through the license agreement, nod your head, and then click the Accept button if you want to use the CD — after you click Accept, you'll never be bothered by the License Agreement window again.**

   The CD interface Welcome screen appears. The interface is a little program that shows you what's on the CD and coordinates installing the programs and running the demos. The interface basically enables you to click a button or two to make things happen.

6. **Click anywhere on the Welcome screen to enter the interface.**

   Now you are getting to the action. This next screen lists categories for the software on the CD.

7. **To view the items within a category, just click the category's name.**

   A list of programs in the category appears.

8. **For more information about a program, click the program's name.**

   Be sure to read the information that appears. Sometimes a program has it's own system requirements or requires you to do a few tricks on your computer before you can install or run the program, and this screen tells you what you might need to do, if necessary.

9. **If you don't want to install the program, click the Back button to return to the previous screen.**

   You can always return to the previous screen by clicking the Back button. This feature allows you to browse the different categories and products and decide what you want to install.

10. **To install a program, click the appropriate Install button.**

    The CD interface drops to the background while the CD installs the program you chose.

11. **To install other items, repeat Steps 7–10.**

12. **When you've finished installing programs, click the Quit button to close the interface.**

    You can eject the CD now. Carefully place it back in the plastic jacket of the book for safekeeping.

In order to run some of the programs on the *Creating Web Pages For Dummies* CD-ROM, you may need to keep the CD inside your CD-ROM drive. This is a Good Thing. Otherwise, the installed program would have required you to install a very large chunk of the program to your hard drive, which may have kept you from installing other software.

Using the CD with Mac OS

To install the items from the CD to your hard drive, follow these steps:

1. **Insert the CD into your computer's CD-ROM drive.**

   In a moment, an icon representing the CD you just inserted appears on your Mac desktop. Chances are, the icon looks like a CD-ROM.

2. **Double-click the CD icon to show the CD's contents.**

3. **Double-click the License Agreement icon.**

   This is the license that you are agreeing to by using the CD. You can close this window once you've looked over the agreement.

4. **Double-click the Read Me First icon.**

   The Read Me First text file contains information about the CD's programs and any last-minute instructions you may need in order to correctly install them.

5. **To install most programs, open the program folder and double-click the icon called "Install" or "Installer."**

   Sometimes the installers are actually self extracting archives, which just means that the program files have been bundled up into an archive, and this self extractor unbundles the files and places them on your hard drive. This kind of program is often called a .sea. Double click anything with .sea in the title, and it will run just like an installer.

6. **Some programs don't come with installers. For those, just drag the program's folder from the CD window and drop it on your hard drive icon.**

After you have installed the programs you want, you can eject the CD. Carefully place it back in the plastic jacket of the book for safekeeping.

What You'll Find

Shareware programs are fully functional, free trial versions of copyrighted programs. If you like particular programs, register with their authors for a nominal fee and receive licenses, enhanced versions, and technical support. Freeware programs are free, copyrighted games, applications, and utilities. You can copy them to as many PCs as you like — free — but they have no technical support. GNU software is governed by its own license, which is included inside the folder of the GNU software. There are no restrictions on distribution of this software. See the GNU license for more details. Trial, demo, or evaluation versions are usually limited either by time or functionality (such as being unable to save projects).

Here's a summary of the software on this CD arranged by category. If you use Windows, the CD interface helps you install software easily. (If you have no idea what we're talking about when we say "CD interface," flip back a page or two to find the section, "Using the CD with Microsoft Windows.")

If you use a Mac OS computer, you can take advantage of the easy Mac interface to quickly install the programs.

A quick overview

This book includes a CD-ROM with a variety of PC and Macintosh programs and demos that you will find useful while creating your Web pages. You can use some of these programs for one of the most important tasks in Web authoring: using HTML tags to create the text file that will be seen by users as a Web page.

The programs on the CD are either free, try before you buy, or demo versions. Some of the programs are HTML focused, and others hide the HTML tags and give you a more intuitive interface to work with.

And while all the programs on the CD-ROM are free in their current form, some require you to pay a fee to get a fully functional version by registering the program. Other programs are functional and ready to go "as is," with no payment required.

The HTML file "Resource.htm" contained on your CD-ROM and described in Appendix D has links to numerous online resources which you will find useful as you create your Web pages.

In this appendix, you find a brief description of the contents of the *Creating Web Pages For Dummies* CD-ROM. Each program listing also includes a pointer to the URL of the program's Web site (if available) where you can check for the latest upgrade and support information. Have fun!

Web resources

Resource.htm, from Arthur and Bud, your humble authors.

For Windows 95/98/NT and Mac OS. This is probably the most useful file on your CD-ROM. This HTML file contains links to many great Internet resources of use to the Web page creator. To use this file productively, you'll need an Internet connection and a Web browser installed on your computer. Conveniently, this CD-ROM includes Internet Explorer and Netscape Communicator browsers. You will find links to all sorts of HTML and image editing tools, to sources of information, and to Usenet newsgroups dealing with the Web. Appendix D covers some of these resources in more detail. To use this file, simply open it in your browser using the File⇨Open menu.

HTML editors

BBEdit Lite and BBEdit Demo, from Bare Bones Software, Inc.

For Mac OS. BBEdit Lite is a Macintosh freeware text editor with powerful features that make creating HTML scripts for your Web pages easy. The commercial version of this program has stronger HTML editing features. We include a demo version of BBEdit on the CD. This demo is fully featured but cannot save files. Incidentally, they have a great motto: "Software That Doesn't Suck." Their Web site is `http://www.barebones.com/`.

Dreamweaver, Trial version, from Macromedia

For Windows 95/98/NT/2000. Dreamweaver is a serious, award-winning professional Web page authoring program. It has many advanced features and is a great product to move to after you've mastered the simple Web page design techniques in this book. This is a trial version of this sophisticated and popular program. Its Web site is `http://www.macromedia.com/software/dreamweaver/`.

FrontPage Express, from Microsoft

For Windows 95/98/NT/2000. Commercial version. An easy-to-use graphical HTML editor tightly integrated with Microsoft's Internet Explorer browser. Good program for beginners. Its Web site is `http://www.microsoft.com/windows/ie/default.htm`.

HomeSite, 30-day evaluation version, from Allaire Co.

For Windows 95/98/NT/2000. Allaire HomeSite is an elegant and easy-to-use Web page creation tool that includes wizards to handle common but complex tasks, such as table or frame creation. Its user interface can also be easily customized to fit your own way of working. This evaluation version is good for 30 days of use. Check out the Web site at `http://www.allaire.com/products/homesite/index.cfm`.

HotDog Professional, Trial version, from Sausage Software

For Windows 95/98/NT/2000. The HotDog HTML Editor from Sausage Software is a fast, flexible, and user-friendly HTML editor that has been getting rave reviews on the Net. This fully functional demo expires in 30 days, after which you have an opportunity to register for the full version. Chapter 12 describes how to use HotDog for Web publishing. For more information about HotDog software, and the latest versions, go to the Sausage Software Web site at `http://www.sausage.com/`.

HTML Pro, from Niklas Frykholm

For Mac OS. HTML Pro is yet another nifty freeware Macintosh Web page editor that lets you work on the graphical view of a page and the HTML source code at the same time. Its Web site can be found at
`http://www.acc.umu.se/~r2d2/files/mac/html_pro.html`.

Graphical tools

GraphicConverter, from Lemke Software

For Macintosh OS. GraphicConverter is a Macintosh shareware program that converts pictures to various formats. The program also contains features that you can use for image manipulation. If you're using a Mac, GraphicConverter is a very useful utility for manipulating images you'll use in your Web pages. Check out its Web site at
`http://www.lemkesoft.de/index.html`.

Paint Shop Pro, from JASC Software, Inc.

For Windows 95/98/NT/2000. Evaluation version. Paint Shop Pro is a powerful and easy-to-use image viewing, editing, and conversion program, which also happens to include many sophisticated drawing and painting tools. This evaluation version will give you an idea of its power. Contains features normally found in programs hundreds of dollars more expensive than this. A great value for your money. Its Web site can be found at
`http://www.jasc.com/psp.html`.

Reptile, from Sausage Software

For Windows 95/98/NT/2000. Reptile is a cool little freeware application that lets you create funky backgrounds for your Web pages. It can produce any combination of wavy, bubbly, organic, big, small, wide, narrow, rough, or smooth textures. And besides generating a vast range of shapes and surfaces, the program also features a great way to color the textures to suit the look and feel you require. Check out the Web site at
`http://www.sausage.com/reptile/reptile.html`.

Ulead GIF Animator, **15-day trial version**, from Ulead Systems

For Windows 95/98/NT/2000. A fast and powerful GIF animation program that will help you add some motion to your Web pages and graphics. This is a fully functional 15-day trial version. Its Web page is at
`http://www.ulead.com/ga/runme.htm`.

Web page utilities

CSE HTML Validator Lite and CSE HTML Validator Pro Demo, from AI
Internet Solutions

For Windows 95/98/NT/2000. CSE Validator is a powerful, easy-to-use, and
user-configurable HTML syntax checker. After you create your Web pages,
simply run them through the Validator, and it will tell you if you have any
errors in your HTML. Validator Lite is an ad-supported free version, while the
Pro version is more powerful and has extra features. We include the Validator
Pro demo version here, which can be used for checking up to 50 Web pages.
Check out its Web site at `http://www.htmlvalidator.com/`.

Mapedit, Mapedit Java, from Boutell Communications

For Windows 95/98/NT/2000 and Mac OS. Mapedit is an elegant utility for creating image maps for Web pages. An image map is simply a picture that can
have clickable image areas linked to other Web pages. You can find out more
about Mapedit and image maps by visiting the Mapedit Web site at
`http://www.boutell.com/mapedit/`.

SiteCheck, Pacific Coast Software

For Windows 95/98/NT/2000. SiteCheck is a useful application that provides a
fast and convenient way to check all the hypertext links at your Web site to
make sure they still point to valid pages.

Web browsers

Internet Explorer, from Microsoft

For Windows 95/98/NT/2000 and Mac OS. We won't insult your intelligence by
telling you what a browser is, and we'd be very surprised if you've never
heard of Microsoft Explorer. However, just in case you don't have the latest
version (at the time of publication), we include a copy of Microsoft Explorer
5.0 on this CD-ROM. You can always find the latest information about
Explorer at the Microsoft support site at `http://www.microsoft.com/`
`windows/ie/default.htm`.

Netscape Communicator, from Netscape/AOL

For Windows 95/98/NT/2000 and Mac OS. This is, of course, the other major
browser, and the most popular one on the Mac (and Linux!). Again, we're
including the latest production version at the time of publication, and you
can always download the latest and greatest from the Netscape
Communicator Web site: `http://www.netscape.com/browsers/`.

Internet access

MindSpring Internet Access, from MindSpring

For Windows 95/98/NT/2000 and Mac OS. In case you don't have an Internet connection, the CD includes sign-on software for MindSpring, an Internet service provider with an excellent reputation for customer service. Also check out its Web site at `http://www.mindspring.com/` for help.

Fun stuff

Astro3D, from Jarrod Davis Software

For Windows 95/98/NT/2000. We know that you'll be working hard creating your Web pages, but it's hard to be creative without some relaxation time. So just because we like it, we threw in this nifty arcade-style shareware shooter onto the CD-ROM. It's kind of like Asteroids but instead of looking down on the action, you see the game from inside the cockpit of your ship. Have fun!

If You've Got Problems (Of the CD Kind)

We tried our best to compile programs that work on most computers with the minimum system requirements. Alas, your computer may differ, and some programs may not work properly for some reason.

The two likeliest problems are that you don't have enough memory (RAM) for the programs you want to use, or you have other programs running that are affecting installation or running of a program. If you get error messages like `Not enough memory` or `Setup cannot continue`, try one or more of these methods and then try using the software again:

- ✔ **Turn off any anti-virus software that you have on your computer.** Installers sometimes mimic virus activity and may make your computer incorrectly believe that it is being infected by a virus.

- ✔ **Close all running programs.** The more programs you're running, the less memory is available to other programs. Installers also typically update files and programs; if you keep other programs running, installation may not work properly.

- ✔ **In Windows, close the CD interface and run demos or installations directly from Windows Explorer.** The interface itself can tie up system memory, or even conflict with certain kinds of interactive demos. Use Windows Explorer to browse the files on the CD and launch installers or demos.

✔ **Have your local computer store add more RAM to your computer.** This is, admittedly, a drastic and somewhat expensive step. However, if you have a Windows 95/98/NT PC or a Mac OS computer with a PowerPC chip, adding more memory can really help the speed of your computer and enable more programs to run at the same time.

If you still have trouble installing the items from the CD, please call the IDG Books Worldwide Customer Service phone number: 800-762-2974 (outside the U.S.: 317-572-3342).

Index

(continued)

Notes

Notes

IDG Books Worldwide, Inc., End-User License Agreement

READ THIS. You should carefully read these terms and conditions before opening the software packet(s) included with this book ("Book"). This is a license agreement ("Agreement") between you and IDG Books Worldwide, Inc. ("IDGB"). By opening the accompanying software packet(s), you acknowledge that you have read and accept the following terms and conditions. If you do not agree and do not want to be bound by such terms and conditions, promptly return the Book and the unopened software packet(s) to the place you obtained them for a full refund.

1. **License Grant.** IDGB grants to you (either an individual or entity) a nonexclusive license to use one copy of the enclosed software program(s) (collectively, the "Software") solely for your own personal or business purposes on a single computer (whether a standard computer or a workstation component of a multiuser network). The Software is in use on a computer when it is loaded into temporary memory (RAM) or installed into permanent memory (hard disk, CD-ROM, or other storage device). IDGB reserves all rights not expressly granted herein.

2. **Ownership.** IDGB is the owner of all right, title, and interest, including copyright, in and to the compilation of the Software recorded on the disk(s) or CD-ROM ("Software Media"). Copyright to the individual programs recorded on the Software Media is owned by the author or other authorized copyright owner of each program. Ownership of the Software and all proprietary rights relating thereto remain with IDGB and its licensers.

3. **Restrictions on Use and Transfer.**

   (a) You may only (i) make one copy of the Software for backup or archival purposes, or (ii) transfer the Software to a single hard disk, provided that you keep the original for backup or archival purposes. You may not (i) rent or lease the Software, (ii) copy or reproduce the Software through a LAN or other network system or through any computer subscriber system or bulletin-board system, or (iii) modify, adapt, or create derivative works based on the Software.

   (b) You may not reverse engineer, decompile, or disassemble the Software. You may transfer the Software and user documentation on a permanent basis, provided that the transferee agrees to accept the terms and conditions of this Agreement and you retain no copies. If the Software is an update or has been updated, any transfer must include the most recent update and all prior versions.

4. **Restrictions on Use of Individual Programs.** You must follow the individual requirements and restrictions detailed for each individual program in Appendix E of this Book. These limitations are also contained in the individual license agreements recorded on the Software Media. These limitations may include a requirement that after using the program for a specified period of time, the user must pay a registration fee or discontinue use. By opening the Software packet(s), you will be agreeing to abide by the licenses and restrictions for these individual programs that are detailed in Appendix E and on the Software Media. None of the material on this Software Media or listed in this Book may ever be redistributed, in original or modified form, for commercial purposes.

5. **Limited Warranty.**

   (a) IDGB warrants that the Software and Software Media are free from defects in materials and workmanship under normal use for a period of sixty (60) days from the date of purchase of this Book. If IDGB receives notification within the warranty period of defects in materials or workmanship, IDGB will replace the defective Software Media.

   (b) **IDGB AND THE AUTHOR OF THE BOOK DISCLAIM ALL OTHER WARRANTIES, EXPRESS OR IMPLIED, INCLUDING WITHOUT LIMITATION IMPLIED WARRANTIES OF MERCHANTABILITY AND FITNESS FOR A PARTICULAR PURPOSE, WITH RESPECT TO THE SOFTWARE, THE PROGRAMS, THE SOURCE CODE CONTAINED THEREIN, AND/OR THE TECHNIQUES DESCRIBED IN THIS BOOK. IDGB DOES NOT WARRANT THAT THE FUNCTIONS CONTAINED IN THE SOFTWARE WILL MEET YOUR REQUIREMENTS OR THAT THE OPERATION OF THE SOFTWARE WILL BE ERROR FREE.**

   (c) This limited warranty gives you specific legal rights, and you may have other rights that vary from jurisdiction to jurisdiction.

6. **Remedies.**

   (a) IDGB's entire liability and your exclusive remedy for defects in materials and workmanship shall be limited to replacement of the Software Media, which may be returned to IDGB with a copy of your receipt at the following address: Software Media Fulfillment Department, Attn.: *Creating Web Pages For Dummies,* 5th Edition, IDG Books Worldwide, Inc., 10475 Crosspoint Boulevard, Indianapolis, IN 46256, or call 800-762-2974. Please allow three to four weeks for delivery. This Limited Warranty is void if failure of the Software Media has resulted from accident, abuse, or misapplication. Any replacement Software Media will be warranted for the remainder of the original warranty period or thirty (30) days, whichever is longer.

   (b) In no event shall IDGB or the author be liable for any damages whatsoever (including without limitation damages for loss of business profits, business interruption, loss of business information, or any other pecuniary loss) arising from the use of or inability to use the Book or the Software, even if IDGB has been advised of the possibility of such damages.

   (c) Because some jurisdictions do not allow the exclusion or limitation of liability for consequential or incidental damages, the above limitation or exclusion may not apply to you.

7. **U.S. Government Restricted Rights.** Use, duplication, or disclosure of the Software by the U.S. Government is subject to restrictions stated in paragraph (c)(1)(ii) of the Rights in Technical Data and Computer Software clause of DFARS 252.227-7013, and in subparagraphs (a) through (d) of the Commercial Computer–Restricted Rights clause at FAR 52.227-19, and in similar clauses in the NASA FAR supplement, when applicable.

8. **General.** This Agreement constitutes the entire understanding of the parties and revokes and supersedes all prior agreements, oral or written, between them and may not be modified or amended except in a writing signed by both parties hereto that specifically refers to this Agreement. This Agreement shall take precedence over any other documents that may be in conflict herewith. If any one or more provisions contained in this Agreement are held by any court or tribunal to be invalid, illegal, or otherwise unenforceable, each and every other provision shall remain in full force and effect.

Installation Instructions

The *Creating Web Pages For Dummies* CD offers valuable information that you won't want to miss. To install the items from the CD to your hard drive, follow the steps outlined in Appendix E of this book. Appendix E includes instructions for both PCs and Macs. You'll also find descriptions of the software and utilities included on the CD-ROM in Appendix E.